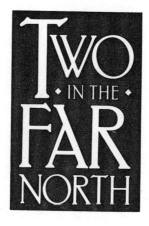

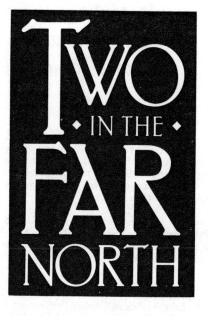

TWO · IN THE · FAR NORTH

MARGARET E. MURIE

ILLUSTRATED BY OLAUS J. MURIE

Alaska Northwest Books™

Anchorage • Seattle • Portland

To Mother
who took me there
and to Olaus
who came

Two in the Far North was first published in the United States by Alfred A. Knopf, Inc., New York, and in Canada by Random House of Canada Limited, Toronto, 1962. Fourth printing, 1970. Ballantine Books, Inc., Comstock Edition, 1972. Published with additional text and illustrations by Alaska Northwest Publishing Company, 1978.

Portions of Chapters 1 and 2 of Part IV appeared originally under the title "A Week at Lobo Lake" in *Animal Kingdom*. Portions of Chapters 1, 2, 3, and 5 of Part IV appeared originally under the title "A Live River in the Arctic" in *The Living Wilderness*. Some of the illustrations first appeared with "A Live River in the Arctic" and in *Audubon* Magazine.

First printing 1978
Eighth printing 1993

Library of Congress Cataloging-in-Publication Data
Murie, Margaret E.
    Two in the Far North.
    1. Murie, Margaret E.   2. Frontier and pioneer life—
Alaska.   3. Natural history—Alaska.   4. Alaska—
Description and travel—1896–1959.   5. Alaska—Biography.
6. Pioneers—Alaska—Biography.   I. Title.
F909.M94   1978   979.8'04'0924 [B]   78-16407
ISBN 0-88240-111-4

Cover design by Cameron Mason
Design by Jon.Hersh

Alaska Northwest Books™
An imprint of Graphic Arts Center Publishing Company
Editorial office: 2208 NW Market Street, Suite 300, Seattle, WA 98107
Catalog and order dept.: P.O. Box 10306, Portland, OR 97210
    800-452-3032

Printed in the United States of America

Preface

What, after all, are the most precious things in a life?

We had a honeymoon in an age when the world was sweet and untrammeled and safe. Up there in the Koyukuk there were very few machines of any kind; but there was joy in companionship and in the simple things—like the crackle of a fire, having tea and bread while the rain pattered on the roof, a chance meeting with a friend on the dog-team trail.

What made us happy to go back to Fairbanks? Was it the new buildings, strangely tall, the blocks of beautiful modern landscaped homes, the busy traffic, the neon signs? All this we saw with our eyes, but it does not touch us. What did touch us deeply is the thought that Ted and Audrey, Otto and Ivar, and Jim and Katherine may be there at the gate as we walk, wondering, from the plane; that the next day when we walked the old familiar streets in the middle of town we might meet Bobbie Sheldon or Freddie Johnston by the post office steps; that down the street we might meet Eddy Davis, that we would see Al Polet in the bank, Les Almquist in the N.C. store, Dave and Benjie Adler in their bookshop; and that when we walked into the lobby of the Nordale, Eva McGown would meet us with outstretched arms.

Here in Alaska people still count, as much today as in the twenties. I would love to think the world will survive its obsession with machines to see a day when people respect one another all over the world. It seems as clear as a shaft of the Aurora that this is our only hope. My prayer is that Alaska will not lose the heart-nourishing friendliness of her youth—that her people will always care for one another, her towns remain friendly and not completely ruled by the dollar—and that her great wild places will remain great, and wild, and free, where wolf and caribou, wolverine and grizzly bear, and all the Arctic blossoms may live on in the delicate balance which supported them long before impetuous man appeared in the North.

This is the great gift Alaska can give to the harassed world.

ACKNOWLEDGMENTS

To my husband, Olaus J. Murie, and to our three children, Martin, Joanne, and Donald, who all joined Angus Cameron, my editor at Alfred A. Knopf, Inc., in urging and encouraging the writing of this book, my earnest thanks.

But also to Mother, again to Joanne, and to my friend Mildred Capron, who helped give me *time* for it, and to Margaret Demorest, who in a few words quickened a desire to try to write our story. To Harriett Willard, who typed the manuscript with interest and zealous care; to the editors of *The Living Wilderness* and *Animal Kingdom* for permission to draw upon material previously published as articles in those magazines; and finally to the other members of our 1956 and 1961 Brooks Range expeditions, to Otto William Geist, and to Fairfield Osborn and the other officers of the New York Zoological Society, who made the whole of Part IV of this book possible.

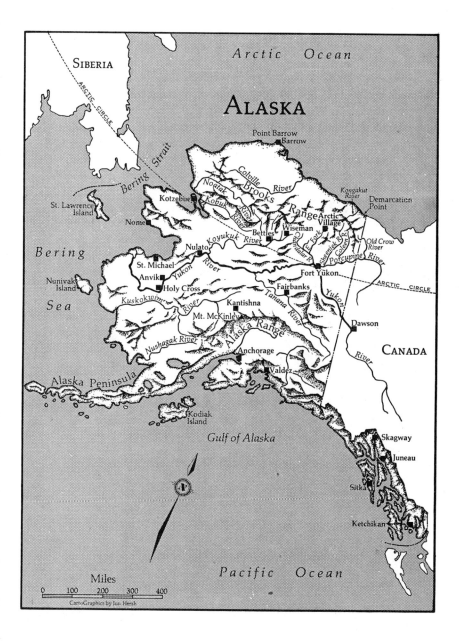

SIBERIA

Arctic   Ocean

ARCTIC CIRCLE

ALASKA

Bering Strait

St. Lawrence
Island

Nome

Bering

Nunivak
Island

Sea

Point Barrow
Barrow

Colville   River

Noatak

Brooks

Kotzebue

Kobuk   River

Range

*Kongakut
River*

Demarcation
Point

Arctic
Village

Bettles   Wiseman

Old Crow
River

Koyukuk   River

Chandalar R.

E. fork

Sheenjek R.

Coleen

Porcupine

Porcupine   River

Nulato

St. Michael

Anvik

Yukon   River

Holy Cross

Fort Yukon

ARCTIC   CIRCLE

Fairbanks

Kuskokwim

River

Kantishna

Tanana   River

Yukon

Dawson

Mt. McKinley

Nushagak River

Alaska Range

Anchorage

Valdez

CANADA

River

Alaska   Peninsula

Kodiak
Island

Gulf of Alaska

Skagway

Juneau

Sitka

Pacific   Ocean

Ketchikan

Miles

0   100   200   300   400

CartoGraphics by Jon Hersh

Contents

PART I:
FAIRBANKS

1

To the North

A nine-year-old girl can see and hear a lot. Too old to hold the center of any adult group with the charm of babyhood, too young to be considered a hazard to conversation, sturdy, round-eyed, my dark hair in a Mary Jane bob with a big butterfly bow on top, I could be quietly everywhere at once. I saw and heard.

So the Alaska most vivid in my memory is the one I saw first as a nine-year-old, traveling from Seattle to Fairbanks with Mother, in September, on the last trip before "freeze-up."

Daddy, my loved and loving stepfather, was already up there, at work on his new job as Assistant U.S. Attorney. One morning as I came downstairs to breakfast I saw a Western Union messenger boy standing with Mother in the front hall of our Seattle home. The telegram said: "Can you catch Str. *Jefferson* September 15th? Last steamer to connect with last boat down the Yukon. Will meet you in Dawson."

I remember running the several blocks to the dressmaker's. "We're going to Alaska in three days and Mother wants to know can you get her a traveling dress made." In those days you didn't just go downtown and buy a dress; it was a project.

Three days. My stepfather had faith in the calm efficiency of that sweet brown-eyed woman. The dressmaker friend came and went to work in the midst of trunks and boxes. My grandmother came and flipped from room to room amid a torrent of words. "I

just don't see how Millette can *expect* you to catch that boat!"
And: "Minnie, do you think you should *try* to do this—in your
condition?" Even while she feverishly stowed linens and clothing
and dishes in the big round-topped trunks.

"In your condition"—that was a queer-sounding phrase. What
condition? But then I was sent running on another errand. And
finally, on the afternoon of the third day, there was
Grandmother, still in a torrent of words, and between tears and
laughter, sitting atop the largest round-topped trunk so the
dressmaker's son could get it closed, while the dressmaker sewed
on the last of the black jet buttons down the back of the brown
wool "traveling dress" with garnet velvet piping around the neck
and sleeves. I remember how soft to the touch that brown wool
cloth was.

The boats for Alaska always sailed at nine in the evening, and it
was like going to the theater—a real social occasion for the Seattle
folks—going to the pier to see the steamer off to the North. Down
through the great cavern of the dock warehouse, brightly lighted
for sailing time, smelling of salt sea and tar and hemp and
adventure. A great crowd of people, and stevedores with hand-
carts pushing their way through, yelling: "Gangway! Gangway!"
A great wave of noise compounded of the churning of engines and
the hissing of steam, and voices in every key, shouts, laughter. At

last to the long opening in the side wall, and there was the ship's white side and the red-and-white gangplank.

I was dressed in my new black-and-white "shepherd check" dress with brass buttons down the front and a red collar and red cuffs, and my new red coat with black silk "frogs," and a red hat with shirred satin ribbon around the crown (and I knew the red Mary Jane hairbow would be crushed by it), and shiny black boots with patent-leather cuffs at the top and a red silk tassel. My stomach was tied in a knot of breathless, almost-not-to-be-borne sensation, and I was clutching all my going-away presents— coloring books, paper-doll books, crayons, a new volume of *Black Beauty*. Mother stood in the midst of a cluster of friends, looking so pretty in her new dress and her coat with the green velvet collar, and she too had her arms full of gifts—boxes of candy, books, the newest *Ladies' Home Journal*. All around us people were carrying or receiving packages. Going to see someone off for Alaska always meant bringing a parting gift. The first moments of letdown after the ship was under way would be brightened by the opening of packages.

For a nine-year-old, no sorrow, only excitement—being hugged all around, and nearly jumping out of my skin when the deep-throated, echoing five-minute whistle blew and set off a crescendo of squeals and shouts and admonitions from the crowd.

"Here you go!" A perkily blue-and-gold uniform sets me up onto the first cleat of the gangplank—really, really going somewhere! Step down onto the deck, find a spot at the rail. Every passenger is at the rail—why doesn't the ship roll over? Hang on to the packages. What if one should fall? From some mysterious realm above come heavy voices of authority; bells clang far down inside; down slides the gangplank to be rolled away onto the pier. That was the last tie being cut. Now it is really happening. Looking down over the ship's side, I see water, and it widens and widens, and faces are looking up, handkerchiefs waving, voices and faces fading away. "See you next June." "Don't take any wooden nickels." "Tell Joe to write." "Hope Queen Charlotte won't be too rough!"

The faces of Grandmother and all our friends are only white blurs now. We are out in the cool black windy bay and the ship is heading out and all the passengers are moving now—moving into their new little world, the Str. *Jefferson*, Gus Nord, Master.

To a nine-year-old, a ship's stateroom was a wonder of a place, such fun—the berths with their railings, the washbowl that pulled down into place, the locker seat with its red plush cushions. Our room opened into the "saloon," and that was another wonder— red plush-covered soft divans and big chairs, soft carpet underfoot, a broad stairway with a shining brass railing that curved down into the dining saloon.

There were other children aboard, and here on the carpeted floor at our mothers' feet we played our games while the women sat with their "fancy work," all of us in a cozy yet adventurous little world of our own. We children cut out paper dolls, and played Parcheesi, and colored pictures, and the women discovered one another, old Alaskans telling new ones all they knew, while fingers flew. Mother was crocheting a long black-and-white wool shawl; the huge amber crochet hook fascinated me.

A lovely routine that was over too quickly. Then, as ever, the days of ship life flew by too fast. Meals, and naps, and always the falling asleep and waking again to the sweet pulse and throb of the ship's engines and the muted hiss of water along her sides. Then racing about on deck, and hide-and-seek on the forward deck, and quiet hours in the lounge, and "dressing for dinner"—which meant, for me, being scrubbed, and having my hair brushed till it shone, and a different bow tied and fluffed into a butterfly, and either the pink challis or the shirred white China silk dress, and the "best" shoes, black patent leather with high tops of brown-calf buttoned straps. Then stepping out to wait for the musical dinner gong and to see what the three other little girls had on this time!

After four days of this delightful life there was talk of about what hour the *Jefferson* would dock at Skagway. I remember it was daytime, and we had been sliding for hours up a long channel of glass-smooth water edged on either side by the ever-present dark green forest that lay below shining white mountains.

Skagway nestled into the delta fan at the mouth of a canyon, embraced on three sides by steep wooded slopes. In front, the very blue waters of the Lynn Canal, which is not really a canal but a long fiord. A long pier extended out to deep water. The little town seemed to sparkle in the September sun. Many of the buildings were of white-painted lumber; some were half-log structures. Back toward the canyon, in a grove of cottonwood trees and spruces, stood Pullen House.

In a frontier town, the feature least frontierish is likely to be the most famous and admired. So Pullen House, looking like a southern manor, with lawns, flower beds, a pergola, a little stream flowing through the lawn and spanned by a rustic bridge. Inside, no homemade frontier furnishings, but heavy Victorian walnut and mahogany and plush, walls crowded with pictures, bric-a-brac, and souvenirs. For here was the whole history of Skagway. Pullen House was the tangible dream of a woman who had come there in the gold rush only fourteen years before, a widow with a daughter and three little sons. She had lived in a tent shack and made dried apple pies and sold them to the hordes of pie-hungry, home-hungry, adventure-hungry men of the days of '98. Thus her grubstake, and Pullen House.

Harriet Pullen, once met, could never be forgotten. She welcomed Mother as a beloved daughter come home, for she remembered Daddy from the days when the District Judge from Juneau came up to Skagway twice a year with his retinue, including his young court reporter, and held court. They always stayed, of course, at Pullen House. "Ma" Pullen, tall, red-haired, statuesque, with suffering and strength and humor in every feature—even a nine-year-old sensed this.

We slept in a room full of overpowering furniture, in a great ark of a bed with headboard reaching toward the ceiling. But this was the special room, the room many important people had occupied when traveling north. The commode had the most gorgeous basin, and a pitcher, blooming with red roses, so heavy I could not lift it.

In the morning Mrs. Pullen ushered us out into the long pantry behind the immense kitchen. "My favorite boarders always get to skim their own cream. Mr. Gillette always loved to when he stayed here," she said.

Here was the other unfrontierish feature of Skagway. Ma Pullen's great pride was a Jersey cow, the only cow in that part of the world, and in the pantry stood the blue-enameled milk pans. The guest was given a bowl and a spoon and allowed to skim off cream for his porridge and coffee. Skimming your own cream at Pullen House in the land of no cream was a ritual talked of all over the North in those days.

Being on a train for the first time provided more excitement. I had to examine every detail of the red plush-covered seats and curlicue-brass-trimmed arms, and jump from one side of the aisle to the other, trying to see everything, yet my only clear recollection from that day is looking down into Lake Bennett near the summit—such turquoise water, such golden birch trees all round it. I think all other impressions were drowned in my rapt absorption in the gorgeous uniforms of the two Northwest Mounted Policemen who came aboard to check us through at the border of the Yukon Territory.

This same impression dominates my memory of the three days traveling downriver from Whitehorse to Dawson. There was one of these gorgeous creatures aboard, and he suffered the company of an adoring small round-eyed girl. I remember sitting with him on the stern deck. I don't remember any of the conversation.

It was dusk at five o'clock, for it was late September in the Land of the Midnight Sun. The passengers on the sternwheel steamer *Casca* were all crowded at the rail on one side while the *Casca* huffed and puffed in the great surge of the Yukon and was maneuvered with uncanny skill toward the dock at Dawson. Her stern wheel chuff-chuffed rapidly in reverse, bells clanged, and with a great swoosh of water the wheel chuff-chuffed forward again. Her high-pitched, exciting whistle blew three times—a greeting to the "Queen of the Klondike" and the crowd of her citizens standing all expectant on the dock.

The *Casca's* passengers pressed closer to the rail, straining to look, straining to recognize loved, feared, or dreaded faces. Squeezed against the white-painted iron mesh below the rail, new red hat pushed askew, heart beating fast, I stood, determined to see everything.

Mother stood quietly beside me, but I could feel her excitement too. We were both looking for the big tan Stetson hat that would tell us Daddy had managed to catch that last upriver steamer and was here to meet us.

The Yukon begins to widen at Dawson; the hills are farther apart and seem bigger and higher, and certainly more bare. Here we were sensing a quite different world, the world of "the interior." The hill behind Dawson seemed to be sitting high above the town, with arms spread about the sprawling clot of man's hurriedly built, haphazard structures. Even then, in 1911, the gold towns had electricity, and now at dusk lights were beginning to show here and there all over the delta shape of the settlement.

The *Casca*, having chuffed upstream above the dock, was now sliding down closer in, closer in, a young Indian poised to jump with the bowline. There arose cries of "I see Jim!" "There's Mary!"

And shouts from the crowd on the dock: "Hey Doc, you old so-and-so, I *knew* you'd be back!"

A bell clanged once somewhere inside the *Casca*, the engines stopped, the Indian boy jumped, for a few seconds more the great wheel turned—over and over—and then how quiet it was! Everyone seemed impressed by the silence for a moment. That is the kind of moment which lives on forever after, when you are nine and in an utterly new and so different world. Then Mother cried out: "There he is!" And there he was, indeed, right at the front, where a crew of Indian boys waited to hoist the big gangplank.

There was moose steak for dinner that night, in Dawson's famed Arcade Café. Under the white glare of the many bulbs, amid the great babble of a happy crowd, everyone talking to everyone and calling back and forth among the tables—I remember most keenly that huge thick slab of meat with a heap of fried potatoes beside it. We had arrived in the North. What the steak cost, I do not know. But that was the Yukon, that was Alaska. I think my gentle mother began to learn about the north country that night. All was costly, everything was done on a lavish scale, life was exciting and each day a story in itself, and nothing was worth worrying about. The finest things that could be hauled into this country from Outside were none too good for these pioneers who were braving the climate and the terrain of this untamable land. If all might be lost in a season in the diggings, then they would have the best while they could.

The hotel rooms reflected this spirit. The wallpaper was likely to be a Greek amphora design in gold, all fluffy with curlicues, on a deep-red ground. There might be a flowered pink Brussels carpet on the floor, a white bedstead with more curly designs and brass knobs on each of the four posts; chairs with more fancy designs and turned legs. There was one with a lion's head carved in its back. At the windows, lace curtains which scratched your nose and neck if you wanted to part them to look down into the street.

The street. The next morning I stood looking down at it. It was full of big-hatted men, fur-capped men, men in Derby hats, men with beards, men in breeches and bright shirts and high laced boots, men in long city overcoats, men in denim parkas. Some were hurrying along, boots clattering on the boardwalk; others were standing about in small groups. There seemed to be a lot of talk and gesturing and much laughter, a feeling of excitement and of things happening. A team of big gray horses came down the dusty street to the dock drawing a load of luggage. Behind them came a team of Huskies pulling a long narrow cart on wheels, also piled with luggage. "See? They use dogs when there is no snow, too," Daddy said.

The three of us were at the window now. Across the street the carts were disappearing into the dock warehouse. The autumn stream of old-timers leaving for Outside for the winter, and of others moving in, was at its peak. One more boat from downriver was due in. It would really be the last one upriver for this season; and on it we would be going downstream, to Tanana, and from Tanana up the Tanana River to Fairbanks. "The *Sarah* should be in any time now," Daddy said. "Look downriver."

I already knew what direction that was, and over the roofs of the row of docks and warehouses, the broad brown river was there, filling our view, the brown hills beyond seeming far away. Downstream, around a sand-colored bluff, a puff of white wood smoke, then a beautiful three-toned whistle, sad and sweet and lonely. "There she is! Only she and her three sisters have that voice!" exclaimed Daddy.

In 1911 the river steamer was queen. There was a great fleet then, nearly all with feminine names, churning and chuffing their stern wheels up the rivers and sliding briskly down them. When the great two-stacker Mississippi-style steamer came in to any dock, she came like a confident southern beauty making a graceful curtsy at a ball. There were four of these on the Yukon—the *Susie,* the *Sarah,* the *Hannah,* and the *Louise*—and they lived their lives between St. Michael at the mouth of the river and Dawson, 1,600 miles upstream. That part of the Yukon is very wide all the way, with plenty of water, a great river. There was another of the big boats, bearing a masculine name, *Herman,* but "he" seemed a bit dirty and a little slower.

Now in the street below there was shouting and calling, and all the town emptied in a rush toward the dock, where the beautiful huge white *Sarah* was sliding in to make a landing.

We left Dawson early the next evening. There was still some daylight, and it seemed that all of Dawson was on the dock to see us off. Back in those times "the last trip of the year" was no meaningless phrase. It meant that all the supplies for the community, enough to last until "the first boat in the spring" came, had to be already delivered and safely stored away in the warehouses and stores—and everyone hoped he hadn't forgotten to order something important. It meant that everyone who felt he could not stand another soul-testing northern winter had better be leaving on this boat. It meant that all those who had been Outside all summer and felt they couldn't stand any more of the tinsel and heartless life of the cities Outside were there, on their way back downriver, or on beyond to Fairbanks, or to wherever they felt they belonged and could try it again. These were aboard the *Sarah*. They were mostly single men, but there were a few families, like us, going into the country to make a home, to follow a career.

How vivid that scene! Again squeezed up against, and almost under, the rail, among all those grownups, I tried hard to see and hear everything.

"Sure you got all your suitcases aboard?"

"Hope that winter dump's a good one."

"Say hello to Charlie."

"Oh, we'll winter through all right."

"See you in the spring!"

Everyone was smiling, tossing jokes back and forth. That was the way of the North always, but even a nine-year-old could sense the sad things too. Maybe we won't see you in the spring; maybe that winter dump won't be so good; maybe this country is too tough for us. Maybe . . .

There is one thing gone forever from our world—the irrevocability of those departures, before the age of the airplane. This was the last boat, and Nature would take over from now until the middle of June. Freeze-up was coming. There would be no chance of seeing any of these faces until another year had rolled away. The *Sarah*'s stern wheel, so huge I was afraid to look at it, began to turn. The swirl and push of water, shouted commands from up above us. The young freight clerk in his navy-and-gold uniform came hurrying up the gangplank, papers in hand, always the last one aboard. A voice from up above shouted down to him: "Sure you got everything? All right, cast off!"

The big cable fell into the river with a splash that must have sent a shiver of finality down many a spine. Up came the gangplank, and the two gorgeous Mounties stood alone and calm down where its lower end had rested. The *Sarah* slid rapidly into the current, and there was a great hissing and churning as bells rang and she slowed, and turned, and straightened out into midstream. Then the three beautiful blended tones, long-drawn-out and echoing from the domed hill behind the town, and from the dock an answering chorus of shouts, and big hats waving.

The *Sarah* was even more exciting than the *Jefferson*. From all the adult conversation I listened to, I gathered that we were lucky to catch her on this last trip, that she was the queen of the fleet, that her captain "knew the river," that she "had the best food." She was, it seemed to me, enormous, both long and broad, and with a great space up front on the main deck, under the upper deck, where everyone gathered when there was anything interesting outdoors, and inside, a large "saloon" all done up in green plush and white paneling and gold trimming, like a drawing room in a fairy-tale palace. Besides this there was a card room, where the men gathered, and a ladies' lounge, where the women sat with their needlework and their talk.

To me, and to the two little boys about my own age who were the only other children on board, the card room and the big deck were the more interesting places. And here we first came in touch with the early Alaskan's attitude toward all children. Children were rare; they were a symbol of everything that many of these men had given up in heeding the call of gold and adventure; they were precious individuals. Out on the deck there were always two or three men eager to play hide-and-seek with us, with shouts and merry antics, swinging themselves about the steel poles which held up the upper deck above us. And inside we were allowed to sit beside someone at the Solo table, and play with the chips while the game went on, and because Daddy knew these men and their big hearts, we children were not forbidden any of these joys.

Life was almost more interesting than one could bear. Every day there were stops, at wood camps when the *Sarah* had to take on the many cords of birch and spruce that kept her huge boiler going. Daddy took me and the little boys ashore to walk about a bit, among the long stacks of wood cut in four-foot lengths; to watch the Indian deckhands so cheerfully going up and down the wide plank into the boiler room of the *Sarah* with their trucks loaded, racing down with a shout and a laugh with an empty truck, straining up the slant with a full one, still smiling. Life seemed a big happy game for everybody in that land. We saw red squirrels in the thick woods behind these wood piles, and sometimes had time to pick a handful of bright red low-bush cranberries before the *Sarah* sounded a short blast which meant her appetite was satisfied for now.

There were Indian villages. A row of tiny log cabins in a straggly line atop a cut bank, backed by the forest, and down below the bank, usually, on the little strip of beach, all the village dogs, chained to stakes, howling their loudest at the approach of the steamer, for it meant food thrown out from the galley for them to fight over.

Sometimes the *Sarah* pulled in to these villages to let off some prospector or trapper going into the far back country for the winter. One of these I remember well. He was called Red Rodgers, a tall, lusty, loud-voiced extrovert with flaming red hair and a long beard. His few boxes of provisions had been quickly wheeled down the plank and onto the shore, but he himself carried his gold pan and pick and shovel and with a great shout leaped from the gangplank onto the beach, and turned to shout a few last lusty, cheery words to friends aboard as the *Sarah* slipped out into the current. Behind him, black spruces stood out against a gold sunset which somehow looked cold. Even then, in my child's mind, I wondered: Did he feel a bit sad, too, as the big white ship slid away downstream?

Everybody went ashore at the towns—Eagle, with the beautiful hills near by; Circle, atop a high bank, a cluster of log buildings where not long before had been a tent city of ten thousand. We were there in the evening in a misty rain; the wide freight plank and the warehouse of the Northern Commercial Company were hung with kerosene lanterns so the freight could be unloaded. We were in the United States now, and the Law was not a beautiful red-and-blue uniform and a strong impassive face, but a jovial round face, a hearty voice, heavy brown woolen trousers, a bright plaid shirt—the U.S. Deputy Marshal. He and his pretty wife came to take us to their bright log-cabin home, and she laughed at Mother's city toe-rubbers: "Those are cheechako rubbers—they won't help you much up here!"

The two little boys and I would have gone happily on and on into the future aboard the *Sarah*; it was a perpetual birthday party. Shining white tablecloths, gleaming silver, white-coated waiters urging all kinds of goodies onto our plates. We all must have had stomachs of iron. We were even allowed to stay up sometimes for the "midnight lunch," which was served at ten in the evening. And at every town, our sourdough friends were eager to buy candy or anything else at the trading posts. My coat pocket bulged with lemon drops.

But one day in warm yet crisp September sunshine, the *Sarah* reached Tanana, where the river of that name poured a wide flood into the Yukon. From here on down to the sea the Yukon would truly be a great river, and the *Sarah* could push five barges of freight ahead of her if need be. Here those who were traveling on downriver to St. Michael and Nome and the Outside must say good-by to the rest of us, and we must say good-by to wonderful *Sarah* and go aboard the *Schwatka*, which was not really so tiny, but looked like a midget beside *Sarah*.

But the *Schwatka* had pleasure for a child which made up for her small size. It was cozy; there was only one small "saloon," and everyone gathered there. Though I had sadly waved good-by to the two little boys, who were staying in Tanana, where their father was employed at the army fort there, Fort Gibbon, some of the good sourdough friends were still aboard and always ready to play games and tell me stories (and how I wish I remembered the stories!). I was invited by the captain up into that mystical place, the pilothouse, from which I could watch the whole river at once, and the deckhands working, and the Huskies tied on the bow, and the man taking the soundings, hour after hour. For now we were in a different river world—a river swift and swirling and carrying a great load of silt and now in its autumn low-water stage, with long sand bars nearly all the way, on one side or the other.

Here river navigation was a fine and definite art. There was a certain expert sweep of the sounding pole, a certain drone to the voice: "Five" and a pause—"Five" and a pause—"and a half four"—getting more shallow—"Four" and a pause—"and a half three." And here the face would be lifted to the pilothouse. What was next? A bell, and a slowing of the engines, and the pilot leaning out the window, looking. And sometimes an awful shuddering thump. We were on the bar! Always at this point Daddy took me down out of the pilothouse. I realize now it must have been to allow the officers free rein in their language as they wrestled with the river. Sometimes they could reverse and slide off. Sometimes they sent a crew in a small boat to the other side, or to some point on the bank, to sink a great timber called a deadman; a cable was attached to the timber, and the freight winch would begin to whine, and slowly, so slowly, the *Schwatka* would be pulled off into deeper water and we could go on again for a spell.

Slow travel, in the Alaska of 1911, provided plenty of time for books and games and paper dolls, for dressing and undressing the brown teddy bear, for visiting the galley and watching the baker rolling out pies and cookies; for peering down into the engine room to watch the play of the long shaft attached to the paddle wheel, sliding forward, knuckling back, terrifying, fascinating— but so long as we heard the chuff and whoosh of that wheel, we knew all was fine, and I know, to this day, of no more soothing, competent, all-is-well sound.

To Mother, arriving in Fairbanks must have been fraught with all kinds of wondering and half fears; she must have been feeling very far away from all she had known. To me, it was just more excitement and more new faces, and new conversation to listen to, often quite interesting.

As it was the fall of the year, there wasn't enough water for the *Schwatka* in the Chena Slough, the small tributary of the Tanana on which Fairbanks had been built. So at the little village of Chena, twelve miles below the town, passengers and freight had to be loaded onto the intrepid Tanana Valley Railroad. Yes, a real train, a real engine, two cars full of people now old friends, reaching the end of a three-week journey together. Even when the train came to the end of its twelve-mile journey, we were not yet at the end of ours, for the main town was across the slough, and horse-drawn carts were at the station to meet the train. So was "Dad" Shaw, owner of the very respectable hotel of the town, the Shaw House, where Daddy had been living and where we were now welcomed as part of the family. There was a big lobby, full of men who all knew Daddy; there were some friendly women too, for on Sunday nights it was a custom with many families to take dinner at the spotless and cheerful Shaw House dining room. Some of the sourdoughs of the journey were staying here too.

Yet when Mother tucked me into a single bed in Daddy's high-ceilinged room, I felt a bit strange. What were the captain and the cook and all the rest on the *Schwatka* doing now? And how empty and quiet the little lounge must be. And where, by now, was the *Sarah*?

2

Freeze-up

Such a final sound—"the last boat," "the freeze-up." But in Fairbanks that year it was an unusually late, mild, sunny autumn. Daddy knew everyone, it seemed, and there were even some picnics with his friends who had horses and buggies, driving out through the golden birch woods and the green spruce forest which extended thick and untouched behind the town, out to the Tanana River, four miles south, a marvelous place of sand and stones and bleached logs to sit on and serve lunch on and clamber over.

After a few days of this exciting life (and without school too!) Daddy found one vacant house—one way out on the edge of town, eight blocks from the river, the last house on the last street of the Fairbanks of that year. It was log of course, and sturdy, but with only four rooms: a living-dining room about sixteen by twenty; behind it a bedroom and a kitchen; and off at one side, a lean-to bedroom built of slab wood. This cabin was home for ten years.

The back door opened into a woodshed-storage place. All such places were called caches, and off one corner of this was what in those days sufficed for sanitary convenience. That was one of the first phenomena of the northern towns. Late in the night on certain nights we might be awakened by a clatter out there. The most heroic soul on the frontier was emptying the can. Lying curled down warm in the middle of my bed in the lean-to bedroom, I would hear the stamping and clatter, the jingle of harness, the low "giddap" to the horses, the creaking of sled runners on the snow, out there in the cold dark.

Added to this was the problem of water. I know Mother really wondered about this life sometimes! Oh, there was a well, and a hand pump in the kitchen sink (the sink drained into a slop bucket which had to be carried outdoors). But the water was so terrifically red and rusty and hard and smelling of iron that Mother could not use it. So we had a big whiskey barrel, with a cover, just inside the kitchen door, and "Fred the Waterman" came every day with his tank wagon or sleigh. First he looked at the kitchen window, to see if the square blue card said two or four, then filled the buckets hanging at the back of his tank—five gallon oil cans fitted with handles of thick copper wire; after this he quickly hooked them onto the hooks of his wooden yoke and came stamping in. "Cold today, yah, yah." Fred's last name was Musjgherd—nobody ever tried to pronounce it. Nobody knew his nationality or how he had come to this far place. But he owned a well which poured forth clear, sweet water, and this directed his life. He was our friend, Fred the Waterman, and his black horses the fattest, sleekest, best-cared-for in town.

So that was the water situation. As for the rest, Mother by some magic touch made it home—colorful and warm and somehow, with everything we owned in those four rooms, still uncluttered.

Neighbors told Mother of how the living room had looked before. The house had belonged to a Mrs. Jackson, a nervous woman with a background of luxurious city life, who had brought her city furnishings along. True, she didn't belong on the Alaskan frontier, and now was gone, but she had not taken it all with her. Even Mother was dismayed about the wallpaper in the living room. As in all the cabins of those days, over the log walls was tacked "house lining"—unbleached muslin cloth—which was also stretched across from eave to eave, making a low ceiling, called a "balloon ceiling." Then the whole was covered with wallpaper. In this case Mrs. Jackson had consented to have *some* light, and the ceiling was white with a "watered silk" silvery overlay, very popular then for ceilings. But the walls jumped at you. They were of a deep red paper with a sort of coat-of-arms figure about a foot high—in gold! The tall front window and the little square ones on each side were curtained in what was called scrim, in a very fancy pattern in red, blue, and tan. On the floor was a Brussels carpet, all roses on a tan background; in one corner was a wide couch "cozy corner" affair, the mattress covered with red rep; in another corner a tall corner cupboard, the bottom part hung with red-and-white-striped material. Mrs. Jackson, the neighbors said, had had this filled with hand-painted china— altogether a lively room. As soon as possible, Mother had the walls covered with light-tan burlap.

I think my mother felt the unspeakable isolation more than she would ever say. She kept it locked away inside, while she went serenely about the task that was hers—adapting her very civilized self to creating a home and bringing up a family on this far frontier, with the man she loved. I realize now that I felt this in her, even while not feeling it myself at all. To an eager, curious child, everything was interesting here.

One thing I remember is that Mother could hardly stand the howling of the dogs. Not too far from our house, across the fields and beyond a slough and some spruce woods, was the dog pound, down on the river. Alaska was a dog country then; there were always plenty of strays, or whole teams being "boarded out" there, so whenever that famous six-o'clock whistle blew there was a chorus not to be ignored—it was too close to our little log house—and Mother thought they "sounded so mournful." To me it was just an interesting noise. The trouble was that the "six-o'clock whistle" blew at six A.M. and seven A.M. and at noon and one P.M., and finally at six P.M., and the chorus was just as great each time, to say nothing of the frenzied tune when that awful fire siren stopped us all in our tracks. That one was enough to make any dog howl; it made all of us want to, besides stabbing us with cold fear each time. Perhaps to the dogs those whistles signified the ancestor of all wolves howling to them. They had to respond. Anyway, I am sure that later, when we moved down close in to town, Mother was glad to have put some distance between herself and that opera.

She had enough to do, that first winter, to adjust to this new life. I can see clearly now that things that were of no thought and little trouble to me, a child, were a daily series of battles for her, gentle and sweet and straight from the city and expecting my first half sister in the spring, and with Daddy gone through Christmas and far into January, traveling by dog team on the Yukon from village to village, for he was the field man for the

U.S. Attorney, and the Law had but recently come to this part of the wild North.

Temperatures, and stoves. On one side of the living room stood the indispensable stove of the North, a Cole Airtight Heater. This took in big heavy chunks of spruce wood. In the kitchen, close to the back window, we had the big wood range. This took endless feeding with split spruce. When the thermometer went down to minus 20, and 30, and 50, and sometimes stayed there for weeks, the pattern of life was set—feeding the stoves. But, since the houses were small and low-ceilinged, and had storm windows and "bankings" of earth about three feet high all around the outside walls (where a riot of sweet peas grew in the summer), we were warm. But Mother's feet were always cold. She would go busily about her housework for a half hour, then open the oven door and sit with her feet in the oven for a few minutes, then back to work. Thank heaven for the nine cords of good spruce wood all neatly ricked up in the back yard. And for the cellar under the kitchen, where all the supplies were stored—vegetables and canned goods, jams and jellies. And out in the cache, in a special cupboard, we had cuts of moose and caribou, all wrapped and frozen oh so solid, and bundles of frozen whitefish. We were fairly self-contained, in a little bastion against the 50-below-zero world outside.

We did have some helpful things: electric lights, so Mother could use her new electric iron, and a telephone, so that during those very cold spells she could talk to her friends—and there were fine friends, but most of them lived on the other side of town.

The house nearest us was vacant that first year. (Later our wonderful friends Jess and Clara Rust moved into it.) Across the street there was only one house, and after Daddy left for his long winter journey that house became a source of worry to Mother. One day we saw six enormous mustachioed, fur-coated, fur-capped men moving their gear into that house—six of them! They were what Fairbanks called "Bohunks"—Slavic men of some kind—tremendous in stature and strength. They worked in the mines in the summer. I don't think Mother had ever seen such huge men before. For weeks the only sound from them was the terrific noise they made late each night, coming home from an evening in town, stamping the snow from their boots at their front door, which sounded as though they were stamping on *our*

front doorstep and coming right on in. Then one day there was a
gentle knock at our back door. I opened it and there stood one of
these giants. He looked at me solemnly and said one word: "Ax!"

I flew in terror to Mother, but when she came, the giant made
her understand by a few gestures that he would like to cut some
wood for us. And he did. After that the stomping and the singing
in Russian, or something, meant only that *our friends* were home
from a convivial evening on Front Street.

3

The Town

Every one of the gold-rush towns had to be unusual. All the factors which combined to produce them were unusual. First, the presence of gold in the earth—call that providential or geologic as you will. Second, the character, the climate, the topography, of the land itself; a land more difficult to conquer could hardly be imagined. Third, the people—the many kinds of people who would be attracted to the promise and the challenge of the gold and the land.

Most important to the story of Fairbanks is a consideration of the conglomeration of people who *stayed* in the country. For it was a conglomeration—it was more than merely an assortment. It was a mixture which made the town like no other perhaps, and in that era, from 1902 to 1922, the town was all theirs.

Growing up in Fairbanks, one knew no other town. There were no others nearer than eight days by horse sleigh or ten days by river steamer. So we children of Fairbanks were early accustomed to all the kinds of people—they were taken for granted, part of the environment we knew. Not until I was nearly grown and at last went Outside to school did I begin to realize that our town was indeed different.

Fairbanks in 1911. Of course it was built on the river bank, the bank of Chena Slough, that offshoot of the mighty Tanana, which swept on four miles behind the town. The story is that

Captain Barnette, bound for the upper Tanana, with his new flat-bottomed boat *Isabelle* loaded with supplies, to establish a new trading post where the trail of the Klondike gold seekers from Valdez crossed the Tanana, got into the Chena Slough, got stuck in the shallow water, and at the same time met two or three prospectors who gave him the news that Felix Pedro had just made a strike on a nearby creek. Here was the place for his trade goods, here was the site of a new camp, and since Barnette's friend James Wickersham, then federal judge for that part of Alaska, had asked him to name his trading post after his friend Senator Fairbanks, of Indiana, the new camp was named accordingly.

The slough was navigable except in low water. Out in the States it would be quite a river, but Alaska is a land laced with great rivers. The slough drew a great shallow curve here; the first street of the new camp followed that curve, so that the pattern of the whole town reflected it, with streets slightly bent. Along Front Street there was a long row of false-front business houses, built of green native lumber, painted white, and green, and ruddy ocher trimmed in red. Opposite these, on the very bank of the slough, a few warehouses on piles, where the steamers tied up just below the bridge. There were more of the same kind of buildings on Second Avenue and a few on Third. That made up the main part of the town. Beyond these, spreading out into the great slightly curved half circle, the buildings diminished from a few two-story frame houses to the low log ones in which most of the people lived.

As though they were the first things the early settlers thought of, the saloons were nearly all on Front Street, some twenty-three of them! The real ladies of the town never walked up Front Street; they turned down and walked on Second. Here and on Third and along Cushman, the main street that bisected the avenues, were the respectable shops.

And then, in the very center of the town, beginning at Fourth and Cushman and extending downstream two or three blocks, was the red-light district, known as "the Row." I guess it was there before many families arrived. With the coming of wives, and churches and schools, a feeble attempt was made to put a respectable face on the town. A high solid board fence, with gates in it, was built right across the street, one on Fourth where it left Cushman, and one across Fourth where it emerged on Barnette, two blocks down, and the big dance hall on Third and Cushman was closed and turned into a dry-goods emporium. Immediately beyond the Row on Fifth and Sixth and Seventh, especially along Cushman, lived the elite, the very respectable leading citizens, in two-story houses which tried to look almost like conservative middle-class homes back in the States.

In the first place, the miners were the source of life. Amazingly soon after them came the followers, to cater to every real or imagined need of those hardy diggers and to share in their diggings. First the traders, who set up stores—grocers, butchers, hardware merchants (who dealt in all the heavy tools and machinery of placer mining), dry-goods dealers, saloon keepers— and, right along with them, gamblers and prostitutes. Restaurants and bakeries and laundries came next, and two newspapers, and all the while anyone who could put two boards together and would stay in town and do that instead of going prospecting was in great demand. And by this time, to keep all these interests in worse or better order, but in any case to make a living from them all, came the lawyers, and in Fairbanks these made a colorful story.

Eventually these energetic pioneers realized they must take time to set up a government of some kind and to accept some representatives of the federal government. After all, the town did belong to the United States. So the next thing they knew they had all helped build a monstrosity of a courthouse on Second and Cushman, right in the heart of the town and just a block and a half from the Row. A monstrosity built in the only style known to the frontier it seemed, a straight box, two tall stories high, of native lumber, with a recessed entrance porch on one corner. To make it supremely attractive it was painted a sickly muddy olive green, and Justice was set up in business in the Far North. In the front corner of the second story of this building was the suite of offices of the U.S. Attorney, Mr. James Crossley, and his three assistants. They were supposed to enforce virtue and observance of the law throughout the Fourth Judicial Division of the Territory of Alaska, an area of 220,000 square miles!

Not surprising either that, as "the Creeks," the mining district around Fairbanks, kept on producing, two banks should soon be established and housed, in cracker boxes not so tall, near the Courthouse. Banks, drugstores, grocery stores—above them the doctors, the lawyers, the dentists, yes, even real estate men and public accountants. This town was pretty solidly built up now. It

had five churches and two hospitals. And all this just nine years after Captain Barnette's *Isabelle* got stuck on the bar and Felix Pedro found a certain spot in the tundra wilderness.

Busy place. Happy-go-lucky place. No place for too much concern over morals—plenty of room for all the characters.

So there you have Fairbanks in 1911. It was a place to draw questions from nine-years-olds—"Why does that part of town have a fence around it?"—and it held various terrors for me.

Soon after our arrival a friend of Daddy's gave me a beautiful, sweet-tempered Husky named Major. He was my companion and protector. He could lick any dog in town. I had a long rope tied to his collar, and if we met a loose dog and there was a fight, I merely stood holding the end of the rope, well out of the way, and waited until the other dog went off whimpering; then Major and I went on about our business. He and I, with the little sled, were sent on all the errands for Mother.

Well, I was forbidden to go up Front Street because of the saloons. I was supposed to go up Second or Third, but each of them held a fear for me which I would never confess to Mother. On Second, the back part of the big corrugated-iron buildings of the Northern Commercial Company housed the town power plant and was the home of the big deep "six-o'clock whistle" and the terrifying fire siren. I had almost a pathological terror of loud sounds, and if I did force myself to go up Second Avenue, I fairly scuttled past, sure the siren was going to blow just as Major and I came abreast of the huge open doors and the terrifying sound of the big dynamos.

The Fire Department fronted on Third Avenue, in the two-story City Hall, whose back door opened into the Row. At street level were the two great double doors, and I was sure that when I reached the exact middle of those doors the alarm would sound within, the doors would fly open, and both teams of huge gray horses would dash out, over my prone body.

So I went clear up to Fifth Avenue and hurried along those two blocks behind the Row—not too fast to cast fearful yet wondering glances at the backs of all those close-ranked little log cabins—and emerged on Cushman Street, and its open, harmless, respectable stores, with a deep breath of relief.

I suppose it's the good women who do it. On the frontier, before the wives arrived I don't think Society was organized. They were a motley group of men, all there for the same two things—adventure and gold, or gold and adventure—and their spare hours were spent in whatever bunch, in whatever saloon, they happened to wander into.

But soon, almost immediately in Fairbanks, there were women, and churchmen, and thus the whole mixed-up population began to fall away into groups—Presbyterian church, Episcopal church, Ladies' Aid, Guild. Also whist clubs, sewing clubs, a Women's Civic Club. They gave the men the fever too. Masons became very active, and along with them, Eastern Star, then Eagles and Lady Eagles, Moose and Lady Moose. And in those early days throughout the North there flourished two strictly indigenous lodges, the Arctic Brotherhood and the Pioneers of Alaska.

The A.B. was quite a plushy lodge. Their functions were examples of how much luxury can be laid over the wilderness. All the "best people" were there. An A.B. dance was a top social event; the ladies' gowns were described in the Fairbanks *News-Miner* the next day. One of the sharp, ecstatic memories is of Mother, ready for one of these balls, in pale blue marquisette over Alice-blue satin, a sprinkling of gold sequins over the bodice, black velvet ribbon about the waist; and then, next day, listening wide-eyed while Daddy read the whole account from the paper, with chortles and dramatic expression. I remember he was so impressed by the fact that every other gown was "a creation," and he had a way of reading "crepe de Chine" that made it sound like the silliest, most ridiculous kind of stuff imaginable.

All that crepe de Chine at the A.B. New Year's ball of 1913 turned into a family joke which has persisted through the years. "Mrs. J. J. Crossley was radiant in a creation of pale pink crepe de Chine with black velvet streamers." To a ten-year-old, every word was straight from the mysterious world of grown-up doings. Mothers had to tell me every little detail—how at midnight the orchestra played "Auld Lang Syne" and they formed a great circle about the big Eagles Hall, hands clasping hands clear around; how she found herself clasping the hand of Jack Robarts, a local newspaperman, and how they both remarked how far they had come on this New Year's Eve from their native New Brunswick, and how that got her to thinking about all the others, from what far distant places they had all come. Here was this gay scene, this little huddle of homes, one little working, whirring piece of civilization set down in almost the exact center of this enormous land, the great wilderness, thousands of miles of it, surrounding that tiny, whirring, alive spot. It was as though a great clock somewhere had exploded, and one little cogwheel had been flung through space, landed in the arctic tundra, and continued spinning.

But of course, Mother told me, while this queer thought was running through her mind they were all trooping upstairs to the dining hall, where a real "collation" was spread. These people on the little cogwheel were of the strongest, most alive, most carefree breed—"Eat, drink, and be merry! We've come a long way; we're different from the stodgy folk; let's take all we can get from life."

4

Winter

Thirty below zero this morning. Frost has crept through the walls and caused the bedclothes to stick to the wall on that side, and it is mortal agony to crawl out of the warm nest in the center of the bed when Daddy calls. It is still dark of course. He turns on my light, opens the draft of the little stove in the corner, puts in more wood, says for the third time: "Come, now, if you're going to school you *must* get up right away," and goes out to stoke the range in the kitchen some more. Mother will be out there making the pot of porridge. I can hardly stuff it down, but I am not allowed to go to school without it. Barely a tinge of pink down in the east when my friends Irene and Lily and Marguerite come by for me. They have already walked four blocks and their faces and scarves are framed in frosty white. We all learned to be fast walkers, growing up in Fairbanks.

Walking into the sunrise on the way to school, half a mile, smoke going straight up in the perfectly still air, which meant 20 below or more. Some days it will be 50 or 60 below and sometimes it will be 50 below for weeks. But life goes on. Businessmen in coonskin overcoats and caps hurry to open their stores and build up the fires in the big stoves. In the Model Cafe or the Arcade it is steamy warm, and the bachelors and the miners spending the winter in town are eating hotcakes and ham and eggs. The Judge, the Marshal, the District Attorney, and all the others are hurrying into the Courthouse to start the day's work, for in winter the court is in session, with some trial or other going on all the time. There is little lingering on sidewalks, no standing in doorways, but there are cheery voices.

In the afternoon, no matter what the temperature, some brave women will be on the streets, in long fur coats and black felt shoes, scarves or veils over their hats, some of them pushing babies in "baby cutters"—a winter version of a baby carriage. The women are shopping in the stores; they are on their way to "pay calls" or to attend the Ladies' Aid or the Guild. If they worried about temperature they would be completely housebound.

The respectable society of Fairbanks was very proper. Every house no matter how small had a "card tray" on a little stand by the door, and the ladies all left cards, another fascinating little facet of life for a small girl. After the callers had left I would study the cards—"Mrs. Louis Kossuth Pratt," "Mrs. John Knox Brown." To me these were somewhat awesome, symbols of a world I could not know for some years.

The "respectable women" of the town, unconsciously perhaps, made a definite answer to the situation in which they found themselves. Here they were, far from their safe and ordinary homes in the States, surrounded by a wilderness so vast it could not be visualized but which did make itself felt, keeping house in log cabins or small frame houses without bathrooms, running water or central heat. Whatever a housewife might be doing at any time, she must remember to stop and stoke more split wood into the kitchen range, another big chunk into the Cole Airtight Heater. When the temperature went down to 30 below and more, frost formed on the nailheads in the walls of the kitchen; when the heavy kitchen door was opened a wave of white frost hurried in and scuttled across the floor, white and very visible. If you forgot and took hold of the kitchen doorknob with a wet hand, you froze to it and "burned" your hand.

Washday was a business of putting the yellow card in the window, for Fred to bring in extra buckets, and warning the small children to get in by the living-room stove so they would not catch a chill while he was carrying in all that water and pouring it into the water barrel. Then you had to stoke up the stove and heat water in the copper wash boiler, and get the washtubs set up in front of the stove, and the Fels-Naphtha soap melted in a pan on the stove to pour into the wash water; then sorting the clothes in piles on the floor and starting in over the washboard. It was impossible to dry the clothes outside, for they would freeze almost immediately; so the kitchen would be hung with lines just below the ceiling and diapers draped on racks by the living-room heater. I remember Mother laughing almost hysterically one fall when a package came from my grandmother containing a warm wool hood and a note: "For you to wear when you are hanging out clothes in winter."

Tuesday was better. There was electricity, and ironing was more a normal procedure and a warmer one. And that was a good day to bake the bread, too. On Wednesdays there were the meetings of the Ladies' Aid or the Guild. On Thursdays many ladies went out calling on the ladies who had "Thursdays" engraved on the lower corners of their cards. On Fridays many of them would take their baskets of mending and go to "spend the afternoon" with a friend. This is a custom which I imagine is nearly dead in the land. The friends came about two o'clock. The hostess brought out her mending or crocheting or knitting, and they all sat and "visited" until four, when the hostess served tea and cookies. The friends had to "go home and get dinner" at five. That was Friday. Saturday was baking and cleaning day. When I was nine and a half, during that first winter in Fairbanks, I made my first batch of molasses cookies. After that nearly every Saturday morning found me making cookies. Mother baked pies, many of them, and doughnuts. These were put out into the cache or the screen porch and frozen, the same as the meat and the fish, and the many loaves of bread. All over town the women would be doing the same kind of thing.

A regular routine, a definite project for each day, a regular program with other people—all this helps. It is all part of the bulwark the women built, consciously or unconsciously, against the isolation, the wilderness, the cold, the difficulties of housekeeping. They set the pattern for the kind of town Fairbanks was supposed to be—the town you could talk about.

Of course the other town was right there too. Mother had one friend, Mrs. Aiken, who did dressmaking for the elite of the town. She was also one of those geniuses who knew all that went on in both towns. She often came and sewed for Mother all day, and talked as she sewed, above the whir of Mother's "New Home," and I, curled in the big chair in the corner with a book and apparently oblivious, took in knowledge of life. I learned that there were different kinds of people, who acted in many kinds of ways.

There was the town of the homes and the schools and the churches and the library, and there was the town of the saloons and the Row—and in between these, in a way, an institution known as the "cigar store," where men played pool and solo and fan-tan in the back part of the store, and where there were hotel chairs scattered around in the front part, where men sat and smoked and chatted or read the old papers from the Outside, and watched the passers-by through the big front windows. Tobacco and cigars were actually sold too. These places were open to the street and the world, not closed in blankly like the saloons, and the family men, the shopkeepers, and the professional men all frequented them, to buy tobacco, to chat, to gather up the news. But in the winter the cigar store also served as a daytime hangout for the miners and workers in from the creeks who were just passing the months until mining opened up again. Most of these men lived in tiny log cabins, which were cramped and dark, and if they did not want to spend their time in the saloons, the cigar stores were a haven and their contact with the life of the town.

Mrs. Aiken seemed to know who spent their time in the saloons, who in the cigar stores, who on the Row, as well as the few unusual and conspicuous ones who were to be found spending their afternoons in the big reading room at the library or reading or writing in the lobby of the Shaw House. These people might find themselves being taken as welcome dinner guests into many of the homes!

I don't think Mother was especially eager for all this information, but she got it anyway, and so did I! We also heard about the Tanana Club, upstairs over the Model Cafe, where the men tried hard to copy the gentlemen's clubs back East, with huge leather easy chairs, a private bar, a white-coated Filipino steward and "big" Solo and poker games. According to Mrs. Aiken, the moving spirit behind this plush establishment was Charlie Thompson. He was perhaps an early forerunner of the "gentleman" czar of the underworld. He owned a good deal of the property on the Row, and dictated the lives of a good many of its occupants; he had a finger in mining ventures, in gambling, in the saloons. When he appeared on the streets of the town he was always impeccably dressed in business attire and high white collar, equipped with a Derby hat and a big cigar, handsome, serious, quiet. In winter he wore the finest of huge coonskin coats, but still the Derby hat. According to Mrs. Aiken, the games at the respectable Tanana Club relieved many of the town's respectable professional men of a good deal of their cash, but it was quietly, fastidiously run, and the ladies of the town were thrilled to accept the adventure of a "Ladies' Night" there, which was held once during the winter. It was an occasion for all the crepe de Chine and velvet bows.

There were the two kinds of town, but they were mixed up too. What would the men have built if no wives had come along with some of them? Fairbanks had both the easygoing, grabby, lusty, frontier philosophy and the striving for some order, for personal recognition perhaps, for justification of the accepted Outside kind of culture. All through the years Fairbanks was torn between these two—mainly cut off from the world, immersed in its own life, with the "proper" and "improper" lives constantly intermingling. The ladies of the church and the home could not speak to the ladies of the Row, but when there was an emergency of any kind, a drive to raise funds for a hospital or a library or relief for a destitute or "burnt-out" family, they gladly accepted donations from the Row; and if one of the cabins on the Row burned down, the respectable ladies would contribute clothing and funds to the unfortunate one. There was a good deal of live-and-let-live, a good deal of gossip, but of a rather humorous, casual, unmalicious kind. We were all far way from the rest of the world; we had to depend on one another.

Mining and trapping were the basis of the economy, the reason for all the rest of it. All the merchants (and there were really fine stores of every kind in Fairbanks almost from the beginning) depended on the miner and the trapper, but in turn the miner and the trapper depended on the merchant. This was the grubstake system. The miner had a prospect, but had no funds for food or tools to continue searching. The merchant "grubstaked" him with the food or tools he needed; there was usually some scrap of paper involved. If the miner struck it, the merchant was repaid, and usually had an interest in the future earnings of the mine or trapline besides. Everyone was gambling; nearly everyone had some kind of lien on or "interest" in mines or mining claims. If the miner or trapper had need of any legal services, he found himself caught in the web of a lawyer. Some of the lawyers in those early

days could have stepped from the pages of Conan Doyle—
brilliant, unscrupulous, colorful. They destroyed, and they built
up.

The colorful tapestry that was life in this far place was woven
of man's yearning for wealth, for power over other men's lives,
for status in the community, or for the chance to go back and
"show" the folks Outside or in the Old Country. Or, sometimes,
simple kindness and concern for a hard-working prospector or
trapper. There was this too.

And there were the children. We were pampered by the whole
community. We were few in comparison to the adults, for the
frontier population was so largely made up of unattached men,
and apparently they all loved us. Nearly every one of us had a
dog and a sled. On Saturdays we were all over the town, racing,
doing errands for our mothers, taking for granted the smiles, the
jovial greetings, the stories about dogs, the help with our tangled
harness, the fifty-cent pieces thrust into our palms—"Here, go
buy yourself some candy."

When conditions were right and the skating rink was open—it
was on the river just below the bridge in front of the town—there
were always plenty of sourdoughs watching the fun, helping us
with our skate buckles, keeping fires going on the edge so we
could warm ourselves, saying sometimes: "Here, you, your nose
is white. Come rub some snow on it."

We lived in an atmosphere of tolerance and love. I wonder if it
affected our grown-up lives? Every family, I think without
exception, had some miner or trapper friend who became more or
less a member—who came in from the creeks for special days, who
was there for Thanksgiving and Christmas. And what Santa Clauses
they were!

Winter was long—October to April—and things happened. We
made our own excitement. We also lived through excitement we
did not make.

In the early days Fairbanks had no bricks and no cement. The
buildings were of wood, from the big logs that served as
foundations to the boards that made up the roofs. Some of the
buildings were sheathed in corrugated iron, but inside they were
wood, locally sawed green spruce lumber. There were no brick
chimneys. The pipes from the many stoves went out through the

roof though galvanized-iron drums called "safeties." In the case of the little cabins, the safety was often merely a gasoline can through which the pipe passed. The next problem was that all the wood burned, especially birch, had a high oil, or creosote, content, depositing a black crust on the inside of the pipes which sometimes caught fire. On a cold winter night just about bedtime, we could hear the neighbors pounding the stovepipes with the stove pokers, "knocking down the creosote." Consider further that the log-wall interiors of the houses, of the hotels, of the saloons, many of them, were all lined with muslin and then with wallpaper. A pretty inflammable town.

We were especially aware of all this perhaps because of Clara and Jess Rust, our nearest neighbors after our first year, who lived two vacant lots away from us. They were cheery hard-working young folks with two little girls the same ages as our Louise and Louis. Jess was an engineer at the Northern Commercial Company power plant, and his particular responsibility was the smooth operation of the big pump which pumped water from under the ice of the river for the fire hoses. I spent a lot of time at the Rusts', taking care of their babies when I wasn't busy with our own, and Clara and Mother shared all their household problems and recipes and ideas.

The winter I was fourteen we had a long spell of 50-below weather. After a while this gets on people's nerves. No one spoke of fire, but everyone was especially careful about knocking down creosote and firing the stoves carefully.

In the middle of the night, into our dreams it came, the blood-chilling siren. I lay in a tight knot under the covers, listening for the other one, the deep-toned "six-o'clock whistle" which would give the signal. One long, one short; the first block this side of Cushman, between First and Second, right in the heart of town, only a block from the power plant itself.

I heard Mother and Daddy stirring, the light went on, I heard Daddy lift the telephone receiver. The operator would be sitting, with all keys open, saying over and over again: "McIntosh Building, McIntosh Building, McIntosh Building."

Now there was hurry in the other bedroom, and I got up too and put on my robe and my fur slippers. Daddy was pulling on his clothes and Mother was saying: "I see lights on over at the Rusts'; I suppose Jess is on his way running by now. Mardy, bring Daddy's overshoes and mittens."

The office of the Red Cross was located in the McIntosh
Building, and in addition to other duties Daddy was secretary,
and responsible for the papers. He was out the door, then back
again—"My pipe!" It reminded me of the time Mr. McCauley's
horse broke away from the post in front of our house, and
Mr. McCauley had to run back into our house and get his hat
before he could run after the horse! But right now I had scraped a
patch of frosted window clear, and there it was, a red glow
against the black night, the snapping clear 50-below-zero night.
There would be no sleep for anyone in Fairbanks now. Mother
was dressing. She called: "Can you hear the pump yet?"

"Yes, it's going; the night fireman starts it, you know, but Jess
has to get there to watch it."

"You'll be cold by that window; do go get your clothes on."
And just then our ring on the phone. Fumbling and trembling and
getting my woolen underwear on wrong side out, I heard Mother
say: "Yes, of course, I'll send her right over."

"Clara wants you to come stay with the children; she's making
a big pot of coffee to take down to the men in the boiler room."

When I ran across the crackling crisp snow between the houses,
the red glow was taller and wider and there were all sorts of
strange sounds mingled with shouts, and beneath it all, the
steady, deep "chook-choom, chook-choom" of that pump, like
another heartbeat.

Clara was plump and rosy-cheeked, and so pretty, but she was pale and a bit breathless now, pulling on her big overshoes, tying a fur cap under her chin. "Looks bad, doesn't it?" she greeted me. "Can you hear the pump?"

I was helping her pack the coffeepot and some cookies into the big basket, and suddenly we both stopped and looked at each other. The pump had stopped! Like one's own heart stopping. Clara lifted the basket and made for the door. "I have to get down there. Do watch the stoves and be careful. I'll be back as soon as I can."

Too quiet, and the red glow taller; the children were asleep and the house so still. I carefully put a few sticks of wood into the kitchen range and sat down by the big kitchen table under the window, the one that looked toward town and the fire; then the pump started—"chook-choom, chook-choom." What a relief, I thought, for Clara, hurrying and hurrying in that bitter-cold air—seven blocks she had to go—thinking of the fire, the fire fighters, the pump, and Jess, on whom the whole town perhaps depended right now.

I still had my coat on, and I stepped out the back door. There was a kind of crackling, and a kind of roar, and shouts. I knew how it would be: the water from the hoses freezing immediately, so that when the fire was burned out, there would remain in the morning a great edifice of ice and charcoal. And the firemen, living icicles themselves, hardly able to move about, and the streets a glacier. Had Daddy got there in time to save the books? Had he got out all right? I looked over to our house, all the lights on; Mother would be watching too, and praying. Just then that space between the two houses seemed a long way. I went back in. I must watch the stoves. The phone rang. Clara's voice: "I'm in the telephone office. Margaret said I could make this one call. Run over and tell your mother your daddy got the books out, and he's O.K., but he's helping across the street. The fire jumped the street—it's the Model Café and all that block now. And then come right back to the kids will you? I can't get home for a while. We're making more hot coffee, for the relief firemen. Just pray the pump keeps going."

I ran. I remembered Daddy's words: "Don't ever run in 50 below zero." But had *he* walked tonight? Had Jess?

And halfway back again—the heartbeat stopped. Mine? No, the pump. The pump. It ran by steam power; if there was a great drain, with all the hoses in action, it took a lot of steam to keep the pump going. There in the dark, another red glow, apart from the first—the fire must have jumped another street. Sparks were rising high in the air; a good thing there was snow on all the roofs. I went in and tucked the covers around the two little girls; somehow my teeth wouldn't stop chattering. And then: "chook-choom, chook-choom."

In the gray half dawn they all came wearily home, and Mother had more hot coffee and sourdough pancakes for all at our house. Jess and Daddy were crusted with both ice and soot, but the fire was under control, and we heard about the pump. The first time, it had been a mechanical breakdown, which Jess spotted and was able to fix in a few moments. The second time, the steam pressure was not sufficient. The manager of the Northern Commerical was there in the boiler room at the time, and the order went out: "Bring in the bacon!"

Into the long corrugated-iron warehouse went the file of volunteer helpers; out they came, arms full of bacon. Onto the little flatcars on the little narrow track went the bacon, into the great door of the boiler room, right into the maw of the enormous boiler; and more wood, and more bacon, carload after carload; and in a few minutes the pressure went up, the pump could start again; the fire was brought under control.

Three corners had burned, but later, when the iron fist of the cold spell had relaxed, there would be crews cleaning up the terrible mess; in the spring there would be new buildings, better than the old—never any question of that. This was just one of the hazards, just one of the exciting events, of business and life in the North.

5

Mail Day

Fairbanks had one lifeline in winter. There lay the little town, a flat platter of hodgepodge buildings and low log cabins, a fan shape on the lonely land, fog over the river, smoke plumes rising straight up from all the impudent little iron stovepipes defying the cold and loneliness and all the powers of the unbeatable North.

From the river, and exactly bisecting the town, ran Cushman, the main street of the town. In those days it stretched for ten blocks. On the eighth one stood the schoolhouse. At the tenth the street was leaving the town, but it did not stop. It became a road, a winter road, narrowing and narrowing and turning a bit, entering the black spruce forest, disappearing to the south. But we knew it went on; it was the lifeline, the Valdez Trail, later named the Richardson Highway, now part of the Alaska Highway.

Those days were different, the early days, days of men and beasts and no machines. Health and stamina and nerve, in the men and in the beasts they drove, were what counted, and on this form of transportation all else depended. The tradesmen, the housewives, the children, the ministers and missionaries, the miners and the lawyers, the gamblers and the prostitutes—we were all hanging on that lifeline, although perhaps none of us ever thought of it exactly that way.

To us children it was like this:

In winter the whole town revolved around one day in the

week—mail day! It was usually Thursday. In the afternoon, after the last class at school, there was an extra flurry to get into our coats, caps, overshoes, muffs, and mittens. We poured down all three sides of the square school porch and raced to the corner. If we were lucky we'd be in time to "see the stage come in." It usually reached town about three-thirty. We stood carefully at the sides of the snowy street, every head turned out down the "trail." It was nearly pitch dark at this hour, but on the snow we could still see a lot. We were used to it. Presently a voice would pipe up: "I hear the bells!"

Quiet now, everyone listening. From far down that mysterious ribbon of road is a sound, a beautiful tinkling sound, growing stronger. Then: "I see 'em! Here they come!"

A dark shape draws toward us, the bells louder. Someone yells: "It's Harry Martin today!"

Delicious excitement! Harry Martin always made a dashing entry into town. He was the most glamorous of the drivers. And here they come—four beautiful big horses at a fast trot. Behind them the long "thorough-brace" bob sleigh, its high body bright yellow, looms unreal in our eyes; three sets of seats and a great boot in back for mail and luggage. In the seats are the passengers, every one of them in a huge bulky coonskin coat and cap, furnished by the stage company, and all wrapped in wolfskin robes; strange giant furry shapes leaning forward, gazing at us. But our gaze is on Harry. He sits higher still, and besides the coonskin coat he has fancy fur mitts and a marten-fur cap with the tails flying out behind. Just as he reaches us he flings out his arm and makes a fine singing coil of his long whip. It cracks like a rifle shot; the horses lunge into a gallop. Harry yells: "Hiya, kids!"

"Hi, Harry, hi!" The lady passengers squeal. The stage is flying down Cushman, right through town, bells jingling, everyone all along the way calling: "Hi, Harry!"

It is Harry's moment, and it is the highlight of the week for us, and it is fresh eggs "over the ice" and a few apples and oranges, and news from home to many a homesick pioneer.

6

Spring

October to April is a long time. But there is a great compensation. Spring in the North comes with a leap and a shout and a surge of excitement. The change begins in February, the month of the returning sun, with glorious sunsets and a softening of the air. In March all the dog mushers are burned to a deep brown by the intense sun reflected from the snow. In April the snow, never very deep in interior Alaska, is going away fast and it is daylight-dusky nearly all night. In late April we school children are having adventures every morning on the way to school, with huge puddles of water and slush to wade in, to sail chips of wood on, to build makeshift bridges of planks across. And then, off with the winter underwear and the overshoes; cotton dresses blossom forth and life is all lighter and freer, and there are pussy willows to pick on the way for the teacher's desk, and the smell of sap and balm of Gilead in the air, snipes in the little ponds, and the call of geese and sandhill cranes overhead and in the evening, the bone-thrilling elfin quavering call of the Wilson snipe high in the sky.

Now comes the agony of sitting in warm chalky-smelling schoolrooms while the eaves are drip-dripping steadily outside and the last and best coasting of the year is melting away out on Birch Hill. Birch Hill, two miles distant, is the nearest hill, and guardian of the valley. In these first weeks of warmer weather the snow roads are slick on top, good sledding, and great towering loads of birch and spruce are being brought into town to be piled up for next winter in the great woodyard not far from the school, where hundreds of cords of four-foot lengths will be stored, fuel for the power plant of the Northern Commercial Company.

These are warm days for sledding. Horses are shining and steaming when they come across the bridge; the big Russian teamsters have doffed the cumbersome coonskin coats; they tramp along in the honeycombing snow beside the sleighs, rubber pacs splashing through into water below the road level. As the big loads drag along up Cushman Street the runners often grate and squeak over protruding patches of gravel and dirt. The store-keepers are out in shirt sleeves, chopping the firm beaten snow and ice of winter off the wooden sidewalks, throwing it in big slabs along the street. Here and there you can see the yellow glint of sawdust piles left by the busy gasoline woodsaws throughout the long winter.

As the wood teams go creaking past the school yard they are greeted by small boys, just let out, who clamber with shouts onto the loads, stand on the runners, dig their toes in between the logs, and ride to the woodyard. If they help unload they may get a ride out to the Hill before supper.

These are the great days for coasting and sliding and snow-balling—it is light until after eight o'clock. Every kitchen stove has a row of wet shoes, socks, and mittens hung behind it, and we hear about "tracking in all that wet snow and sawdust." But April is short and must be used.

To add another thrill to these days, dog teams are coming into town. Long strings of Malemutes lope down the streets pulling basket sleighs twelve and fourteen feet long loaded with the fruit of the winter's trapping or prospecting. Those who have wintered in the hills must hurry in now on the last snow or wait a weary six weeks for summer travel. On this same "last snow" other teams are leaving town carrying supplies for spring work in the mines and camps. Every day sees less snow on the level, and all of that honeycombed, and more bare brown spots on the hill slopes. On these bare spots woodsmen find the ptarmigan, with the first brown of summer on their necks, feeding on last year's crow-berries.

Even the fearsome glorious Alaska Range looks softer, warmer; its peaks seem to blend with the sky; and in all directions there are the hills showing patches of heliotrope and reddish brown on their slopes, and that, say the old-timers, means sap coming up. In the North there is no coy advance and retreat of spring, as there is in the western states, with hot sun one day and a blizzard the next. When the snow has gone the sun has come to stay, and the nights are never cold. Pale green buds appear on the birches, and one day a homesteader from the Hill announces that "the crocuses are out," and the whole school takes a day off for the annual "crocus picnic."

Lunches in hand, pupils and teachers cross the river, tramp out along the dirt road through the birches and willows, climb up onto the broad breast of the domelike Hill, roam through the birch groves, clamber over the little rocky bluffs on the south slope. From these slopes one may look across the broad flat valley of low spruces to the still frozen white ribbon of the Tanana, curving below the misty peaks of the Range one hundred miles south. The air up here is warmer, holding a faint but sure promise of awakening life.

At last, in the light fragrant evening, we come trooping back, each with a bouquet of the soft blue pasqueflowers for our mothers—official notice of the arrival of another spring in the north country. How the flower beds of nature withstood this annual visitation, I have ever since wondered.

The crocus picnic was always around the twenty-ninth of April, and by this time we were all watching the river for signs of the break-up. Wouldn't it be fun if the ice went out while we were on the Hill and we had to wait for the ferry to start operating? By this time the men of the town would have been prepared for the break-up. With the fire horses and all the other horses available, they would already have pulled the superstructure of the bridge across the slough off its pilings and up the street. This much of the bridge they saved from year to year. The pilings went ripping and tearing out and down to the ocean with the first big pans of ice that hit them. After all the ice had run, the barge piledriver would be put into the water from the Garden Island side, opposite Fairbanks, and would go to work, with a fine clangor, driving in new piles.

But we never got caught in delightful misadventure on our crocus picnics, and all the break-ups I can remember occurred during school hours. This by no means meant that we missed them! There was a tradition about this. Perhaps in the middle of the afternoon grammar lesson, the fire siren would sound, and at the same instant the "six-o'clock whistle" in quick short blasts. The ice was going!

We were going too! Books were thrown into the desks. Out of the room, down the wide stairs, down the hall (Mr. Gerth, the janitor, would by this time have the front doors thrown wide), and teachers and pupils, *and* Mr. Gerth, would pour forth upon the street. Down to the corner, to Cushman, down Cushman in a tide that spread across the street—no traffic to get in our way in those days. It was eight blocks to the river, and as we reached Fourth or Third we could hear it—the roar, the hissing, the surge of spring. By the time we reached the river front the rest of the town was there too, and if we were lucky we could wedge ourselves under someone's elbow and watch the spectacle.

If it was a "good" break-up, there would be the sight of huge pans of ice many feet thick being raised on edge, carried along, thrown down upon other pans, many of them piling up, pushing upon the bridge pilings. Away go the pilings—a great show! And then, if it was an extra-special break-up, there would come a wildfire whisper through the crowd. "The ice is jammed down at the shipyards!"

Then we would see some of the men in a wagon, driving fast downriver. And someone at the edge of the river with a pole. Was the ice slowing up, was the water rising up the bank, closer to the top, to Front Street, to the rest of the town? Perhaps they would have to blast the ice loose down at the slaughterhouse. There was one wonderful spring when people had to move out of their houses on Front Street, and rowboats were the thing, but this was fun only for children.

Anyway, spring had now come to the Tanana Valley. The end of school might conceivably come also!

On the last trips of the winter stages the merchants would get in their supplies of seed, and the three men who had greenhouses would begin their operations, and the other townspeople would begin to plan what they would plant in the outdoor gardens, after the break-up, perhaps about May 20.

So with the arrival of spring, on with the annual big spring salad, and don't think about the cost! Paul Rickert drove the streets in his neat green-painted wagon behind his sleek bay horse, and in the wagon a thrilling sight—flat boxes of ripe tomatoes,

shiny green peppers, cucumbers, small green onions, lettuce! At a price. But this was the spring fling, and that evening there would be the big wooden chopping bowl full of the first taste of the earth. There are no words for the special joy of this taste, after a winter of root vegetables, potatoes, canned corn and peas, dried apple sauce and prunes.

Fairbanks is, of course, built on an old river course; the soil seems just like sea sand. And yet, what things grow in it! As though to compensate for its inability to produce all the exotic things which cannot grow in the North, this soil brought forth such carrots, peas, turnips, beets, lettuce, onions, spinach, and rhubarb as have never been seen elsewhere. Everyone had a garden. Carrots and parsnips grew fourteen inches long and as wide across at the top as a teacup, and crisp and sweet all the way through. Turnips grew to weigh six pounds, just as crisp and sweet, and cabbages, though they had to be started in flats inside, grew to fill a dishpan and weigh twenty-five pounds.

So now, after break-up, to plant the gardens. In the mild daylight evenings all the neighbors would be out until late, spading, raking, planting—it never got dark any more. A man could work all day at his office or in a store and then work six hours more in the garden, and all his neighbors would be out doing the same thing, and shouting comments to one another. This was a part of the general wakening and loosening—no longer housebound, no longer mindful of stoking fires, no longer swathed in heavy clothes. Easy to run from house to house, from neighbor to neighbor, draw deep breaths, fling your arms wide. Spring!

After the break-up of the Chena, we waited for news of other break-ups, for they meant much to all of us. The sooner the ice went out at Tanana, the sooner it went out at Dawson, the sooner the boats would start running up and down the river; from St. Michael up, from Whitehorse and Dawson down. On the front of the U.S. Signal Corps telegraph office, a yellow-painted building on Cushman Street, would be posted each day the bulletins: "Ice moved at Fort Gibbon this morning 8 A.M." "Ice went out at Kokrines 4 P.M. May 8." And finally: "Ice went out at Dawson 3 P.M. May 9." The first downriver steamer would be on her way!

Then: "Str. *Yukon*, downriver at Eagle, 3 P.M. June 1." Let's see—five days to Tanana, four days up the Tanana. When could we begin to listen for the blood-stirring chirr-chirr of a paddle wheel, to look downriver, over the tops of the spruce trees, for the puff of white wood smoke from her stacks?

Around our yard Daddy had built a picket fence. The two-by-four railing brace behind the pickets was a vantage point. On those spring evenings all the neighbor children—Mary and Frank and Stella Shafer and Billy Godske from up the street—and my friend Cleora and I would stand and look, jump down, play hopscotch out in the sandy road, go back to the fence for another look. What prestige, to be the first one to see that white smoke!

Every steamer, all summer, was exciting, and its arrival and departure was attended by almost the whole town. But the first one—that brought Christmas! First-class mail we had had, yes, via the jingling bells and the frosty-breathed horses—but packages, very few. Now came Christmas packages from all our relatives and friends out in the States, bundles of magazines and papers, and new clothes, ordered from mail-order catalogues months before. And more mail-order catalogues, to order more clothes from before the freeze-up should catch us again.

It also brought friends who had wintered Outside, and there

would be reunions, and dinner parties, and all the news of the outside world at first hand. So, as soon as the lucky one on the fence spied the smoke, the family would begin to get ready to walk downtown to the river and the docks, to share in the excitement of the first boat. We watched the smoke moving along over the trees; we listened to the blessed sound of the wheel. We listened to the chorus of howls when she was passing the dog pound—then we started for town.

And down on Front Street we found most of the rest of the town gathering—men, women, children, dogs, chatter and laughter, and a tangible wave of excitement. Some were expecting relatives, some friends coming back, some business partners. We all wanted to see everyone who was on board; we children wanted to watch again the clever backing and filling and hear the chuff-chuffing and shouted commands of the boat and her crew; and everyone was looking forward to the mail, the fresh food, the packages.

As for the passengers on the boat, most of them would be straining eagerly for a glimpse of the town and the familiar buildings, the dock, the faces of friends. But a few perhaps were returning with empty pockets and wondering about unpaid bills left behind in the fall; and for them, one figure stood out in the crowd by the foot of the gangplank—Waterfront Brown, collector of bills, nemesis of all deadbeats, always on hand to greet every incoming boat, and to speed every departing boat, looking for his prey. Thus had he gained his name, and he was always there, portly but ramrod straight, in a brown business suit and high collar and brown Derby. To us children, he was a somber and portentous figure. He spoke kindly to us on the street, but we scuttled past him. Too often we had seen him walking inexorably beside some harassed, unhappy-looking passenger up the dock to the street!

But the first boat was mostly pure joy and excitement, followed by waiting outside the post office while mountains of mail were being distributed, then carrying home packages, letters, and magazines by the armful, and, in the long summer evening, Christmas on the big screen porch, being allowed to stay up till all hours, having a lunch at midnight. Life was all good.

After the very first boat we began to wait for word about the Waechter Brothers' barge, the slaughterhouse boat, and, when she came up the river, to the chirr of the wheel and the howling of the dogs on shore would be added the lowing of cows, the baaing of sheep, the crowing of roosters, and the squealing of pigs. To children growing up in Alaska in those days, this was the opportunity to see what these animals really looked like, and we were all grateful that for some reason the *Robert S. Kerr* with her two big barges always came uptown and made a landing before dropping back down to the slaughterhouse. Added to the usual interest of a boat with barges making a landing and tying up was the vociferous life she carried. Inside the enclosed barges were the cows, the steers, the sheep, and the pigs. On top, in crates and making a great cackling, were the roosters, the hens, the ducks, and the geese. They had traveled a week on the ocean from Seattle to Nome, had been unloaded and loaded again, and had traveled another week or more—more than a thousand miles, up the Yukon, up the Tanana, to be food for a booming mining camp.

7

Summer

Winter had its cold and its great isolation from the outside world. Summer had heat and mosquitoes. Winter was long and sometimes became a real adversary to the spirit and temper. Summer was a glorious season. We were determined it should be so, and in spite of the mosquitoes. Fairbanks has no mosquitoes now, thanks to the Army. It has jet planes shrieking over instead. In 1912 it was a quiet place; the hum of the mosquito was heard in the land.

We had three weapons against them. Nearly everyone had or soon built a large screened-in porch; in the houses we burned Buhach like incense; on outings we wore head nets or smeared ourselves with Citronella. Life would have been pretty hard without Buhach. I think the only recourse the early Klondike miners had was to build smudges where they were working. I don't think they had Buhach or Citronella those first years. In front of a miner's cabin there would be an old tub or wash boiler; in this would be a smoldering fire fed with green branches or grass or weeds (and there were various theories as to which vegetation made the best smudge). The hope was that this smoke would deter the bugs from going through it into the cabin. On the early homesteads upriver from Fairbanks, where the farmers raised grain and vegetables and harvested the great natural meadows of red-top hay, there were always large smudges going for the farm horses too, and they soon learned to come in from feeding whenever they could not stand the bugs any longer and to stand right in the smoke.

In town the insects were not so terrible, but if you lived, as we did, on the edge of town near the lovely birch woods and the willows and the sloughs and ponds, they were worse. Sometimes we children wore scarves of cheesecloth soaked in Citronella round our necks when we went out to play; sometimes we just swatted and forgot them. If we went into the woods or out berry picking, we had to wear hats and head nets. But life went on, in defiance of these bugs. There were picnics, outings, ball games, tennis, and even the theater. Traveling stock companies made the long journey from the States, playing a week in each Alaska town, to packed houses of course.

There was the tennis club, which was very active, with two sets of courts. The children could play in the daytime; the grownups took over in the evenings. This was perfectly possible, for it was broad daylight all night, a soft, warm, faintly pink beneficent sort of daylight that cannot be described. The days were often so warm that people were content to sit with sewing or a book on the porches in the afternoons. But after dinner, that was a wonderful time. There was a ball game going on at the ball park, which was only three blocks from our house, or they were playing tennis down by the Shaw House. Children were everywhere, afoot or on bicycles, playing games, watching everything. Eventually parents might catch up with us and insist on our going to bed; but how horrible, to go to bed when the world was at its most enticing and the white-crowned sparrows were singing their loudest and most incessant!

There were two occasions in the summer when no parent thought of making us go to bed. First, the twenty-first of June, Alaska's own day. Beginning at six in the evening, it was a holiday for everyone and went on all night. There was the parade, a band playing, the floats and flags of all the clubs and lodges, especially the Pioneers and Pioneer Women, and, most important of all, the "Native Sons and Daughters of the Golden North." None of these was very old yet—some of them were in baby carriages all decorated in gold and white—but all were in the parade. When my sister Louise was a little over a year old, she was in the parade, in her carriage, in a gold-and-white lace bonnet; a few years later she was a princess in waiting to the queen and rode on the big float in the parade. Unfortunately, I had been born in Seattle!

The parade always ended up at the ball park, to be followed by the midnight ball game, the greatest ball game of the year. And after that, a dance of course, all through the night, the doors and windows of the big "Auditorium" thrown wide to the soft midnight daylight.

Fourth of July in Fairbanks came at just the right time for a holiday, so they made it a good one—three days. Spring work at the mines was over; most of them had made their first clean-up of the season. Everybody was ready to come to town, money or dust or nuggets in their pockets, for a celebration before settling down to the hard work of all the rest of the mining season until the freeze-up. So there was a grandstand erected on the bank of the river, facing Front Street, and for three days things went on in the street all day, and in the saloons and dance halls all night, and on the fourth morning the wagons and the Model-T Fords were loading up with sleepy, satiated, tired, but happy Russians, Serbs, Swedes, Irishmen, all the rest—and back to the creeks, and the town back to work.

On one Fourth of July, I was "Liberty" in a float made up of children. We were smothered in bunting and I had a tinsel crown and a "torch" and felt terribly solemn and important. And instead of going home afterward, as was probably expected of me, I stayed on, and with all the other kids found a place in the grandstand and watched all the races and contests and tricks.

Of these, the event still most vivid to me is the tug-of-war. This was the great event put on by the miners, and every year there were the same two teams—the "Bohunks" and the "Swedes." Six dark, swarthy giants on one side of that long wooden cleated platform; six blond ones on the other. I can't remember who won that year I managed to be there, but the thing itself, the straining, bulging muscles, the grunted commands of the captains, the clenched teeth, the grimaces, the breathless tense silence of the holiday crowd—these I remember. Perhaps it was my first good look at Conflict.

For all the women, and all the children old enough to toddle, the other main occupation of the summer was berry picking. Nature made it impossible for fruit trees to grow in the North. But she

compensated for this with the most lavish gift of berries, and in those early times, because fresh fruit from the States was so rarely seen and more costly than jewels, it was necessary for each household to put up berries for the winter. Right after the Fourth of July celebration the picking began, blueberries first. Walking out from town in almost any direction in the open tundra, you came to blueberries; of course, there were some extra-special places, and people had their favorite places to go. One good place was downriver toward the slaughterhouse and Leah Bar. We would go tramping through the thick spruce and birch woods to get there, head nets on, mosquitoes humming, the air warm, carrying our buckets, and in one of them our lunches. We would come out of the woods into an opening full of blueberry bushes and go to work. The bushes were low, and loaded. You hunkered down, or sat, or knelt; you wanted to get your pail full as quickly as Cleora or Irene or Lily did. It was hot; you were sweating; the net made it hotter. You snatched it up onto the top of your straw hat, smeared on some Citronella, and went back to picking. "If you start eating them, you won't get your pail full," the mother in charge of the party would say. "Wait till we stop for lunch, and then eat all you want."

By lunch time you hoped to be near enough to the river to go over to a gravel-bar peninsula sticking out into the stream, where it would be dry, with no vegetation, a little breeze, and few mosquitoes. How we loved the gravel bars! We knew every one of them, and boat trips on the river and berry-picking trips and ordinary picnics all focused on a gravel bar for lunch. Here we had rest and relaxation and fun. But not all relaxation for the mothers. The river, like most Alaskan rivers, was swift and treacherous, and children could not be allowed to go into the water. We could only stand on the edge and paddle in it a bit, and throw rocks into it. Then back to the berry patch. And home late in the afternoon, hot and tired, with full pails dragging at our arms.

Mother made blueberry pie, blueberry muffins, blueberry cobbler, blueberry syrup for the sourdough pancakes. We ate bowls of blueberries with canned milk and sugar on them. (Mash the berries into the cream until it is all a purple mush, then eat it!) But more than all this, they must be put up for the winter. Berries and sugar were put in a fifty-pound butter barrel—a layer of berries, a layer of sugar, and so on clear to the top. The best scheme for this project was to go out to some friend's on the creeks and spend three days picking the berries and packing them out there. Then you put them down in one of the mine shafts, where it was very cold. When winter came, the friend brought the barrel in and you put it in your own cellar under the kitchen, and all was well. A quart measure dipped into the barrel brings up a quart of juicy berries, almost like fresh ones. In addition to all this, there had to be jars of specially "hot-packed" big luscious berries and glasses of jelly.

While the blueberries were still being picked, the beautiful big red raspberries would ripen. They grew on the hillsides in dry woods where stands of birch had burned. We had to travel farther to get them, but they were worth it, and plentiful. They were carefully packed in hot syrup and sealed away for the winter, but in the meantime the family had quite a few raspberry shortcakes.

Farther out, along "the Trail" to Valdez, in favored places in the open woods, grew both red and black currants. In the edges of the birch woods, not so numerous but prized above all, there was the berry we called dewberry. It was a tiny plant, with two leaves, in the bract of which grew one large glowing red ruby of a berry; its flavor was somewhere between that of the blackberry and that of the raspberry, a thing of joy. These berries were made into jelly for the very special dinner party, the birthday, the special occasion.

In August came the cranberries—first the Viburnum, which we

called high-bush cranberry, and then, on into September, the real low-bush cranberry. The high-bush, related to the "wayfaring tree" of the East, grew in fat red clusters on tall bushes and was easy to pick. It grew along the water courses and on the hillsides and around the lakes; there was no end to it. The mothers made jelly of it; they put the pulp through sieves, added spices, and made "apple butter" of it. They added more spices and vinegar and made ketchup of it. Picking both kinds of cranberry was a joy, for by that time there weren't so many mosquitoes and being out in the woods was pure pleasure.

In the case of the low-bush cranberry there were other procedures. Some were made into jelly of course—such a glowing Christmas red. Some were made into fresh pies immediately. But mostly we picked them after the first frost had turned them dead ripe, packed them in shallow wooden boxes, and put them down in the empty rain barrel at the corner of the house. In the winter we would go out and dip out a panful, frozen solid like marbles! These were for cranberry sauce, or for mock cherry pie, which was made with cranberries put through the meat grinder while still frozen—no muss, no fuss, with the same amount of raisins, cooked with sugar and flour and spice into a delectable filling for a pie.

So went the glorious summer, short in days but almost of double length thanks to the heavenly, stimulating twenty-four-hour daylight. We children knew no other kind of summer, yet even so we sensed a special enchanting dreamlike quality. If you consider all the night ball games and all the berry picking, and the tennis, and running down to meet every stern-wheel steamer that puffed and tooted up before the town, you can see how swiftly summer flew by for us children.

8

The Trail

On March 12, 1914, on an afternoon when Mother and I were quietly at home with the two babies, Louise and Louis, all the town whistles suddenly burst into sound. We rushed to the windows. What kind of fire? The telephone rang. Daddy was calling. The telegram had just been received; the railroad bill had passed Congress!

Here ended years of work on the part of Alaska's first delegate to Congress, that dynamo of determination James Wickersham, and here began the new era.

The town of Fairbanks greeted the news with its usual vigor. The whistles kept on blowing, the fire bells were ringing. Everyone flocked to Cushman Street, to Front Street. There began a purely impromptu parade down the whole length of Front Street. Dog teams, horses and cutters. People snatched up any strange costume they happened to have, any instrument that would make any kind of noise; they were playing and singing "Casey Jones"—they were shouting. The railroad would open the Healy River coal mines, and the man who had found a coal scuttle and was marching along banging it merrily received the most applause from the side lines. That was probably the only coal scuttle in Fairbanks on that day.

From that day, all was talk of the railroad, the plans, the route—from Seward to Anchorage to Fairbanks, 477 miles from the sea, twenty-four hours from the coast, one week from Seattle—tremendous! Work would begin from both ends. A great many men would be employed. Uncle Sam was at last going to do the big thing for interior Alaska. Each person in the country was thinking of just what this would mean to him.

One thing it meant, by the spring of 1918, was that we were nearing the end of the era of dependence on the horse-drawn sleighs that came over the Valdez Trail in winter—the jingle of sleigh bells, the crack of Harry Martin's whip. The Northern Commerical Company was closing down that part of its business. The spring of 1918 was to be the end of the chapter. By the next winter enough of the railroad would be built so that mail could be carried between ends of steel by dog teams or horses, and the railroad would then be the lifeline to the outside world.

Another thing it meant was something almost too tremendous for the nine-year-old grown to be fifteen. Fifteen, and shy, yet eager for adventure—scared, yet determined to go ahead. For it had turned out that of all the eager crowd who had stood spellbound as the stage went by, week after week, winter after winter, I was to be the one to go over that mysterious Trail on the last trip of the stage line, the last trip before break-up, the very last trip of all. The mere thought of it went whirling round and round all day long in my head. With Ruth and Marguerite and Irene and the other schoolmates and neighbors, I was trying to act as though it really were not very much; I must not act too superior before their half-envious questions. Actually, of course, I felt I was the favored one of the whole universe, at the same time wondering how I could possibly leave Mother and Daddy and the babies. How I finished up all the school work early, I don't remember at all. And added to the thought of seeing all that outside world again was the thought that at the other end of the Trail I would be met by my own father and my older half brother, both of whom I barely remembered.

The last stage was leaving at midnight on May 4. From that date until the first steamer churned its way up Chena Slough was a lost period of time—nothing, no one, no mail. The Signal Corps would be the only link.

Travel must now be at night, while the trail was frozen. The trail was going; the snow would not hold up the horses in daytime. Daddy and Mother visited the Northern Commercial office, bought my ticket, arranged all particulars. They laughed over squeezing all my things into a suitcase and traveling bag, and over Daddy having to sit on the case to get it closed. He was making his Irish jokes, Mother was laughing at him, and when all was ready they went to the piano and started practicing his solo for Sunday. How could they be so gay? I was leaving at midnight! I was going out into the great unknown overwhelming world!

Now that I have sent my own children off to school many times, I understand all that brave play acting. But then I wondered whether they were doing their whole duty by me. All this jollity and no special instructions—only how to take care of the (to me) enormous sum of money in the little crocheted bag inside the big purse. Finally I had to ask: "But, Mother, aren't there any things you should tell me before I go?"

Mother looked at me for a moment; then in her sweet laughing voice she said: "No, you're going on sixteen. If I haven't raised you properly so far, there isn't much use trying to start now. I'm relying on your good sense." She paused. "I talked to Roy Rynearson; he's the driver you're to start with. He's a nice man, and I know all the others will take good care of you too. I think you'll find that most any man will be a gentleman as long as the girl is a lady. Now, look what I found for you today! Slip them into your bag."

And she went to the cupboard and brought out a striped candy sack full of lemon drops! Here was the memory of 1911, and the sourdough friend of Daddy's, Mr. Furstenau, who had bought me lemon drops at every little town along the Yukon. They were the symbol of travel to me, and Mother had remembered.

But I never did ride in one of the gorgeous yellow thoroughbrace stages! This was break-up time. The vehicle was what we in Alaska called a "double-ender," or Yukon sled. It was a low, flat framework of narrow but strong hickory slats, which formed a platform above the three-inch-wide ironbound runners which curved up over the end of the sled, both front and back; it could be pulled or pushed either way. This type of sled came in all sizes, for hand pulling, for dogs, for horses.

This one was about fourteen feet long and four feet wide and had a seat nailed on at the rear. At least there were some wolfskin robes on the seat! The sled had four large sleek horses harnessed to it, and it stood, loaded with mail sacks and luggage, behind the Northern Commercial Company warehouse on Second Avenue on that May 4. When Daddy and I arrived just before midnight, the driver and a warehouse man and the one other passenger were drawing up the big tarpaulin over the whole load and lashing it all tight to various parts of the sled. It was exactly like one tremendous package, neatly tied in waterproof canvas. It wasn't long before I found out why. "But we've got the young lady's bags well stowed in there too."

Roy Rynearson, stalwart and good-looking, had twinkling blue eyes in a face burned to leather by the spring sun reflected off the snow. "She may get pretty tired before we make our first long stop—got to get across five rivers before they go out—but we'll take good care of her. Guess we're ready, Joe."

The other passenger, fortunately, was someone I knew—Gus Conrad, a genial German baron apparently of means, one of the interesting types to be found in the North, "interested" in some mines, but never actually working in them. He was going only forty miles to Salcha Roadhouse, to go on a spring bear hunt. He assured Daddy I would be well looked after and helped tuck the wolfskin robe all round me in the seat beside him. Roy climbed up onto the front of the big bundle, settled himself in his big fur coat, and then sang out, not "Giddap," but "Ish!"

The horses started at a trot; the warehouse porch and Daddy and the warehouseman standing there watching us were quickly lost to sight. We were moving through the dusky half-dark quiet streets, pulling over bare ground. The snow was all gone in town. The panicky emptiness inside me fought against the enormous thrill of unimaginable adventure ahead. I could fairly feel the presence of the big square schoolhouse when we passed Eighth Avenue. The kids would all be there in another few hours, and I—I would be way out on the Trail somewhere.

There was now a little snow on the trail; the double-ender slid along with a tiny swishing monotone tune. It was still rather dark. Gus Conrad said: "Listen here, you might as well get some sleep. I bet you've been pretty excited. Lean over this way, or we'll lose you over the side!"

"'Fraid she's gonna be another warm day. Only thing to do is keep going till we get to Little Delta."

I heard these words through a dream. Where on earth was I? Oh yes, on the big adventure; it was real after all. I *had* slept. It was daylight, the early-spring daylight of the Arctic, and Gus and Roy were talking.

"I figured these rivers were about ready to go when I came in on

Monday. Old John at Salcha thought we could make one more trip. Well, we'll soon see."

I rubbed my eyes and sat up. It was still the familiar kind of country, the kind in which I had often gone snowshoeing or berry picking; flat black-spruce forest, little willow-bordered sloughs. But ahead of us loomed a long ridge of hills billowing back into the sky. Gus pointed. "See that notch up ahead? Just below that is Salcha. You'll stop there awhile and have a good meal, and find out whether you can cross the Tanana."

We were crossing a side stream now. The old worn trail marked by many winter crossings was still there, but the ice and snow looked darkly damp in patches at the sides. The horses didn't hesitate, and we were quickly across and plodding along through the forest. Early morning, bright daylight—the snow and ice beneath the runners began to lose its clear slick sound, began to sound muffled and damp. The snow was beginning its day's thawing; winter was receding, spring pushing on. We moved more slowly, on and on through a quiet world. I began to think I was dreaming. Maybe I was. Suddenly the sled gave a great lurch and I felt Gus's arm around my shoulder. "Look out now—I *said* we'd lose you out!"

We were bumping down a steep creek bank and the ridge of blue hills had moved to meet us. At the base of the hills, here across the creek, there were some neat log buildings, one of them two stories high. Salcha. And out in front of the buildings, stretching along at our right, the Tanana, broad and white.

"Well, she's still there! Got some mushy spots though."

Roy was leaning toward the river, blue eyes flicking over it judiciously, while the horses sped along, crossed the bridge over the creek, and stopped exactly in front of the two-story house—George Hillar's roadhouse. A wizened old man in a big sheepskin coat was right there to take the horses—Old John, the barnman. There was also dapper, mustached little George Hillar, a German, who ushered us into the house with a lot of clucking quick chatter.

Salcha was one of the "better" roadhouses. They had to be pretty much alike, however. They were built to suit the country. The big front room had a box couch in one corner, a long table piled with all kinds of magazines under the one low window, several round-backed hotel-lobby chairs, a large Cole heater, too hot for this weather, on the back wall, and beyond it in the back corner a wash stand, oilcloth-covered, with the usual five-gallon can of water, the long-handled dipper, and a washbasin and soap. Here we all washed up a bit. Roy combed his thick red-blond hair carefully with a wet comb. I tried to push the hairpins back into my "figure 8" hairdo (very recently it had all been hanging down my back in one thick braid). Then we all went into the room beyond to a long white oilcloth-covered table, very clean, with benches on either side, and loaded with oval vegetable dishes and platters of thick hotel china, a great array of food.

It was eleven in the morning and we had been going since midnight. Everyone piled in with great joviality and a steady stream of talk despite steady eating. Could we, or could we not, cross the river? Everyone had an opinion or a report. Some Indians had brought in reports about other streams. There were tales of other springs and other break-ups.

I was more interested in watching George's new wife. Gus had told me that George had been back to Germany to find a wife and this was her first winter in the strange land. She hurried from kitchen to dining table, small but plump, round-faced, very blonde with lovely skin. She spoke not at all, only smiled shyly with a slightly bewildered look in her blue eyes. Surely the long winter in this place, a continuous round of cooking for troops of hungry men, with silent Indians appearing at her back door frequently, must have been a contrast to all her former years. Even my fifteen-year-old mind sensed something of this. I was shy enough myself, but something urged me to go to the door of her clean, scrubbed kitchen after the meal and say: "Thank you. That was a very good dinner."

She really smiled then, and said: "Ah, dat's fine." And when we went out to climb onto the sled again, she stood in the kitchen doorway and waved to us.

Good-by to Gus, who had been so kind. He and George both walked to the edge of the bank to watch our luck. "Now, young lady," said Roy, "I'm going to have you climb right up on top of the load here behind me. Hang on to the lash ropes and get a good grip, but don't be scared. Whatever happens, *don't jump off.* Stay right with the load."

He settled himself firmly, got his feet braced at the front of the load, and we started slowly down the long incline onto the river. Ahead of us was Old John, walking, holding a long pole, which he continually drove into the ice, testing. The horses, a fresh

team, were very wise too. They went slowly, I thought even reluctantly. The off leader kept tossing his head as though to say: "Don't you know this is silly business?"

Out over the ice we went. There were dark-looking spots here and there, with water on top. The river here was about a quarter of a mile wide. We kept going. I looked back and saw Gus and George and several Indians in a frozen, still row on the bank, growing smaller. Now I looked ahead again and realized that Old John had on hip boots, and that he now walked through water, very slowly, probing each step. Roy looked back at me and grinned and said softly: "Scared?"

"No, I think it's fun!"

But my fingers were wound pretty tightly around those lash ropes. We were in the water now, but Roy was reassuring me. "This is just surface water, on top the anchor ice. So long as John finds the anchor ice we're all right."

Out of the water now, John was wading through slush, but he didn't sink out of sight. In a sudden burst he fairly ran up the far bank, turned, and yelled: "Lay it on 'em, Roy!"

Roy did, and in a great splashing, tipping, rocking flurry we were all on the bank and up among the black spruces again. Old John started right back. "Better get myself back now," he called.

"Hope you make it across the Delta O.K. I bet you're the last outfit across the Tanana this year!" He waved his long pole and disappeared down over the bank.

We were winding through forest again, shady here and a bit of frozen snow for the runners. I was still on top of the load, feet curled under me. Roy turned and smiled at me. "Sleepy? You didn't sleep more than two or three hours back there in the night."

"No, I think I'm too excited. What about you? You haven't had *any.*"

"Oh, us fellows are used to it—make it up when we get in somewhere. I've gone forty-eight hours lots of times in the fifteen years I've been on this trail. Sometimes be stalled in a storm and wouldn't dare let myself sleep for fear some fool passenger would try to go afoot for a roadhouse and get lost. Worse than a bunch of kids, some I've had."

The horses plodded on through the warm afternoon, pulling over dry ground in spots, plunging through softened deep snow in others, and Roy talked on: "Go to sleep any time you feel like it. Don't mind me. It just helps me to stay awake, to talk."

But his talk opened a new world to me—the world of the Trail—and my imagination followed his words through blizzards and overflows and hurricane winds, injured horses, sick passengers, insane passengers, murderers in the custody of deputy marshals, broken bridges and fires in roadhouses—there was no end to the drama which would happen and had happened on the Valdez Trail.

The afternoon was going. We were still in the endless flat valley of the Tanana, pushing through the black-spruce forest, across slushy sloughs and willow-bordered creeks, the sun high and hot and the going softer and heavier, so that Roy stopped the team for a breather every so often. He seemed to know just when they had to rest. He had discarded the big coat by now and drove in flannel shirt and leather vest, and I had loosened my wool coat and taken off the green angora tam-o'-shanter. It was nearly six, but there was no danger of darkness overtaking us. Even on May 5 the arctic day had no evening. Everything was dreamlike and unreal, and I knew I'd have to sleep soon. Maybe I could crawl back to the seat and curl up . . . and then we stopped. There was an opening in the trees ahead, and Roy began pushing his fur coat under the lash ropes. "Well, here we are—the last river. Three little ones and two big ones makes five, doesn't it? If we get across the Delta now, you can soon catch up on some sleep."

He looked back at me then, smiling. "But don't go to sleep right now. You sit up here, right close behind me, and we'll pull out here and take a look."

Out of the trees—there was the Delta River, snow-covered still but somehow looking pretty soggy and gray, and at least half as wide as the Tanana at Salcha. Roy stood up and looked across. I rose to my knees and peered over too. Over against the opposite shore was a black streak, about thirty feet wide. The off lead horse snorted. Roy said nothing, settled the reins in his hands, turned and looked the lashings over, and said very calmly: "Ish!"

As we went out onto the ice, through slushy snow, he spoke again: "Remember what I told you before—stay with us. They may have to swim a few feet, you know, but just hang on to those ropes."

Now we were reaching that black streak, and as if in a daze I heard the sound of water, and Roy's voice talking softly, urgently, to the team. But they were old stage horses; they plunged in. I felt the whole sled lift and float; a terrific churning, a great heave and a thump, and up the steep bank we went in a rush. The horses stopped as soon as they were up on the level again. They knew they rated a rest there.

"Whew!" said Roy. "That does it!"

And we both sat there, laughing. He looked at me steadily for a moment. "I guess you'll do."

We went on now; the horses were suddenly trotting. "They know they're nearly there now. Only a quarter mile to Little Delta."

He paused, then said, gazing steadily ahead: "Think I ought to tell you—don't know just how you've been raised an' all that—but there'll be nothing but men at this place. Just want you to know, you'll be as safe as though you were in God's pocket. I had a young sister-in-law of mine along on a trip last year—scared to death and whining all the time. Wouldn't let me out of her sight. You'd a thought every man on the trail was plannin' to eat her alive. I finally told her that next time she went out to the coast she could sure enough go on some other fellow's rig—it'd be good for her. Crazy foolishness, that's what. I tried to tell her that the old sourdoughs always treat a lady like a lady, but she wouldn't listen. Probably die an old maid. Well, here we are, and there's old Charlie lookin' for us. He can hear a team coming two miles away, they say."

The horses raced right up to old Charlie, who was standing in front of a long, low log cabin; the Huskies chained behind the cabin set up a chorus. Three more men came out of the cabin and greeted Roy loudly, then stopped, looking, a bit discomfited, at the passenger. One tall lean one with twinkly gray eyes said: "Didn't know you were takin' any passengers this last trip."

Roy laughed. "This one's special. She likes tough trips. Had a lot of fun back here, swimmin' the Delta. Don't need to worry about *her!*"

Thus I was admitted. The proprietor of this little low log cabin was a slightly bewildered-looking young Englishman—at least he was young compared with the three others. He carried my small bag in in silence and turned and looked at me rather helplessly. Roy and Charlie the barnman had gone with the horses. We stood there, both wondering what to do next, I guess. The tall grizzled one, whose name was Tom, spoke from the door. "Put her bag on that far bunk, why don't you, Dinty? We'll fix a blanket in front for a curtain later on. Here, give me your coat an' stuff. We'll hang 'em on this peg here. Sit down now; I'll take your overshoes off for you. Pretty long pull, wasn't it? Roy says you came all the way from Fairbanks without a sleep stop. Bet you're starved too."

He stooped and worked at the fastenings of the overshoes. I felt suddenly limp and blank and comfortable all over. I leaned back in the homemade easy chair. Dinty had ducked into the kitchen and was rattling pans as though greatly relieved. Tom put the overshoes by the stove and shouted toward the kitchen. "Better hustle up that dinner, Dinty. These folks must be plumb starved."

He turned and looked me over now. "Dinty's not used to having any females around much. You see, this is always just a lunch stop on the regular run. There's really no accommodations for women folks. But don't you worry none; we'll make you comfortable as we can."

"I'm not worrying. I was brought up in this country; and I could go to sleep right here on this floor!"

We had ham and eggs and fried potatoes and dried peach pie— very good pie—and then Roy ordered me to bed. "You crawl in there and get some sleep, young lady. Have to wake you up at midnight, you know."

Tom the nursemaid had fastened a blanket across the front of one bunk. Charlie, the little old Irish barnman, came over to me where I sat unlacing my high shoes. "I noticed your lips are pretty chapped. If you haven't got any salve with you, rub some wax from your ears on 'em—that'll help. And after these fellers get settled, pull that blanket aside, over this chair—give you some air. It'll be all right."

He shuffled back to his game of solitaire. I crawled into the bunk. The conversation around the table dropped to a low tone, and Dinty tried to be quiet with the dishes in the kitchen, but before I drifted off to sleep I had a new outlook on this trip.

I had known that the Northern Commercial Company was selling out, that the railroad was nearly completed, that this was the last trip of the Company's mail, passenger, and freight business. These were the cold facts; but now, from behind the blanket, I listened to the men.

"What d'you plan to do now Charlie?"

"Damn, I dunno. Gettin' too old for most jobs. Might take what little I got in the bank and go 'Outside' when the river opens up. I got a niece out in California, but I dunno if I'd want to stay there very long. . . ." Charlie's voice trailed off, as though Roy's question had made him think about things he really didn't want to think about.

Tom's voice picked up his thought. "Trouble with this country, you stay so long you don't fit in 'Outside' any more. I know I couldn't stand that city life any more. A man's free to come and go as he damn pleases up here. I was brought up in Detroit. Dunno how I stood it long's I did. Think I'll go down the railroad right-of-way; they say they're usin' some horses and packers between steel. What you gonna do, Roy?"

"Well, there's a war on, you know. Guess I'm too old for the draft, but Harry Martin says they're askin' for experienced packers and teamsters to teach the young ones in some horse outfit at Fort Lewis. Harry and I thought we might enlist for that."

Dinty's soft English voice joined in: "That's what I think I'll do too—but not for horses. I'll probably get put in as cook somewhere, but there's nothing more right here for a while. A man might as well take a whirl at something different, don't you know. A bit hard to leave the old place here though. . . ."

There was a silence. He had left unsaid what they all understood. He would miss the place—the snug cabin, the broad free land, the men of the Trail, the horses and the dogs and the

comings and goings of the Trail. It was the end of a chapter. For
the old barnmen it was one of the last chapters. "The Company"
was going out of business; the railroad was coming. Hard for an
old dog to have a whole bag of new tricks shoved at him.

There was a sudden scraping of chairs. "Well," Tom said, "it's a
great life, a great country; just like a woman; can't live with her or
without her. I've cussed the country and the cold and the job and
the Company, and now it's all about to end. Damned if a feller
don't feel bad. But we've got to get some shut-eye if this outfit has
to pull out again when it freezes."

In about ten minutes it seemed, I heard very groggily, through a
haze of sleep, stirrings and low voices and a careful muted clatter
of pans, and then Roy's voice: "Dinty, you got nerve enough to
go wake up my passenger?"

Someone had fastened my curtain up again, but faint light from
the kerosene lamps came through. It was time to start off in the
frozen early hours again.

Sometimes the trail was all bare, sometimes it went under water
when crossing sloughs, and we had to make detours, with Roy
standing, guiding the horses here and there around through the
woods. Only in the dusky hours would the trail hold up; after
that it was going fast, for we were moving south. The horses
plunged and bucked their way when the bottom went out, and we
sank through soft snow. Then it took skillful handling of the reins
and quick, calm words to the horses. When it was broad daylight
I stayed on top, hands clasped in the ropes, for the sled often
dipped and plunged up and down like a dory in a choppy sea.
Surely Roy's arms and shoulders must be aching.

Mid-morning, and another blue May sky and hot sun. "One
thing sure," said Roy, leaning and watching the runners, "we'll
have a good rest at Sullivan's because there'll be no trying to
travel in this stuff this afternoon; have to wait till she tightens up
again, tonight. Don't think we'll mind having a rest, either of
us—'bout four hours last night, wasn't it? And Ma Sullivan loves
to take care of folks. You'll have a real bed and a clean one this
time."

Sullivan's was in a wooded dip among the low hills. We were
getting into the foothills of the Range now. The roadhouse was
low and sprawling, so comfortable-looking, larger than the others
so far, with a wing extending out at the back. Pa Sullivan himself
and a barnman came out to greet us, both looking well fed, rosy

of face, both in shirt sleeves. "Where's your wheels? Don't you know spring come day before yestiddy?"

Pa helped me off the load. "Pretty tough guy, this driver of yours, ain't he? Now you run right along in to Ma. She'll fix you up, and we'll bring in your stuff."

Ma was at the door, neat, roly-poly, pretty in a crisp blue-and-white checked gingham dress. "My land sakes, I bet you're all in. They let you get any sleep at all at Delta, all those old fellers? You come right in here now."

She bustled me on through the front room and the dining room and into the wing, which seemed to be two rows of curtained cubicles, each with bed, chair, table, and washstand. The one she ushered me into looked like heaven.

Yes, that was the difference. There was a Ma at Sullivan's. I think even the toughest old sourdough preferred the roadhouses where there was a Ma. I had seen the difference while walking through. Cretonne curtains at the windows; rag rugs on the floor; lots of fancy pillows on the big homemade sofa; floral lampshades on the oil lamps; big old-fashioned rocking chairs with flowered cushions in them. Not so fancy that a man of the Trail would be afraid to sit down and relax, but cozy, a home.

And now a bed with sheets and a white counterpane. Ma came bustling back with a pitcher of hot water. "Now then, have a good wash, and soon as we have lunch you get into that bed. I know that's what your mother would say."

Sweet sleep and delicious food—moose steak—at Sullivan's. We left in the dusky dark again, at midnight, but the dark and the cold didn't last long enough in that north country, not long enough to tighten up the trail very much. There were a couple of hours when I lay curled in the wolfskin robe on the seat, half asleep while the sled whispered along fairly smoothly, a sleepy sound, broken only once in a while by a quiet voice: "Ish—get in there, Brownie."

Only a couple of hours; then the world began to wake up and we were reminded that spring was here, relentlessly, stageline or no. Gray to rose; gold gleamings in the birch woods we were passing through, and bird chirpings all about. I told Roy I could not sleep any more, and we began to talk again. It seemed we had been traveling along like this for weeks. But this morning I was faced with the knowledge that in a few hours, at Big Delta, I would be turned over to another driver. Roy would have to turn back. I had a cold, apprehensive sadness inside me. But Roy was preparing me for the next chapter. "Now, when you get to Rapids, the dog mushers will be there to take you and the mail across the summit of the range. You be sure you go in French John's sled. You'll have the time of your life. He's the most comical character you ever met; don't be surprised at anything he says, but he'll take good care of you too. There'll likely be three dog mushers waiting at Rapids, but you go with French John!"

9

And Over the Mountains

After Sullivan's, Big Delta, and what I remember of that is the kindness of Mrs. Robertson, the cook, and the big cheery front room with windows looking out across the Big Delta River and the high peaks of the Alaska Range beyond. But even more vivid in memory is Roy cranking the big phonograph and putting on records: "They've got some pretty good music at this place. I sure like Alma Gluck's voice."

So I heard Alma Gluck singing Tennyson's "The Brook" and another lovely old thing called "Fiddle and I." I remember the melodies of both and I remember most of the words, but I have never in all the years since been able to find the records or the songs. "Fiddle and I, wandering by, travel the world together!"

There was a sudden breathless knot in the pit of my stomach when Roy helped me up onto the seat of a little buckboard. I was leaving him here, and for the first time I felt I was leaving home and all the familiar things—yet at the same time eager for the next adventure. Roy took both my hands in his then and smiled and said: "Well, we've sure had a time, haven't we? I'll always remember this last trip. You have a fine summer, now. Maybe I'll see you in the fall. Archie here will take good care of you."

Archie did. He was red-haired, portly, and jovial, and he told me all about the country as we rattled and bumped over the wide gravel bars of countless streams. We were on wheels, but we were very slowly climbing, and coming in closer and closer to the mountains; they were all around us. Late in the afternoon we arrived at Rapids, and there was deep snow all around, and outside the two-story log roadhouse were a great number of dogs, chained and howling at our approach.

"They keep three teams here," said Archie, "but this will be about their last trip too. Remember, you want to go with French John. Young Hudson and Milo will be disappointed, but John is one you shouldn't miss. And here he comes now! Hey, John, *bo-jour*. Gotta real nice passenger for you. Roy says tell you to take real good care of her or he'll see to you later! Told me to tell you for sure!"

Big strong hands were lifting me bodily down from the seat of the buckboard. Piercing black eyes under thick grizzled brows were looking me through and through. "Hah! Hello, young lady. You traveling all by yourself dis time o' year, heh? Don't worry—John take care of you, dat's a fact. Come now, I got you bag. Here's Flanagan. He's gonna cook one hell of a fine dinner for you—pumpkin pie too. Maybe he was tink somebody nice comin', eh?"

While he spoke he ushered me in, introducing me to round-faced, red-cheeked Flanagan, and then to the two young mushers who stood solemnly by the door. "Dis here's Ray Hudson, and dis one, he Milo Hadjukovich. Dey pretty good boys too. But you boys don't stand a chance; da young lady gonna ride in my sled. Roy, he say I gonna take care of her. Takes ole man like me you know to take bes' care dese young ladies!"

The handsome, prematurely gray Hudson and the equally handsome Montenegrin Milo smiled at me; they said nothing, but looked fiercely at John.

There was caribou stew and pumpkin pie, and a great deal of talk from French John and Archie and Flanagan. Milo gazed at me from big melting brown eyes; Ray Hudson looked at his plate, ate with beautiful manners, and said nothing.

I had a tiny cubicle with clean blankets. After a few hours' sleep, I was tucked into a big wolfskin robe in John's basket sled sometime around midnight. For now the snow even high in the mountains was thawing and we must still travel at night.

But not silently, for John poured forth one story after another of the North, of his dogs, even while he struggled to keep the sled on the thawing, sliding trail which led up and around and ever up, with the high peaks glistening above us. Sometimes John talked to his seven beautiful Huskies in French, and I almost drowsed, snug in the furs, in spite of the bouncing and sliding of the sled on the soft trail. Once I roused suddenly with John's face close to mine; he was crouching under the side of the sled, his shoulder under the rim of the basket, his voice exhorting the dogs. He was fairly holding the sled by main strength from turning over and rolling down the mountainside, for here the way led across a steep mountain face and the trail had thawed away. "Jus' sit still; don' be scare. We soon get to Yost's now; dis place here de worse one. Ah, dere's de bell!"

Bell? I sat up. We had come onto a level pass, and out in the middle hung a large bell in a framework of heavy timbers. A few yards away there was a black hole in a snowdrift, and above the hole, smoke.

"Funny places in dis worl', eh?" said John. "You know, snow still very deep up here, roadhouse still mostly covered. Dis is top of Alaska Range—summit. And dat bell, she is save much people since early days. Wind, she blow like son of gun here in winter—roadhouse always cover in snow. Bell, she only ting to tell us where Yost's is, you see? Wind so strong she ring bell. Whoa, Blackie, don' you know roadhouse when you right dere?"

Milo had already arrived with his load of mail, and came over to help unload. "You, John, you slow today. You mus' told plenty stories to young lady on way over."

"Yes, dat's right, and I tell her pleny more too, from here to Paxson. Pretty nice for de old man, to have young lady passenger on las' trip I ever make for N. C. Company!"

They had shoveled the snow away from the windows; the big front room was still cavernlike but warm, and the two old sourdoughs in charge were at once fussing over me, bringing me hot water to wash in. Was I all right? Was there anything more they could do for me? No pie this time, but fresh sourdough bread and caribou steaks, and four men urging me to eat: "You still got a long way to go you know!" Young Ray Hudson, a man of mystery, fired my romantic imagination by saying absolutely nothing. I was sure he was a millionaire's son, disappointed in love, seeking escape, solace, adventure, in the Far North. He showed no sign of wanting any comfort from me!

But John continued in exuberant spirits. "I tell you 'bout one time, big bunch of us mushers here at Yost's; big storm she snow, she blow like all hell. I have to go see is my dogs all right; put on snowshoes, go feed my dogs just behind roadhouse. Man! She blow and snow so I can't find roadhouse no more. I try to go, I find nothing. Then bang! I run into stovepipe, up on roof. I bang, bang on stovepipe with snowshoe; old Jim he get out through front shed and open door and holler like all blazes and I come tumble down to door. Dis place, she look good to me dat time! I bet you wonder why we old mushers stick with, eh? Crazy, whole bunch of us, Milo, you too! Now I quit; my last trip. Feel pretty funny. Going mining out Goldstream with my brudder now. I dunno will I like it. Miss my dogs, I betcha—maybe even miss dese fellows, eh? Gonna keep three my dogs."

He ladled a big spoonful of jam onto a slab of bread, and the black eyes twinkled. "But I think maybe good luck, having young lady passenger my las' trip!"

Four days had gone. There were to be five more. From Paxson's I was with Lloyd Becket, and a double-ender sleigh and horses again. Lloyd was tall and blond and twenty-six, and had his passenger ride right beside him at the front of the sleigh. One whole day we were together. Did I think ten years' difference in ages too much?

Down out of the mountains now, from one broad valley of rushing streams and spruce and birch forest into another. It seemed months since Roy and I had crossed the Tanana River at Salcha.

George Markham was next. At Meier's roadhouse he stood at the head of the team after I was settled in the seat at the back of his double-ender, and said to Lloyd: "Well, go say good-by to your passenger."

Lloyd came back, leaned over me, his blue eyes troubled, and took both my hands in his. "Good-by—good luck—remember me." He turned quickly and was gone.

George was older, serious, educated, of solid opinions. He took wonderful care of me and discoursed on life and love and marriage and Alaska as we dragged along, and then wheeled along in a big wagon, for three days. He was divorced. "She was too young. The man ought to be at least ten years older than the girl. You remember that. Whatever you do, don't go into it too fast; you want to be sure. See the fellow in as many kinds of circumstances as you can. See how he does in each one."

He gave me a long look from keen gray eyes. "You'll be meeting lots of fellows. They all want to get married. Just take your time!"

A few of the so-called roadhouses were usually avoided, but at break-up time one could not avoid any of them. On the second day with George, in a one-room cabin of monstrous untidiness, we had warmed-over fried potatoes and warmed-over moose steak. George made a face at the coffee. But the horror here was lessened by our meeting jolly Beezwanger, another teamster, with merry black eyes and round face, who was always smiling. He loved potatoes; he enjoyed them in any form. He told me that he had once spent two years in the Arctic with never a potato, and he had been crazy about them ever since. "Beez" also brought George the news that the bridge just beyond was out. They were bringing a wagon and team from the south, but we would have to leave our team and sleigh here. The mouselike proprietor of this strange hostelry had one old horse, also mouselike, and a small Yukon sleigh. "Beez" set off to meet the oncoming wagon. George and I walked behind the Yukon sleigh, on which the mail and my luggage were piled. It was wet underfoot, but I had my overshoes and the air was warm and sweet. I threw my coat onto the load; the flannel middy blouse was warm enough. Here to the south the birch and cottonwood were already in bud; pasqueflowers and white anemones dotted the slopes.

George suddenly turned and said: "Do you get dizzy easily?"

"No, I don't think so."

"Well, I just wondered, because we're gonna cross this stream on a whipstick—what's left of the bridge. Here we are. Think you can make it? I'll take the old pony through the creek."

The two logs were about eight inches wide. It was fun. On the other side the poor old pony was pulling over bare ground. We had left all snow behind. The country ahead, green hills rising to snowy mountains, looked inviting and different. "Well," said George as we slogged along, "we'll be in Copper Center tonight, a real nice place. There's a whole village there, and the Copper River Indians school and store. It's on the river, real pretty. And tomorrow we'll be in Chitina and I'll take you to Mrs. Handy at the hotel and you'll catch the train to Cordova next afternoon. The train gets into Cordova about midnight, but I bet your dad will be right there waiting for you. So your big journey is about over—nine days of it. Whoa there!"

The old horse was only too willing to stop. George stooped to the ground by the horse's left hind foot. There in the clod of mud raised by the hoof shone two silver dollars.

"Well, young lady, speaking of luck—here's ours, yours and mine!"

He wiped the coins off on his trousers and handed me one. "Keep this always. It's your lucky dollar. I'll keep the other for mine. Good luck!"

I still have that dollar. Every once in a while a grandchild goes through my jewel box, handling, admiring, and always: "Oh, here's a dollar!"

"Leave it alone. That's my lucky dollar."

And the scene comes back. A warm, fragrant spring day near Copper Center, near the end of those nine days "safe as in God's pocket."

I wonder if George Markham kept his?

PART II:

THE UPPER KOYUKUK

1

Home to Romance

Before I came home in June 1921 after being away two years at Reed College, the family moved to another house, a square story-and-a-half bungalow, close to the center of town on Third and Wickersham. It had screened porches halfway around it, beautiful birch trees all round the rim of the yard, and a large vegetable garden in back.

After four days of bumpy, hilarious, stuck-in-the-mud pushing and shoving travel in a four-cylinder Dodge over the old Valdez Trail, which was then trying to become a summer road instead of a winter one, I arrived at the family door early in the morning, in a daze from excitement and lack of sleep. Breakfast with the family seemed like a happy dream. Those two years had seemed an age. So much had happened to me, or so I thought, that I was quite amazed to find that Mother had not turned gray, Daddy was not stooped over with a cane, the neighbors who stopped in to say hello looked just the same as they did when I left! And the children, Louise, Louis, and Carol, beautiful and loving, looked different, but were still little children!

After breakfast my precious "Weezy," now nine years old, and Carol, the black-eyed beautiful minx who had been only nine months old when I had gone away, proudly showed me how Mother had fixed up the big dormer room upstairs for all three of us. It was a happy house and a happy homecoming. For two

whole months I could be at home and keep house for the family before going off again, this time to Boston, which seemed like the other side of the planet, and almost was.

Mother was working as a secretary at the Bureau of Mines Experiment Station. I would be her housekeeper. Daddy showed me how fast his garden was growing and warned me that I would have to watch Carol; she was fascinated by all those little plants and wanted to investigate both ends of them.

Mother and Daddy departed for their offices. Louis ran to snatch Carol out of the garden. There was a voice at the back door, a high-pitched, urgent, dearly beloved voice, and there was Jess, tall, lanky, sparkling-eyed, the same as ever! "Where's this college girl? Have you gone high-toned on us? By golly, you look just the same! How are you anyway?"

Now I knew I was home! How were Clara and all the kids—the new baby, the first boy, Jesse, Jr.? Yes, I would go up that very afternoon and see them all. And then Jess said: "How many fellers have you got? You engaged yet?"

"Heavens, no, I want to look at a lot of them first."

And then he looked at me rather soberly and said: "I've got a new pal I want you to meet. His name's Murie and he's with the Biological Survey."

I stared at Jess blankly. "Biological Survey! What's that?"

After a while I found out.

The next evening I was at the Rusts' for dinner. It was wonderful to be with Clara in the big kitchen again, to see the three little girls again, to admire their rosy little son. Clara was peeling potatoes. Jess, Jr., began to howl. She said: "Mardy, will you fix his bottle please—just half milk and half water."

So I had the baby bottle in my hand when the front door slammed and we heard Jess's voice: "Hey, Mardy! Come here!"

In the living room stood Jess with a slim blond young man, not handsome in my schoolgirl eyes, but with the freshest complexion and the bluest eyes. I shifted the bottle from right to left and shook hands with Mr. Murie of the Biological Survey, while the thought raced through my mind: "How can he be a scientist and look so young?"

I think Olaus must have said a few words that first evening, though there wasn't much chance, with Jess and Clara and me all going at once about the happenings of two years, but I remember Clara saying: "Your name is Scotch, isn't it?" and Olaus answering: "No. Norwegian," and I remember thinking what a pleasant voice he had.

We walked home together in the rosy northern evening; all I can remember is that we agreed we didn't care to live in cities. He did not say: "When may I see you again?" as all the rest of them did. He was not *like* any of the rest of them, and it took me quite a while to learn this. But in a few days we went on a trip upriver with Jess and Clara in their motorboat, and at one place in the

quiet water of Moose Creek, Jess cut the motor and we heard a
great horned owl hoot far off in the forest. Olaus answered him.
Again the owl spoke, a bit closer this time. Olaus hooted again,
and so it went, until suddenly out of nowhere the dark soft shape
floated into a treetop right above us on the riverbank and sat
silhouetted against the golden sky. What kind of magic did this
man have? And when we made camp later that evening he took
out his notebook and made me a sketch of that owl. So he was an
artist too? He did all this quietly, with few words. I remembered
Mother saying: "I like that young man; he's so unassuming."

But Olaus was in Alaska to study caribou, to learn all that
could be learned about these truly northern animals, and in a few
days he was gone into the hills; and in what seemed like only a
few short days to me, I was leaving the family and Jess and Clara
and all the other good friends again and setting out for Boston.

Once during the winter I received a letter, with a hand-tinted
snapshot of our group camping at Moose Creek—"which I
thought you might like to have." Sitting there in my college room,
I suddenly remembered that sunny day on Moose Creek. We were
picking high-bush cranberries and I, of course, was prattling on in
schoolgirl fashion, trying to "draw him out"—asking questions
about his work. He told me a story about a scientist who had
falsified the label on a bird specimen to make it appear to be a
very rare find. The deception was uncovered; a short note
appeared in the leading ornithological journals, and that scientist
was never heard of again in scientific circles. I remembered
Olaus's quiet voice saying: "You see, all a scientist has is his
integrity."

Somehow, in my foolish young self-absorption, this made a
deep impression.

The next July, I was home again, to stay. By now the railroad was
completed and travel was by steamer to Seward and then by
railroad. Mother's boss, John Allen Davis, superintendent of the
Bureau of Mines station, was on the same train, and we walked
uptown together in the new booming town of Nenana, where
there was a layover and a ferrying of train and passengers across
the Tanana. On the board sidewalk walking toward us came a
slim blond Norwegian with the bluest eyes. I think Mr. Davis did
most of the talking; we just looked at each other. For once I was

not prattling. But Olaus was headed in the opposite direction, to study the caribou in the newly created national park, Mount McKinley.

It was September before we saw each other again, but then there were two whole months before the trails were ready for dog travel, and he and his younger brother Adolph, who had come from Minnesota to be his assistant for a year, had a little cabin only a block from our house.

I was not in love with this young man—not yet—and I had no inkling of how he felt about me. There were some others hanging about in the outskirts of my life too. But he was there. Clara and I taught him to dance. It seemed strange to me, in dance-mad Alaska, to find a young man who had spent so much of his life in the wilderness that he had never learned to dance, but he learned very quickly—he was as light on his feet as a cat. His brother liked to dance and we all formed a happy group. We went to dances and hiked out to the Tanana for breakfasts or wienie roasts, and gathered at our house for games or at the Rusts' for photography work and hot cocoa afterward.

So the beautiful autumn went on, and snow came in late October and Olaus and Adolph were busy taking their two dog teams out for exercise and training and getting ready for the big trip they were to make into the arctic part of Alaska.

Somehow I still did not know this quiet young scientist, always sweet and pleasant and agreeable. Something was missing. One evening the gang were all at our dining table making Christmas cards, Olaus helping us with the drawings. Over some question of mine and his usual sweet answer, I suddenly snapped: "Oh, what everlasting good nature!"

He turned to me, and the blue eyes were steely: "Look, if you want a fight, you can have it!"

Here was more than a pleasant companion. Here was a man— gentle but with steel within. From that moment everything was different.

I was clerk to the U. S. Attorney, "Uncle Guy" Erwin, that year, a fascinating job, especially in midwinter when the District Court was in session and the deputy marshal and plaintiffs and defendants and witnesses from all over the 220,000-square-mile Fourth Judicial Division arrived by train or dog team in

Fairbanks. Part of my job was keeping a daily check on all the witnesses. There were Indians, Eskimos, and even one Negro, and all types of whites too; they were frightened of the big city, or happily excited to be seeing it at government expense, or overcome by its offerings—some mornings some of them were missing. I learned quite a few things about life on that job.

But my mind and more and more of my heart were reaching way up north somewhere. I wrote long letters expounding my young romantic thoughts about life and love, and sent them off to various far stations to the north where the dog-team mail went and where a young naturalist and his dog team might eventually arrive. And once in a while the dog-team mail arrived in Fairbanks and there were letters from the north. In this way we came to know each other. By the time the twenty-fourth of April arrived at long last, I was pretty sure.

In late July, Mother and Daddy and Louis and I visited the boys' camp on the Savage River in Mount McKinley National Park. One of the objectives of Olaus's caribou study was to find a place where some of the wild caribou (a larger animal) could be trapped alive to be transported to the coast of the Bering Sea, where they could be bred with the reindeer of the Eskimo herds in order to improve the reindeer stock. In Mount McKinley National Park, Olaus and Adolph had found a suitable place and had built a trap and a corral and were awaiting a caribou migration.

At the end of five days of tramping about in a rosy haze in those enchanted mountains, we both knew there was no life for us except together. But at the same time we were faced with what seemed an impossible decision. Olaus knew he had to return to Washington, D. C., in the fall, to report on the caribou work and to receive new orders. I had been planning to finish work for my college degree—I had one more year—and the two-year-old Alaska Agricultural College and School of Mines (now the University of Alaska) was that year inaugurating its School of Business Administration; so I could finish college right there at home. We felt we could not bear to be separated ever again, but we made that decision.

The college occupied one large frame building and two or three smaller ones, with a bungalow for Dr. Bunnell, on a hillside three and a half miles south of Fairbanks. As the tracks of the new railroad ran along at the foot of the hill, the railroad operated a little bus on wheels on the tracks, the "dinky," to serve the college. Students and faculty all lived in town and traveled together on the dinky to school every morning. From "College Station" by the tracks, we trudged up the hill along a trail to the main building, and from that hill we looked out across the vast forested expanse of the Tanana Valley, with here and there a glimpse of the river winding its way, and beyond, stretched clear across the southern horizon, the lofty rugged snow rampart of the Alaska Range. And on clear days, far to the south, one mountain looming alone and unbelievable, Denali of the Indians, the "Most High"—named by the white man Mount McKinley.

Until December, Olaus and Adolph were in the little cabin not far from our house, and in their off hours managed to become nearly as involved in the new college as I was. Adolph was coaching the girls' basketball team; Olaus was painting a huge geological map for the Geology Department. And in the evening he was helping me with the bewildering mathematics. Because I had dodged math and science all through college, I was now faced with taking it all this last year—advanced algebra and trigonometry at the same time, with calculus coming up in the second semester. The other subjects were chemistry and botany, business law, sociology, and advanced typing. When the boys left for the States on December 10, I was not only emotionally bereft but also mathematically overwhelmed. I was the only senior in that second year of the college's existence, but I was taking math with boys who were training to be civil engineers and who knew a lot more of the fundamentals than I did—anybody would have! I did try, and the boys were kind, and so was the professor, and somehow I got through with a C. I had to get through; I had to be ready to marry Olaus in the summer. In addition, Dr. Bunnell had such touching faith in me and such a strong desire to have a graduate every year. (The first graduate had been Jack Shanly, a volatile and brilliant Irishman from New York State and Cornell.)

This is where Elizabeth came into my life—sparkling, irrepressible, brilliant, fun-loving Elizabeth—sensitive to all beauty, frank in her love of life, full of pranks, full of affection, and with a long string of lovesick swains in her wake. She was just what I needed to sweep me joyously through that strenuous winter of study. In addition to all her other traits, Elizabeth was a fine student, and except for the horrible math, we were in all the same classes together.

There weren't many classes in that fledgling college of fifty-two students and ten faculty members, but what an eager, energetic, excited group we were! Dr. Bunnell, with his tremendous vision and optimism, made us all feel we were partners in a great adventure; he and the young teachers made us all feel so important. We were in on all the plans; we were making a university. And there was amazing talent in that small group. Whatever needed to be done for the college, we plunged in like horses going to a fire. The two Roth sisters were not only good basketball players, they played the piano superbly; the boys' basketball team was made up of two sets of brothers, the McCombe twins from Quebec and the three Loftus brothers from Wisconsin; and we all thought we had acting ability! We put on a complete variety show, we and our young faculty, to raise funds for the college. We had a box social at the Masonic Hall in town and raised five hundred dollars in one evening to buy a piano. We started the college magazine, *Farthest North Collegian*, and worked after hours till late at night getting it ready for the printer, and in the course of these sessions, naturally, the young English professor fell in love with Elizabeth.

But everyone was in love with Elizabeth—all who were not already in love with one of the other ten girls. I was enjoying a wonderful relaxed period; I was wearing Olaus's diamond by that time. All the boys danced with me and were good friends, and they also cried on my shoulder about Elizabeth. I was already in the position of having a matronly understanding of life's problems. With all this and the studying, and skiing on Sundays, the days did go by, and on an evening early in March I had a phone call from Jess: "Hey, Mardy, I just got a wire from Olaus! He wants me to buy two teams of dogs for that expedition to the mouth of the Yukon; and he says he and Mr. Brandt and Mr. Conover will get here on the tenth!"

The Biological Survey was sending a big expedition to the mouth of the Yukon to study and band waterfowl, and Olaus was to be in charge. This whole region had proved to be one of the continent's outstanding nesting places for waterfowl, and the Biological Survey felt they should have a more complete knowledge of the area and its life, on which at that time there was little data. Two wealthy men interested in ornithology were going along, paying part of the expense in order to visit this famous waterfowl breeding area.

Jess found the dog teams. Captain Klinkenberg, the famous

arctic trader, had just arrived in Fairbanks. He and his Eskimo helpers had come from Victoria Land, pulling four thousand white fox skins on two toboggans, with four tough Huskies to each toboggan. Jess bought these eight dogs for the government. Out at Chatanika, on the Creeks, young Morris O'Leary had trained six half-year-old pups, all of one litter so they would not fight, beautifully matched, just broken to harness. This was the second team.

Olaus and his party were in town for one week, but inexorably the morning came when they and the whole student body and faculty were on the railroad platform, everybody saying good-by all round. Then the conductor of the dinky tooted his whistle— time to go to school! Elizabeth came and took my arm and said: "Come on, you may as well get out of sight. They have to get on the train in a minute anyway."

And as the dinky moved off toward the college young Ernest Patty, the geology professor (later to be an illustrious president of the University of Alaska), leaned from the back platform and shouted to Olaus: "Don't worry about her; we'll take care of her for you!"

There had been, in that happy week, one frustrating evening when we had tried to make plans, and when I had finally said, half in tears: "I don't think you're going to have *time* to stop and get married this summer!"

Olaus had replied, in his soothing voice: "Now look, your birthday is August 18; let's take a chance on that date. I can't tell, but gosh, I should be able to get out of Hooper Bay and up the Yukon by that time. It will *have* to be about that time, because I have to catch the last trip up the Koyukuk on the *Teddy H.*". . . .

"*Teddy H.*! What's that?"

"It's trader Sam Dubin's little stern-wheel steamer. I'm going to send the dogs out from Hooper Bay with an Eskimo before break-up, to some village where they can be boarded for most of the summer, and then I'll have them sent up on an earlier trip of the *Teddy H.* to Bettles, so we'll be sure to have them up there for freeze-up for the caribou-collecting trip. Let's *plan* at least on being married by Dr. Chapman at Anvik at the Episcopal mission on the eighteenth; then whatever river boat you come downriver on can take us on up to Nulato and we can wait there for the *Teddy H.* It's the best I can think of. I talked to the Chief about your going along."

He paused, and then leaned toward me with a rather questioning smile: "You *do* want to go, don't you?"

Mother and Daddy sat there looking first at Olaus and then at me, rather dubiously, rather puzzled, but I looked at Olaus and there was no question. "Yes, I want to go."

Nothing about this whole romance was conventional in any sense, except for the lovely parties which were given for me and the fact that Mother, with immense faith, did go ahead and order engraved wedding announcements from Lowman & Hanford in Seattle, with "August 18, at Anvik, Alaska" on them. There was even an announcement party given by Edna Lewis and Vide Gaustad, later the wife of Senator Bob Bartlett of Alaska. The bridegroom was not there of course—he was halfway down the Yukon by dog team; his photograph stood on the table by the Gaustads' front door. But it was a beautiful party, with all our friends, old and new, asking quetions about where and when, and Elizabeth explaining: "Her trousseau is going to be fur parka and fur boots and flannel pajamas and wool shirts and hiking boots!"

She was right. All Mother's friends said: "What a funny trousseau!" But they all dropped in later on in the summer when I had it assembled, to look and laugh over it: a tent, a Yukon stove, duffel bags, pack sacks, snowshoes, fur parka, wool knickers, wool shirts, big socks, flannel pajamas. Not a dress, not a bit of lace or a ribbon.

I graduated on June 13. Though I was the only senior, there was a beautiful, full commencement ceremony, for which notables of the Territory came and the whole town, it seemed, turned out. After that Elizabeth and I took part tearfully in several "seeing-off" parties as the faculty members departed for a summer "Outside" and the students left for summer jobs. We had all had a memorable year together, fun and accomplishment and sharing of new adventures, and it was heart-tugging to have it end. Elizabeth went to work at the photography studio in town, and I went to work for Dr. Bunnell in the now too quiet main building at the college, cataloguing the library of 5,000 volumes (now 60,000!).

The government-operated stern-wheel steamer *General Jacobs* was leaving Nenana, seventy-five miles downriver from Fairbanks, on August 13, bound for Holy Cross, near the mouth of the Yukon. In all the five months since March, I had had two letters, and no recent word.

But on August 12, in the still broad daylight of 7 P.M. when the train left for Nenana, at the same spot where Mother and I had arrived in that faraway September of 1911, we stood in a crowd of happy chattering friends. For the wedding ceremony at least, I would be feminine-looking; there was one bag filled with my wedding things. And here at the train I was wearing my beautiful new gray coat that had come all the way from Franklin Simon in New York and a delectable small hat of iridescent purple and lavender silk covered with pink and rose silk flowers, and in my arms a great bouquet of Mrs. Hess's sweet peas. Clara and Jess were there, with their children. Louise and Louis and Carol were clustered beside them, for they were going back to the old neighborhood to stay with the Rusts and Shafers while Mother accompanied her oldest daughter on this journey to join her bridegroom. Daddy had been called Outside on legal business a month before. Tears were on Clara's cheeks, and tears on mine as I hugged them all a last time, but the children were only wide-eyed and interested; they were going to have a fine time with the Rusts, and seeing Mardy off was exciting fun.

While I was being hugged and kissed and handed more flowers and candy and magazines, I kept looking toward the bridge, hoping and praying Elizabeth would make it. I wanted her for my bridesmaid, but it was still in doubt whether Dr. Romig would decide he could do without her for ten days, for in the evenings, after her other work, she did his laboratory work. But the famous "Dog-team Doctor" was my true friend, for at the last moment his Model T shooshed up to the platform and Elizabeth, followed by two young men carrying her bags, rushed up to us. "Come on! Let's get this train started before Daddy changes his mind again!"

So now I had Mother and my bridesmaid, and Harry Watson, superintendent of transportation on the river and one of Olaus's dearest friends, would be on the boat at Nenana to go downriver with us and be best man.

I also had Olaus's suitcase, which he had left with me in March; it contained his good suit and shirts and other items. I had a wedding ring, purchased by Adolph back home in Moorhead, Minnesota, and sent to me in July. I had the "funny trousseau." I had several hundred dollars of the bridegroom's money (he had left me a blank check in March!), and above all, I had the marriage license, which he had been thoughtful enough to procure in March also. Now if we could only find out where he was and whether he was going to come up the river or not!

At Nenana, three hours later, there on the platform was our beloved Jim Hagan, deputy marshal for that district. As Elizabeth and I came down the steps off the train he held his arms wide to take us both in. "Hey, acushla, I've got the news you're lookin' for, I think—just forwarded down from Fairbanks!" and he handed me a yellow sheet. "Ah, look at her face, eh, Elizabeth? It's good news!"

Good news! Olaus was in St. Michael and would be on his way upriver in the little gas scow that served as the mail boat. And with him was the associate chief of the U. S. Biological Survey, Mr. Henderson from Washington, D. C. "Well, how wonderful," said Mother. "Just what we need, since Daddy couldn't be with us—someone to give the bride away!"

At that moment Harry came up, black eyes sparkling. "Word from that fella at last, hey? Well then, we're all set—pulling out in half an hour. Come on, Jim, let's get these folks aboard and stowed away and you can have a mug-up with us before we leave."

Happiness and excitement and the enveloping warmth of kindness—everything any girl could dream about—here it was. The crowning joy, that both Mother and Elizabeth could go with me down the great river looking for my bridegroom.

2

Anvik

Five days later, on the afternoon of August 18, the *General Jacobs* was tied up at the end of her downriver run, in front of the Catholic mission village of Holy Cross, a good many miles down the Yukon from the Episcopal mission at Anvik mentioned in the wedding announcements. Mother, outwardly serene as always, was sitting up in the pilothouse, hemming wedding-gift napkins. Elizabeth and handsome Captain Looney were promenading through the Indian village playing with all the Malemute pups. Harry was on the beach teasing the trader's pet bear cubs with a can of milk.

I had hoped to escape all the joking sympathy over the gas boat *Tanana's* failure to arrive from St. Michael, by retreating into my stateroom—I was beginning to feel a good cry coming on. But the Norwegian steward poked his head in the door to ask if he could give the wedding cake to a young Indian bride he knew of on shore, and the charming, irrepressible chief engineer called through the window wanting to know how it felt to have so much faith in one man that you would travel eight hundred miles with a whole wedding party when you had hardly heard from the man in three months.

They did all this, I knew, to hide their deep friendly concern, to help me pretend that waiting was bearable, to reassure me that that gas boat from St. Michael had not hit a snag, that it would come, that there would be a bridegroom on it. We sat at Holy Cross for twenty-four hours. Harry and Captain Looney had been talking, in whispers loud enough for me to hear, about the fact that by law they were supposed to wait only twenty-four hours for the connecting mail boat and then turn and go back upriver to keep on schedule!

At eight o'clock that evening, my birthday, we were all in the pilothouse as usual, everyone making forced, unconcerned remarks, when in the middle of a sentence the captain yelled: "Gas boat *Tanana!*" and pulled the whistle cord, which hung over the wheel. And the tension snapped. I fell on the captain's neck, and Mother on Harry's, and everyone hugged Elizabeth of course, but she reached for my hand and began pulling me out of the pilothouse and down the companionway. "Come on, get into your room. I'll tell Olaus where you are."

Behind us I heard Harry cry: "There's Olaus! I see him!"

Alone inside the stateroom, I listened to the shouts of greeting, and the bumpings and chuggings as that clumsy craft came along-side the *General Jacobs,* and tried to make myself realize what this moment was, but all I could think of was how loud my heart was pounding. Then the door opened quietly, and we were together and there was no thinking.

Suddenly, over our heads, we heard a loud thump, and then the *General Jacobs*'s whistle, the fifteen-minute whistle, and Olaus said: "Gee whiz, I've got to get out there, I guess, and get my stuff loaded!"

We went out on deck into the happiest, noisiest excitement— greetings and explanations, people rushing back and forth above and below deck, the luggage and mail being unloaded. The Indian deckhands were moving from the scow to the steamer with the speed and grace of cats, but managed to look over their shoulders to grin at us. The captain leaned from the pilothouse window— "Get that stuff over here now; step on it!"—and looked down at me with a wonderful smile. From his bedlam down below the engineer shouted up that he didn't blame me for coming all the way down the Yukon. In the midst of all this confusion we met Mr. Henderson and knew at once how fine he was.

So at last the party was complete, as we steamed back up the river in the deepening dusk of arctic August toward Anvik.

Olaus and his suitcase disappeared for a time, and when an absolutely jubilant group gathered for "midnight lunch" at ten

o'clock, the bridegroom really looked like one. Mr. Henderson looked all round the table as we finished eating and said in his deep, authoritative voice: "Now, we're going to have a rehearsal. Elizabeth, go get your prayer book; you told me you had it with you."

We had a rehearsal, and it was then we discovered that everyone in the wedding party, including the captain and the chief engineer and the purser, was a member of the Episcopal Church— except the bride and groom and the bride's mother!

After that Harry sent us all away for a rest, assuring us that the cabin boy would wake us in plenty of time. I fell at once into a deep sleep, and it seemed only moments before there came a rap-tapping at the door: "Anvik in half an hour!" and Mother, leaning over me: "Are you ready for your wedding? It's half past two."

I suppose the most unusual thing about this wedding was the

hour at which it was held. I felt a great wave of gratitude when Mother and I stepped out on deck and found all the rest of the party waiting, perfectly groomed, at that hour, and for us! Under the deck lights stood Elizabeth, in cream lace and a flowery cloche, the light glinted on the captain's gold buttons; the engineer was startlingly handsome, having scrubbed away the engine-room grease and sporting gray suede gloves and a fedora. The whole crew too was ready for the occasion. And the bride, in seal-brown crepe touched here and there with blue and orange, and a brown straw cloche trimmed with orange silk flowers. As the *General Jacobs* blew the landing blast the gangplank swung out, I turned to catch a happy reassuring smile from Mother, and saw that she was wearing a big pink rose Mrs. Webster had given us from her hothouse at Tanana on our way downriver. Roses were rare, precious gems in Alaska, and yet here was one at our wedding far down the Yukon.

In the beam of the ship's light on the black shore stood the minister, dear Dr. Chapman, and all the mission family, six of them, up at this hour to welcome us. So we knew that our Signal Corps friend at Holy Cross had been able to get through to Dr. Chapman. How fortunate that this clergyman was a ham radio operator also!

We walked up the bank under the glow of lights strung miraculously from ship to shore, in those few minutes of landing, by that same teasing engineer and his crew, and we came to the little log church. The lights showed us its sturdy outline, low and square, its rustic bell tower, its tiny windows. What a comfortable quiet there was about it. Willows crowded thick beside it, and beyond them at this most silent hour of morning there spoke the voice of the great river flowing by.

Here Mr. Henderson took my arm, and we stepped over the threshold and into soft yellow light from the many tall candles shining on the brown log walls and the hand-made benches and chancel carved of tawny birch. From two large candelabra at the altar, candles shone also on bowls of ferns and pale-gold arctic poppies. This was like a dream—pausing but an hour in the night and finding all this beauty prepared for us.

Now came Dr. Chapman, in gown and stole, and while I was trying hard to realize the perfection of this hour, we were going on: "Dearly beloved, we are gathered together . . ."

What greater joy could life ever hold than to be able to repeat

those words—"I, Margaret, take thee, Olaus"—with a sure heart?

Then there was Elizabeth, clinging to me and weeping, and the captain with tears in his eyes, and Mother, not crying, but with shining eyes: "Oh, I'm so glad, and I can tell Daddy all about it!"

We went almost reluctantly out from that gracious candle-lit place; some happy tears were dropping upon the mass of ferns and arctic poppies that Dr. Chapman's daughter Ada had put into my arms, but there was someone to guide my steps, and we were saying "Thank you," not knowing how to say it enough, and "Good-by," and the *General Jacobs* was blowing a salute as we went up the gangplank.

As we slid away from the shore Dr. Chapman shouted up to the captain: "Four o'clock. Just one hour. And there's the sun!"

Out across the wide gray river, over the low willows, there was a bright splash of rose and molten gold. Mother and Olaus and I stood in the bow and watched a sunrise of promise. A beautiful world was waking to light here on the Yukon.

3

Nulato

As though it were the last time any of us would see one another, there was steady talking, talking as the *General Jacobs* churned her way upriver against the mighty current all that day. The past five months to tell of, the next five to plan. Olaus had to tell them all about the expedition at the mouth of the Yukon, the life in an Eskimo village, the rare birds banded, the adventures and mishaps. Then we had to repack all our bags, sending all the civilized clothing back home with Mother, packing all our wilderness equipment into the duffel bags, to be ready for disembarking early next morning at Nulato.

The whole ship, from the captain and the engineer to Mr. Henderson, supervised and advised; they rolled sleeping bags, tied knots, and gave us plenty of suggestions. Harry, old dog musher that he was, and calmly efficient, had to make sure we had all the important things for a winter journey. The "funny trousseau" was being inspected and repacked into the rucksacks.

Finally, when evening came, there was a surprise wedding supper. The Norwegian steward, all the while smiling at his countryman ("Ah ya, you got a good boy here; he's a good Norsk boy!"), brought in melons and strawberries, which he had kept safely in the ice box all the way from Nenana. But Harry and Elizabeth had disappeared—oh, here they came, through the galley door, carrying between them a huge wedding cake! I had known of no cake; I had thought the steward was simply joking when he asked if he could give the cake to the Indian bride. The little Filipino baker had made this marvelous thing in secret, with the connivance of Harry and Elizabeth. It consisted of three stories of fruitcake, covered with filigreed frosting, the whole surmouted by a miniature log cabin, snow-covered, with icicles of frosting hanging from the eaves!

Olaus and I went out in the galley after supper to thank the baker, but we only flustered him. He waved his hands at us: "Tha's all right. Tha's all right. Go way now, go way now."

We lingered long over that late supper. It seemed there must be many more last words to say; but words are weak; we use many of them and never really express what is in our hearts.

At 5 A.M. the *General Jacobs* pulled into Nulato, and again the whole wedding party was there on the deck to see us ashore. They had done their duty by us, and now they topped it off by showering us with rice as we walked down the gangplank.

On the way downriver Nulato had been basking and twinkling in the sun, but this morning at five o'clock the straggly row of log cabins, the Indian graveyard on the hill upstream and the great river were all shrouded in misty rain. So, standing close together on the riverbank, Olaus and I watched the dear faces grow dimmer and dimmer in the mist, and as we waved, the wedding ship sounded her last salute to us and disappeared around the bend in the rain, the churn-churn of her wheel severing us from all the known and familiar things and leaving us to start our first chapter in the wilderness.

Following Olaus into the trading post, I sat down rather tearfully on our piled duffel bags. My sitting there like that brought to mind such a ludicrous "immigrant at Ellis Island" picture that we both burst out laughing, and the mist of confusion and rain and overexcitement seemed to lift and we suddenly looked at each other with laughing eyes, knowing that we were together and ready for anything!

The thought came to me that I was thankful that the trader had to get up to meet the boat, for here was shelter, for the moment at least, and here was the kindly German trader, Charlie Steinhauser, hovering round us with helpful murmurs. No, not even a roadhouse here—the deputy marshal and the postmaster were the only other white people except for the missionaries at the Catholic mission above town. But we might be able to find a

cabin suitable for white people where we could keep house while
waiting for the *Teddy H.*

I heard footsteps overhead; they descended the staircase into
the front of the store, and Mrs. Steinhauser appeared, all in
immaculate white, as she had been when we had met her on our
way downriver, her golden hair curling out from under a starchy
white housecap, her comely face smiling a welcome. In two
minutes we were relaxing in the warm comfort of her cozy living
room. Indian baskets spilled green vines in all the corners; two
gorgeous grizzly-bear skins lay on the floor; there were bookcases
across one end of the room, a piano, plump easy chairs, bright
curtains at the big windows, which looked out onto the river. A
cold rain was beating in against them now. There was no sign of
life in any of the little cabins facing the road that wandered along
the riverbank. I turned back from the window and curled down
gratefully on one of the bear-skins. From the adjoining room
came the odor of coffee and bacon, and the eager voice of our
hostess. Now we must come and eat, and tell her all about the
wedding!

We sat at table a long time, the three of us, in that shining
kitchen.

I awoke to find myself in a strange room, alone, with sun
streaming in through starched white curtains. Then I heard a low
murmur of voices from the kitchen, and remembered. I was in
Mrs. Steinhauser's bed, in Nulato on the Yukon; I had had a
wonderful sleep, the greatest adventure was beginning and I felt
ready for it! From outside came the many sounds of a fully awake
village, out to bask in the sunshine after the storm. Below, in the
store, the murmur of more voices, low and strange, the Nulato
Indians.

I did not try to put my hair into its usual Elsie Ferguson puffed-
and-rolled style; I parted it in the middle and combed it into two
long braids to hang over my shoulders; this was the way it would
have to be for the coming months.

Olaus was in the kitchen eating cake, luscious coconut layer
cake just out of Mrs. Steinhauser's oven, while waiting to take me
to our first home. A few hundred yards upstream from the trading
post, and back from the river, in the second tier of cabins, there it
was, a neat two-room cabin with bright blue window and door

frames. Olaus and the young Indian who owned the cabin had already moved all our gear, and now we went gleefully to buy our first order of groceries from Mr. Steinhauser.

It was like playing dollhouse again, rearranging the few dishes and clearing the cupboard and trying the four pieces of furniture first in one spot then another. The bedroom was no more than the word implies—we had nothing in it but a bed. The front room had the four pieces of furniture—a big oilcloth-covered table, a tall cupboard, a couch, and a rocking chair—besides, of course, the little cookstove and two straight chairs. There was also a washstand made of boxes and a big woodbox which could also serve as an extra chair—what more could we need?

For our first meal we had macaroni and cheese, biscuits, and canned peaches. Thanks to my being used to cooking for at least six people at home, we ate macaroni and cheese for days to come; but that was unimportant. What was important was that finally we were apart from the world, with a dream come true. We had the warm light of a kerosene lamp on the table, the cheerful crackling from the stove; and to make it complete, as darkness fell the rain came again, a soft patter on the tin roof, with a whisper of wind.

Day came sparkling clear, calling to us, and before the waterfront had come to life we laced up our hiking boots, took a sackful of mousetraps, some rolled oats for bait, and the shotgun, and went swinging up the grassy old winter road south of the village. As we followed this road for several miles through the spruce woods, now aflame with high-bush cranberries, I had my first lesson in being a field assistant to a naturalist. I learned where to look for mouseholes and feeding places and was shown their tiny runways, like an intricate street system for fairies. What delightful discoveries can be made beneath a mossy stump or under the dense mat of water rushes! I had never seen a mousehole before; the unknowning eye is unable to see. In addition to his main assignment, studying the life history of the caribou, Olaus was interested in learning all he could about the distribution of several species of meadow vole, the red-backed mouse, the bog lemming, and the brown lemming. I had never known there were so many kinds of mice; I had known only the kitchen-cupboard ones. Nor had I known that these were true wild animals, which ranged throughout the wilderness and belonged there, nor that at that time there was not much known about the distribution of the various species. So everywhere Olaus traveled he set out mouse traplines! I learned that to the scientist these little creatures are interesting and important, for they have a relationship to bigger creatures and to the land and are part of the great chain of life.

We collected some plant specimens. This too I learned is part of the usual routine of any field naturalist, for plants are also part of the great chain of life. We also collected a good many blueberries, and I had my first taste of bird watching. I learned to identify two chickadees, the Hudsonian and the black-capped, the arctic three-toed woodpecker, and the pine grosbeak, so sturdy and vivid and at home in his world. Even that first day I began to feel the magnetic charm of birds, of *knowing* them.

After Olaus had set his trapline for mice, we looked northward toward the beautiful dome-shaped hill rising off the tundra. "Let's go over, shall we?"

An Indian hunting trail led across the summit of this dome, through evergreens made glorious by silver birches in their autumn gold and cranberries in a riot of red, and underfoot the rich colors of all kinds of moss dotted with orange toadstools.

Up there on top we found a broad stretch of flat hilltop covered with deep, deep reindeer moss and nothing else; no little dwarf birches or dwarf willows sticking up through. Olaus was looking for lemming runways, but then he straightened up and looked around and said: "Did you ever try falling straight backward without bending? We could do it here."

And he showed me. He stood with hands at his sides and tipped back on his heels, holding his body in one straight stiff column. Over he went, describing a perfect quarter circle, and there he was, lying perfectly straight and flat on that fine soft bed. "Now you try it," he said, grinning up at me.

I did. It takes a little courage to trust that the moss is really going to be soft, and to keep your body perfectly rigid. I didn't make it the first time, but afterward it was great fun. And I learned something else that afternoon: my husband thought I could do anything—and he expected me to do it!

Walking through Nulato in midafternoon was like walking down a long stage peopled with "villagers, townspeople, and others." But these villagers were brown of skin and parti-colored, with shapeless clothing, and too many of the younger ones were bowlegged and cross-eyed. A noisy ball game had been going on on the riverbank, but all activity ceased at our approach—strangers. Olaus was used to this sort of thing, and tramped along calmly, smiling at them all. I felt we should do a dance or respond in some special way to such attention, but perhaps my knickers and long braids were interesting.

The next afternoon when we came back from our trapline, the population of the village seemed to have doubled in our absence. The waterfront had become a lively scene indeed—children, dogs, old people, costumes of every color, shouting, ball throwing, racing, more shouting, sounds as of a cataclysmic emergency. When we entered the store, we must have had curiosity written on our faces, for Mr. Steinhauser laughed and said: "Didn't you know? There is to be a big potlatch here in two days. The hunters are out after bear meat now. Nulato, Kaltag, and Kokrines natives will all be here."

The river looked like regatta day. The motorboat is to the Yukon Indian what the automobile is to the Oklahoma brave. There were no gray or white hulls; the river's breast was specked with the gayest of blues, yellows, reds, and the attire of the occupants of the boats made the pattern even more colorful. We stood on the bank for a long time, watching, listening to a great chug-chugging and coughing and back-firing of engines, against an orchestral background of howling Malemutes, for the village dogs were tied along the beach below the riverbank and greeted every approaching craft with impartial raucousness. Most of the boats arriving contained dogs too, heads and front paws bobbing, looking as though they had been thrown from a long distance, had landed among piled household effects, and had not dared to move a muscle since—except for their lungs, which they used wildly in answer to the shore committee. Olaus said he was sure the Indians reveled in all the noise, and the excitement was contagious.

In the "front yard" of our cabin, another cabin was being built, and the next morning we were wakened early by a great yammering and hammering and thumping. It is amazing how boisterous five young Indians can be. I did the breakfast dishes to the accompaniment of splutterings of Indian words and American slang all mixed up in great good-natured energy. They were raising the roof beams, and as Olaus said, each one was an

emergency. I kept running to the window, thinking someone was
about to be demolished, as they pulled on ropes and lifted and
heaved, their language a succession of urgent, violent explosions
most upsetting to listen to. Olaus thought some of the gusto might
be for our benefit. One of the boys had to stop every so often,
take off his shoes, and rearrange his socks. The feet were a
heliotrope shade, with blue toe and heel; the legs were a bright
green with red and yellow stripes around the top.

After breakfast we began the job of sorting all our gear again
and trying to sew a new cover for the braided rabbit-skin lining of
Olaus's sleeping bag. I was never a seamstress, and as I sat there
on the floor with big quilt spread all around me, Olaus was no
help. He was unpacking Eskimo artifacts from Hooper Bay and
telling me funny stories about some of them, and we both got to
laughing over nothing—just laughing in the sheer joy of all our
happiness.

We had forgotten all about the carpenters outside, but when, a
while later, I went out to go see Mrs. Steinhauser and get some
things from the store, one of the boys looked up from his
hammering and said to me: "Lotsa fun, eh, Margaret?"

How did he know my name? Perhaps our young landlord
knew. We had had a call from him the day before. It is the custom
of these people to enter a house unannounced and sit placidly,
responding only to questions. But our landlord, a handsome lad,
was more responsive; in fact, one of his responses was fun. I had
given him a piece of our wedding cake. He smiled at us and said:
"Oh yes, you fellas just got married!"

On the morning of August 27, the day the potlatch was to begin,
the ship of adventure arrived. The *Teddy H.* was one of the
remnants of the stampede days, when small stern-wheel steamers
were nailed together for every new "strike." The ship was white,
and neat, and was shaped like an oblong box. She was tall enough
to be divided into two "stories"—the engine room, the wood
storage room, the freight room, and the crew's quarters below,
with the open bow protruding in front; the "second story"
consisting of four staterooms fore and the galley aft with a fairly
large open space behind that running all the way to the stern; and
on top of all this, the little pilothouse. Her arrival in Nulato

furnished more noise and commotion for an already uproarious
waterfront. The shore was lined so thickly with elements of the
potlatch flotilla that the little steamer had to edge in very
cautiously, with much tooting and jingling from the pilothouse,
her native deckhands scurrying importantly and shouting
greetings to friends on shore at the same time.

When we returned from our trapline in the afternoon we met
the *Teddy H.*'s owner, Sam Dubin, the principal trader of the
Koyukuk River country and one of the northland's famous
characters. As he came up the gangway to the store, I thought of a
black bear. His short stout body was clad in a huge turtleneck
sweater of black wool and black breeches of some blanketlike
material laced below the knee; he had thick lips and heavy jowls,
and he was smoking a big black pipe. But he was very kind. He
told in a rumbling heavy voice with a Russian kind of accent of
the hard trip they had had and of the many delays, and trouble
with the motorboats they used at the head of the river. He hated
"gez boats," but they had got some "geeze" and would we come
aboard for dinner? We certainly would.

The galley was combination galley and dining saloon, a huge
restaurant range on one wall, a long table along the other, various
cupboards along the sides. We ate with the officers, I at the place
of honor at Sam's right. The captain, Fred Clark, was tall and lean
and rather young and reminded us of Jess; the chief engineer was a
powerful gray-haired man whose name was Bill Finger and who
had only one arm. The second engineer and the fireman were
young Germans, Otto and Heinie. The cook and I became friends
right away. He seemed to have stepped out of a Bret Harte yarn;
tall, lanky, with a droopy brown mustache and keen squinty
black eyes, his name was Frank Smith and he was a miner in the
Koyukuk in the winter. Everyone was shy and polite that first
night. The roast goose and stuffing were delicious and there was
even pumpkin pie.

After the meal Sam took us on a tour of the *Teddy H.*, and we
chose the port-bow stateroom for our home. It measured seven by
five feet and contained two berths, small windows front and side,
two small three-cornered shelves and a mirror, and two camp-
stools. Olaus looked at me and read my mind. He pointed to a
narrow space at the end of the double-decker bunks. "We can
stack a lot of our stuff in here," he said hopefully.

Suddenly there was a new kind of sound, coming from the

crew's quarters below, an alluring rhythmical singing in Eskimo to the accompaniment of cymbals and the beating of gasoline cans. Sam laughed and said: "Come on, I show you the *Teddy H.* orchestra!"

He led us down the outside companionway to the lower deck and through the big sliding door, and there Olaus found he knew all the performers. They were Kobuk Eskimos whom he and Adolph had met on their big winter trip two years before. The music stopped. They were all smiles to meet Olaus again and to find he remembered their names and the names of most of their people, after whom he inquired. I had, of course, heard a great deal about these people, one of the two inland tribes of Eskimo in Alaska, and I liked them at once. They were tall and well built, reminding one more of Hawaiians than any northern type. They immediately spoke to Olaus about the dogs, and we were glad to learn that the seven Victoria Land huskies had been safely delivered at Bettles on the previous trip and that the roadhouse keeper was taking care of them. Bettles would be the farthest north that the *Teddy H.* would go, eight hundred miles upriver from Nulato; from there we would travel north by scow or "gez boat."

The next day was a busy one. We made a last trip to our trapline and the beautiful forest and the beautiful mossy dome and then did some packing. But it was a temptation just to watch the village. There were cooking fires everywhere, over which hung huge iron pots filled with bear meat. The villagers' costumes had added even more color; new head kerchiefs, new neck ribbons, a great many beads. We thought the children might have been washed; they seemed to shine with a new light. The dogs had become innumerable and fights were so frequent that it was just one continuous battle. The Kobuks were busy loading the last freight for upriver into the *Teddy H's* big covered scow; Olaus was out paying for smoked dog salmon, some eight hundred pounds of it, shipped upriver earlier; and Sam was rolling animatedly from store to waterfront, the big pipe replaced by the fattest of black cigars.

Mr. Steinhauser explained to us that this potlatch was caused by the temerity of President Coolidge in declaring Indians citizens of these United States. The Kokrines, Nulato, and Kaltag tribes were by no means sure they were pleased with being no longer wards of Uncle Sam, and despite Mr. Steinhauser's repeated explanation that it was too late to do anything about it, they had to have a powwow. Two envoys came to our cabin. The chief had heard that Olaus was "government animal man." Would he please attend a meeting in the store that evening? They wanted to hear about the new laws on "beaber and muskrap."

At supper time we noticed that there was great interest centered on one cabin near the store. This was the chief's house, and issuing from it were the men, each with a heaping plate of bear meat and other food, which was being dished out by the women of the chief's household.

When we walked up to the store later, there was a buzzing crowd about the door. The "business meeting" was about to begin, and Olaus was escorted in to meet the chief. I sat upstairs with Mrs. Steinhauser and gave her the news of the village, feeling rather strange to be doing so, but I had learned that she rarely went out into the village. I gathered that her kindly husband preferred a woman to be very secluded. Her place was in the home; her three pleasant rooms, her pet canary, her plants, her piano, books, sewing, and housework—these constituted her life. She told me she went for walks in winter; there were "fewer people" about then! Yet she seemed content. We listened to the rise and fall of the many speeches down below—a long harangue in the Indian tongue, a low, even voice which I knew well, then a long period of murmur and babble and more harangue. Olaus came up to us then, and we heard the noisy exit of many feet and voices dying away toward the kashima in the rear of the village. The dance would be beginning.

In a few moments Otto Geist, the stocky, keen-eyed young second engineer of the *Teddy H.*, arrived to tell us that the Indian chief sent word that "if the young white bride would like to come," they would do some native dances for her.

As we walked with Otto into the pitch-black night and down a narrow alley to the kashima, little did we realize how our lives were to be intertwined with his forever after.

The dimly lighted log kashima seemed packed with humanity. All around the log walls ran a high shelf or bench; here sat the men. I spied our Kobuk friends with their oil cans, established on the shelf at the front of the building. On a sort of dais at one side sat the old men, the chief and his counselors, all in white man's dress but with the Indian's flair for color. All round the room on the floor were the women and children, hundreds it seemed at first glance, packed in close in a wiggling jumble, but remarkably quiet—the men were making the noise. Someone brought a box for us, and we sat on it near the door.

Just to watch that colorful crowd would have been enough, for though they were not very noisy, their faces shone with pent-up excitement, and a feeling of suspense filled the air.

The two Kobuk Eskimos with the oil cans finally began, a fairly fast beat of sticks on the cans, the rhythm broken into short phrases as in a song. Their Kobuk companions sat as quiet as cats; so did all the Indians. On they went for what seemed a long time, and I was wondering why the signal for a dance was not given when suddenly a little short Kobuk in overalls and a red shirt jumped to the center of the floor and began to sing and dance at the same time. Olaus whispered that this was a descriptive dance and urged me to try to figure out what the story was about. Anyone who has tried to sing while dancing could appreciate the performance of this square-built Eskimo, for their dance is a muscle dance, a series of quick jerks, contortions, and startling gestures of the arms accompanied by continuous quick jumping with both feet at once. We could gather that the story was about a hunt of some kind and, at the end, about someone who ate so much that he became all swelled up, with a great stomach, and at this gesture the audience burst into laughter and the performer ended with a broad grin, his face shining like polished walnut. The drumming continued.

A strenuous mad business, yet an authentic outlet for energy. Eskimo drumming rhythm is compelling; as it goes along it increases in power. I could readily see the psychology of it. You sit stolidly listening, until your savage love of rhythm, your pent-up life, can stand no more, then out you jump and go at it. I had hardly finished thinking this when Oscar, the *Teddy H.*'s cabin boy, leaped out upon the floor. He did a similar kind of dance, with no song, only now and then an explosive "Ay, ah, ah," in which his companions joined. By this time the whole crowd was swaying in time to the drumbeat; so were we. I glanced sideways at Olaus; he was leaning forward, keeping time with his fist on his knee, and I would not have been surprised if he had jumped out there and joined Oscar, for I knew he had learned this dance two years before at Alatna. We were both captured and carried along in that demanding, insistent rhythm, there in that smoky log hall, with flickering light from oil lamps lighting the fierce animation of all those brown faces.

Oscar's dance was followed by a speech, which sounded like a scolding, by the Indian chief. Evidently he was exhorting his people not to be outperformed by the visiting Eskimos, for there was soon a change in the program. Big Ambrose, an Indian deckhand from the *Teddy H.*, stepped out to the floor, oil can and stick in hand, and there followed a mass dance in which all the Indians participated. It was somehow poignantly touching. To begin with, Big Ambrose was built like a football player, with a broad jovial countenance, his thick black locks hanging over one cheek. He wore a black felt hat, slapped on at an angle, and a bright bandana knotted at his throat. He led the way, singing an Indian song which sounded like a wild chant from the puzzled heart of an untamed soul, and he was followed by the Indian youths, crowding up about him in disordered file; then came the women and children in a compact group. Around and around they went, to the beat of the drum and Ambrose's song. Their dance was a slumping, loose shuffle, as of someone dancing in half-drunken sleep, and indeed Ambrose looked intoxicated with emotion, shuffling along, leaning backward, head to one side, his big lips curling back in a sleepy triumphant grin.

Suddenly, without warning, it all ended, and they scurried to their seats. A messenger was then sent across to us to say that that was the end of the native dances. All the rest of that night the "ceremonial house" would resound to the scraping of a fiddle, the clapping of hands, the shuffling of moccasined feet performing the white man's square dances, reels, and quadrilles; these the Indian had seized upon as his own. Times change.

We asked Otto to come to our cabin. Olaus built up the fire and I made cocoa, and as we sat there in the cozy warmth Olaus told us of another potlatch he had attended. Two years before, when he and Adolph were up in the Kobuk's Alatna River country, they had been invited to witness a real one, one which demonstrated the real meaning of the word "potlatch." It was just after the New Year. Hunters had brought in caribou and moose for the feast; the women had been busy cooking and making ready. The night of the potlatch was cold and clear with a hint of the aurora in the northern sky. The potlatch was an Indian affair, but the Kobuk Eskimos had all been invited and they were crossing the river in groups, from their village to the Indian village on the opposite shore of the Koyukuk—dark blotches moving along the village trail over the white snow.

"What's this for, this potlatch?" Olaus had asked an Eskimo companion.

"Little Andrew, he lose his little boy last summer. Now he give big potlatch; he give away all his stuff."

That indeed was the purpose of the potlatch. In the assembly hall a great crowd had gathered, men, women, and children, all out for a night of celebration. The grownups found seats on the benches along the walls; the children sat on the floor. Great tubs of cooked meat were brought in. These were carried around by two stalwart Indians and each guest helped himself. Olaus picked a caribou rib and found it delicious. Then came a tub of moose meat, and that was delectable also. Presently hardtack was passed around; then came buckets of fruit—canned peaches, cherries, raspberries, from the store, all mixed in the same bucket. This was a convenient innovation made possible by the coming of the white man.

Such festivities, with chatter and laughter, gave no indication of any bereavement, and Olaus and Adolph wondered about this; but presently there was a hush and they noticed that quantities of household goods were being carried in and deposited in a heap in the middle of the floor. Little Andrew and his wife knelt quietly beside their worldly goods, their heads bowed. There was a pause. Then the chief of the Indians arose and made a speech, earnest and apparently very eloquent. He sat down, and there was another pause. Then the medicine man, wearing a fur cap, arose. Olaus said that he was bald, the only bald Indian he had ever seen, and was never without his cap. He gave a long, fiery harangue. He was followed by others. Then old Tobuk, the chief of the Eskimos, arose and spoke in Indian. Olaus understands a little of the Indian language, and quite a bit of Eskimo, but these formal orations went over his head. He would have given much to know what they spoke about so earnestly.

After a due pause, Little Andrew and his wife began to pick over the pile of goods. Little Andrew was one of the best hunters in the tribe and was considered well-to-do. There were piles of new blankets, evidently just bought at the store; there were cooking utensils, bolts of cloth, traps, and the hunter's own rifle. All must go. A little boy acted as messenger. There would be a few muttered words, perhaps a brief consultation, and the boy would carry the article to the guest that had been designated. Slowly, as the wearisome process went on, the pile diminished until the floor was bare. Even then, the bereaved parents brought forth some money and distributed that. They had now done their part. There were a few short speeches; the potlatch was over; Little Andrew and his wife were to begin over again. Olaus noticed, however, that some of the guests, as they walked out, dropped some coins beside the destitute couple where they sat in the middle of the floor with bowed heads.

4

Willow River

At midnight on August 31 we went aboard the *Teddy H.* after spending the evening with the Steinhausers. They came down to the shore with us. It was impossible to tell those kind people how much they had enriched our first ten days. Nor were they through heaping good things upon us, for a few minutes later Sam, who had also been their guest that evening, knocked on our door and presented us with one of those huge baskets of chocolates, tied with yards and yards of white satin ribbon, "with the Steinhausers' compliments."

David Tobuk, the good-looking young Kobuk pilot, was waiting to give us a gasoline lamp for our stateroom. He had cleaned the room and made up the berths for us himself, and its tiny warm interior looked inviting.

At three o'clock in the morning, once more, we took the second step in our journey when the *Teddy H.* pulled away from the sleeping village of Nulato. So we woke to that most beloved sound, the churning of a stern wheel, and heard Oscar's soft voice at the window: "Breakfast ready."

Breakfast was in progress, and here we met our only fellow passengers, Mr. and Mrs. Long. He was middle-aged and very English, despite twenty-six years in the Koyukuk; she was younger, dark-eyed, attractive and animated. They had met the year before, when she was teaching school at Wiseman, at the head of navigation on the Koyukuk.

Frank, the cook, stood before the huge range, dish towel tied round his middle, pouring from a pitcher the thin batter that makes those delicious sourdough hotcakes, flipping them nonchalantly while discoursing with Mrs. Long: "So you're glad to be leavin' the States behind, huh? I'd like to take a look-see down there again someday, but I guess the old Koyukuk's not so bad. Oscar, pass these folks some syrup. Fella can't starve to death up here anyway; even if your claims don't pan out you can always get plenty of firewood and plenty of rabbits and trap a few furs for another grubstake. You think these cakes are good? Huh, I've made better; dough don't work so good sometimes."

Soon after breakfast that first morning we "opened up" the mouth of the Koyukuk when we passed below a green-and-red-streaked sandstone bluff, and there was the Koyukuk, the "Willow River" of the Indians. I was surprised at its size, for at its mouth it seemed as wide as the Yukon we were leaving. Oscar, passing along the deck, paused beside us. "You see that red color on hill there? Old people say that's blood from Indians killed in fight, long 'go. Long time 'go Koyukuk Indians all time fight Yukon Indians. Yukon Indians sneak up, kill big bunch Koyukuks one time, that hill."

After lunch we sat on the coal box at the stern, basking in warm sunshine and talking to Oscar and David about Indian and Eskimo dances. Oscar had brought out a tub filled with potatoes to peel and squatted beside it; David was off shift and lounged at the rail near us. We asked them about the dances we had seen at Nulato. The Kobuk's songs had seemed so sprightly, so full of vigor. David said: "Oh yes, our people like to have fun. Indians songs all about somebody dead. Ambrose's song he sang in kashim is about his sister, died last year. Before Kobuk came over from the Arctic, Indians had no fun games—we teach 'em all games they have now. Yes, they like cry, feel bad. We like laugh, have fun. Lots of things funny."

He laughed, and we laughed with him. It is so easy to laugh with the Eskimos; and it was a joy to be getting acquainted with our shipmates. We swung our feet from the coal box and felt at home on the *Teddy H.*; and we felt the tremble and lift of the paddle wheel under us, churning to foam the glassy waters of that lonely and beautiful river. We had left the muddy Yukon; this water was crystal clear.

Sam came rolling along the deck. "Well, how you people like

this river, eh? I tell you, Mrs. Murie, make yourself at home on
this boat; anything you want, just ask for it."

He leaned against the coal box and pulled on his big black pipe.
"You like to cook, so? Sure you go ahead and make a cake; I'd
like a good cake for supper myself—hey Frank?"

Frank appeared in the door of the galley. "You bet. Come right
along; we need some fancy touches put on around here!"

So we had fresh salmon for supper, and devil's food cake, and
as we were finishing Frank called us and the Longs out on deck.
Four foxes—two reds, a silver, and a cross—were loping and
playing along the beach. Their holes could be seen right there
behind them in the sand bank, and above the bank the mixed
thick forest of yellow birches and dark spruces was silhouetted
before a golden sunset.

"Why are three different colors all playing together like that?"
asked Mrs. Long.

"Oh well, you know, it's just like blondes and brunettes in the
same family," answered Olaus. "All these colors can happen in
the same litter; there's no difference in species or subspecies. I'm
sure that's one family there."

We sat with the Longs on the locker outside our stateroom,
watching the sky and the forest, and Mr. Long suddenly began to
speak of the river in different guise, in different days.

"Oh yes, some of us came down the Yukon and all the way up
the river here. Someone had struck it rich up at the head of this
river, but no one knew the best way to get in here, don't you
know. We were the ones who had drawn blanks on the Klondike
fuss, and came on to the new strike—umm—'99 it was when I
came. Some of us pulled our sled load of stuff on the ice here; jolly
long way to pull, you know, eight hundred miles by river, cold
wind blowing all the time, deep snow some places, miserable;
didn't look much as it does now."

And we all gazed at the riotous rose of the western sky, the
inviting shimmery green of a grassy shore. Mrs. Long murmured:
"Oh, John, how could anybody live through such an awful test?
Just think!"

"Oh well, the lure of the gold, you know, my dear. Jolly young
adventurers. We were all young then, young . . . Now we're all
looking for overland trails, short cuts, airplanes."

We sat silent. The rosy sky dimmed to saffron; two red-
throated loons flew across the bow; ducks marched Indianfile

along the sand beach. "Yes, the prospectors are going in in airplanes these days; but the Koyukuk country is still the same as in '99. Civilization will not get to it too much for quite a while yet."

He spoke this last in a satisfied manner, conveying the feeling held by all of us: civilization, meaning many comforts, many people, speed, efficiency, thought of as an enemy. Selfish, no doubt, and "ornery," we would stand and cheer so long as our spot of wilderness could repel the invasion. Why shouldn't one corner of the earth remain "unconquered"?

Day after gleaming day, cloudless, windless, the *Teddy H.* churned her way up the river; it was like a dream world, achingly happy and so beautiful that there is hardly any way to tell about it. Here is a typical day, from the diary:

"We went ashore into woods gold and dark green. Olaus went up the slope and shot a varied thrush and a three-toed woodpecker to paint and make specimens of. Then the chicka-dees, camp robbers, and squirrels started a great fuss, and a big blue-gray goshawk sailed over my head, so he was added to the specimens and we came aboard well supplied with work for the biologist-artist. Now I saw the reason for the kind of shotgun Olaus had—a 16-gauge double-barreled one, in which one barrel had inserted into it a little auxiliary barrel which carried a .32-shot shell for small birds; so there was one barrel for the hawk, the other for the thrush. He is painting the thrush now while I sit on the locker outside our open door where I can talk and write and at the same time watch the activities of our little floating world. Ambrose the inimitable and a tall Kobuk, David's brother, are winding up cable on the capstan just below on the bow, Ambrose shuffling a dance step and singing the crew's favorite, 'Oh, it ain't gonna rain no more, no more,' as they work. I know they hope Sam, in his cabin with his bills and business troubles, will hear, because we are all supposed to be praying for rain, to raise the water in the river. Capt. Fred leans from the pilothouse and calls some instructions and jingles his signals; he must know every foot of this river trail. In the suddenly lessened noise of the engines I can hear the engineer and his assistants, Otto and Heinie, all shouting German and laughing. At the stern deck stands Oscar, picking ducks for dinner and throwing the feathers over the rail, at the same time doing a Kobuk dance and singing: 'Ah, yunga, yah, yunga, hunga, ah, hah.' Suddenly Frank appears in the galley door: 'Ah, yah, hah, yah,' and flings his long lanky limbs in burlesque.

"While he skinned and stuffed the hawk this afternoon Olaus had the whole crew and passenger list for audience; even Sam emerged from his world of invoices and cigar smoke for a few minutes. Oscar said to Olaus: 'Everybody watch *you.*' The Kobuk inflection is quite like French Canadian.

"There is below decks a tall raw-boned silent man, one of those solitary characters who live along the rivers and earn a living of a kind by chopping cords and cords of wood to feed the *Teddy's* boiler. He has with him two little half-breed sons who look like forest creatures. They are going back to their wood camp for another winter of chopping and trapping. I wonder what has happened to their Indian mother. One of the little boys kept smiling up at me very shyly and finally consented to come up and have some of the chocolates from the big basket and to converse in quaint halting phrases. When we reached his father's wood camp just before supper we went ashore with the boy. This is his home; just one cabin, and wood piles. I asked him his name and he answered: 'I got no name.' A flock of ruffed grouse whirred up before us in the trail and while Olaus followed them little No-Name gave me a short course in woodcraft, leading me from one favorite nook in the woods to another. He told me how the squirrels run round in their clearing all winter, showed me two of their nests in a big spruce, and countless holes in the soft mossy ground, packed full of white spruce cones, fitted in like canned asparagus, tips up. He told me how ermine and mink make their holes, and how he snares rabbits; last winter he caught four by just running after them. He showed me how the Indians chose birch wood for their sleds and told me he had made a sled all by himself. 'I see how to make it.' He also pointed out the juicy inner bark of the birch—'Taste fine.'

"All these things he showed me with a certain eagerness, yet all easy joy seemed to have been left out of him. As the *Teddy* pulled away from shore little No-Name stood quietly beside his silent father and his older brother, clutching in his arms the box of candy I had given him, watching the boat out of sight. He had been so reticent about any family; it seemed as though no human being had ever mattered much in his life. As we watched the three still figures on the bank, looking after us fixedly, I saw beyond them a picture of winter—bare trees, deep snow around that tiny cabin, the pile of steamboat wood growing and growing on the shore."

For us the days went by in a golden happy haze. Every wooding-up stop was a chance to explore the forest and the hillsides, to identify birds, to collect a specimen or two perhaps, and for all this the sunny warm days were ideal. But what was perfection for us, we came to realize, was a cause of worry for Sam, and finally to the Longs also. Perfect days and freezing nights meant that water was dropping rapidly at the head of the river; without rain it was a question whether the *Teddy H.* could get to Bettles; and beyond Bettles all the goods would have to be reloaded onto the motor scow for the seventy-five miles to Wiseman, the northernmost village and the center of mining on the Koyukuk. Aboard the *Teddy H.*'s scow we had, besides goods for Sam's posts at Alatna, Bettles, and Wiseman, the furniture and household goods for the cabin which the Longs would still have to build after they arrived at his mine above Wiseman.

For five days the *Teddy H.* churned along, stopping only for wood, or so that the Indian hunter they carried along could drop off into his birch canoe and go speeding off after some geese or ducks someone had spied. Big Bedis in his birchbark, sliding swiftly over water made gold by the sunset, a honey-colored moon rising over the black spires of spruce across the river, while a black fox streaked across the pale sand—this was a picture to treasure.

But our gold-bordered pathway to the Arctic held other things too. An hour after Big Bedis had come back in the moonlight with five widgeon and the *Teddy* had started again, she found a sand bar smack in the middle of the river and landed the big scow on it with a sickening lurch.

There followed a night of maneuvering and hard work on the part of the crew. We watched until it was too dark to see what they were doing, but far into our dreams followed the rumble of chain, the splashing of oars, hoarse commands, shouts from the engine room, scraps of Kobuk songs. As they tugged and pulled, the Kobuks still sang.

The next morning we reached Hughes, a few cabins against a high hill. We climbed the hill and had an inspiring view of the country we had been passing through. It was good to have a

larger picture, after days of churning quietly along the river, seeing only crystal shimmering water bordered by forests of tall spruce shot with the flame of high-bush cranberry and the gold and white of birches. From the hilltop we saw rank after rank of shelved and peaked hills, little lakes and streams, all gold and green, a quiet empty land seeming to speak mutely of the lonely but seeking lives lived there in other days. Below us, the *Teddy H.*, like a toy, loading wood; two Indian birchbark canoes slipping downriver toward the ship, wondrously graceful. When they landed they laid one paddle across the canoe and stuck one in the bank to steady it.

On the seventh morning, as we neared our first destination, Alatna, we woke to sounds of commotion. Olaus reported that the hog chain on the fantail refused to stay in place. This meant nothing to me, but I was impressed with all the running about and shouting in English, German, Indian and Eskimo, in the midst of which the engineer very earnestly and robustly wanted to know where the blankety-blank water bucket had gone. "Bring that bucket back here and leave it here, blankety blank." He then retired and proceeded to blow off steam for half an hour, which made further sleep impossible, but I was glad to be up to witness the migration of about two hundred Canada geese winging into the morning mist over the river and out again against the blue sky, and to realize that we had at last come in among the hills we had been seeing in the distance for days—rolling hills covered with gold and green and scarlet.

5

Alatna

On the morning of September 8, Frank said to us at breakfast: "You can tell we're getting near Alatna, can't you? All these fellas bloomin' out in new shirts and singin' love songs!"

Ambrose, in a red shirt, was swabbing the deck with mighty flourishes, an irrepressible grin on his broad cheeks. Frank told us that one day he had found Ambrose sitting way off in a corner of the barge by himself, singing, big tears rolling down his cheeks. "What in heck's the matter with *you?*" asked Frank. "Yuh sick?"

"Me? Oh no, just sing love song, dat's all."

Evening came clear and beautiful with plumes of smoke rising over the trees ahead. The first of Sam's three trading posts, Alatna—the site of both Kobuk and Koyukuk villages and of the famous Episcopal mission, "St. John's in the Wilderness," or Allakaket—was just round the bend. We heard the howls of dogs; they had heard the *Teddy H.* coming. But between us and Alatna lay Malemute Riffle, a ticklish bit of going in low water. Ambrose, sounding pole in hand, was poised on the bow of the scow; the rest of the crew were stationed by the steam winch, anxious and alert. Slowly, slowly—"puff, puff," the wheel hardly turning, as though the *Teddy H.* were tiptoeing over the riffle. Sam, silent and ponderous, strode from one side of the deck to the other, watchful and worried. Then "scrunch-ch"; the barge was grating on the bar!

The tense group came to life as though someone had touched an inner spring. Anxious as they were to arrive and greet their wives and sweethearts, first this chore must be done. For us it was like a play, a study in wilderness atmosphere: yellow dusk dimming behind needle-pointed spruces, a yellow moon shedding its glow over the river where the unruly water flung itself down over the bar; the *Teddy H.*, a futile monster fuming there, spitting red sparks into the night; David leaning philosophically alert out of the pilothouse window, the glow from the binnacle lamp on his brown skin. And on the deck below us—quiet orders from Captain Fred, the rattling of snatchblocks and chains, the whir of cables, the splash of oars as the dory slipped across the moonwake to fasten a line ashore, the oarsmen leaning back with eager glances toward shore, where shone two or three lights of home.

With all the effort, it meant work until after midnight. In the morning we found ourselves docked at the store, a big two-story building flanked by all sorts of small cabins up and down the riverbank. This was the Eskimo side of the river.

Everyone was congregated about the store in the warm sunshine, and we met the rest of Olaus's old friends and many new ones. We sat on the porch watching the unloading of the new goods, conversing with all those agreeable smiling people about the news from downriver. When the unloading of the goods for Alatna was finished, the pretty young wives of Oscar and David came aboard. Then the *Teddy H.* dropped across the river to unload supplies for the mission and the Indian village, and our whole party descended upon the two young women missionaries, Miss Hill and Miss Uben. Here in this far place they ran a busy establishment; they held school in the winter, administered to the health and well-being of every native family, taught all the domestic arts to the women, ushered all the babies into the world, and tended the sick, continually passing out first-aid supplies, advice, and clothing. David told us that Miss Hill, a slim attractive young Irishwoman, mushed her own dog team in the winter, visiting outlying camps of trappers.

The mission house was a long log structure, charmingly furnished with homemade furniture and bright hangings. We went through the office, first-aid room, supply room, pantry, and kitchen—all on one side of the building; and on the other side were the living room, dining room, and three bedrooms. On the

big screened porch across the front was a huge box couch filled
with magazines, and here we found Frank and Otto rapidly filling
a gunny sack to take along. "Here's where we get our winter's
reading matter." It seemed that was the purpose of the big chest,
so we helped ourselves too, taking some copies of *Scribner's*,
Harper's, and the *Atlantic Monthly*.

When the *Teddy H.* departed at three that afternoon for Bettles,
at the head of steam navigation, the people of the village and the
mission folk waved us good-by from the high bank. Backed by its
forest of tall spruces, the mission village was a neat and pretty
picture. David's wife waved a laughing good-by and called to
him: "You'll be back pretty soon. I know this river; no much
water up above!"

An hour above Alatna, going over one riffle after another, but
still going, we heard cries of "Ambrose, Ambrose, ay-yah-yah"
from the whole crew. A birchbark canoe was tied up to a bar, in it
a pretty Indian maid, an orange kerchief tied round her head.
"Atta boy," cried David from the pilothouse. Ambrose was at the
winch, and Captain Fred said: "I've got a chain on his leg now, he
can't go."

All the while Ambrose, in a red plaid shirt and a green silk
bandana, was hanging to the cable, but he never took his eyes
off that canoe. There was a wonderful grin on his face, and he had
a big cigar and was going through that wonderful crook-fingered
manipulation of his. All the rest of the crew were smoking Sam's
cigars too, ribbing Ambrose, chortling, waving to the canoe.
Oscar rushed out from the galley, also with a cigar, the huge
salmon that was to be our dinner dangling from one hand. Finally
Ambrose could stand it no longer and burst out into a love song.
Then a mighty cheer went up.

What company for a wedding journey! They were back in their
own country, and all were smoking cigars because we had
reached Alatna intact; it was Sam's treat.

Two days later we were stuck on a bar eleven miles above
Alatna, and Sam had to make another decision. The Longs were
worried about their furniture in the barge, and seemed to feel that
Sam *could* deliver them to Wiseman if he only would! But a
northern river is an inexorable foe. Sam called Olaus into his
room to tell him all his troubles. He said: "Nobody knows what I
have to contend! Now you can see *my* shoes!"

Olaus assured him that we were not frantic to get anywhere so long as we reached Bettles and the dog team by trail time, and we then went ashore to watch the moon rise and escape from an atmosphere fraught with worries about freight and furniture. We came back to find that it had been decided to send the Longs on in the *Chicken Chaser*, the motorboat we had picked up at Alatna and had been towing alongside. Fred Clark would take them. But the next problem was to get the *Chicken Chaser*'s motor to run, and Otto, Fred, and Bill Finger, the Chief, worked on it all the next day in a downpour which raised everyone's hopes for more water in the river. Mrs. Long and I sat in the galley, the only warm place above decks, and I made a devil's food cake. Olaus went ashore with his shotgun to hunt rabbits for the larder. Up in the pilothouse David was having a musical session all by himself, alternating fiddle and banjo, playing "Casey Jones," "Tipperary," "The Irish Washerwoman." "Now play it backward," yelled the Chief.

The next day was clear again and the water still low, but the *Chicken Chaser* was running and it departed right after breakfast. The Longs were glad to be moving northward; this would at least give them a chance to get their new cabin up before freeze-up. Aboard the *Teddy H.* everyone was full of joy except Sam, and he was patient with our fun and foolishness and glad of one thing, that the Longs were on their way north. I heard Frank say to him: "Think we're gonna spend the winter on this bar?"

Sam replied: "Oh, go on! We're not going to stay here everlasting!"

We took a long tramp ashore, through deep woods and around many little lakes. Through every mile of the Koyukuk, Olaus was opening my mind and heart to the little-known teeming, rich life going on in the trees and streams, in the mossy tundra, and in the grassy sloughs. By a beautiful little lake bordered with golden birches and tall spruces, we stood counting muskrat houses and saw a gray jay dart out and seize one of the many dragonflies which were flitting over the water. From the woods came the songs of myrtle warblers and tree sparrows and the plaintive note of the varied thrush; as we tramped along, robins flew across our path, making us feel that winter was not yet too near, and always there was the rat-tat-tat of the arctic three-toed woodpecker.

We came home to the *Teddy H.* feeling completely alive and hungry as bears. We were late for dinner, but Frank had heaping plates of fried grouse and vegetables kept hot for us, and the whole gang was there to talk with. They sat around watching Olaus skin a mink and a raven he had collected for specimens, and later we had a concert. We felt simply saturated with happiness and good will, and it was as though the *Teddy H.* had been our home for a long, long time and all former things had passed out of ken.

Oscar had been down to Alatna and back by canoe, and had brought chewing gum, tobacco, and news of the villages. He reported that the hunters had come back from Old Man Creek with eleven caribou, seven moose, and four bears. Around noon that day three more hunters from Henshaw Creek had come floating past the *Teddy H.* They had two bears. Oscar said: "Well, we did pretty well today—got news from all directions."

While Olaus made a sketch of the mink, conversation ranged from ducks, fossils, mastodons, bears, and fish to Alaska in general and freeze-ups they had known. Then the Chief and Frank and Olaus began to live over their boyhoods in the Midwest and it sounded like the book "The Court of Boyville" come to life. The Chief said: "I wish them days were back. I'd know how to enjoy them now."

We had another idyllic day of hiking and hunting ashore. Olaus brought in three scaups and a baldpate. The *Teddy H.*'s larder had to be replenished from the country, and every man in the crew not needed aboard spent time hunting rabbits. Frank fed huge heaped-up platters of rabbit to the crew. "You can see these fellas are stockin' up for a hard winter."

After supper Olaus and I walked up the bar on which we were stuck, and found a beautiful sandy spot and did some gymnastics in the dusk. I was watching him stand on his head when I saw a canoe suddenly round the point from upstream, a lone Indian in it, silhouetted against the golden sky.

When we went aboard a few moments later, we found the Indian in the galley with all the gang, and he never took his eyes off Olaus. I suppose it really had been something of a shock to come round a bend of the river and see a lone white man standing upside down on a sand bar!

We had heard the *Teddy H.* orchestra before, but this night we could watch as well as listen. Frank sat cross-legged against the wall, a typical old-time fiddler with his big mustaches; Ambrose was beside him, bronze cheeks shining, ecstatically twanging his banjo; David sat on a milk case with the cymbals; young flaxen-

haired Heinie, the fireman, held the triangle between his knees; and Otto, sitting on an oil can, beat on it with two monkey wrenches, his keen gray eyes sparkling. We all sang, and Olaus and I danced in the middle of the floor. They even played "Three O'Clock in the Morning" for us to waltz to.

On September 15, with no rain yet, Sam gave the order to drop back down to Alatna to await the other gas boats, which Fred was supposed to bring down from Bettles as soon as possible. The village of Alatna showed no surprise at our second arrival; David's wife stood at the gangplank with a smug smile on her rosy cheeks.

To us it did not matter; Olaus was studying and collecting and learning wherever he was, and the country, whether upriver or downriver, was beautiful and full of interest. But we felt sorry for Sam—with winter coming on quickly and part of the winter supplies for the settlements above us still in the big barge, not moving. It was hard to think of any pleasant remarks at mealtimes which would not suggest the weather or our situation—awful when you can't even talk about the weather.

At Alatna the *Teddy H.* was still our snug home, and we had meals and visits at the mission—with candlelight and willow-ware china—and Miss Hill and Miss Uben came aboard the *Teddy H.* for roast goose and lemon pie, which Frank did in fine style. We spent part of each day on a mouse trapline, collecting specimens, and visiting with the people. Olaus and Oscar spent some hours in the galley making a list of Kobuk Eskimo names for various animals. Oscar would very patiently say the word over and over and then laugh and turn to me and say: "He don't *listen*; he just watch my *mouth*."

It is almost impossible to represent the Kobuk sounds with our letters, and Olaus was trying to see just how they were formed. He would take his sheaf of sketches and show one to Oscar. "You know this one?" he would ask, showing him a raven.

"Oh yes, *Too-loo-aluk*."

While this went on, Frank and I would be preparing a meal; and in the doorway, nearly always, a quiet, wide-eyed group of small boys from the village would be watching. One afternoon Olaus was painting a sketch of mergansers the Indian hunter had brought in. Frank said to the boys: "You think that white man can't make picture of duck? You look 'em."

They all filed in, silently looking over Olaus's shoulder, and one finally said in an awe-struck tone: "All same duck!"

These were Kobuk boys, for we were tied up on the Alatna side of the river. Miss Hill had told us that the two villages were friendly and got together for all special occasions, and co-operated on any work that had to be done for the mission, but they had serious objections to any of their people intermarrying. Olaus one day heard David and some of the other Kobuk boys speaking of one Kobuk who had married an Indian girl, and David said: "Oh yes, he's lost, that fella."

Yet in all superficial matters there was no friction, and the Kobuk chief and the Koyukuk chief were great old friends.

6

"And Beyond"

Three days later we were sitting on the benches on the sunny little front deck writing notes when the dogs of Alatna suddenly began to howl, a chorus of children's voices along the bank shrilled out: "Gas boat!" and around the bend came a flotilla. Captain Fred was at the wheel of the thirty-foot *Black Maria*, a small roofed scow with side walls of canvas, pushing another covered barge, the *Dooley*, and towing the *Chicken Chaser* alongside. The *Black Maria* looked not much more reputable than her name, but Bill Finger told us she had a five-thousand-dollar engine in her.

Captain Fred's report was that it was "nice and dry" upriver, so we all knew something drastic would have to be decided, and soon. Two mornings later we were wakened by voices. Sam was shouting out orders to the men, while Captain Fred was issuing quieter, more precise ones. We hurried into our clothes.

The *Maria* was being loaded with perishables (she had a stove), and there was great running back and forth and jabbering in Eskimo and Indian, everyone with arms and hands full. We got our gear out on deck, and then I helped Frank prepare an early dinner in the galley and pack enough food into boxes for the next adventure. It was fun to be busy again, and everyone seemed to feel the same way. We all carried bedding onto the *Maria*, and each picked a bunk from among the canvas-and-pole affairs that ran in two tiers along the sides of the scow. Sam loudly proclaimed that I was to have the best one and that Oscar was to put a mattress in it.

At twelve-thirty we made our second departure from Alatna, the *Maria* pushing the *Dooley*, which was loaded with bacon and lard and other supplies badly needed at the head of the river. Olaus and Otto and I stood on the tiny stern deck of the *Maria* and watched the villages and the *Teddy H.* pass from sight. "Yes," said Otto, as though reading my mind, "kind of hard to leave the old ship; we had a good time on her, yah? And there's Ambrose too—leaving him behind too; see, he's waving there by the *Teddy*. We'll miss him too, but I guess he and that girl want to get a cabin built before winter."

We waved to Ambrose until we went round the bend and the whole scene was gone. Then we turned to the new adventures ahead. The day was clear and cold; the beautiful nickel-plated machinery in the stern of the *Maria* purred along sweetly until sundown, then suddenly stuttered and died. A bearing gasket, whatever that might be, had burned out. Otto and the Chief, after making a few appropriate remarks in both German and English, went to work, and the rest of us gathered up front among the boxes of apples and eggs and enjoyed ourselves—all but Sam, who returned to his bunk, morose and speechless.

A funny craft we were. Eggs, potatoes, and apples were piled to the ceiling, leaving a narrow corridor on each side beside the canvas-and-pole bunks. The galley was back near the engine; the "social hall" was up front near our bunks and consisted of a short table, a fat little sheet-iron stove, and boxes of apples for seats.

The next day it snowed! And all day we sat tied to the bank while Otto and Bill Finger labored over the engine. Sam stayed in his bunk. Frank, the Kobuks, the Indians, and Olaus and I enjoyed ourselves immensely. Our levity must have driven Sam to distraction, but he said nothing. Our crew had been augmented by Sam's two favorite Indians, Billy Bergman and Little Henry, both middle-aged, tall fine specimens of strength. They and the Kobuks and Olaus had a great session of talk about birds and mammals. They told us stories and sang songs for us, and Olaus sang songs and told stories from the Hudson Bay country. These men were the best of companions, so responsive, so quick to see a joke and enjoy it. I got one of Billy's stories down in shorthand in my notebook, but that created a distraction, for David, sitting next to me, noticed what I was doing and had to know what "those funny marks" were, and then they all had to see and have it explained.

David told us the legend that had grown up around the semi-palmated plover (he identified it from one of Olaus's sketches). The plover is a famous bird in this part of the world, on account of the ring around his neck. The people say this ring consists of the precious beads that were the first things that came to the Kobuks when they lived out on the coast, long, long ago, when they used stone knives. No one knows where or from whom these beads came, perhaps from Siberia, but they were the greatest thing a person could have. Some big chief might have a string of them. They were a clear light or dark blue, and never changed color. David's mother had some from her parents. Thus, because he has this ring around his neck, the people say the plover is the medicine man of the river fish; that they give him things as sacrifice so he will let them get back to the sea before the river freezes up in the fall. And David, articulate, trained in the white man's ways, sophisticated in manner, sat there on an apple box with a very earnest look on his face as he told us these things about his people.

Oscar pushed the canvas at the front of the *Maria* aside and brought in another armful of split wood from the front deck. "Oh yes, still snowing outside," he said cheerily, and we all settled more gratefully about the little stove. It was a cozy little world up front there around the little table; the mutterings from far back on the other side of the piled-up freight came to us only faintly, and were offset by Frank's cheery rattling of pans. Billy Bergman lit his big black pipe. "Yes, lotsa story, the old folks had, lotsa story about raven."

All the natives, both Eskimo and Indian, have the legend that the raven created everything in the beginning, but it is a long story and very few old people now know it all. David and Billy both agreed that with both the Indians and the Eskimos these stories of creation and early history are so long that the old people take many long nights to tell them. They would start every night when they couldn't work any longer, and talk until midnight, and next evening take up the story in the same place and go on. Up until the past two generations the stories were handed down and learned by rote. Thus these people had the history of how and where they had lived, how they had hunted, what they ate, and what they believed in times past. But since the white man and the missionary came, the young ones have had so much else to learn and remember that they have not learned the old stories. David told us that his father, Chief Tobuk, told his children: "You might as well go ahead now and learn all you can of the white man's ways and go to school what you can, because you have to live among white people now."

"I and my brother as children," said David, "were not taught any of the Eskimo stories or customs, but we like to know about them, and have learned some anyway. We don't like to forget it all."

"Dat's right," said Billy. "Same with us Indians; too bad for all old stories to lose 'em."

Shortly after supper two things occurred. It stopped snowing and the beautiful engine suddenly began to purr again, so we traveled on until nine o'clock and then tied up for the night under a very high cut bank. Billy and Henry made their camp on top of the bank. The night-blue sky was still warmed by a hint of yellow just ahead of us, due north, a hint of the Northern Lights and of winter on its way. The Dipper sat above our bow and pointed to the North Star, which hung over one tall spruce. Under this same tree the Indians had built a fire. Warm red stars flew up against the cold white ones of the autumn sky, and the rosy spruces stood out distinctly. Inside the barge the gang was clambering into bed with sighs of contentment and a few last words and chuckles. From behind the blanket curtain in front of my bunk I listened to the few gurgles of Indian floating up from the other side of the pile of egg crates, and to the low conversation of David and Oscar, who were sitting up late to keep the fire going. The Kobuk language is a joy to listen to; it sounds like the close-together speech of two lovers; it has that lilting yet pleading rising inflection at the end of a phrase.

Next morning I again lay behind the blanket and listened to the life of this floating home from the time Frank yelled: "Stand by, you fellas!" until the whole crew had eaten and we were on our way. They gathered up front at the little table for breakfast, all very jovial, jabbering in three languages. Once in a while the humorous, authoritative voice of Frank burst out: "Hey, you guys, don't fill up on bacon. Lay off a little."

Oscar, banging a spoon against a kettle, called out: "Poultice, poultice, who wants cackle berries?"

Cries of: "Here," and "Me, me."

David, being the pilot, expatiated in a benevolent tone on subjects of his choosing. "I bet you fellas never see hen lay a egg. All got little house—all sit there; pretty soon jump down, and there's egg lying there, and people come round and pick 'em up."

Someone, impressed, said: "Dat so?"

Someone else called out: "Cow, cow, drag the cow down here, another one, Oscar, this one's empty," and began a tune on the empty can with his fork. Then the engineers were ready and there came a call for the pilot: "How long is he going to eat?"

But they needed to eat. In the course of the morning we fought our way over six riffles. There was a tiny deck on the stern of the *Maria*; here I sat and watched the river and the steep wooded shores, with now and then a vista of green river ending in dazzling white mountains, the Endicotts, our goal. I also watched the process of getting the *Maria* and the *Dooley* nearer those mountains. There would be a lovely straight stretch of river, then a bend, then a riffle. Here everyone went into action, and I understood why Sam had added more men to the crew. We managed to scrape over some of the riffles with the aid of eight men with eight poles. Olaus cut himself a pole and joined the crew. On some riffles, a steel cable had to be run ashore and fastened around a very sturdy tree or stump; then brawny arms on the bow of the *Maria* would begin to wind the capstan and the *Dooley* was pulled over the riffle into the deeper water above. The *Dooley* had the heavier load and took more water than the *Maria*.

Thus we went on for three strenuous days, with clear skies and no moisture. At noon on the twenty-fourth the whole outfit came to a determined stop. The *Dooley* refused to be budged off the bottom of the Koyukuk. The *Maria* let go and dropped over to the shore and tied up while they pulled and hauled around the *Dooley*, everyone in hip boots. Sam appeared in a bright red pair and went splashing and spluttering around in the water, slipping and floundering and getting in everyone's way, and bossing the job very futilely. I wondered whether he realized what a grotesque figure he was in those red boots. When the *Dooley* was finally loosed and brought to the shore also, Sam was of the mind that further progress with his load of merchandise was impossible.

The whole afternoon was spent in indecision—arguments, counterarguments, suggestions, refutations—everyone participating in Sam's business. He even appealed to me: "Mrs. Murie, what would you do?" And not being as wisely self-controlled as my husband, I couldn't resist a few suggestions even while chuckling inwardly at the comedy of the whole scene—everyone from engineer to Eskimo deckhand telling the owner how to run his business. But at this point Olaus said: "Come on, Mardy, let's see what's up on this hill."

We climbed the hill, a very steep wooded one, and when we came back Sam was still sunk in indecision. Sitting on an apple box by the stove, he was repeating himself. "I know this river; we can't make it; we have to go back to Alatna, I guess."

Bill Finger, oil can in hand, was arguing: "Well, you gotta make up your mind quick or David and I can't get this tub here back downriver even. I've seen it do this way in this country and then rain for two weeks. You may be able to come up next week with the *Teddy* and the scow—you can't tell a damn thing about it and you know that."

Whereupon Frank, whacking up rabbits with a huge butcher knife, put in his bit: "What I say is, with all the men you've got here I don't see why you can't load your lighter stuff, the perishables, into the *Dooley*—she's light draft—and pole her up to Bettles. Unload the canned stuff here on the bank and pole it up later. Looks to me like the weather means business and you'd better get this bunch on up before she freezes solid. Let David and the Chief go on back with this valuable ship before they have to haul her on bare gravel."

Sam protested: "I don't believe you can pole the *Dooley* any further."

Frank replied: "Aw, I bet yuh anything we can do it if she don't drop any more tonight. What yuh got all these savages for anyhow, just tuh eat up your grub? Why, Ike Spinks an' Roy King an' me poled a boat most as heavy up Lost River all by ourselves one year. Huh!"

Suddenly Sam stood up and threw up his hands. "All right, I give up. I resign. You take charge, Frank. I don't think you can do it, but if you want to take a chance, go ahead. Here, all you fellas, you're under Frank now—I'm through!" And with this speech he clambered ashore and disappeared in the woods.

At that moment I became the cook, and proceeded to make a huge roaster full of Swiss steak out of caribou meat while Frank took charge of the expedition. Bacon, lard, and all the rest of the non-perishables were flying out of the *Dooley* and being built into a great pile on the beach. Apples, potatoes and eggs were then loaded into the *Dooley*, with our gear and the mail. This would be the load for the poling trip.

That night we all froze, for the heater had to be transferred from us in the *Maria* to the eggs and apples in the *Dooley*. We were all more than ready to rise at the first light of dawn, and Frank and I threw some breakfast together, mostly oatmeal, and assembled a camp outfit of dishes and food and loaded them into the *Dooley*. I finally took the big coffeepot with me and climbed into the *Dooley*, and waved good-by to David and the Chief, who were already dropping downstream with the *Maria*. We had all been impressed by Billy's announcement that he thought the water had dropped about eight inches during the night!

Otto and Frank and Olaus went ashore with the line. All the rest, in hip boots, lined up on either side of the *Dooley*, and here they spent three hours of back-breaking effort in pulling, hoisting, lifting, or otherwise persuading our little ark over the very first riffle! Indeed, the water *had* dropped!

Finally, in order to get the scow off the gravel and back to shore, they had to put their backs under the sides of the *Dooley* and wiggle and jiggle and push until it seemed to me they would every one of them burst a blood vessel. Billy Bergman and Little Henry, who is anything but little, would brace their toes in the gravel and, with a great "heave-ho" in Indian, fairly lift the *Dooley* up on their backs.

All this time I was inside, trying to keep the hot stove from tipping over. When the men heaved up on one side I braced myself with a piece of stovewood against the other side of the stove and tried to keep my balance. About noon we were finally loose and tied to shore again, and I put the coffeepot on and stoked the fire and the whole crew came aboard. Frank said cheerfully: "I'm fair shivered to the bone," and reached for a cup of coffee. We fed them all as best we could, everyone finding something to eat and balancing on an egg crate or a mail sack, all happy, laughing at their failure. They knew better than to worry about tomorrow. It was all a good adventure. Only Sam paced the shore, looking ominous. And suddenly he came aboard and took charge again, vociferously.

Oscar was dispatched on foot upriver to Bettles to bring Frank's big poling boat and meet us. Young Heinie and one of the young

Bergman boys were left to keep the barge and the eggs warm and guard the groceries, and the Murie gear and some mail and the personal baggage of the others were loaded into Little Henry's poling boat.

Fortunately it seemed to be the practice in the Koyukuk for a larger boat always to have in tow some smaller craft for use in an emergency. Thus had we come from the steamer *Teddy H.* to the motor scow *Black Maria*, to the unmotorized scow *Dooley*, to Little Henry's poling boat. While the crew unloaded and loaded again, and Frank and I hurried to pack three boxes of camp dishes and food for two days, Sam paced up and down on the shore, yelling: "Come on, come on; we can't stay here all day. We got to get to Beddles!"

Billy Bergman and Little Henry stood bow and stern in the boat, each with pole; the rest of us walked. The day was clear and spicy-warm, and it was good to be hiking again, to be actively doing something, after the cramped quarters on the *Maria*. We walked along bars, through willows, through spruce woods. When the boat reached a riffle a line was thrown ashore and we all walked on it, "necking it" along. When we all came together for another meal at two o'clock, we had come five miles of the twenty-seven which separated us from Bettles. The boys built a big fire; I started roasting chunks of caribou meat and bacon on a stick and they all followed suit, laughing like children. Sam took a piece of meat about the size of a ham, roasted it black on the outside, consumed it quickly in great mouthfuls, and then announced he would "take the short cut" through a dry slough and meet us at camping time. We all thought he probably couldn't stand our jollity any longer!

Otto suggested that Olaus carry his .22 and get some rabbits during the afternoon, for he knew food was going to be low. This was easily accomplished, for rabbits were darting about frequently in the river-bottom willows; they were approaching the peak of their usual ten- or eleven-year cycle. Then the men decreed that I must ride in the boat the last hour. At six-thirty we camped on a fine beach; it was too dark for further travel.

The only sign of Sam was his tracks, going on; he was apparently trying to get through to Bettles, still not feeling the need of our company. We roasted the last of the caribou over a big campfire, and Olaus made a fine bough bed under one of the huge spruces. Little Henry, sitting by the fire smoking his pipe, cocked his eye at the sky and said mildly: "I tink maybe lain tonight, maybe snow."

Olaus said nothing, but went to the boat and got out the big tarp we were going to use later in the dog sled, laid it on the boughs, spread our sleeping bags, put the other half of the tarp over them, and when I crawled into this cozy place, said "Put your boots and everything under the tarp."

We woke after a sound dreamless sleep. I felt water trickling down my nose, and put up my hand—into snow, an inch or so on top of my head! Just then we heard Otto in his chuckling young German voice saying: "Hey, Frank, about time for you to get up and get breakfast for us, isn't it?"

It was snug around the big fire under the trees. More serious was the discovery that in our great haste to leave the *Dooley* we had forgotten to pack any salt, and had brought only two cans of milk; so we had meat and bacon, rice and oatmeal, lots of butter, and that was all. Except that Frank presented me with an orange! He had sat and slept and rolled on it, but it was still a rare and welcome gift.

At six-thirty we were traveling again, and before long we began to see slush ice floating in the Koyukuk. It was snowing, and blowing, and the beach was slippery, and I was given orders to get into the boat again. This was a pleasure. Billy and Henry talked to each other in Indian, discussing the water and the best route to follow; then they talked in English to include me. They talked about Sam, and laughed merrily. Henry said: "Nobody cry for Dubin. Evelbody say, 'Let 'um go.' His own faul', nobody's faul'. Oh, Dubin, *he* don't know much; he know money, where it go, but he don't know how to trabbel. Maybe not lost but maybe too much scare, tha's all."

Billy liked to talk about his family. His wife had made the beaded mitts he wore; they had nine children and had lost a boy and a girl. He told me about the rabbit-fur coat he wore in winter to hunt—"so anything can't see in the woods, look like rabbit or ptarmigan"—told me how they were so glad to get a bear in late fall before they hibernate, such fine grease it made, and how he had to "hunt, hunt, hunt, all time in winter, to food the family."

All the men were pulling on the line the whole time that morning; Billy and Henry called them "the dog team." The wind was driving fine snow in their faces and it was pretty cold; we had to laugh at their struggles to stand up on the ice-coated pebbles, and at the slope of the team, from tall Frank in the lead to Otto at the end, so much shorter that he sometimes had a hard time even hanging on to the line. The slush ice was running thicker and thicker all the time, and often we had to take the whole "team" aboard and pole across to a better channel. The snowstorm was becoming a blizzard and at one stop Olaus insisted on digging into our duffel bag and handed me my ground-squirrel-fur parka and the beautiful caribou-leg-fur boots from Nulato. I sat in state, wrapped in the absent Sam's wolf-skin robe.

At ten o'clock we met Oscar coming down with Frank's poling boat, all smiles at being with us again. Frank decided we should divide the loads and take both boats back up, since the ice was running so thickly. Olaus and Otto built a big fire in a spruce thicket out of the growing blast of the storm. We sat on spruce boughs; the wet ones got dried out and we combined all the remaining food, making a mulligan in the brand-new aluminum roaster which Frank had brought all the way from Nulato as a present for Mary, his Indian wife at Bettles. We made the mulligan of two rabbits, rice, and oatmeal; everyone dug in and pronounced it grand; I had discovered in my big mackinaw pocket a tin of chipped beef which I had snatched at the last moment on the *Dooley* and then forgotten; it helped give a bit of salt to the mulligan.

After that there were riffles which were almost fearsome. Billy and Henry got out into the icy water and pushed and lifted the boat through the churning rapids while those ashore tugged manfully on the line. The two boats were taken one at a time through these places, but we kept on without a stop, and at three o'clock the storm abated, just as we pulled up over Kobuk Riffle to the village of Bettles.

All the villagers were there atop the high bank, and in the forefront, the familiar burly figure in a black turtleneck sweater, smoking a big cigar. He had made his way through, had come out on the shore opposite Bettles early that morning, and had yelled and shouted until one of the Indians had gone across in a boat to get him. We were introduced to Billy English, the quiet-spoken gray-haired storekeeper, and to Jack Dodds, the roadhouse keeper, even quieter but with the kindliest smile. The men immediately set to work unloading and carrying things up the high bank, but the women and children, about twenty of them, followed me into the store and just stood there gazing at me amiably. I gazed amiably back, but couldn't think just how to start a conversation, and somehow was suddenly feeling quite tired. I was glad when Olaus and Jack Dodds came to take me and our luggage over to the roadhouse, a few cabins downstream from the store. Here we found everything prepared for our coming, and felt a real gratitude to Sam for getting here first and notifying Jack. In a sort of courtyard at the back of the roadhouse was a one-room cabin cozily furnished as a bedroom. A fire was roaring in a little heater, buckets of water heating on top of it!

Here was a bit of heaven—to be alone, to have a bit of luxury frontier-style, to be really clean, to have reached our first destination. And then to go, clean and rested, to join the whole crowd at supper in the roadhouse and live over again all the fun of the poling-boat expedition, to the delectation of the local people.

There was a pool table in the big front room, a phonograph and card tables, big homemade chairs fitted with moosehide cushions. Here the entire white population of five miners, and a good many of the Indians, spent their spare time. This was the interim season, during which the men waited for the freeze-up to come so they could go to their mining or trapping grounds for winter. Frank came over with Mary, his wife, a kind-faced Indian woman a good many years past her youth but clean and bright-eyed. I liked her and I liked the kindness and respect with which Frank treated her.

7

Bettles

Next morning we moved into a new home, a big one-room cabin next to the roadhouse. It belonged to Jack Dodds, who kept bringing over more chairs and wooden boxes, dishes and towels and pans, "which you might use in your settling up." He had scrubbed the floor white, and there were lots of clean bedding and extra pillows. The walls were covered with white muslin house-lining cloth, like the early-day cabins of Fairbanks, and someone had decorated them profusely with every kind of magazine illustration from around 1915. We took these down, and wiped the walls, and there are no words for the happiness we felt as we worked.

The cabin was furnished with two homemade beds, a sheet-iron stove, two tables, a big cupboard, a homemade easy chair, and some straight chairs. We made a bedroom out of one back corner; next to it was the kitchen; in one of the front corners we fixed the other bed as a couch, using a brightly colored blanket cover and the extra pillows. Beside it, by the one long window in the front wall of the cabin, we placed the second table, which became Olaus's work table. The other front corner, behind the door, soon became the specimen and storage space, where Olaus spread the clean tarpaulin and kept whatever specimens he brought in, and along the wall there, all the miscellaneous camp gear was stacked.

By now it was midafternoon. We went up to the store and

bought some groceries, paying $6.25 for a twenty-five pound sack of flour, $5.25 for half a case of condensed milk, twenty cents a pound for sugar and for beans, eighty-five cents a pound for butter, and the same high prices for other items. Compared with 1961 prices they don't sound so outrageous, but compared with 1924 prices in the States and even in Fairbanks, they were staggering.

We now had supper in our own home once more, by the light of a kerosene lamp. Afterward I got out the little sewing kit and made covers for the couch pillows from some bright blue-and-red percale I had found at the store.

On this day too the Kobuks and the Koyukuks and Sam had all gone back downriver, taking with them all the poling boats available in Bettles, for the weather had cleared again, the ice had stopped running for the time being, and they now had their chance to rescue the rest of the supplies left on the beach.

Also on this first day we began to get acquainted again with our companions for the winter journey, the Victoria Land Huskies, grown fat and eager under Jack Dodds's care, and all chained, each to his own post, behind our cabin. These dogs had been our goal; now there was nothing to do but settle down here with them and wait for freeze-up, when we could start the dog-team chapter, the continuation of the caribou study which had been Olaus's chief assignment for four years.

The dogs seemed glad to see us; I am sure they were always glad to see anyone who would stop and rough them up and play a bit, but we felt that perhaps they really did remember Olaus. Certainly it seemed to me they should have, after having him run beside them for eight hundred miles down the Yukon and over to Hooper Bay six months before. There were Fuzzy and Mally, Ungiak and Wolf, Mayuk and Bingo, and Pooto, the black leader, more slender than the others, a little worried and sober and responsible-looking. If they had names in their Victoria Land days no one had known them, so Jess and Clara and I had named them that past winter. We had heard Olaus and Adolph talk about Pooto, the Eskimo with whom they had traveled two years before; so the leader became Pooto, and Mayuk and Ungiak were named for children of his. We never dreamed that these dogs would come up into Pooto the Kobuk's home territory, for the team of young brothers had been designated as our team. But they had all died of distemper during the summer on the Yukon. So when these dogs had come upriver on the *Teddy H.*, Oscar and David had been much amused to find on the tags attached to their collar the names of their friend Pooto and two of his children!

Jack had mentioned to Olaus that he had been in the habit of feeding the dogs each evening at five o'clock, and at five o'clock there arose from behind our cabin a concert of howling and yelping. They knew what time it was. During that afternoon while we were getting settled in the cabin, Olaus had had a five-gallon oil can of rice and "dog bacon" cooking on the stove, and he now carried it out and we both ladled out portions. Each dog had his own dish, a container about three inches deep made from the cut-off end of a gasoline can. One after another the five-o'clock singers became quiet and contentedly busy. We said good night to them and went around to the front of the cabin, where we stood a moment watching a lone Indian in a birchbark slipping down the river against a bright gold sky. It seemed that we had dwelled in that world along the river for a long happy time; it was hard to believe that less than a month had passed since we left the howling banks of Nulato.

In the northeast a gold moon was rising, and near it the great red eye of Mars, which in 1924 was closer to the earth than in many years. It was a very quiet world. We turned and went into our snug new home.

From the day of our moving in, we lived in our cabin in Bettles as though we were to live there always. The village, the people, the back country, all became familiar and loved. We met nothing but kindness and good cheer. Whatever frustrations or sorrows these Alaskans may have had, they were, in the presence of their fellows, happy, objective, quick to laugh over failures and hard luck, intensely interested in one another's welfare.

We soon had a happy routine. To the trapline in the morning, then back home to build up the fire and cook the big can of corn meal or rice and bacon, adding to it the cut-up rabbits from my snareline. One of the first things Olaus did was to teach me to set rabbit snares. Our smoke-dried fish from Nulato, which had been transported up the river earlier, had to be saved for the dog-team trip north. "Mary-the-wife-of-Frank," as Otto called her, chuckled when she met me coming in from my line one morning. "All same squaw, you!" she laughed.

After lunch we might go out again for a while, exploring for new mouse-trapping territory, perhaps stopping at the roadhouse on the way back to chat a while and have a cup of coffee with Jack and the other old-timers. The rest of the day Olaus would be busy with specimens or notes or drawings; he soon taught me to do the labels and the cataloguing, though my printing would never be as neat and clear as his. Each mouse label had to contain the date and location of the catch, the Latin name of the animal, and its sex; then the conventional scientific data without which it would not be a scientific specimen: total length, length of tail, and length of hind foot. And all this then had to be entered in the proper columns in the catalogue, a hard-covered blank book in which the notes for Olaus's mammal collection now amounted to some 1,940 entries.

In midafternoon Otto would come in with the results of his morning's hunt, a raven or sea gull or something else, and would receive a lesson from Olaus in preparing museum specimens. Otto was going mining that winter after freeze-up, with Frank and Mary and Heinie, up the Wild River, where Frank had a mine. He did not know what he was going to do after that, but he had, we soon saw, such an intense interest in all things of the wild, such a desire to do something for science, such unusual powers of observation, and such abounding energy that we both felt there must be an interesting, full career ahead for him somehow.

Two days after we had settled into the cabin, I went on a fishing expedition with Otto, Frank, Mary, and Ludie, a friend of Mary's. We went upriver for about two miles in Frank's poling boat, and it was such a brisk morning that I was glad Olaus had insisted I wear my fur parka. We reached a place where the ice was beginning to form along the shore, extending out about twenty-five feet, and under this shelf the grayling were in the habit of lurking.

Frank and Otto handed out lengths of fishline with hooks on the ends baited with bits of bacon. I sat there pulling my line up and down as Frank had instructed, but mostly I was watching Ludie. Ludie was huge and round-faced and happy. She was Indian, married to Pooto's brother Sammy Hope, and they had adopted a baby. Like all the native women, Ludie carried her baby in the hood of her parka. At this time of year the women were still wearing their "summer parkas" of blue or brown denim, and the baby was laid on his mother's back, his head bobbing

over her shoulder inside the hood, which was pushed back from her head. He was held there by a wide knitted woolen sash tied about Ludie's waist.

Ludie sat in the stern, a great hulk, jiggling her line energetically and singing lustily: "Ay-yah, hotches; ay-yah, hotches!" The baby, named Henry, called "Henly," bobbed owl-eyed. Frank laughed. "That's the stuff, Ludie, you call 'em," and said to me: "That means in Indian: 'Come on, fish, and get hooked!'"

Mary quietly caught a nice grayling. Ludie sang louder and her whole body swayed in eagerness. From her parka hood came a whimper, then a howl, then more howls. "Ay-yah, hotches!" sang Ludie, and reaching her free hand around, jiggled Henly up and down in rhythm with the fishing. "She holla," she informed me, laughing. "She" continued to "holla" while Ludie flopped a big fish into the boat, rebaited, and went at it again. Singing and howling went on together until Ludie paused long enough to reach into her bosom and draw out a baby's nursing bottle. This she passed back over her shoulder into Henly's mouth, just opened for another "holla." Quiet seemed to descend upon the Koyukuk. I had forgotten all about my fishline.

"What do you feed your baby?" I asked Ludie.

"Oh, Eagle blillik" (Eagle Brand condensed milk) was the reply, and she began with more vigor than ever: "Ay-yah, hotches!"

And just then *I* caught a fish, and before the morning was over I had five nice ones, and came home to Olaus quite frozen and very proud, and we had grayling and creamed carrots and chocolate pudding for dinner that night.

From the diary:

"September 30: After the day's work we took a ramble up over Lookout Mountain behind the town, following the wood road up, coming back through the woods. The day was fair and from the top of the mountain there were spread the Koyukuk Valley and the Endicott Mountains in blue and white tranquillity, broad brown and green valley, twisting river, high snowy peaks; soon it will surely be a picture in black and white. Olaus called down to us a flock of both hoary and common redpolls and we had a sweet visit with them and with three pine grosbeaks swinging merrily in one graceful old birch tree. We came home at sunset time; the air is tingly smoky cold these days, the mountains where lies Wiseman, far upriver, flooded in sunset pink.

"October 1: Today we went to find mouse-trapping country, around the bluffs above the village, up a little slough, through mossy woods to a lake. We gathered juniper from the rocky bluffs on the way back, to decorate our cabin walls. I picked up two more rabbits in my snareline and put them in the small packsack which I carry. A few minutes later Olaus turned around to say something to me and then ran back and put his arms about me: 'My gosh, darlin', what's the matter? What are you crying for?'

" 'One of the rabbits is jumping, in my packsack, just as though he were alive, and I know he isn't alive, but it's an *awful* feeling!' and I collapsed on Olaus's shoulder.

"Olaus was patient with me. 'There, gee whiz, it's only reflex action, you know about that don't you—just the muscles—do you want me to take him?'

" 'No, boo-hoo—I have to learn about these things, but it's just such a terrible feeling, right against my back! But he was in my snare, and I'm going to carry him home!'

"In the afternoon while I was hanging out clothes I heard some commotion around the roadhouse, and Olaus came out and joined the group, greeting his old friends of the winter on the Alatna; Olaus's former guide, Pooto Hope himself in person, Johnnie Edwards, and Napoleon, all Kobuks. They had just tramped down from Wiseman, where they had been working all summer on the horse-drawn scows which freight Sam's goods through the Kobukuk's swift headwaters to Wiseman. I was much interested in meeting Pooto, for I had heard Olaus and Adolph both tell many stories of their journey with him and his family. He had features purely Caucasian, it seemed to me, and quite a casual worldly manner, but speaks English after a style of his own. Olaus asked him how far upriver they had been able to take the scow on the last trip. 'Oh, Wiseman below five mile got dere.'

"He and Napoleon called on us after supper. I set out a plate of homemade penuche. Pooto ate one piece after another very methodically as though he were eating a meal, the while he told Olaus all about his family. He and his companions are tramping on down to Alatna tomorrow, for Pooto says: 'Been gone long time to Annie.'

"October 3: Now we shall watch the freeze-up happen. The last poling boat got in yesterday, pushing a careful way through thick-running ice cakes, the boats heavily loaded with the last of the hams and bacon and lard and coffee from the *Dooley*. The river is running almost bank-full of ice now and river travel has come to an end. The rest of the freight from Alatna will have to wait until the Kobuks and Koyukuks can use their dog teams. It rained all night, and this morning there is 'lain-half,' as Pooto called it, half snow; the temperature is falling. Oscar and Little Henry and Billy Bergman all came to say good-by before starting their hike overland to Alatna. We hated to say good-by to them; this was the very end of the *Teddy H.* chapter. We went outdoors with them and watched them disappear into the woods on the downriver trail. Three days ago we said good-by to Sam and waved him and his party as the last poling boat to go back downriver made its way through the ice. Now we people of Bettles are left alone to await the freeze-up. But we still have Otto and Frank to talk and laugh with over the *Teddy H.* episodes!

"Otto came in the afternoon, and while mice and a raven were being skinned in one corner, I made an applesauce cake in the other, and also hopefully set a bread sponge.

"We also played for a while with the four red-backed mice which Olaus live-trapped and has in a cage he made from some mosquito screen. They are beautiful little animals and so friendly they have become real pets in a few days. Otto lowers into their cage a table knife smeared with peanut butter and they climb right up the handle and also lick bits of peanut butter off his fingers. Otto chuckles and looks at Olaus: 'Good thing you found that piece of whalebone, eh?'

When we moved into the cabin Olaus gleefully pounced on an old corset stay lying in the back of the cupboard: 'Just what I need for a live-trap!' I had looked pretty blank, I guess, so he proceeded to show me. He bent the piece of whalebone back upon itself, tied the end together with lots of heavy thread, picked up a one-pound coffee can, and, on the floor in one corner, placed one edge of the can just balancing on the top of the curve of the whalebone. On the tied-together ends he had put peanut butter for bait. That night we heard the clink of the 'up' edge of the can falling to the floor, and the scuffling sounds of a mouse, trapped beneath the can! So—red-backed mice for observation and sketching and friendliness; and I hope he will decide to turn these four loose when we leave.

"October 4: The sponge didn't sponge in spite of red damask tablecloth and fur parka I had it lovingly wrapped in. Olaus went over to the roadhouse and when he came back he had a bottle of homemade yeast in his hand and a whimsical smile on his face. 'The fellows over there asked me how "the Missus" was,' he said. 'Sort of startled me—never thought of you just that way—are you my "Missus"?' and he handed me the bottle of yeast.

"But I couldn't pull the cork, and when Olaus exerted his strength on it the stuff hit the ceiling and flew all over us; I snatched the bottle out of his hand and dumped the remaining contents into the pan of dough and kneaded it in quickly.

"Then I stayed home and nursed the dough baby and kept the fire going while Olaus went alone to the traplines in pouring rain. It was a special keen joy to help him into dry clothes when he returned, to build up the fire and hang the wet clothes near the stove to dry, to point with pride to the big mound rising under the red tablecloth, to hear the most beloved voice say: 'Gosh, it worked, didn't it?'

"I could not have held more happiness.

"Otto came and they skinned mouse specimens all afternoon and I did the cataloguing between ministrations to the dough, and by the time Mary and Frank came in at 8 o'clock to see Olaus's field sketches, I had five loaves of bread spread out on the big cupboard, and we all had bread and jam and tea. Mary was deeply impressed with Olaus's drawings: 'Oh-o-o, what kinda man!'

"She smoked her pipe and watched bright-eyed as Olaus showed her one sketch after another. She was so pleased when she recognized a bird: 'Me sabby this one!'

"She also admired the mouse specimens all pinned in a row on a piece of cardboard, and told me how they used to make little doll parkas from mouse skins when she was a little girl. Then, of course, as always in the North, we talked about our dogs, and Mary said: 'When you raise a pup it is just like you raise a kid—you like 'em so much!'

"Mary had brought us a bowl of blueberries taken from the barrelful she had sugared and frozen down for winter use; they are just like fresh ones.

"October 5: Day came bright again, fog lifting over the mountains upriver, revealing them in winter garb dazzling white and lovely with the sun on them. We had to climb up over part of the rocks on the shore on the way to the upriver trapline because the water had risen so much. Took a long hike in the woods beyond the lake and got six rabbits, two in my snares and four by Olaus's prowess. Saw a rough-legged hawk, soaring, dipping, banking, flaunting his graceful power in the face of the north wind, while just below him a quaint grandma hawk owl sat mooning on a dead spruce. On the way home we saw a red-tailed hawk, but Olaus had used all his shells for rabbits. 'We won't see those two hawks around here much longer,' said Olaus. 'They should be on their way pretty soon to the south country.'

"An afternoon of joy, curled up in the 'cozy corner' reading aloud from some of the *Scribners* while Olaus painted watercolors of three rabbits. Otto has just come in now with a raven to practice on and sits on a box in the corner working on it. I have stewed canned strawberries into jam, and made a chocolate gelatin, so in a little while we three shall have a supper of homemade bread and jam and pudding and tea. The antiphonal choir in the back yard has been silenced by a big feed of rabbit, rice, and tallow, the chores are all done, the lamps lit; the fire is crackling a contented snory tune. Outside, the north wind is banging at the stovepipe and shouting at the yellow half moon that winter is treading at his back, and he makes woolly ripples in the moon's path across the black river. Just over the tops of the spruces on the other shore Mars blinks a startling red eye. When I go to the doorstep to stir the cooling pudding it is a joy to gaze a bit at the chilly yellow-and-gray beauty of moon and river, to feel the wind in my hair, and then retreat to the snug warmth of fire and lamp and Olaus, while I think of all the friends up and down the river—are they all snug tonight?—David and Oscar, and Little Henry and Billy Bergman and all the others? And is the

Teddy H. safe in her winter berth in the little side slough above Alatna?

"Olaus just looked up from his work now and said: 'There, that's the last one. Gosh, I'm hungry. How about you, Otto?'

"So I must stop this writing now and, as soon as Olaus clears his table, spread the red tablecloth on it, make the tea, make cocoa for Olaus. What happiness, to be a woman, to spread a table for two appreciative hungry men! To hear the wind howling outside; to be so warm and cherished.

"October 7: She 'froze 'em up' last night and today the slush ice is slipping along in big pans. Ludie brought my new mitts, moose hide trimmed in beaver and lined with flannel. She sat and exclaimed and ohed and ahed over the bird and mouse specimens. She is such an amiable soul, and does such beautiful needlework. She said she guessed she and Sammy would have to go hunting pretty soon. 'We got to get some little gane; we got no beat for winter—maybe we get boose.'

"This evening she came back with my fur parka; she had fixed the sleeves. Olaus happened to be skinning an especially small kind of shrew, and she was completely fascinated. 'Oh, too-oo-oo small! I tell Sammy today: "Dat govmint boy over dere, he got fine fingles, he can do any *ting*: no big at ends, fingles, no big at ends."' And when I showed her the watercolor of the raven she exclaimed: 'Oh, oh, oh, looks like it, looks just like it. Oh, smar-r-t!'"

By October 12 the long slow snake of ice in the middle of the river had frozen solid to the shore ice, and for two days and nights the snow fell heavily and steadily. Now it was time to get the dog harnesses ready; all the collars had to be fitted to the dogs, and what a jubilant hullabaloo that was! When Olaus appeared with his arms full of harnesses, the dogs promptly went into an ecstasy of jumping and howling. After all that long summer of inactivity they knew they were going somewhere, they just *knew* it! Pooto, the leader, was heart-rendingly eager, and insulted and hurt because his collar didn't go on first, as it should have. The dog which was being fitted was importantly, significantly quiet, seeming to know that all his pals were yelling and jumping in an agony of envy. They all yowled the whole time, but when Olaus finally got to Pooto the chorus was deafening and Pooto nearly ate Olaus up in gratitude. And then, when Olaus gathered up the harnesses and took them away, what hurt, puzzled looks of disappointment!

There followed days of waiting for a little more snow, just enough to make sledding possible. Olaus and Otto took the team on trial runs. In all our preparations Otto was a great help, and at the same time he and Frank and Heinie and Mary were busy getting their own outfits ready to leave too. There was the continual excitement of dog teams being tried out and other dog teams wanting to be tried out. Our sparkling black Koyukuk had become a sparkling white ribbon, solid from shore to shore, and on the seventeenth Olaus and Otto crossed it with the team, as rambunctious as they could be, to take a load of dog fish ten miles up the trail.

They returned at six o'clock and supper was ready—baked ham, mashed potatoes, creamed carrots, and apple pie. The carrots came out of a can and the apples were dried ones, but the ham and potatoes were fresh, and the whole affair was dispatched with no fuss at all, and I felt more than repaid for staying home, keeping the fire going, preparing for the men's return. I thought of all the women who have kept a log cabin warm and ready on the far reaches of various frontiers. All afternoon as I worked I thought of these women, feeling a kinship with them.

Next day we finished packing all our gear. Into one packsack went our clothing; into another large one, our food—flour, sugar, beans, dried apples and prunes, oatmeal, cornmeal, rice, condensed milk, powdered eggs, a small can of lard, a small package of tea (Olaus drinks neither tea nor coffee and I decided I could do nicely with only tea), a big bag of Jersey Creams (thick, slightly sweet biscuits about the size of a teacup which were and are the stand-by of wilderness travelers in Alaska), some cheese, many large cakes of real Swiss chocolate, some raisins, some canned butter. In another canvas bag went our tools and the set of nested trail pots of gray enamelware, all with tin lids which fitted inside the rims; these were standard equipment for dog mushers in those days, but I don't suppose they are even manufactured any more. We decided to take half a ham instead of bacon, and that about completed our list.

Into the little rucksack Olaus had given me I packed our toilet articles and personal things and the sewing kit, the first-aid kit, notebooks, a few books to read. Our stock of magazines, we left at the roadhouse. Another small canvas kit held Olaus's skinning

tools and his paints and sketchbooks. We gathered together the
tent, the two sleeping bags, the Yukon stove, the rifle, the
steelyards for weighing animals. First into the fourteen-foot
basket sleigh made so sturdily from seasoned birch by our friend
Nels Jensen in Fairbanks, would go the big tarp, lining the sled;
into this would be laid a whole layer of bales of dried salmon for
the dogs; on top of that all our gear. Then the tarp would be
pulled up and over and around and tucked in snugly and tied
across and across up the whole length of the load. Finally, on top,
tucked under the ropes, the ax, the guns, the big iron skillet. Into
the canvas ditty bag hanging at the back of the sled below the
handle bars and under the bow would go a supply of chocolate
and Jersey Creams for lunch, a hunting knife, extra snaps for dog
harnesses, extra rawhide for emergency repairs to sled or harness,
an extra waterproof match safe, canvas moccasins for all the dogs
in case we had to go over sharp splintery ice anywhere, and a
chain for each dog.

So we were ready, and here is the last entry in the diary at
Bettles:

"Tomorrow we leave Bettles and hope to get through to King's
fox farm and roadhouse, nineteen miles, with the whole load by
tomorrow night. King's is the first and only roadhouse between
here and Wiseman. Fun to be packing up for another step in this
together journey; yet what aching-sweet memories will linger
around the dear log cabin in Bettles!"

8

One Day of It

Behind our log cabin next morning a great welter of sound was going up. The sled was loaded and Olaus and Otto were beginning to hook up, with Pooto and his followers trying to turn themselves inside out with joy.

It was a fine frosty morning to hit the trail. I took a last look around our happy home—clean and neat and bare, empty, all empty, of our possessions, tables, chairs, beds, cupboard; even the juniper branches were gone from the walls. And it was already becoming a bit cold, for the fire was out. I pulled on my new moose-hide mitts and swallowed a big lump in my throat. It had been perfect here, and was I going to measure up as a staunch and capable enough partner in the next chapter? Confusing, being a woman, eagerness for new adventure fighting within one with love of cozy home-keeping. Did men ever feel pulled this way?

I closed the door quietly. The yips and yowls were coming round to the front of the cabin, and when Olaus shouted "All right," I had to be ready to run along behind. Otto was going a little way with us, and he took the handle bars.

We had said our good-bys and thank you's to Jack Dodds and the others at the roadhouse the night before, but now they all came out, in shirt sleeves, to stand in the frosty air atop the steep bank and wave to us as the team fairly shot down the cleft in the bank and out onto the river in a wild swirl of dogs and thumping sled. Pooto headed straight out over the ice hummocks, and I had a lively time getting my moccasined feet over the sharp edges fast enough. Before we climbed up onto the portage trail we turned for a last look at Bettles, a staunch little row of log cabins. Three or four old-timers were still there on the bank waving good-by. They had watched many a dog team disappear through that gap in the forest!

Now we were really on the trail; yet what we found could hardly be called such. There was only a light skim of snow as yet and the original contours of the portage mail trail were quite evident, even prominent. They included sizable tussocks, good solid stumps, numberless stubs of brush and trees once supposedly "swamped out," humps and hollows, all in rapid succession. I was supposed to ride and conserve strength here for worse trail farther on, yet riding that fourteen-foot sled, hanging on to the ropes, resembled riding a bronco. But it was exciting, and so long as our tough old Huskies could trundle along so unconcernedly, so happy to be in harness again, I could enjoy it too. So I tried to put out of my mind the cabin back there, growing cold—tried to look ahead.

Olaus ran in front for a while, to ward off sudden forays that would be led by Bingo, the huge black-and-white dog, on a rabbit snareline we were passing. Otto had to fairly gallop at the handle bars to keep our swaying craft upright; and I was busy keeping my weight on the "up" side and jumping quickly when the "up" side suddenly flopped over. As soon as we had passed the snareline, Olaus called back to Otto: "I guess I might as well put on a gee pole right now. Can you get them stopped?" Then he disappeared into the woods.

In a few moments he returned, carrying a small smooth dead spruce, pulled out a small coil of rope from under the front of the load, and knelt beside the sled. I had heard of gee poles; this was the first one I had seen installed. Olaus held the larger end of the pole about a fourth of the way back from the front of the sled, and tied it securely to the short wooden braces above the runners, in such a way that it slanted upward and forward and the end of it was at a height convenient to his hand. He then stepped over the towline, behind the first pair of dogs, took hold of the pole, and smiled back over his shoulder at us. "O.K., let's try it now."

Olaus trotted along holding the pole, and this was a great help in keeping the sled on the trail and preventing it from tipping over. All the while the sun was climbing higher, glowing through the purple willow branches, gilding the yellow grass of occasional sloughs. Every few minutes our winding trail gave us a glorious vista of white peaks, our goal, rosy and beckoning on this first morning on the trail. We traveled five miles in this colorful world, the three of us, but on the next rise Otto was to leave us.

On top of the little hill we pulled off our mitts and clasped hands with Otto. Suddenly we all knew we could not speak. In that moment I think we all realized what a deep, foreverafter friendship it had become. Otto stood on top of the little hill, striped parka and red wool cap bright against the blue sky, as we reluctantly slipped down the slope toward the deep woods. Suddenly his rifle went to his shoulder and the three shots of farewell salute went crashing through the silent woods; off went his red toque, and he stood there at attention while our sled traveled on toward the new country and the forest came between us.

We traveled in silence for a long time.

An hour later we came up the shoulder of a long hill and there, amazingly, curled just below us, was the Koyukuk again, terraced on either side by gray graceful skeletons of cottonwoods. Our trail on up the hill led through a thick forest of all the northern trees, more lovely than I had ever seen them—spruce trees, black in shadow and emerald in the light, willows full of purple shades and alive with gossiping redpolls. There in some tall poplars were some pine grosbeaks, yellow and red caps lighted up by the sun. They were very busy about their own affairs and our passing bothered them not at all.

I was no longer a passenger. I ambled along behind the team, parka hood thrown back, bareheaded and barehanded, gazing out from the top of the plateau over the broad valley, which swelled into distant blue hills and more distant white mountains, and stubbing my toe frequently because the trail was not built for scenery-gazers.

Once when I caught up to the sled near a little creek, Olaus said: "Look at old Grandpa." And there was Wolf, the brown patriarch of the team, jogging along with a stiff, stark bunny in his jaws. He had carried it a mile and would go trotting on for more miles with that rabbit sticking out from both sides of his head and poking his partner in the ear, until the team stopped and he could consume his forage. He evidently had little faith in us as providers.

Twenty minutes for lunch! And the dogs knew it was rest time, for they all flopped down, noses in tails, and appeared to lose all consciousness. We were in the middle of a broad sea of tussocks on top of the plateau. It took almost every little dead scrub spruce in sight for a little fire; and our new lard-pail teapot was too new, though I had boiled and boiled it at the cabin. On top of the tea floated grease and spruce needles, but that didn't matter; it was just right for washing down cheese sandwiches toasted on the end of a stick. The sun was shining, the air was crystal clear yet balmy, the far blue hills and golden sky were enchanting. We had the toughest piece of muskeg tussock portage in the Koyukuk right there; but the dogs were tough too, and six more miles would bring us to the haven of King's roadhouse. No setting up camp in a tent or mail shelter cabin this first night. Days on the trail taught us that there is always and forever something to rejoice about. It was a fairyland, this highland, skyland, on a glorious blue-and-gold day. Our seven dogs, the two of us, alone up there, sliding along on top of the world. Out there above the tableland's edge were the tops of white mountains that seemed to rise out of nowhere.

As we neared the end of the plateau the sun was sinking and the coming of night gave us a golden world for a few minutes. Sky, clouds, mountain peaks, spruce forests, all swimming in molten gold—the hawk that winged out into the valley was a golden bird too. This faded to give place to liquid rose and lavender, and we came whirling down the long hill into a river valley bathed in pink. Smooth ice was on the river here, but open water swirled above and below the crossing, reflecting the rose and lavender of the sky.

We had been told that from the river crossing it was only three miles to King's. But it sometimes happens that three miles is thirty! Our trail led us down steep banks into sloughs, up steep banks out of them, across stretches of gravel bar, through forests growing on sand bars, with never enough snow to cover sand and gravel, the hardest pulling known to the dog musher. So we and the dogs were working together for the next two hours; our shoulders under the handle bars—push for all you're worth! All right, Pooto, you're a wonder! This was an awful load for any team, with sixteen miles of pulling already behind them.

What dog musher does not curse a sliding trail! Look out now! Struggle as you may at the handle bars, over she goes; the dogs

stop, look around, too weary to start a fight, glad to just stand. Olaus says nothing, only looks back at me with a rueful smile—after six times this is getting old. Close to tears, I cry: "I couldn't help it; I just couldn't hold it by the bars!"

"I know it. Don't worry, we'll make it."

He goes off to the nearest timber and comes back with a small tree, which he wedges under the runner at the back, heavy end of the sled; then I lean all my weight on the end of the pole, while Olaus tugs at the handle bars. Glory be! Up she goes—we had made it once more.

It was getting pretty dark now; the trees were just black shapes on either side and we had to strain our eyes to see bumps in the trail. I wondered how many more banks and sloughs and creeks and gravel bars there could be. I ached all over; I had a strong impulse to just flop down on one of those dry grass patches and stay there—I couldn't even feel what my feet were doing.

Just then Olaus looked over his shoulder and smiled at me and said: "You know, Mardy, you're doing awfully well. I know this has been a tough day for the first one."

Suddenly I felt much better. And then we came out in sight of the broad river again, dark hills rising behind it and one perfect cone of a white mountain standing there alone against that indescribable midnight-blue sky of a winter twilight, and riding triumphant on the white mountain's shoulder, Mars, flaming red, magnificent.

On the strength of that scene we hoisted the sled up the next steep bank, the worst one of all, and I plodded ahead to encourage Pooto, who was dragging cheerfully at my heels. Thank goodness for tough dogs! Surely we must get in somewhere before that trail became much darker. Then Olaus, back at the handle bars now, cried: "Come back here a minute, darlin'."

I left Pooto and waited for the sled. Olaus put an arm about me: "Look there! I told you we'd make it!"

A warm yellow light was gleaming through the trees; then we heard a dog barking, a man's voice, and there, nestled among mammoth spruce trees, a low rambling log home, a light in the window, another bobbing toward us, and approaching us a man with the cheeriest voice and the heartiest welcome I have ever known, Roy King. "Well, well, well, here you are; that Indian walking upriver yesterday told me you were coming, but I couldn't believe it; didn't see how you could make it on this trail now. Well, I'm proud to shake a white woman's hand! You must be about dead; here, you come with me!"

From the diary:

"Here in the bunkhouse it is warm and light. The dogs have been fed and put away; we have doffed our trail gear, and I have discovered the wondrous comfort of a bunk in the corner covered with a wolf robe. From the kitchen comes a joyous clatter of dishes and pans, and the gracious fragrance of food. Heaven? This is it!"

We had a good rest before we were called in to a marvelous meal. Roy had a garden, and we feasted on cole slaw, fried cabbage, creamed carrots, and rabbit simmered all day in olive oil (delicious!). And we sat and talked till nearly midnight. Roy had seen only that one Indian for weeks and was hungry for talk. He kept marveling that Olaus had got me over that nineteen miles of overland trail in one day, with no snow to "fill up the chinks"—thus bolstering my ego a good deal.

9

On the River Ice

No two ways about it, Roy insisted, he would take his little "kick-sled" and his four bird dogs (Irish setters) and haul the dog fish and the camp stove up to the North Fork cabin for us. He knew his river; she was treacherous just along here. We would have his tracks to follow.

Breakfast was at six—oatmeal and stewed prunes, hotcakes, bacon and fried eggs. Roy wouldn't let me do the dishes. We had a long way to go, and he would have "nothing but time" when he came back from North Fork that afternoon. As we led out our dogs he was already speeding out onto the river. How those dogs could go! Of course, ours started with a leap too, taking us out over the bank and onto the river with a swish and a whirl. I hung to the handle bars for dear life, unable to use the brake in the gravel. As we glanced back at King's, crisp sunshine was pinking the smoke that floated lazily up against the grove of spruces. There would be no other roadhouse until we reached Wiseman.

The dogs with a lightened load and a smooth trail, were running easily, ears pricked, curled tails waving over their backs. Pooto followed Roy's single track with a bored air, as though to say: "This is too easy; why don't you give me something worthwhile to do?"

An ideal day to hit the trail; twelve below, just right for mushing. We were both running and I was soon too warm; I threw back the parka hood and pulled off the red toque; the crisp air felt good on my bared head. How light my moccasined feet felt, padding along on snow-sprinkled ice at a dog trot, exhilaration in every muscle responding to the joy of motion, running, running, without getting out of breath.

Roy had warned us of open places. The first one was fairly close to shore, and the churning water looked black and wicked. It seemed to be fighting a battle to the death with old Winter and the thickening ice. We crossed at the lower edge, Olaus leading Pooto, the team all stepping gingerly in Roy's tracks. I followed, stepping rather gingerly also. "Crack! Boom!" Some old river ogre, out there under the ice.

On the other side of the river, the wind of the Endicotts had been sweeping due south and made a dance floor of the ice next to the bank. Olaus looked back: "There's a trick, you know, to traveling on glare ice. Pretend your knees are made of jelly and that there are really no bones in your feet either, and you don't care if you do fall, and you'll get along fine."

I found myself enjoying it, like learning a new dance step; I began to put variations into it.

"Whoa, Pooto," Olaus suddenly shouted. I looked up. The whole team was trotting off upriver while we and the sled stood there on the ice. The giant spring fastening which hooked the main towline to the sled had frozen open. This might have been serious trouble, had not Pooto decided to stop and see what all the shouting was about. On the ice it was easy for us to push the sled over and connect it to the team again.

Along here the Koyukuk had had to cut through hills, and it had left barren high bluffs on either side. We were finally in the real foothills of the Endicotts now; sometimes, rounding a bend, we rejoiced again in a glimpse of those snow peaks gleaming there due north of us.

We trotted on, chuckling at old Wolf's fatherly expression, at the way Fuzzy's flying hind feet seemed hardly to reach the ground. We passed the fossil banks Otto had told us about, where the old relentless river had cut a cross section through some faraway and long-ago terrain. Otto had heard that there was a big mammoth tusk in the bank that had not been removed, but we searched in vain. The faraway silent valleys of the earth give one tantalizing thoughts; oh, for just one glimpse of this valley, this very spot, as it stood thousands of years ago!

But while we were daydreaming there, gazing up at those high tawny bluffs, we heard the swishing sound of an approaching dog team and Roy's voice: "You've only a half mile more to go. I cached your stuff right by the trail. Didn't take it over to the cabin. You'll find the cabin right near, at the mouth of North Fork, on the right limit of the river. It's no more than a doghouse, but it's a shelter. No, don't thank me; you don't know how much it's meant to me to have you folks with me, and don't forget you're to stay over a day on the way down; stay a week if you can. I'll know when you're coming; I'll see little waves of happiness dancing over the willows! Good-by, and good luck. All right, Mickie!" And he was gone.

I was close to tears, and Olaus looked back with a smile and said: "Aren't people wonderful?"

Now we were on our own, and the first thing Olaus did was take himself and his dog team right through an overflow, very successfully, while I walked around by a gravel bar because I was in my fur boots.

When the dogs smelled the cabin, we went up the little side slough helter-skelter over the frozen hummocks of goose grass. Up on top of the bank stood our first trail home; rather, it squatted. It seemed a trifle higher than a doghouse, although after bending double to get through the square hole which served as a door, you had to stay in that position once inside. I immediately felt like some old witch, and soon was wishing I knew an incantation to bewitch the ancient stove into throwing off enough heat to fry bacon at least; poor thing, it must have been there with rains and snows leaking on it since the early days of the Koyukuk.

Behind the stove and a rude shelf table there was barely room for our two sleeping bags. We wondered about Roy King's story of a spell of fifty-below weather they had had one winter when nine of them were camped at North Fork. All things are possible in the North.

While trying to insert our grub bag into a corner, we heard sudden furious sounds outside, and rushed out to find the team a furry quivering mass emitting frightful noises. Olaus went to work with the loaded butt of the whip, but this was my first dog fight and I simply stood, horrified, and prayed they wouldn't entirely kill one another. He soon had them lying in their traces again, a sullen, snarling crew, panting and ready to spring again. Ungiak, the beauty of the team, lay flattened to the ground like a lizard. Very slowly and quietly, watching the other dogs all the while, Olaus unharnessed him and dragged him away from the sled, looking very serious. "Gosh, I'm afraid they've got him," he said. "They were all on top of him and Fuzzy was tearing at his flank."

My heart quite stood still. But Ungiak didn't seem to be bleeding anywhere, and as soon as he had been dragged away from his persecutors, he got his feet under him and walked up to me as easy as you please; but as we took him over toward the cabin he kept close to Olaus's knees and, dropping down in front of the door, looked up at him as though to say: "I'll just stay here, if you please; I am a very scared dog."

Olaus knelt and talked soothingly to Ungiak while he examined him all over. "I'm sure he isn't really hurt," he said. "I don't know what got into those darn dogs; they never picked on just one like this before; it's usually just a good-natured free-for-all."

"Maybe they're all jealous of Ungiak because he's the best-looking one in the team," I said, with human-female logic.

Olaus smiled patiently. "I don't think they know that, but anyway, I think I had better leave him here with you this afternoon while I relay the fish on upriver a few miles. I don't think we need to tie him. Let's experiment and see if he won't stay around. I'll have to hurry now; it starts to get dark at four. You'll be all right, won't you?"

Ungiak did not seem in the least anxious to go anywhere. He lay down in front of the door hole, I sat on the doorstep, and we just gazed at each other for a while. When I took the folding canvas bucket and started for the river, he got to his feet and trotted at my heels in exemplary fashion all the way to the river, and stood inquiringly but politely at my elbow while I dipped the bucket. But the moment I turned he bounded off, and when I came panting and a bit worried up the bank he was standing at the door with a real Husky grin on his beautiful face.

From that moment Ungiak and I were pals. His beauty and his winning personality were striking, and when you looked at his splendid size and build, at his glorious thick black coat with the creamy underfur, at his typical Husky prick ears and gray face, you forgave him for all the trouble he might have caused. He was a lamb that day anyway and lay curled at my feet as I sat in the doorway and read the magazines Roy had given me and by constantly urging the stove got beans and applesauce cooked.

After a while Ungiak and I went into the slough and gathered dry grass and worked at chinking up the front and one side of the cabin, where nearly all the moss filling was gone. We worked until the walls were really quite well stuffed. The cooking was done, supper all ready. The sun was going down across the river, turning the blue hills and green forest rosy for a moment. Ungiak and I sat quietly content, waiting. A goshawk flopped into the spruces on the main riverbank; far on the other side ptarmigan were gossiping; in the woods a great horned owl had a quiet word to say at dusk. It was very still except for these voices. Ungiak knew no other world, but to me it was a new feeling; the Koyukuk is a long, broad country, and there were sixty-five white people throughout its whole length. That was the joy of it too.

Now we heard a voice, and here they came, the team slipping very softly through the dusk; the hungry man and the ravenous dogs were home.

Next morning Ungiak was back in the team and all was serene. They had had a good fight and were content for a while. The only difference was that from that morning on Ungiak would not have his harness put on until I had said good morning and roughed him up a bit; then he went and stood in place, ready to be hooked into harness.

We traveled three miles to the cache, where Olaus announced that we should see how much a bunch of Victoria Land Huskies could pull. Maybe a good load would take some of the fight out of them! Since we were out on the first river ice in violation of the practice of the Koyukuk sourdoughs anyway (the mailman pulled over bare tussocks overland rather than risk the ice), we might just as well put on our whole load and be content to travel slowly.

What an enormous heap our outfit made, all piled out on the ice! I simply sat on a sleeping bag and watched my magician, methodically, unerringly, with scientific precision, insert that mass of objects into the sled again. First the eight bales of dog salmon as a foundation layer spread out along the whole length of the fourteen-foot sled, then all the rest fitted on on top of that. Lucky for the bride that her trousseau was packed in a small duffel bag! In addition to everything else, the big Graflex and the little movie camera and films filled one large packsack, and that had to be right on top and next to the handle bars. When the whole assembly, wrapped in the tarp and lashed with rope, had been loaded, the iron skillet, the symbol of the frontier, had to be

tucked in, and last of all the ax, the .30-'06, the shotgun, and, finally, the two pairs of snowshoes which we didn't need now but would later on when more snow came.

"Lord, what a load!" said Olaus. "Well, are you ready? We'll just see whether they can move it or not. All right, Pooto!"

Pooto wriggled to his feet, looked calmly back as though to say: "All set?" and they walked off at the same old gait. I was reminded of that motor which used to advertise: "No load too great—no hill too steep."

So we went on quietly throughout that mild, gray, quiet day, the dogs pulling evenly along over the unmarked surface of the snow, Olaus and I trudging along behind. Here Olaus did not need to be on the gee pole. This piece of the world seemed to be our very own. The little sift of snow on the ice was marked only by tracks of fox, lynx, and rabbit, and they were evidently not traveling that day. It was as though all the creatures and the winds and snows of this region had withdrawn to the bordering hills to allow us to pass silently into their land.

Pooto showed himself to be a treasure of a leader whenever there was no sign of a trail. Olaus was able to "gee and haw" him actually by inches as he chose the quickest and safest route for us up a river not only twisting but all cluttered up with sand islands, false channels, and side sloughs. How to choose the good part and cling to the main channel?

Yes, there are tricks to river navigation in winter as well as in summer. Once we were wrong. Such an imposing-looking channel, running up behind a gravel bar, but when we had traced it to its end, we found the open water of a swift riffle. The wide main channel lay white and inviting one hundred feet away, but that hundred feet had to be traversed by main strength and ingenuity. Traveling over bare gravel is an impossibility with a load. Olaus stopped the team, cut willow poles, laid them crosswise in front of the sled, and then, the dogs straining, the two of us lifting and pushing on the handle bars, we proceeded, a foot, maybe five or ten, at each try.

I must be a poor judge of a mile. We were to travel nine miles to reach Frank's old roadhouse on the river—now closed and empty, but a kind of objective anyway. Yet when one's stomach is achingly empty, the miles double themselves and stretch before you, around bend after bend—hours of this, it seemed (it was really only one o'clock, but that is seven hours from breakfast). Finally we sighted a huddled group of cabins and caches. We had not meant to stop, but there was smoke, and sled tracks from upriver.

It creates a special kind of feeling to meet another soul unexpectedly in a very large wilderness. It must be the same feeling our forebears had when, slipping through the primeval forest, they glimpsed the smoke of another camp fire wafting over the treetops.

I was musing on this thought as I followed Olaus up to the cabin, and in the door there did stand a caveman! I felt a quick sensation of unreality, almost fright, when I saw him standing there, in a long parka of striped denim, a gray beard covering his chest, gray hair standing out wildly around a long-featured face. He stood and stared at us from wide gray eyes, but when he spoke, in a thick German accent, I realized he must be South Fork Henry, whom Roy had described, and he was no doubt more astonished to see us than we were to see him. He motioned us right into the cabin, and as we sat on the bunks in there and talked to him I recalled what Roy had told us: that he was alone throughout the year away over on the South Fork, mining an ungracious mining claim, unaided, tending to a bit of a garden,

hunting in the fall, trapping in the winter, seeing no one but wandering Indian hunters except when he came down to the Koyukuk settlements in the spring for supplies. Roy had said the old fellow always talked a blue streak to the first white person he met and that his language was quite unintelligible until he had been among English-speaking people for a while each time.

I understood only about every third word of his outpouring of instructions, distances, and landmarks for our guidance, but Olaus, knowing German, seemed to be doing very well. Henry was quite determined we should stay right there until morning. Most old sourdoughs felt that no camping place should be passed up, no matter how short the travel, perhaps because they had gone through too many days of forced marches and long, long trails. South Fork Henry no doubt thought we were young fools to be looking forward to a night of siwashing (that is, camping outside without a tent)—he implied as much—but when he saw we were determined to go on he insisted on giving us the last of his tiny home-grown potatoes, enough for our next meal, and three rabbits, all beautifully prepared and frozen. We did stay with him long enough to eat our lunch, and he seemed to enjoy some of the last of the applesauce cake we had brought from Bettles.

As dusk came on we noticed higher, bolder hills creeping close to the river. We must be approaching the canyon of the Koyukuk. And I was approaching starvation. I found myself plodding along in a half dream, unable to think of anything but how tired my legs were and how hungry I was. I must try to think of something else; there must be lots of other things to think of. Then into my absorption penetrated the beloved voice with welcome news: "Mardy, aren't you getting hungry too? That next stand of big spruces up there ought to be all right for a camp and we'd better get settled before it's much darker."

One hour later, and there was our siwash camp: a rope was stretched between two big trees and the whole tent thrown over this as a back wall for the camping place. (The reason we were siwashing was that we had not yet sewed ties along the ridge of the tent for attaching it to a ridgepole.) In front of the canvas back wall we placed a thick bed of spruce boughs, and in front of this, the two sleeping bags, still rolled, for seats. At one end of the fly our little Yukon stove crackled merrily and sent a brave plume of smoke skyward; across the whole front of the camping place, a long fire, heaped high, was roaring gloriously.

Here was home; fire and the smell of meat sizzling, the sound of the man's ax blows in the woods near by, the figure of the woman kneeling busily before her hearth fire, and the honest dog faces in a wide circle beyond the fire. Their master had with much effort brought them one by one up the steep bank from the river and tied them near, "because it seems cozy to have them around."

This was total peace and contentment. I sat on a sleeping-bag roll before the tiny stove, grub sack open at one side, dishes arranged at my feet, and the skillet, full of ptarmigan and rabbit, making a great promising hissing; South Fork Henry's potatoes were peeled and sliced in with the meat; the bean pot and the applesauce pan had been put on the back of the stove to thaw out—odors, hunger, comfort! The wood pile was growing in the background, but now came a pitiful voice from the gloom: "Can we eat pretty soon? Those dogs look so darn satisfied!"

They did too. They fairly exuded satisfaction. They had received with loud acclaim one large salmon apiece, had devoured it all, and now lay there watching us with benign expressions.

Food never tasted so intoxicatingly good. Two tin plates, piled high with rabbit, ptarmigan, potatoes, and beans. We sat there on the bags in front of the fire, eating with great enjoyment, tossing the bones to the happy dogs. We ate the last of our bread and whole platefuls of applesauce. There's no such thing as stomach ache on the trail. You simply eat until you think perhaps you can last until morning, and let it go at that.

I awoke at 2 A.M. The new moon was shining through the silhouette of a spruce tree in front of our camp; the sky was fairly white with stars, so close it seemed they might almost speak to this valley in the Far North; beyond the low light of our fire the river was a dazzling white ribbon. A dog stirred, turned round a few times, and settled himself again; far off an owl spoke soothingly, the fire crackled. I remembered reading somewhere a beautiful account of the tropical forest at night. So with the Arctic. I could not analyze my feeling as I lay there watching and listening, but I felt somehow privileged, humble yet triumphant, waking so in the night hours, as though I had found omnipotence at work undisturbed.

It seemed I had fallen asleep again for only a moment when I saw that far-traveler, dressed and building up a big fire. "What's the matter? The stars are still out!"

"Yes, but I think it must be time to start; the watches have both stopped. They have to be wound once in a while, I guess!"

If South Fork Henry's language had been rightly interpreted, we had only about twelve miles to travel from our siwash camp to Tramway Bar and the mine of the French-Canadian Marcel Sheehy and his partner, Swift, about whom Roy had told us.

Pooto was allowed to make his dignified way unnagged while we trudged along behind, gazing at the increasingly high walls on either side of us, the lovely colorings in those rocky walls, and, stretched like a flat roof above the canyon, the sky, blue as only the short-lived blue skies of an Alaskan winter day may be.

We watched for rock pinnacles, or islands, out in the channel. Henry had said we must pass two, then a big one, "Bishop Rock," and after that "Squaw Rock" and then we should be eight miles from "those two fellas." We hoped there would be room on the river for the Bishop and us too. So far the ice in the canyon was splendid, with no open spaces or overflows. We were getting upriver on the first "freeze-up ice" before the dreaded overflows that come with colder weather.

The valley became narrower with every mile, and now we saw the Bishop, seventy-five feet high and towering all alone. But why it was called the Bishop is a mystery, for this old rock was a perfect Turk, even to the tassel on the back of its fez. Even the dogs eyed this thing warily, quick to note a foreign shape in their environment. But the ice was smooth and flawless all about the Turk, and we stopped to take pictures. The dogs lay down, all except big white-and-black Bingo, the strong man of the team. He sat up and gazed at the Turk and the canyon wall behind it as though he expected something to emerge from it. Vigilant Bingo, his was the independent character. When the rest of the team knew it was time to rest for five minutes, Bingo sat up, carefully scanning the countryside. When Bingo stopped they all stopped; when he chose to pull hard they all pulled hard; when he spied a rabbit in the brush the whole team went with him. Today he could locate nothing but a chattering red squirrel on that canyon wall and looked at Olaus in a questioning manner, as though wondering why we had stopped here.

Around the next bend, squatting right in the middle of the channel, was Squaw Rock, with open river boiling all around it. There was about five feet of solid ice next to the shore. Around this point Pooto was sure-footedly taking us, when Ungiak had the misfortune to cast a glance back at Fuzzy, and that little rascal nailed him! Naturally they were all willing to have a big fight right there—all except Pooto, who had seen open water and ice before in his career and tried to keep the team strung out. Olaus gave me some quick commands, and I managed to get past the fight and grab Pooto's collar and pull, helping him keep the team strung out so they couldn't all turn back into the fight, while Olaus went to work on the four who were fighting, and so, snarling and pulling, we got past that tricky spot and all was calm again.

With Squaw Rock well behind us, and with a beautiful cliff as background, Olaus took some movies, with Mardy as the heroine urging her gallant team on over treacherous unmarked wilderness! How blue and bright that sky over the silent canyon, how warm the sun! While Olaus wound film the dogs and I all lay flat on the snow, lazy and comfortable, watching a raven flying back and forth over us, making raucous inquiries as to who we were and what we might be doing in his canyon.

Traveling through the canyon was such fun that we weren't tired at all, and we came to the end of it much sooner than we had expected. There a poling boat was drawn back on the beach, and perched upon the last high bench above it were two cabins and the various scattered equipment of a mine in the wilderness. The top of a shaft showed above the snow, and some new flume. Two black dogs chained on top of the bank went into a frenzy, and there appeared in the doorway of one of the cabins a tall white-haired man. He called down to us: "Come on up!"

This was Fred Swift. Yes, he remembered Olaus from two years before, and seemed to take me for granted, though a little later he confessed to us that had he known there was a white woman coming up the bank he would have run and hidden because he "wasn't dressed up for ladies."

Being from Vermont, he showed no astonishment, but talked along in a steady, quiet way while he got us some dinner. We protested that we had lunched in the canyon, but that made no difference. I took off my parka and mitts and sat on an old sea chest and tried to think of all the news of downriver to tell Mr. Swift. He had seen no one since the last horse scow had gone up to Wiseman. How had Sam come out on his last trip? They were out of ham, bacon, eggs, and kerosene at Wiseman and now they'd have to wait until Jack White started to haul freight with his horses. Yes, there were caribou in the country. This man was a famous hunter, and he and Olaus were soon off on a long discussion of the ways of animals. He stood by the stove, frying ptarmigan, and the coffee boiled and boiled. That's the way they liked it in the Koyukuk. While we ate, our host sat on the chest and regaled us with tales of the fortunes he had made and lost since the early days; how he had gone home on a visit once, and lost fifteen thousand dollars in a speculation, and so had come back to the Koyukuk. But not to stay! "No sir, life's too short; we work harder here for our money than anywhere, and the season is so short. Winter mining is too expensive for most of us; winters I just go off trapping and prospecting. Yes, I'll be hitting out pretty soon. Oh, just take a tent and a stove and the dogs, and live around like a siwash. It's awful, the way a man gets used to living up here. Look at me." I pictured the orderly New England home this adventurer had come from; he still had its mark. "You get so you don't care; there's nobody to care if you do care; you get in an awful rut, and after a while the life up here gets hold of you so you can't fit in anywhere else."

The subject shifted to politics and the coming elections. What did we think about it all? I was careful not to say much, for I had discovered way downriver that the old-timers were far ahead of me on questions of the day. I said as much to Mr. Swift and looked around at the magazines and books strewn over bunks and shelves. "Yes," he said, "I don't know what a man would do in this valley without the magazines we get. Of course, they come all in a bunch, in summer, but we save them for the long winter days. Last winter I was kept in my tent three weeks, account of cold weather, and I guess I read the few magazines I had with me ten times apiece. I know I'd go crazy up here without them. Yes, we all read political stuff up here, but we're too far away to do any good by it; if some of the real voters in the States had as much time to read as we have, they might do differently. I'm not much of a politician myself, but that French-Canadian partner of mine is worse. One night this fall at supper I was trying to tell him some of the news I'd been reading. I said: 'Fellow named Davis been nominated for Vice-President.'

"He said: 'I lose two my rabbit snare today!'

"Well, I thought I'd try him again, so I said: 'President Coolidge's younger son just died.'

"He answered: 'Dese fellas'll have plenty room in dere cellars for all da potatoes dey raise *dis* fall!' "

This story reminded us that the afternoon was running along and we had better get on another mile to the place where the unpolitical partner was building a cabin for the winter freighter. Mr. Swift told us we could stay the night there.

As we were leaving, after assuring him we had all the grub we needed, and candles, he said rather diffidently: "We might run up and see you for a little while this evening, if you won't be too tired."

How starved for new companionship, and talk, just talk!

A mile and a half upriver the trail led us up a steep bank onto a little plateau backed by thick woods. There were dogs barking up there, and our team hauled our big load up that bank as though the sled were empty; nothing equals the curiosity Alaska dogs have for one another. But there was plenty of curiosity, if not astonishment, on the face of the red-toqued man who came out of the woods with two dogs drawing a load of logs.

A beautiful young pup tied to a tree before the door had been barking the riotous welcome, and I'm sure the other two dogs had hauled the load of logs out of the woods in record time. They were panting and quite ready to eat up all seven of our dogs when they arrived.

In a torrent of French-English the man subdued the dogs and tied them to a log, where they lay and muttered at our team while Olaus unhitched and tied them to stumps. By this time I was making overtures to the beautiful pup, and in this way to his master too. This was Marcel, a delightful, joyous, never-to-be-forgotten friend! Olaus and I sat on the new doorstep and gave him all the news of the lower country, and he responded with a delicious French-Canadian commentary on life in the Koyukuk. I leaned my head against the doorpost and listened and looked, quite entranced. The sun was sinking in a golden sea; the whole scene swam in that warm golden light of the North. Across the river, the rolling hills were green with small spruces, brown moss, and little bushes, all snow-sprinkled; while in the foreground the well-fed dogs curled up contentedly among the scrub spruce. Olaus rose and began carrying our gear from the sled to the cabin. Sheehy, in his red toque and blue shirt, his cheeks rosy and his blue eyes snapping in excitement, chattered away as he chopped with fascinating skill and speed with a big chisel affair, trimming the moss chinking inside and out.

"Yes, I guess you tink us ole Koyukuk fellas pretty funny bunch, livin' way we do, eh?"

"Yeh, I been in dis countree twenty-four year, yes. Never been out to de States, me, since I come Klondike in '98."

He picked up a handful of willow branches and, deftly twisting them into a broom, began brushing shavings and sawdust off the hewn-log floor.

"Um, lotsa difference out dere now, I guess—automobiles, airplanes. I never see airplane yet. See two automobiles; see one in Dawson, li'l one, and one in Fairbanks, beeg one, dat's all. You tink dat funny, eh? Well, we have to make our own fun up here; funny way to live, though, yes, I guess so. Now we put dese shaving in your stove, cabin soon be warm; I take my dogs home now; my partner and me, we come back see you awhile dis evening."

We had just finished supper when we heard the scrunching of steps in the snow and in they came, knocking the frost from their quickly doffed caps and immediately sinking to a tarp on the floor, leaving the one log chair for me.

It was cozy in the little cabin; we set three candles on the long shelf of hewn logs; the little stove buzzed and the warmth brought out the friendly spicy odor of new logs and tundra-moss chinking. There soon arose also the odor of boiling fudge; the last of our little can of cocoa, with the last of the raisins thrown in. The men lounged on the floor with their backs against the wall, and there were no pauses in the conversation.

I took the candy outside to cool and stood gazing at those myriad stars laughing over their silent big land again. The whole river glimmered between its jagged black friezes of spruces. The voices inside the cabin were contented yet sounded eager. Olaus was following his usual procedure, in his friendly quiet way drawing out from these men every bit of information they had on animals and birds and the country, always getting round to the topic of caribou: Where had they seen them? How many? In what direction were they traveling? How many years had they hunted them? Did they think they were more or less numerous now than ten years ago?

I took the fudge in, to the most appreciative guests one ever could have.

"Um-mm," said Fred, "I guess this is the first candy I've had for two years!"

Amid the clamor of harnessing up the dogs next morning, Marcel and his dogs arrived, and he stood upon the high bank and shouted some last words about our route: "One fella, Ed Marsan, he been down here other day from Porcupine Creek. You follow his track maybe; maybe wind blow 'em all away—dat Windy Arm bad place for wind, glare ice. I see you sometime, yes. Goodby!"

The Endicotts loomed very near that morning; the bluish streams of timber on their lower slopes were very clear.

Windy Arm was a gay place—four or five miles of blaring wind and a river of gleaming bare ice. Olaus at the gee pole, I on the handle bars—in this way we would cautiously leave the safety of snow surface and start across each stretch of glare ice. The dogs knew. They flattened themselves down and spread their legs until I realized the fitness of the term "crab-hounds." "Whoosh!" came the voice of Windy Arm. Olaus threw his weight against the gee pole; I stood with both feet on the brake, and its big steel teeth only made pretty scratches on the ice as around we went in a flash and came up against a snow bank many yards downstream.

The dogs whined complainingly; off we started again; slow going, but it was the only way we knew; we could not repeat the yanking-across-gravel-bar method any more. As the trail twisted among a maze of gravel bars and islands we did sometimes have a respite from the wind. But then, as we rounded a bend, "Bang! Whoo-oo-sh!" Old Man Wind of the River met us vociferously again. Few travelers came this way; he must amuse himself well with them. Yet by noon we had struggled beyond his reach.

The river was one straight channel again, sheltered by high cut banks. Here we stopped to eat our lunch of Jersey Creams and Swiss chocolate and water. That afternoon we found water too easily—ominous black slits where it boiled blackly, rapids, the last to be smothered by winter. We passed many such places, blessing Pooto as he gave each black gap a wide berth, gazing sidewise worriedly as he led his team past the danger. We were finding more virtues in Pooto every day.

An intriguing thought, how these men of the North place their lives in the keeping of these cousins of the wolf; the wolf, whom they call treacherous, cruel, enemy, whom they have pursued as treacherously and as cruelly. A dozen times that one day, Pooto, by a single false step, might have plunged us into dreadful danger. But Pooto knew the threat of open water in winter.

About three o'clock we sighted a cluster of cabins and a single plume of smoke. That meant Coldfoot. But directly before us lay a bewildering piece of river. The channel that seemed most thoroughly frozen led to the left around a half-mile maze of gravel bars in front of the village, and Sheehy had said to keep to the left limit, which meant our right-hand side. Here, between us in mid-channel and the solid ice near the bank, boiled a stretch of black water thirty feet wide. A bridge of ice no more than four feet wide had formed across this in one spot.

Pooto needed no "Whoa!" He immediately stopped and looked around at Olaus. Olaus slipped the ax from under the top lashings. Pooto lay down. No team can move if its leader lies down. I stood on the brake nevertheless, watching breathlessly while Olaus went across that slippery span, tapping with the head of the ax handle all the way. When he returned he smiled reassuringly and gave me my instructions: "Stand on the brake; that will keep the back of the sled from swerving. If anything happens climb right on top of the load if you can. I'm sure it's all right, though."

With Olaus leading Pooto by the collar, we went over the bridge very slowly in orderly fashion, and this time Fuzzy behaved himself. The ice on either side of the water boomed loudly just to add spice to the performance, but the bridge was safe.

It was a relief, however, a few moments later, to climb up a cleft in the high cut bank and trot over solid ground, between two rows of deserted cabins which had once been the busy mining camp of Coldfoot.

One family still lived there, Minano the Japanese, his Kobuk wife, and their numerous children. The oldest boy came out to greet us and to unlock the big log cabin, once the roadhouse and saloon, now used by the few travelers. A bar still stood along the wall in the front room; in the back room a huge French range occupied one end. Here there were homemade cupboards and four bunks filled with native swamp hay.

Our bean pot and skillet looked quite lost on that great expanse of stove, but the stove threw out gracious heat. We also had the luxury of a kerosene lamp on our supper table and were hugely enjoying talking about the little trials of that day when Minano came in, bursting with apologies and hospitality, all expressed in correct, even ornate, English. He was "so sorry, so sorry" to have been absent when we arrived. Yes, they had been caribou hunting, but no caribou. So sorry there were no better "comdations for a lady—hard trip for a lady—my, my!"

Minano told us, as he drank a cup of tea with us, of his coming across from Manchuria "many years away," of his years on the Arctic Coast with the whalers, of coming over the mountains into the Koyukuk in '99 when gold was struck here. And yet he did not look more than forty years old. The Koyukuk seemed to nurture a perennial population. There were no young white men, yet none seemed old. Roy King had told us that he, forty-four, was one of the "younger set" of the valley, and he didn't think there had ever been "a real young white woman" like myself in the Koyukuk!

Minano anticipated the usual question and informed us that the overland trail to Wiseman was passable. So here we would leave the winding river. But from Coldfoot it was not so winding anyway, for we were at last "in" the mountains; they rose all around us, on both sides of the river, and they seemed friendly and welcoming.

10

Wiseman

It was a beautiful world between Coldfoot and Wiseman, and only fourteen miles to travel. A delight to be tramping along behind the team, to breathe deeply the challenging keen air, to gloat over rugged white peaks glimpsed through an opening in the forest; a joy to feel blood pounding in your cheeks, every ounce alive and going, feeling the ecstatic warmth of vigorous exercise. The load was still heavy; the dogs traveled so slowly that Olaus could point out all the birds. Redpolls and chickadees sang greetings from every side; ravens made patterns across the blue sky, wheeling back and forth over the river below us; pine grosbeaks flitted across the trail; a willow grouse cuddled serenely under some low branches; and flitting through the trees, keeping us company and questioning in liquid rippling notes, were the gray jays, which have been called by various names—Alaska jay, Canada jay, camp robber, whiskey jack—but which are always and everywhere the companionable spirits of the wilderness.

Soon after noon we came out upon a high plateau, or bench, the Koyukuk far below us, mountains rising behind us. Over this bench the trail led down one little hummock, up onto another, and so on and on for about two hours. This was fun, especially the downhill sides, where we both rode on the sled and gazed down at the panorama of river, forest, and snowy mountain slopes spread below us.

We climbed from the plateau up a wooded hill, and among the trees on the top, in the middle of the trail, stood a horse. Our old hunter, Wolf, emitted a gurgled howl of astonishment and leaped straight for the poor old animal. In a second Olaus was at Pooto's head, I was on the brake, the horse's owner appeared on the run from the woods. Someday our savages might learn that all was not caribou which stood so high, but certainly they had seen no horses in Victoria Land.

The woodsman, stout and jovial—"Jack Hood's my name"— had curiosity and surprise written all over his face. We were the first dog-team arrivals of the season, and strangers at that. He was most cordial, and said he would wait at the top of the hill until we got down, "because the trail drops right off to the bottom here." And so it did! Olaus took the brake this time, while I made myself as flat as possible on the load and hung on to the ropes, and we went down a "chute-the-chutes" between stumps, a wild ride made wilder by the fact that the dogs had smelled the town.

So we continued to make good time through the woods at the bottom and arrived at the river, and there, on the other side, lay Wiseman, the northernmost settlement of white miners, snuggled under the mountains in a baylike bend of the river. We went careening out across the river toward the row of cabins. Several men appeared from various cabins as we drew near. A tall fellow, after being nearly knocked down by our eager dogs, directed us to the roadhouse—Olaus couldn't quite remember which place it was, but no doubt the dogs would have found it, for there were other dogs tied behind it and our team swung right round in a great flurry of anticipation and joined in with the chorus of greeting.

The roadhouse was one large cabin flanked by two smaller ones, both connected to the central one by enclosed passageways, so that it was all like one house. We walked through the front door. A long oilcloth-covered table stood along the right side; on the other, a short counter on which stood in solitary state a pair of gold scales. "What a nice reminder of the old stampede days," I thought.

There were voices in the kitchen beyond, and we had barely glanced around when a tall good-looking man with a great shock of black hair hurried in. Olaus greeted him and introduced him as Martin Slisco, proprietor. Although Olaus had stopped here only a day, two years earlier, he was remembered at once; I was greeted with old-world deference and invited to sit by the fire—a huge oil-drum heater—and be comfortable. He would get our room ready right away.

Olaus went out to put up the dogs and bring in our baggage. I sat in utter contentedness, surveying my surroundings and listening to the voices in the kitchen. First a low native guttural, then Martin Slisco's soft Dalmatian accent: "More shells? I give you whole box shells yesterday; you no catch 'em caribou; what kinda hunter you, eh?"

There was response in a low voice, then laughter. I gathered that the native hunter received more ammunition and departed to "catch 'em sure dis time."

Martin then began to bustle back and forth from the kitchen to the cabin which formed the right wing of the house and which was to be our room. All these men of the Koyukuk were a bit tongue-tied at first, but only at first. Martin was soon dashing in and out in a veritable fever of happy hospitality and talk, arms loaded with firewood and bedding. From that room of ours I heard the swishing of a broom, the rattling of the stove, the thumping of furniture, all accompanied by remarks, explanations, and questions about our trip.

In the midst of this Olaus came in with a dapper rosy-cheeked little old man whom he introduced as Judge Huey, the local commissioner and postmaster. Soon we were all chatting like old friends.

There was no constraint in that north country. People were few and had to make the most of one another's company; each individual was important. On first meeting, there is always the trail to discuss. The first question is not "How are you?" (It is obvious that you are in good health; otherwise you never would have arrived.) The first question is "How's the trail?"

And then: "How many dogs have you got?"

And that's the key which unlocks the floodgates. Everyone begins to talk dog. That one subject is sufficient to last far, far into the night. We had talked dog with every man we had met since we left Nulato. We would go on talking dog all through the Koyukuk. And when we had to go back to so-called civilized life again, we would keep it up until our friends would be bored—and then we would be homesick for the old dog conclaves of our honeymoon.

A rocking chair and a bed with springs are to be enjoyed

wherever met. The room Martin had made ready for us had both of these and a real dresser and table, store-made; a colorful carpet was on the floor, flowered stuff at the window, and wallpaper with great green-and-gold scrolls, which had been popular in Klondike days. Beauteous calendar ladies smiled from among the gold scrolls. The room was cozy and warm, and it was fun to play at being civilized lady and gentleman for a bit.

To make the most of the dresser, I spread out my few toilet articles, dug out my long hairpins, and brushed out the Minnehaha braids and did my hair up on top of my head. Folded carefully in the bottom of my little rucksack were my "best" brown plaid woolen shirt and my "better" tan wool knickers and golf socks. I put these on, along with my one pair of shoes, brown oxfords. I was dressed for dinner as well as I could manage. Soon we heard a buzz of masculine voices and a bustle and clatter in the main room, and supper was announced. Martin seated me at the head of that long table, and men began filing in from the opposite cabin, evidently the men's bunkhouse.

All were dressed as everyone was up there: woolen trousers, gay woolen shirts, moccasins or rubber shoe-pacs; but all were so very clean-looking, every hair carefully in place. They were very quiet, but I knew that wouldn't last long. Olaus had met some of them before, and Judge Huey at my right talked on eagerly, and then all the tongues were loosened and we were soon enjoying both Martin's good food and one another's company. I looked down that long table, with five men on each side, and realized I had never been in just this position before. "Are there no women here at all, then?" I asked Judge Huey.

"Oh yes, there are seven white women here, but they are nearly all up Nolan Creek now, at the mines. There are never very many of us down in town; we all have cabins here but are at the mines most of the time." (A new version of town and country home.) "But they will all be down to see you. I telephoned Mrs. Pingel. She remembers Mr. Murie."

I gasped inwardly at this, first at the news that the Koyukuk had some sort of telephone system, and then at the thought that our coming had been broadcast within an hour of our arrival!

Everyone at the table was besieging us with questions about all the affairs of the downriver settlements, and especially about Sam and his freight. When was he going to get some of it up here? Very little freight had been brought this far before the freeze-up. Now it would have to be hauled on the river by Jack White's horse teams or overland by native dog teams. There were no potatoes; yes, they sometimes raised them, but this year they all froze on the vine; no bacon, no eggs, no kerosene; just about everything was in short supply.

"You know," spoke up Bobbie Jones, a rosy-cheeked black-haired little man at the foot of the table, "we've all been in the Koyukuk so long we're afraid to leave it; we cuss the blame place and still we're so darn fond of it we keep on staying and digging and freezing and forking over all our dust to Sam, to get enough to eat to keep on digging and freezing and cursing the country. We've got the gold here all right, but if somebody doesn't find a way to get grub up here a little cheaper we'll all starve and be frozen up for good; a fellow can't eat gold dust and nuggets."

Early in the morning there was a loud pounding on our door. "Mr. Murie, Mr. Murie, get up! Dere's *millions* of caribou up the trail!"

It was Martin, his voice trembling with excitement. Olaus was in the middle of the floor pulling on his clothes before he had finished speaking. By the time I stumbled out to the kitchen Martin was there alone, eyes bulging with excitement.

Tony Borovich had started early for his mine on Porcupine Creek, three miles below Coldfoot. Only half a mile down the trail he had encountered, as he said, "thousands of caribou" blocking his trail. His dogs went crazy, but he managed to get them turned and raced back to give the news to the meat-starved community. He and Olaus had departed immediately, on foot.

Martin was serving me coffee and toast and caramel layer cake while he gave me all this news. Here was a great event. The caribou had not come so near Wiseman in years; they had always crossed over the range much farther north; and to think of their coming then, when meat and everything was so scarce!

Martin piled enamelware plates into his dishpan with a happy clatter. "Yes, ma'am, all the fellas who were here last night are gone caribou hunting. Judge Huey telephoned up Nolan Creek too, and I bet the whole bunch'll be down; won't be much gold mining done in dis neighborhood today. Dis makes lots of excitement for us—you folks coming, and the caribou too! You like dat cake, yes? All de ladies roun' here, dey teach me make

cake and pie. Sometimes I make pretty good. Here's the Judge now. I bet you wanna take Mrs. Murie away, huh? Don't you know I don't get to talk to young white woman very often?"

"Well, we have to make her divide her time, don't we?" replied the Judge.

I did want to see caribou, if that would be possible, so I swallowed the last bite of cake, slid down off the kitchen cupboard, and went to get my parka and mitts.

We had a nice walk and I heard a good deal of the Judge's past, and that of the Koyukuk, but saw no caribou. The trail was all trampled up with tracks of sleds and dogs and men. We returned to find that the Judge's telephone call was bringing results. Three dog teams were tied before the roadhouse, and I was glad to greet Mr. and Mrs. Long again, our fellow passengers on the *Teddy H.* Yes, they had got the cabin up, and it was snug. Mrs. Long said with a gay laugh: "Do come up and see all the beautiful furniture John and I have made out of milk cases. We may get so fond of it we won't even care if the other real pieces ever get this far upriver or not!"

Others were there too—Mrs. Allen, a lovely sweet-faced woman who had also come up here to teach and had married a miner; and Mrs. Pingel, who had been a missionary and had married a miner. We women chatted by the big stove while the men went on down the trail after that elusive herd of caribou, and Martin bustled about the kitchen preparing dinner for a large crowd and talking steadily.

The crowd began to foregather around noon. Most of them had seen no caribou and there was a great deal of light-hearted complaining; the caribou had been invented by Martin and the Judge to get them all down to the roadhouse for a meal! Just then Olaus and Tony Borovich came through the back door into the kitchen.

"Get one?" shouted the whole assemblage.

"No."

What a disappointment! Olaus, in my eyes, always got what he went after. Then someone yelled: "Oh, yeh? Where'd you get all that blood on your parkas then?"

They grinned then, and admitted they *had* got one, two in fact.

When we had finished our noisy, jolly meal, and the Nolan Creek people had departed, we hitched up our dogs and went out to bring in the specimens and meat. This was my first taste of dog mushing as done in the movies—sled empty except for the heroine, muffled in furs, the hero poised gracefully on the runners behind her, dogs racing along over a trail as smooth and hard-packed as white stone. The hunters of Nolan Creek had done this to our loose snowy trail of yesterday.

Out on the plateau the dogs and I watched while the two cow caribou were skinned. Here we found out another thing about our team; they had obviously been trained for hunting in their youth. They lay down quietly, watching every move, while Olaus skinned the two caribou and cut the meat into quarters—that is, all except Ungiak, who stood up the whole time, scarlet tongue dripping out of his mouth, ears and tail quivering with hope-fulness. Old Wolf lay down politely because Pooto did, but he informed us of his desires and hopes by means of comical rumblings and whines which sounded almost like words. All this time a flock of ptarmigan were wheeling over our heads, alighting and rising again with a great beating of wings, their immaculate white plumage shining in the sun.

As he worked away skinning the caribou, Olaus kept repeating how lucky he was. "Just think, I'm right here to see part of this migration, when there hasn't been a caribou migration through this part of the Brooks Range for as long as the older Indians can remember. You remember Old Tobuk, at Alatna, saying none of them could remember the last time a caribou migration had come through there, and that the caribou moss had grown up deep and thick everywhere? Here, hold this edge of the hide out for me, will you?"

"Well, then," I said, "did these caribou know that the lichens had finally grown up ready for the harvest in this part of the country?"

Olaus laughed. "Not individually, no, but racially they have a knowledge of some kind—of when it's time to shift to a new territory. And I'm certainly glad I was here when they shifted; this will give me a lot of interesting information and will fill in gaps in my study."

And he went on blissfully poking about in the caribou stomach he had just pulled out from one carcass. "This will give me valuable data on food habits too." To me it looked like a gory mess, but I had faith in the words of the biologist, and he was a patient teacher.

When the cutting up was finished and the sled loaded, the dogs were given a great feast before we started back to town, and then we traveled back to the roadhouse in our usual slow sedate style.

Back in the roadhouse kitchen, those who hadn't dispersed to the mines were swapping stories of the day's almost fruitless hunt for caribou. The herd was probably many miles south of Wiseman by this time, but the gang at the roadhouse would have liver for supper, and Martin would have meat to serve for a little while; Tony Borovich was on his way home with plenty of meat, and we would have plenty to take on upriver. Olaus had an interested audience while he took care of his specimens on the kitchen floor, having first taken all the scientific measurements. The hide must be complete; headskin to hoofs in one piece. Olaus was explaining how, in all museum specimens, the hide and the complete skull make up one specimen; so the skull must be carefully cleaned of all meat, measured, dried, wrapped, and given a specimen number, so that it can be matched up with the hide.

We all sat around on chairs and on Martin's cot and heard tales of hunting and mining, of drinking and fighting, in this far outpost. In the old days this place must have been like the Wild West of the story books. What a mixture of terrible deeds and kindly deeds!

A tall man named Jim was telling a yarn about the old days. Once, when he had got rather tipsy, he got hold of the only horse and buggy in the Koyukuk and invited two old Indian women to go riding with him. They ended up careening down Wiseman's one street and off the bridge into Wiseman Creek.

Jack Holzer then spoke up: "Speaking of newlyweds, we had

one interesting wedding down at Coldfoot years ago. You fellows remember, when Jack Bridges wanted to marry that young Indian Eva, and the only fellow who could marry people up here was the U.S. Commissioner—this was before Judge Huey's time. It was late at night, but Jack and the girl wanted to start for the mines, so a bunch of us fellas got the old commissioner out of bed. He kept saying he had to have a book; he couldn't marry anybody without a book. He had a Bible up at Wiseman, but that was too far away. So I looked around the roadhouse there and the only book I could see was the Sears Roebuck catalogue, and I handed it to the old commissioner and said: 'Here, Judge, here's a book—now go ahead and marry this pair.' And that's just what he did! They got along fine, too; they're still living together, down on the Yukon somewhere."

All this talk was interrupted by comments, philosophical or otherwise, from the other fellows. These tales were local history well known to them all, but they were enjoying having it told to newcomers. Some of these men had lived together for twenty- six years on this one stretch of river. Their relations were still apparently harmonious; at least they were humorously tolerant of one another. On the frontier, anyone lacking a sense of humor is inevitably weeded out, and only those who can laugh at it all are able to remain. And a delightfully humorous-philosophical bunch these men were. Jack Holzer and Jim, partners since the beginning, a handsome pair they must have been. Here they were, after twenty-five years, still looking for the gold, finding it, spending it. So with all the rest—our friend Jack Hood, the man who owned the terrified horse we had met; George Eaton, seventy-four years old, sitting on the bed in the corner nursing a rheumatic knee; the debonair rosy-cheeked Bobbie Jones. All were bachelors, severed from family ties, all remarkably young-looking, vigorous, laughing at the past, apparently unafraid of the future. Yet I wondered about them. I wondered if they didn't sometimes puzzle about it all, and think the same thoughts expressed by Fred Swift, the Vermonter.

11

The Mountains

From the diary:

"Gold Creek, October 25: We left Wiseman with just a light outfit rather late today, bound for the heart of these Endicott Mountains and the collecting of more caribou. Early in the trip Olaus had tried to explain to my ignorant mind the scientific reasons for collecting specimens of the arctic herd, for studying their food habits in winter, for observing their migration; it would close a gap in his previous three years' work of gathering facts about caribou all over Alaska. He had explained that this northern, or arctic, herd is separated from the herds farther south in interior Alaska, and we don't know much about these northernmost animals. One problem we have is in the identification of the caribou of Alaska. Do they all belong to the barren-ground species? That's why they need specimens from up here. Then, too, they know that the farther north you go, the more room the animals need. That's why the government biologists need to know what the caribou live on, in winter especially, and what is there for them to eat. It is significant that the woodland caribou in the far south do not travel far. But these barren-ground caribou of the Arctic have tremendous migrations. Why? So Olaus has for three years been following the caribou, all over Alaska and Yukon Territory, learning all he can about their lives, and about the motivations they have learned racially. In winter by dog team, in spring by poling boat and raft on the rivers, in summer afoot, with three or four dogs carrying small packs; and now here we are on the trail of the arctic herd."

Olaus had learned that the caribou have traditional migration routes throughout their vast homeland, but that sometimes there is a sudden shift to a new territory. That is why he had been so elated at being at Wiseman at the right moment to see one of these shifts taking place. His study was to be a complete life-history study, to be published as a government bulletin, and it involved learning their migration routes, the sizes of the various herds, their food habits, their winter and summer ranges, their breeding and calving, and the parasites and predators which preyed upon them. Throughout his study, one fact had impressed him—that somehow the caribou had learned, racially, to keep on the move, so as not to eliminate the food supply in any one place, for arctic vegetation renews itself slowly, especially the lichens, or "reindeer moss," which is their favorite, though not their main, food.

"Tonight we are in a cabin at the mouth of Gold Creek (and I am wondering how many Gold Creeks there must be in Alaska!), only twelve miles upriver from Wiseman. We are here because Eskimos are leisurely travelers. We have become cheechakos for the time being and have an Eskimo guide. The lad from the 'arctic' tribe, over the range to the north, who had been hunting for Martin Slisco, has agreed to show Olaus the caribou range, since he is traveling that way anyway—the consideration for this service being some dog fish. Another Eskimo with another dog team is traveling part way with us. Our guide's Eskimo name I do not know—he is called Jack Horner.

"We found the cabin here occupied by Hans Christianson, a Danish old-timer on his way to his mine up this creek. He wanted to move out and sleep in his sled, but of course Olaus would not listen to that. He explained to Hans that 'my wife is a sourdough—she doesn't mind.'

"Hans had his bean pot already on the stove and a good fire going, and I made biscuits for the three of us and we had a good meal. The two Eskimos had their tent up outside and a stove in it, but they came in after supper and as I write are seated immovable and inscrutable on the floor behind the stove, watching us. Olaus is also writing his notes. Hans is making a fancy candlestick out of a milk can. He tells me that he can make a pretty good one out of a coffee can and a dried-egg can, and that he will make me one while I am upriver, 'just for a souvenir of the Koyukuk.' He is a blacksmith by trade and has worked in the mines, but 'a man would rather have a claim of his own, even if he don't make much better.'

"The Northern Lights are sweeping across the sky behind the white mountains and the dogs are restless. Bingo has been chastised twice for starting all four teams into a wilderness chorus.

"October 27—*Our own camp, thirty miles above Wiseman:* So snappily cold that it was joy to run behind the sled all day, to keep warm. I shall never want to ride in a dog sled anyway; it would be like being demoted from first mate to mere passenger. More fun to hold to the ends of the handle bars and pad along, swifter, swifter, as the dogs pace along over the hard-packed snow with a light load, with Olaus running alongside, laughing. Sometimes I thought I surely could not put one foot ahead of the other fast enough to keep hold of those bars!

"We came all the way on the river, and all the way the snow was packed hard by the hoofs of caribou, that herd which so enlivened Wiseman town. In many places a trough almost a foot deep had been worn in the cut banks of the river, where thousands had crossed over. We began to wonder if they have *all* left the mountains!

"About noon the two Eskimo teams ahead of us stopped. Jack Horner's companion was leaving us here, to go east to Bettles Lake to get his little daughter, who is in the winter village of the Arctics. We watched in wonder while Jack Horner with his finger drew in the snow a diagram of the route to Bettles Lake. He drew a few lines, pointed to a mountain across from us, and spoke about ten words in Eskimo. His companion nodded that he understood, walked back to his own sled, hopped on, and was gone.

" 'Why,' I exclaimed, 'if they were white men they would powwow and explain and re-explain for ten minutes before they would be sure!'

" 'Yes,' said Olaus. 'I always marvel at it too, but they are real wilderness travelers, you know. It's their whole life.'

"We traveled on for three hours more. The river was becoming narrow and more twisting with each mile, and we were encircled by mountains, their wooded lower slopes rising directly from the riverbanks. No more could we look far north to snowy peaks; we were among them; we must lift our eyes up, up, to see, beyond the belt of trees, fantastic outcroppings of yellow sandstone, and then white summits.

"When Jack Horner stopped his team, we were in a spot where mountains seemed to close the river in, where spruces marched down to the very edge of the bank. Up on top of the bank, in a little clear space back among the trees, we made our first real tent camp, leaving the sled on the river below the steep bank and bringing the dogs up, one at a time, chaining each to a tree around the clearing. Then I had my first real lesson in making camp in winter.

"Though we had stopped traveling for the day, I put on my snowshoes and tramped back and forth in a ten-foot-square space where the tent had to be, until the snow was packed down nice and smooth. Meanwhile the song of the ax was ringing and Olaus called to me: 'Mardy, do you think you could take the little hatchet and cut the branches from these trees we've cut down? Do be careful not to cut toward your foot, you know.'

"I managed to cut off all the branches without cutting my foot—yes, I was learning a little—and we proceeded to put up the tent. Tent pegs next, and Olaus patiently showed me how to tie them. By the time we reached this point Jack Horner had his wickiup all pitched, under a big tree down the bank, and had come to observe the elaborate ways of white folks. After helping us make a floor and bed of the branches, he must have thought it looked pretty comfortable, for he announced: 'I take some too.' Olaus said: 'Sure, you take some,' and he went off with an armload for his tiny shelter. He came back in a few minutes and cut us some firewood and helped install the little Yukon stove in the tent.

"As we carried up our housekeeping supplies from the sled to the camp, dusk was dropping swiftly—a rose glow tipped the mountains across the river, but mauve shadows crowded the valley; the woods were black. We were hurrying now—sleeping bags, duffel bag, grub bag, the utensils; doesn't it look homey? Throw a fish to each dog, make a fire in the stove, mix some bannock, put on the skillet for ptarmigan and caribou.

"Dark now, and outside are the stars, so close and so bright, and a great horned owl is speaking from woodsy depths where trees are cracking in the increasing cold. The contented dogs make seven black circles in the snow. Jack Horner has taken a gift of bannock and ptarmigan and gone happily over to his own fire. His dogs are well fed tonight and so is he—the Eskimo asks no more of Providence.

"October 28: The hunt began today and certainly Jack knows where the caribou are. At noon they were back with two specimens and spent the afternoon dressing the hides and taking care of the meat. We had delicious liver for supper.

"Now, supper over, our eight-by-ten tent holds a rather interesting scene. While I sit on the sleeping bags writing notes, Olaus, across the tent is cleaning the caribou skulls. I was quite horror-stricken when a cow caribou skull with its stubby antlers was shoved through the tent flap and the operation began, but the process has a fascination after all, and where but in the tent could it be done in twenty below zero?

"I marvel at the deftness with which meat is carved from the jaws, eyes scooped out with one expert dip of the knife, brains pulled out through the foramen magnum with a loop made of baling wire, all deposited neatly on blocks of stovewood. At the end of the operation these will be carried out and the dogs will receive some frozen tidbits later on. And all this has been going to the accompaniment of a discussion of great paintings we have seen!"

For six weeks Olaus and I had been apart for only a few hours now and then. The last two days of October it was all different. The three caribou hides had to be dried for shipment. They were hung on a rope stretched inside the ridgepole from one end of the tent to the other, and for those two days I stayed there to keep the fire going in the tiny stove to dry the hides, while Olaus hunted more caribou atop the mountain across the river. Imagine an eight-by-ten tent occupied by three caribou hides, including hoofs, various camp equipment, one girl, no reading matter, and you have the picture. I was learning a bit more about being married to a scientist.

I kept poking wood into the fire, turned the hides around, draped them in various positions for quicker drying, arranging the little sticks that held the hoofs wide apart so they would dry inside, taking as long for each operation as I possibly could—the first time I had ever consciously engaged in killing time.

Why had I been so zealous in paring down our load at

Wiseman? Here I was without a magazine or a book; the little Dunsany book could just as well have been put in. Oh well, at least there was some enjoyment in knowing how the many lone trappers and miners in that north country must feel. All my life I had heard stories about their having nothing to do but read the labels on cans. That second day I read every label in the grub bag. The milk cans were especially nice; they had recipes on them. I looked them over, but they had all come out of the same case, I guess, so I memorized the recipe for creamed clams that was on every one of them. Hard to tell when we should ever see a clam! Our ham was wrapped in a page from a magazine, and I shall forever be wondering whether the wandering son got back to the old homestead and his childhood sweetheart before his poor old mother passed away!

Well—time to turn the hides over again. I got used to their odor and didn't mind so much having them dangling over my shoulders whichever way I turned; caribou hides were never so carefully nursed. And I did have the dogs for company, and when too stiff from sitting, I could go out for a few minutes' romp with Ungiak; but soon it was time to crawl back in and stoke the fire again.

On the first day, Jack Horner was in camp part of the day, but toward noon he had his sled loaded. He had done his duty by Olaus, and he had all the meat he could carry on his sled. His people at Bettles Lake would surely welcome him! I put into his hands a last little gift of bannock, and stood and watched him disappear down the river. He had seemed so much quieter than our Kobuks; he did not speak much English and seemed perfectly matter-of-fact as he departed, but before his team rounded the bend, he turned, looked back at me, and lifted his arm in farewell. I walked back to our tent—time to stoke the fire again. Pooto, curled in the snow, cocked his white eyebrow at me as though to say: "Only you here?"

At four o'clock it was dark, and by that time it had been a long day in the tent. As I look into my diary of that date I find only one long sentence, which does not tell the truth:

"I sat for what seemed endless hours, listening to the dark sounds—owls, trees cracking in the cold; sat and gazed at the red eye of the stove draft and wondered—if—should I go look for him myself or hitch up the dogs and go to Wiseman for help, and how quickly could I make it?"

The truth was that when Olaus finally arrived at about eight

o'clock, safe and sound, with a big bull caribou head on top of his pack, and dropped his huge load of head, hide, and meat and crawled into the tent, he found his bride in her sleeping bag sobbing wildly.

Now, after all the years, I can't remember just why I was crying. I do remember that after four o'clock, when it was too dark to go out to play with Ungiak or go down to the river and look upstream I couldn't seem to keep warm in the tent any more even though I kept poking wood into the stove. I crept into my sleeping bag to keep warm. As soon as I lay down, my imagination went galloping, not worried for myself—I have never minded being alone in the wilderness; it has always seemed a friendly place—but wondering how it could possibly take Olaus that long to go up to the site of the caribou kill, load up that one animal, and come back. Pictures flashed through my mind of every kind of mishap—the gun, the river ice, the steep mountainside. But above all, the realization that in another hour, surely, I would have to make a decision. I would have to hitch up the dogs— could I manage them? And then—to go upriver or down?

After two hours of this kind of feminine illogic, to hear at last the sudden yelping of the dogs when they heard him coming, unloosed a real torrent. There he was, kneeling, leaning over me, taking me in his arms. "Oh, Mardy, darlin', what's the matter? Are you hurt?"

"Hurt? No, of course not, just worried, worried, worried!

Didn't you *know* I'd be worried? It was so *long*. I thought
something had happened to you!"

"Oh no, you know I'm always careful. It just took so long to get
the hide scraped so I could carry it back. Things take longer than
you think, you know. I'll have to make one more trip up there
tomorrow too. But you can go along; I can dry this last skin when
we get back to Wiseman."

Olaus paused, and lifted my face from his shoulder. "Is there
anything to eat?"

I came out of that sleeping bag in a hurry! A few minutes later
we sat close together by the stove, each with a plate of caribou
chops, beans, bannock, and honey.

Otto and Heinie had given us the honey from a large can they
had brought up from Nulato. They had put some for us into a Log
Cabin Syrup can. And on this night I discovered, scratched into
the lacquer after the words 'Log Cabin,' the message: "Honey for
the honeymooners. May all your journeys be sweet and pleasant.
Otto and Heinie."

This was the message for October 31!

Climbing a mountain on snowshoes is an entirely different affair
from flip-flopping over the tundra on them. It was such a release
to be out of the tent and going along again, such fun crossing the
river, with Ungiak running circles around us in jubilation at being
allowed to go along too. But by the time we were halfway up the
mountain I was puffing outrageously, and had fallen down and
painfully untangled myself seven times while Ungiak helpfully
stepped all over me and the snowshoes. I had also lost a lot of
breath just laughing, and my throat seemed sealed and dry.
Visions of frosty lemonades and ice-cream sodas floated
irrepressibly through my mind.

Ungiak and I were finally left to sit on a hummock and eat snow
while Olaus sped on up to the summit, seemingly as effortlessly as
a caribou. Could I ever achieve that physical efficiency? I
suddenly seemed to hear dear old Jim Hagan's voice back in
Fairbanks that previous winter: "You go ahead and marry that
fellow; he's a fine one. The only thing is, I don't know how you're
ever going to keep up with him. He's half caribou, you know."

But I had kept within fifty feet today, at least halfway! If I
could always keep within fifty feet . . . .

Although I don't remember exactly why I cried in the tent, I do remember sitting on the mountainside the next day having a real session with my thoughts. I had learned something about our life together. I had sobbed into Olaus's shoulder: "Didn't you *know* I'd be worried?" thinking only of myself. And he had answered: "Oh no, things take longer . . ."

There it was, and I knew I had better change my thinking to conform to it or grow into a nervous, nagging, unhappy wife. The work came first. "All a scientist has is his integrity."

The bride who happened to be along on the collecting trip had better learn not to worry. So far as I knew, our life was to be one long field trip; this I had known and been eager for. But I had never faced the fact that sometimes I would have to stay behind in camp, and wait after darkness, and wonder. I must learn to trust, to wait serenely.

That hour on the snowy mountainside was good for me. I came to terms with being a scientist's wife. Since then, in many camps in many mountains, I have waited, and fed the children, and put them into their sleeping bags, and still, long past the normal hour, have kept busy—and waited. "Things take longer than you think, you know."

Usually, by the time I really begin to wonder, I hear a long coyote howl, our signal that he is coming.

That afternoon, from the mountainside where Ungiak and I waited, the slopes flanking the river looked like chalk drawings, chalk-blue lines and ranks of trees filling all the little gullies, reaching up toward the tops of all the ridges, giving way at last to the chalk-white of snowy summits; these two colors. Yet an hour later as we came running and sliding down to the valley, the western sky was flame-red as it so often is in the Arctic in winter, dyeing the mountaintops a rose color, lifting the forest into inky black contrast. Upriver there was Mars again, blinking his red eye at the red sunset. Night comes swiftly and dramatically in November in the North. It was long past dark when we got back to camp, but that didn't matter. I was snowshoeing along with Olaus, not curled up back there in that tent.

But there is one wonderful thing about a tent; it gets warm in no time once the fire is blazing. We splurged and lit three candles that night, and very soon there were caribou steaks, tender and golden brown, with hot bannock and more of the honey. Caribou, no matter how lean or how fresh, is never tough.

Olaus mixed the bannock that night and it was especially good. Flour, lard, salt, baking powder, and water were added together to form a stiff batter, which was dropped by spoonfuls into the skillet and baked to a golden brown, and then turned and baked on the other side. The result: soft flaky biscuits with a crisp brown crust on both sides. To split the bannock and add butter and honey, while sitting on a spruce-bough bed in a warm tent—what more could one ask?

Waking early in the morning, we lay and listened to what sounded like a ladies' sewing circle outside our tent—the ptarmigan, with more variations of cluckings and chucklings and calling than any brood of domestic chickens can produce, and all of it serene and cozy-sounding. "Come here, come here," some seemed to say. "Go back, go back," said others.

Olaus reached out from his bag and touched a match to the shavings laid in the stove. "Go back, go back, that's for us, I guess," he said. "Tomorrow, real early, we'll have to start back."

If it were up to us, we would have gone on farther north, for Olaus would have loved a few days on those northern slopes. From the top of the mountains, on our first day here, Olaus and Jack Horner had looked over to the arctic slopes—more hills, stepping down toward the tundra and the Arctic Ocean. Jack Horner and all his people are called "arctic people"; they are not of the Kobuk tribe, but they frequently travel the hundred or more miles over the Endicotts to hunt.

So, wondering and speculating about that unknown country, we packed our gear and worked some more on the specimens. On the fourth of November we would vote at Wiseman; my first, and no doubt northernmost, vote. Alaskans could not vote for President of the United States, but we would get the returns of that election over the newly established radio station at Wiseman.

From the diary:

"November 3: We rose at four o'clock, when it was still pitch dark except for a moon gleaming wanly. The dogs gazed sleepily at such untimely preparations. By six-thirty our first wilderness home was completely demolished, the equipment all stowed in the sled. The dogs had fully awakened and were putting on the usual ear-splitting harnessing-up chorus.

"Generally we have the sled tied to a tree until the instant of departure, but down on the river this was impossible, and when the wheel dogs, the little fighters Fuzzy and Mally, were buckled in, Olaus crept back stealthily, never taking his hands off the sled and softly murmuring: 'Whoa, whoa,' to Pooto until he had reached the handle bars. I flung myself onto the load as the outfit sped past me. What a wild eagerness to go to work, to get into harness and pull! I wonder if any animal on earth is as crazy to work as the Alaskan dog. If this exuberance could be expressed exclusively in speed, it would be great, but before we had rounded the first bend in the river, the two little rascals in the wheel had pounced on each other and the whole team was in a pile.

"We are perfecting a technique in this dog-fight business. At the first pounce I leave the sled and run up to Pooto, who is always the last one to join in. If I can get there before he turns upon the dogs behind him, I take him by the collar and drag him out as far as possible. This stretches the towline and gives Olaus a chance to get in more effective work with the loaded butt of the whip. That whip is never used except to keep these fight-loving, tough-skinned savages from destroying one another. A good dog musher is never found whipping his dogs to make them pull, but fights have to be stopped no matter how much the dogs enjoy them!

"We had three dog fights this morning, the usual result of having dogs tied up for several days, and we had just got into a peaceful trot after the third one when we struck an overflow. We had rather expected this, for we knew it had been twenty to thirty degrees below zero while we were camping. This meant that the ice had been thickening, reaching down toward the stream bottom, pushing water up through some weak spot, to flow over the surface ice.

"Not far above the mouth of Gold Creek, Pooto stopped and looked around inquiringly. A line of gray stretched before us— water on the river ice and snow with a thin slushy coating of ice on top of it. This overflow extended clear across the river, so we had no choice but to proceed. Keeping close to shore, we went splashing through a few inches of water, but as we traveled downstream it became deeper, until water lapped the canvas-wrapped load, instantly changing to ice. Pooto went on steadily; Olaus had climbed onto the front of the sled, I onto the back. We were both wearing moccasins. We knew that if there were any holes in the solid river ice Pooto would stop in time.

"A quarter of a mile further down we came to the end of the

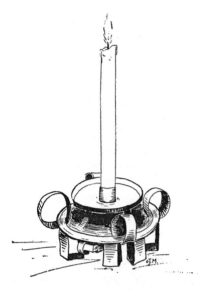

overflow; the snow shone white and dry and safe just ahead. But to get us and the loaded sled up onto this was another matter, for the ice over the flow became thicker; the bow of the sled was breaking through with difficulty and finally, reaching the edge of the solid ice, had to be pulled up as onto a shelf. Here the front of the sled stuck, the dogs trying to get a footing on the edge of the solid ice. There we sat, Olaus and I and the sled, in a foot of water while Pooto tried valiantly to dig his toenails into glare ice, and all around us the ice cracked loudly. 'Wait a minute,' said Olaus, 'stay with the sled.'

"Reaching over the bow of the sled, he pulled in the six feet of towline behind the wheel dogs, pulling the whole team back against the sled. Then, yelling 'All right' in most urgent tones, he let go suddenly, the dogs leaped forward, and by this added impetus the sled bounced up onto solid ice.

"Overflows are the most sinister of all arctic dangers. All the dog-team accidents I have known about have been caused by overflow. Sometimes whole teams have been plunged into a fatal hole; many times drivers have got wet and, unable to start a fire, suffered frozen hands or feet before reaching help. The overflow is more deadly because it is accompanied by cold weather, and only those who have experienced it can appreciate the horror of a plunge into ice water in forty-below weather. This is another reason for the waterproof match safes and the candle stubs or can of Sterno which Olaus and other mushers carry in the big front pockets of their parkas.

"Two more overflows we traveled through this morning, and when we passed Sheep Creek at noon we felt great relief, for it was the last of the creeks along this stretch notorious for overflowing out onto the river. At this happy hour breakfast seemed weeks ago, and we dug out our chocolate and Jersey Creams from the ditty bag; the dogs were given a little snack of caribou. We sat on the sled, munching happily; the contented dogs were lying down; Bingo sat up and gazed at the scenery. These short hours of blue sky and sun are glorious. Stray wisps of cold-weather fog still hung about the snout of the teapot-shaped yellow sandstone mountain we had admired on the way upriver.

"We estimated, or rather Olaus did, that the thermometer had risen to ten below, ideal mushing weather, and we were getting over our route in such good time despite overflows and fights that we stopped to take photographs and to enjoy each hawk owl, each flock of redpolls and crossbills we saw. This is dog mushing at its thrilling best. The dogs were happy too, trotting along with ears erect, tails curled and waving.

"At three o'clock we were off the river, where a cold breeze had just begun to blow, and up on the wooded trail, nearing Wiseman. I stepped up on the runners and stood backward to watch the glory of another short arctic day ending. It seems that to compensate for its fleeting hours, the winter day begins and ends in a riotous prodigality of color—red to rose, to vermilion streaked and fringed with ocher, saffron, lemon—but all so brief, fading as you try to imprint it in memory, now pale green, now the stars; the mountains draw away into darkness, close black ranks of spruce draw near.

"Thoughts slip back to earthly matters. I turned and called to Olaus: 'You know what? I'm going to eat everything I can find in Martin's kitchen when we get in!'

"Olaus looked over his shoulder. (How blue his eyes were under the white frosted fur of his parka ruff.) 'You are huh? Well, I feel that way too, but you know it isn't a good idea. We've been running nearly all day, and it isn't good to eat a lot as soon as you get in. Best to wait a while.'

"While we argued about this matter a yellow light twinkled down the trail, then another, and we were in Wiseman, pulling up behind the roadhouse barn. I snatched an armload of duffle and rushed through the back door.

"Heavenly fragrance! Could it be? Yes, warm golden loaves, round ones, rows of cinnamon rolls, and Martin, rising from before the oven with an enormous pan of coffee cake in his hands, and a great shout of greeting. 'Well, well, I thought you come back today; yes, I had good luck with my bread dis time, and old Jim he told me 'bout cinnamon rolls—you like 'em?'

"Did I like 'em? Did I like the fragrance from the coffee-pot on the huge range, the warm friendliness of the big kitchen? Five minutes later Olaus found me sitting on the corner of the cupboard, a cinnamon roll in one hand, a piece of coffee cake in the other. He said nothing—only grinned and held out his hand—and I put a cinnamon roll into it. Martin yelled toward the bunkhouse door: 'Come on, you fellas—the Muries are back!'

"Everyone was in town for the election, and the supper table was a steady buzz of talk. It was like coming home to a large family—a family really glad to see you again. The mailman had arrived and already departed on his first trip, in our absence, and there was much news of the outside world to be handed round the supper table. 'Oh yes,' said Martin, 'he brought your mail. I hear the Judge say you got twenty-four letter!'

"This was said in a somewhat awe-struck voice. At that point in came the Judge with the twenty-four letters. Personal service in the Far North!"

In Wiseman in those days there was a chapter of the Order of Pioneers of Alaska. In addition, they had a Pioneer Hall, a low square building of logs, with benches all around the walls and a piano in one corner. At two tables near the piano the elections for Wiseman Precinct were going on. Judge Huey and Mr. and Mrs. Pingel were officiating, and it was something of a social gathering. In another corner chances were being sold on a mountain sheep. An Eskimo hunter had learned the money-making schemes of the white man. The sheep was to be raffled off at the big dance that night. We voted, and bought chances, and chatted with the assembled voters. Mrs. Pingel, an intelligent woman, once a missionary, had been in the Koyukuk for many years, and kept a motherly eye on the welfare of all its inhabitants.

The election of 1924, as far as Wiseman Precinct was concerned, was a huge success. Accompanied by most of the roadhouse family, we went to the Pioneer Hall at nine o'clock that evening. (Olaus and I had dressed up as much as we could—he in a new navy-blue wool shirt, I in my good brown plaid and my hair done up on my head.)

The benches on one side were lined with men, forty-five of them, and on the other side sat five women. Mrs. Pingel took us in tow and introduced as to those we had not met. Everyone seemed determined that we should have a good time; there is no doubt in the world that we did, but Olaus had a much less strenuous night than I had, for it seemed that most of the forty-five men wanted to dance—and only five women to go around! Two of these were the daughters of Minano of Coldfoot, very pretty girls. One of them was married to the local deputy marshal, a good-looking middle-aged giant, who seemed cordial and kindly.

There was a sixth woman, an auburn-haired lady, but she was the music; her piano provided quite good dance music, and soon the hall was reverberating to laughter and the shuffle of feet. Olaus and I stepped out on the floor for the first dance; we had danced about ten steps when Jack Holzer tapped Olaus on the shoulder. "You can dance with your wife the rest of your lives; we can only dance with her tonight!"

Wiseman folk knew how to make the most of their social events. The scarcity of women was cleverly compensated for by the marshal, who announced "tag dance" nearly every other dance. There would follow a mad rush of all the stags, and a raucous melee, in which we women changed partners about every five steps, and when the music ceased we were led breathless to our seats. The revelry went on, everyone entering in with childlike glee.

After a while there was a pause. I had to sing a song for them, Mrs. Pingel insisted. There was no dissuading her, and the pianist found a popular song I knew, "Little Love Ship." Then one of the younger prospectors, a man named Miller, who had just come in from the creeks, sang "When I Leave the World Behind" in a very good tenor. The best number was a jig danced by old Dad Eaton and one of Minano's children, a sober-eyed little lady of ten years. Here was a picture: the twinkling-eyed old fellow and the little girl with shining black braids, whose serious eyes never left her partner's feet as she stood opposite him and followed his steps perfectly with the unconscious grace that all these girls had.

The mountain sheep was the next event. It was lugged in by four stalwarts and placed on a table at the front of the room. Then the drawing took place. It was won by Mrs. Green, the marshal's young wife, and we were promptly invited to eat some of it with them the next evening.

It was now midnight, and the Judge announced that supper was being served at the roadhouse. We had all danced up an appetite and attacked with jolly fervor the cold meats, sandwiches, and cakes spread on the long tables. During the supper someone kept running between the roadhouse and the Signal Corps office, bringing the election returns from the faraway States. The citizens of Wiseman could not marvel enough at this. "And usually, before, it would be a month before we knew who was President!"

After that the dance went on and on—that auburn-haired lady had staying power! It was five o'clock in the morning when we said good-by to a memorable party and with Martin and the rest hobbled over to the roadhouse in the darkness—that is, I hobbled; the men were all fresh and still voluble—they had not danced *constantly* since nine o'clock the night before! But we felt so grateful to be able to take away with us the memory of a real frontier party in a little log building on the last real frontier. Here was I, raised in "Alaska's Golden Heart" yet only now having my first taste of life beyond the "comforts" of civilization. We had found that life good and we were thinking regretfully of our trip southward; we had not had enough of this Koyukuk, of these people who had so taken us into their lives.

In Martin's kitchen that afternoon we all gathered again, and there were gifts. Hans Christianson arrived from up Gold Creek bringing the "Koyukuk candlestick" he had promised, and a treasure it was; there is even a tiny matchbox which slides in under the base of the candlestick, all made from two cans!

The Pingels came to say good-by, bringing a beautiful nugget for me. Our jolly friend Jack Hood brought me three quaint nuggets, one a strange thin one shaped like a curled whip, "to beat your husband with"! The three nuggets were presented to me in a tiny poke made of ermine with the figure of a mountain sheep appliqued on it, the work of an Eskimo girl.

In the midst of all our visiting, old Dad Eaton came into the kitchen carrying a canvas sack such as banks use for holding gold coin. He came to me and dumped the contents into my lap—gold nuggets, none smaller than an egg, and all of weird, unusual shapes! Collecting large and odd-shaped nuggets was this sourdough's hobby. Whenever he met anyone with such a nugget he traded him the equivalent in dust and added the nugget to his collection. So for a few minutes I held in my lap fifteen hundred dollars in large nuggets, a pretty heavy lapful! I had learned that the gold scales I had thought merely a relic of the early days were an everyday necessity here in the Wiseman roadhouse; after each meal we had watched some miners pouring the price of a meal from their leather pokes into those scales.

Then in came that handsome pair Jack Holzer and Jim. They wanted me "to have something to remember the two renegades of the Koyukuk by," and there it lay in my hand, a perfect replica of a lucky horseshoe nail, beaten and carved from pure Koyukuk gold. Olaus and I both exclaimed in wonder, and Jack then explained that he had "learned the jeweler's trade once, and still knew some of the tricks."

We had a delightful dinner at the Greens'. I had heard that the young wife, Mamie, had been a protegee of Mrs. Allen's when she had taught in Wiseman. She had poise and a natural quiet charm. The house was well and tastefully furnished, the table set correctly and prettily with shining silver and china. Mamie told me that her father, Minano, had been a chef in his youth and had taught all his girls to cook. The mountain sheep, the most delicious meat of the wild, was roasted to perfection, and more important, there were real vegetables from the marshal's own garden. Afterwards we had fine music from a beautiful big phonograph. As Marshal Green put it with pardonable pride: "Pretty nice, we think, to be able to hear John McCormack singing all these Irish songs way up here in what most folks would call 'nowhere'!"

These people were living in grace and comfort far north of the circle. They had serenity.

As we walked back to Martin's we were both silent. At last I said: "You know, darlin', if you were a gold miner instead of a scientist, we could just stay here!"

12

Southward

We were traveling south on the overland route, jogging along over the best trail we had had so far. I could ride on the runners at the handle bars most of the way, and often Olaus left the gee pole and sat on the load up front while we talked over the past weeks, which would light our lives forever. We rather missed being down there on the river, but Marshal Green had warned us that the river along this stretch was too dangerous since colder weather had come—too many overflows.

Twelve miles below Coldfoot we found the mail relief cabin, more spacious by far than the North Fork hovel, nestled among big trees at the foot of a hill. We were pretty tired after all the social life at Wiseman and went to bed immediately after supper, planning to rise at five o'clock to get a good start on the thirty-three miles of notoriously rough going we had to get through the next day in order to reach King's.

My sleeping bag was next to the outside wall, and I was roused from a deep sleep by a sudden *crunch, crunch* of snow. I thought: "One of the dogs is loose. I'll have to call Olaus."

Then came a loud, hearty voice: "Hello, here! Who's here?"

Fred Swift, of Tramway Bar! He crawled through the square canvas door covering and loomed giantlike in the gloom. "Hope you weren't asleep yet. I'm camped half a mile across here, on the river, trapping for a little while, and I heard your dogs. Had to come on over and see who it was and get some news. Who's the new President?"

All this time he was building up a fire in the stove and lighting a couple of candles. Olaus and I propped ourselves up in our bags against the wall, tried to come awake, and relayed to Fred all the news—local, territorial, national, and international—that we could remember. I think I went to sleep a few times during the conversation, but we told him of all the doings and he related his activities since our last meeting. Toward midnight he blew out the candles and rose. "Well, I hate to think you folks are leaving our country, but sure glad I could have this little visit. Marcel is down at King's, building a barn for Jack White's freighter horses, so you'll be seeing him. Tell him I'm O.K."

He stooped to crawl through the door. "Good-by—good luck to you. Don't forget us old Koyukukers!" Then he went crunching away in the darkness, out of our lives.

Almost immediately, it seemed, it was six o'clock and we were laboriously making ready for the trail again, feeling more tired, both of us, than we had the night before. Olaus says that's always the way if one doesn't get fully rested between days on the trail; the human engine has to be kept at peak efficiency for this winter travel. Trying to hurry, trying to boost the grub bag and myself through the door hole together, I cracked my head on the log and nearly knocked myself out, which helped a lot!

An uphill start is no cause for rejoicing on any day, for the morning enthusiasm of the dogs is too soon spent. This morning we were winded the first hundred feet; all our limbs ached; the fatigue poisons were still present. Yet up and still up the trail went, rough and sidling, so that it took all my weight on the handle bars and Olaus's against the gee pole to keep the heavy sled from sliding off against stumps. This continued for what seemed hours, upgrade for three miles.

The descent on the other side was worse. Stubs and bumps and hummocks dotted the middle of the barely snowed-over trail; the dogs went faster and faster, Olaus hopping over obstructions and trying to hold back on the gee pole, while I stood with both feet on the brake, accomplishing nothing. The brake kept bouncing over the bumps until the soles of my feet were aching. Olaus shouted back: "Don't try to; it doesn't do any good anyway." So we went drunkenly on to the bottom and straight going again.

Straight going did not mean smooth going. No attempt was

made to smooth over the surface when an Alaskan mail trail was slashed through the forest. Before sufficient snow falls, willow stubs, small stumps, tussocks, hummocks, and bumps have to be negotiated as best one can. We had a load of five hundred pounds with only seven dogs, and a fourteen-foot sled to manage. The mailman was required to carry no more than two hundred pounds of mail on this route. Even at that, I will still swear that all Alaskan mail carriers of that era were heroes.

This straight going we now had was through scrubby spruce and willow woods, up and down little hummocks, across creek beds, down a precipitous bank, up a precipitous bank, with the dogs clawing for footing and the two of us shoving and tugging. But the sturdy old savages never stopped, going on eternally at their steady slow freighting pace. I was kept at a steady trot behind, hanging on to the handle bars, trying to hop over each obstacle as it appeared behind the end of the sled. Every willow stub seemed to be pointed upstream, and padding along so close to the sled, I could not see them all quickly enough to dodge them, and occasionally my moccasin would get caught underneath one. This kept up until my toes felt skinned, cut, and bleeding, if not broken. Tears seemed near the surface anyway today. Olaus said: "Never mind, I've often felt like crying myself from that same thing. Do try sitting up on the handle bar for a while."

So I tried this, and the results were even more distressing. The rear end of the sled was continually being thrown back and forth from one hummock to another. I was thumped in the ribs by each handle bar, and finally there came a mighty lurch and I went flying off into a willow bush. I picked myself up with the hysterical declaration that I would now "*travel by myself!*"

But that was impossible too, for Olaus was having such a time trying to keep the top-heavy sled from going over that I felt too guilty, plodding along behind alone, and once more took hold of the obstreperous handle bars. So we went on. Sometimes we traveled along a ridge that gave a glimpse of the country on the other side of the foothills—snowy slopes and humps and hollows dotted with scrub spruces and little white lakes. The sky was overcast, so it was a quiet black and white and gray symphony— no wind, a still, workaday kind of world, yet even through fatigue and the ache of bruises, I felt its beauty. It was the North as it so often is, gray, quiet, self-sufficient, and aloof; you couldn't help feeling the strength of the land in it.

At noon Olaus stopped the team in a little clearing in the forest and started to build a fire. This didn't suit me at all. "I don't want any lunch. I just want to keep going to King's. If I sit down now I won't be able to get going again. I just want to get to King's!" Then came the tears again.

Thoughts of that warm cheery kitchen, that bunk with the big wolfskin robe spread on it, lamplight, rest, were singing through my brain, excluding all else; I had gone into a half-awake, stubborn trance. Of course, I didn't realize how many miles still lay between us and King's. And, of course, Olaus knew better. The frying pan was filled with snow and set on the fire; the Jersey Creams and the chocolate were brought from the ditty bag; a log was rolled over to the fire. He made me sit there quietly and rest, and drink and eat. Pretty soon somehow the trance lifted, and my outlook began to change. The Jersey Creams were delicious, so was the chocolate, so was the melted snow water. I looked over the rim of the cup at Olaus. He smiled at me. "Feel a little better?"

Suddenly I began to laugh; we were both laughing. As for the dogs, they lay and chewed their meal—half a fish each, extra rations for a hard day—and fairly oozed contentment. They asked little of life.

Darkness came early that cloudy afternoon. At dusk, at three o'clock, we passed the North Fork cabin, that tiny old nook of memories, and came out onto the river once more. Olaus turned and called back to me: "We're going to make it!"

Gone were those treacherous stubs and stumps and tussocks, that strain of watching every step, of yanking and tugging at handle bars which flounced around as though alive. We had come through on our feet, and my husband was saying lovely words about its being the toughest trail he had ever seen and there weren't many women . . .

So now I could sit on steady handle bars and go into a wonderful dream of work done and good things coming, and feel some remorse, too, over my vile noonday temper. We slid along mile after mile of smooth snowy river, past all the landmarks on the upriver trip, sixteen thrilling days before. Olaus still trotted at the gee pole, and I marveled at him. It was very dark now, and the stars were out, but after a long time we saw the outline of a group of tall spruces on the opposite bank, then a yellow glimmer, and the dogs broke into a trot. At the end of the longest, hardest day, they could still break into a trot at the smell of cabins. We were running up the bank now amid the yipping of dogs tied in the barn, and there came the lantern swinging along again, and that hearty voice: "Well, well, well, here you are. This is great! You pretty tired? You go right on in now; I'll help your man put the dogs up."

The big front room was just as warm and welcoming as I had dreamed it would be, and I quickly pulled off my parka, mitts, and fur boots. There was a jumble of happy voices outside, and soon the men came stamping in, carrying our luggage, Roy with his lantern, Olaus and Marcel grinning broadly, and all fussing around to make me comfortable. "My lord," Roy exclaimed, "I didn't realize you meant you had come overland when you said yes, you were a little tired! Why, that's the worst trail in Alaska right now. My goodness, you must be about dead, both of you. You lie down in your same old bunk, Missus. I'll hurry with dinner. This is Bill Creecy."

In the doorway a giant figure was pulling off a red cap. We had heard about Bill Creecy up above. A mulatto, he was a veteran of many campaigns with Uncle Sam's troops, and now was a miner in the isolated Little Squaw region west of King's. He came in slowly, gazing bashfully at me and regarding me timidly as I slipped on dry moccasins and began to brush my hair. "You a cheechako, ma'am?"

I said, emphatically: "Oh heavens, *no*, I was raised in the country!"

"Oh, dat's all right den. You unnerstan' us ole sourdoughs den. I'se afraid you was some city lady."

He heaved a sigh of relief and began eagerly taking part in the rapid conversation going on, Marcel continuing his monologue of "By gar, dat's a tough trail for lady to come over, my, my, my, dat's terreeble!"

All this was refreshing and would have made me feel quite a heroine if I hadn't had the memory of my noon tantrum! But warm water and soap and the hairbrush made life new, and when we trooped into the kitchen with its bright lamps and laden table, Olaus and I looked laughingly at each other and realized that all was well again, and we were *so* hungry!

Dinner was a gala affair, such a happy reunion, so much news to relate, so many questions to ask and answer. Here were a French Canadian, a mulatto old-time Alaskan, an American Hoosier Alaskan, with a good meal, a warm bright room, an

admiring audience of two newcomers who had never heard any of
the stories before. Such an entertainment comes few times in a
lifetime, and cannot be retold properly, but I will never forget
Marcel's tale of the cake.

Roy had made a very good chocolate cake, which we were all
enjoying, and that made Marcel remember. "One time I make a
cake, long time ago, out at de mine. I get to teenk 'bout cake, and
I teenk: 'By gee, I make one!' So I make, and put in de oven. Dat
cake, I donno. She go UP—she go DOWN! My partner, he say he
don' wanna eat 'im. I say to him: 'You eat 'im! Lotsa good teeng in
dat cake. You eat 'im! Butter, sugar, egg—all kinda good teengs I
put in. You eat 'im!'"

From the diary:
"Now we have adjourned to the front room and become a bit
more sensible, but an eager conversation touching a wide array of
subjects goes on about me as I sit curled up here in the wolfskin
robe. Bliss and serenity! Roy has just come in with an armful of
wood and replenished the heater; a wraith of frosty air follows
him in. 'By George, the spirit's goin' down fast; she'll be thirty at
least before morning. I'm sure glad you folks got in tonight!'

"The logs in the wall by the bunk give a loud crack—winter
speaking! . . .

"November 10: Good-by to Roy King, to Marcel, to Creecy,

those good companions of some of our happiest hours on the Koyukuk. Through the frost-laden beautiful forest, down the white ribbon of river, we went to Bettles. We avoided the trail over the plateau, the scene of the unforgettable first day on the trail, but we missed the beauty of that above-the-world bit of country where we had had such views of the mountains, then far and beckoning, now known and loved.

"Winter is enthroned in the north country now—a frosty veil hangs over the hills, the sunny hours are but as a few minutes, then night again. Tonight we are in the cozy cabin back of the roadhouse once more. Bettles is well-nigh deserted, cabins empty, everyone gone to mines or trapping grounds. Otto and Frank and Mary, all gone, but gentle Jack Dodds is all eager kindness, wanting to hear all the news of the upriver country. And the Kobuk crew of the *Teddy H.* are all on the river these days with their dog teams, finishing the hauling of that precious barge load of provisions to the upper river. David is here tonight and will be our trail companion to Alatna tomorrow; pleasant to hear again his soft lilting accent as he talks about 'dog *teams*.'

"I think we shall be glad to travel on; our cabin next door looks too lonely—it hurts to think about it all, to wonder whether we can ever come back.

"November 14, *Twenty-four mile cabin:* I crawled into this place tonight on hands and knees, but it is nearly miraculous what a few moments rest, knowing you don't have to get up and go on again in a few minutes, will do. We have had supper and are now both able to sit here by the little stove and laugh at those tussocks. Twenty-four miles from Alatna today, and for eight of those the trail led across a piece of real tundra, a sea of tussocks, with just enough snow to make each one frosted, so that the whole expanse as far as one could see looked like thousands of mammoth frosted cupcakes set out to cool. We had a touch of gentle life at Alatna for two days, staying in friendly Hank Kroeger's spare room up over Sam's store. Sam had gone back Outside, to Fairbanks. We had dinner at the Mission with those two charming women—dinner on willow ware, by candlelight, again with much talk about books and learning. We hated to say good-by to them, to Hank, to Alatna, to the Kobuks, to Little Henry and Billy Bergman.

"Having picked up various belongings stored at Bettles and at Alatna, the sled is still heavily loaded, and the task of getting a

fourteen-foot sled over eight miles of muskeg when there is not
enough snow to fill up the chinks was almost too much for us. It
was impossible, of course, to stand on the runners at the back, yet
necessary that Olaus be at the gee pole and I at the handle bars to
keep the sled upright. Nerve-wracking to flounder along, trying
to step from one 'head' to the next, sliding off, trying to walk in
the interstices below, stubbing your toes to pieces—then over
goes the sled—heave-ho! Up again. 'Well, darlin', these things
can't last forever,' I said hopefully.

" 'Oh yes, they can! That's what Alaska is made of!'

"I think this was the first discouraged remark Olaus had made
on the whole trip! It was nearly noon when we crossed Kanuti
(Old Man) River, but the muskeg was behind us for the time being
at least; dusk when we reached the foot of this long hill fronting
the Koyukuk; dark when we labored up the last steep pitch to the
mail cabin, twenty-four miles from Alatna, dogs pulling and
puffing, we pushing and puffing; and when we were within a few
yards of the cabin my legs seemed to go out from under me, and I
crawled the rest of the way and through the square door hole and
collapsed on a straw-strewn bunk. Olaus, who is never 'all gone,'
put up the dogs, brought in our beds and the grub bag, and
started a fire.

"After twenty minutes I decided I wasn't completely all gone
either, for I was suddenly so hungry that I rolled off the bunk and
started rummaging in the grub bag for the last package of caribou
chops. The fire was buzzing encouragingly. I lit two more candles
and stuck them on the little shelf table near the stove, and went
to work.

"Tomorrow we leave the Koyukuk Valley and start across the
hundred and twenty miles of winter trail "brushed out" through
the willows and spruce, which cuts off the twisting and
meandering of the Koyukuk and makes a line for the Yukon at
Tanana, far upstream from the mouth of the Koyukuk.

"November 16: We made such a flying start this morning that I
was nearly left behind; no chance for either of us to look back
toward the beloved valley. The hill went down as steeply on this
side as it went up on the other, and the dogs were especially
jubilant and eager to go. Such jumping and leaping and wild
clamor of voices, and when Olaus finally gave the desired word,
off they went in a mad leap. Fortunately I had my arm through
the bow above the handle bars, but I couldn't get my feet up onto

the runners for several yards, and then had to get busy immediately with the brake as we went tearing down the steep narrow way between the trees.

"At the foot of the hill the trail dipped down into a creek bottom and turned at a right angle. The dogs never slackened pace; I couldn't keep my feet on the brake, and when those fourteen feet of sled turned, I was thrown off, 'like a rag doll,' as Olaus said, and landed up against the snowy bank of the opposite side of the creek. I had hit my shoulder against some protruding roots, and the tears were oozing down my cheeks in spite of myself, but I knew Olaus couldn't leave the team—he had finally got them stopped a few yards further down—so I picked myself up and rejoined the expedition, and was comforted with words from the front of the sled, and took a very firm hold on the handle bars again.

"Less than an hour later we were winding down a little hill, the trail very narrow between trees, when Bingo smelled a rabbit or something, and suddenly speeded up. So the whole team speeded up and went round a turn, and off I went again, slamming against the trunk of a large spruce. This time Olaus did leave the team and rushed over, expecting, as he said later, to 'pick me up in little pieces.' I had landed head down and was half buried in snow, but when he dug me out and lifted me up, all anxiety, he found me laughing, and gasping through the laughter: 'Oh boy, that must have looked funny!' Women!

"Thus the first two miles every morning are real sport—first the dreadful racket; then, suddenly, complete silence, the energy now taken up in legwork. How their little feet twinkle along, and what a pretty sight, all those furry backs, rippling with the play of muscles, those prick ears alert for a rabbit or whatever adventure the trail may bring, tails curled stiffly over backs.

"The trail is much better, with more snow, but the way to Tanana seems to be up hill, down dale, all the way. Sometimes we cross a broad white expanse of lake dotted with black muskrat houses, sometimes we follow a winding slough with yellow grass still standing above the snow and exquisite silvery birches frosty on knolls above it; then up another wooded hill through spruces getting larger as we travel south. These are beautiful hills, and always from the tops there are views which lift the spirit and make the long climbs worthwhile. Southward we gaze on terraced slopes, splashed with crystal-shining birches and magenta-hued willows, dropping gently away to a stream valley far below; beyond that more wooded slopes and the pink and snowy peaks of the Beaver Mountains far over the Great River."

On our fourth day south we caught up with a part of that same caribou herd which on its southward migration had caused such excitement in Wiseman. We were bumping along down a rough slope full of those tussocks again, when old Wolf's ears pricked up and Mayuk, his partner, gave a yelp and in a flash they were all off on a mad run. Over on the next slope we saw twelve or fifteen buff-brown caribou, and on slopes further off, more and more. One small band was feeding along close to the trail ahead, and the Victoria Land hunters were straining every muscle to reach them. There was nothing we could do but hang on to the sled and pray it wouldn't tip over. "Be ready to jump," Olaus called back. "Don't get in the way of the handle bars."

A wild ride. But when the hunters reached the slope they found they still had their driver along, and by the time we reached the plateau on top, Olaus had them under control for the moment and the caribou were angling off far away from the trail. I stood on the brake, and Olaus stayed by Pooto's head. Good old Pooto had at least kept them on the trail—still a hard job, for Mayuk and Wolf were straining and whining and jumping in harness. Looking through the binoculars, Olaus exclaimed: "Gosh, there's a big bull I must get if I can!"

He returned cautiously to the load, quietly drew out his rifle, took a slow aim, and fired. The animal, which was so far away he was just a black blur to me, fell! The dogs were trembling with excitement, but Pooto lay down in the trail. Up got the caribou, and Olaus started after him, admonishing Pooto: "Lie down now, lie down, good boy!"

But seeing Olaus start off, rifle in hand, was too much for Mayuk and Wolf. They made a wild lunge off the trail; I stood on the brake with both feet and all my might and yelled "Whoa! Whoa!" in the fiercest voice I could muster. Pooto, who had been fairly yanked to his feet by the others, kept them running on the trail for a few yards, but then turned and gave me an eloquent look as though to say: "I just can't do it!" and away we went, five hundred pounds of load, Mardy standing with both feet on the brake and yelling wildly, and that crazy team dragging the sled

through two feet of loose snow and over the tussocks faster than they had ever been known to travel on legitimate business on a smooth trail! On they galloped toward Olaus, yelping in eagerness. Then Mally got a foot tangled in the tow rope, and instantly there was a fight! Olaus immediately turned back, and when peace reigned again the caribou was a black dot disappearing over the far rim, evidently not badly wounded. Olaus hated to leave a wounded animal, and had never done so, but this one was apparently going to recover. He was traveling so fast there was no chance to catch up with him.

Now the dogs seemed to feel they had had their daily adventure and trotted along meekly until we met another group of caribou feeding near the trail. But this time Pooto was able to keep them straight and they just raced madly along as though they expected to meet the caribou any minute. So we made fine time all day, for there were either caribou or their tracks or their scent all the way; great sport after the laborious freighting pace we had held to for the past month.

They were still going at a good pace when we neared the mail cabin at dusk that fourth day, and this time the cabin was at the foot of a slope, and from somewhere above the trail water had flowed down from a spring and had frozen over the trail. The dogs smelled the cabin of course, and speeded up, and just then

Olaus slipped on the slick ice and went down, disappearing under the sled. I stood on the brake and dug in and screamed at the dogs, and had a flash picture in my mind of the teeth of the brake going into his body—a terrible moment, for the dogs merely went faster. Then Olaus's head emerged at the front of the sled, then his shoulders—he had kept his hold on the gee pole and chinned himself up and out from under. Then the team came to a calm stop in front of the cabin.

From the diary:

"November 18: So short are the days becoming that the fiery glory of the red sunrise seems almost to merge into the delicate rosy saffron glow of sunset, so that we travel across a colorful stage setting and watch green spruces, red willows, snowy birches, undergo strange and delightful changes of color. Out across the snow-covered tundra a snowy owl sits calm and inscrutable on a birch stub, the startling, beautiful ghost of the Arctic. Behind his whiteness the western sky is shell-pink. Words can never tell the peace, the strength, the triumphant beauty of this land.

"Then very soon the sky is midnight blue and fully spangled with stars, and the moon is rising brighter and brighter behind the pointed trees. In the north a flicker of green and yellow; then an unfurled bolt of rainbow ribbon shivering and shimmering across the stars—the Aurora. The dogs begin to speed up; we must be nearing a cabin; yes, there it is, a little black blotch on the creek bank. The air is cold and tingling, fingers are numb. A great dark form flops slowly across the trail—a great horned owl, the speaking spirit of the wilderness.

"A little later, when warmth and light and food and our few possessions had made the tiny cabin our home for another night, we listen to that 'whoo, hoo, hoo—hoo, hoo' from the forest; it makes a day on an arctic trail complete. I am sitting on a low log stool near the stove. On the other side of the stove Olaus bends studiously over his notes. The owl hoots very near out there. The fire crackles. Olaus looks up. He still has the bluest eyes, the nicest smile. And I remember that evening in Jess's boat on the Chena the owl floating out of the forest, settling in the treetop over the river.

"November 19: We had traveled five hours before daybreak; hours of misty moonlight in an unreal quiet white world. In silence we were sliding out of our beloved North. The dogs padded softly along, slowly, steadily, up a long hill, through black silent forest, and out upon a bare summit.

"Standing close together at the handle bars, we looked to the south. Below us wooded terraces descended to the Yukon. The river was a glimmering expanse in the faint light of a gold horizon glowing brighter each moment. Looming against the yellow sky, above the smokes of Tanana, the great granite promontory where the Tanana, a smooth white avenue, merged with that greater white ribbon, the Yukon. There lay our road to civilization.

"But we turned away from all that, turned back north the way we had come—looked down into the white valley we had just traversed. And through our minds ran the picture of all those other valleys beyond, of rivers bordered with woods, grassy sloughs, wide white lakes, on and on to the white Endicott peaks—to that happy valley of the Koyukuk, the river of golden autumn, golden dreams, and brave laughing souls. While our hearts went winging back over those miles, and our tears brimmed over, our feet had to turn south.

"'All right, Pooto!' And the sturdy dog feet padded swiftly on toward the sunrise—once more a rosy sunrise over the willows of the Yukon."

PART III:

THE OLD CROW RIVER

1

Tanana and Yukon

One day in March 1926, I was sitting by a baby crib in our Washington, D.C., apartment making a list of hot-weather clothing. The phone rang and I heard Olaus's voice: "Don't hurry with that packing, Mardy. We're not going to Arizona. We're going back up North instead, and we won't leave so soon!"

"Back North? Where?"

"Old Crow River, to band geese. I'll try to get home early tonight and tell you all about it."

I turned from the phone to my desk and somewhat dazedly pulled out the map of Alaska. Mother and Daddy had moved to the States while we were up in the Koyukuk and had settled in their new home by the beautiful Twisp River in north-central Washington, the apple country. There, Martin Louis Murie had been born. At the time, Olaus was far out at the tip of the Alaska Peninsula studying, collecting, and taking photographs of the big Alaska brown bears. He went away three months before Martin was born, and didn't receive the telegram announcing the birth until his son was eighteen days old; he didn't see Martin Louis until he was three months old. Olaus later realized that on July 10, the day of the baby's birth, he and his assistant had been stranded on a little sand island with their dinghy adrift beyond swimming reach. They were on that island for twenty-four hours, until an abnormally low tide the next night saved them. These six months

were the longest separation we have ever had, and it began only eight months after our marriage. Martin has often teased me about having him born in a place with such a queer name—Twisp in Indian means "hornet"—but that big comfortable house, with its garden and fruit trees beside the tumbling river, and the loving family, was a real haven. And when Olaus came back to us in the fall, we took Weezy along with us for a term of school in Washington.

"Now," I thought, as I leaned over the map, "Weezy's school is going to be interrupted again. The family in Twisp will have us with them sooner than they expected."

Funny thing—Alaska was home, but I couldn't remember the Old Crow River. Let's see, it must be far north; yes, there it was, starting way up on the northeastern corner not far from the Arctic coast. My finger traced that thin line winding down; it crossed the International Boundary, spent most of its twisting length in the Yukon Territory, Canada, then joined the Porcupine, still in the Yukon Territory. The Porcupine is a big river; it runs southwestward and joins the Yukon just below the village of Fort Yukon. So that was it. We'd have to go by boat all the way. I leaned closer over the map spread there on my desk. In my mind's eye I saw a little craft leaving Fairbanks, sliding down that wiggly line which was the Tanana, into the "great river"—even my finger went more slowly now; the boat would be bucking the current of the Yukon all the way to Fort Yukon, some four hundred and fifty miles. Up to this point I knew the country a little. But then, the Porcupine. What had I ever heard about the Porcupine? It was a beautiful river; it was the country of the valuable dark marten skins; I couldn't remember any more.

Just then there was a gurgling sound from the baby crib. Our eight-month-old roly-poly was waking, reaching his arms to me with a big smile. I lifted him up. "Well, old sweetie, you want to be an Alaskan too?"

And then came a terrible thought. Maybe the baby and I couldn't go. Maybe Olaus wouldn't think it possible. What would the chief, Dr. Nelson, think about it? I suddenly remembered the letter Dr. Nelson had written from the Cosmos Club in Washington, D. C., ten days after Martin's birth, addressed not to me but to "Martin Louis Murie." I had read this letter so many times I knew it by heart: "An old settler welcomes you as a newcomer to this mixed-up old world. With such good scouts as your father and mother to guide you on the trails you must follow, you will miss many of the rough places, but for your own sake I hope you will find enough of them to make life interesting. You have all my best wishes for a happy and prosperous journey. I hope you will be at least enough of a naturalist to appreciate the infinite variety of interest the world provides and to get from it health, happiness, and contentment. With congratulations on your arrival and all good wishes for your future I take pleasure in recording myself as one of your first friends. E. W. Nelson."

Six weeks later we were on our way north. Elizabeth, then living in Seward, met us at the dock, and then rode all the way to Fairbanks on the train with us—just to have a visit and play with the baby! "I'd like a dozen like this!"

As usual, lovesick swains were trailing in her wake. One, a young doctor from the States, also rode all the way to Fairbanks with us—he wasn't going to let Elizabeth out of his sight. But it was a mining engineer who next year won her heart and still holds it. (She doesn't have a dozen. She has five.)

It was early May when we arrived in Fairbanks, and the United States Biological Survey expedition to the Old Crow River was soon getting under way. This was to be a real wild-goose chase, to band young geese and molting adult geese on their Arctic breeding grounds, in the hope that these birds, if later shot on migration or wintering grounds, would add to the fund of information of migration routes. The purpose was to help Canada and the United States set up fair protective regulations. Banded birds which are shot perform a final service, for science.

But a bird bander must be very mobile. A good inboard motorboat was the first requirement. When Olaus had come home that March evening after his phone call, the first thing he said as he came through the door was: "I'm going to write to Jess tonight. If I can just get him and his boat! I think the Northern Commercial Company might give him six months' leave."

Olaus and Jess had talked for years of a real big trip together. Here it was. Olaus and Jess and I felt we knew each other well enough to be willing to put our friendship to a test. So, under the hot sunshine of May in Fairbanks, the two men worked in the Rusts' back yard building a twenty-five-foot deep-sided scow, poling-boat style, to be pushed ahead of the twenty-five-foot motorboat.

Martin Louis crawled about on the grass while Clara and I sat on the back steps and made lists. That is, Clara, from her years of housekeeping and camping experience, dictated while I wrote: lists of food, lists of clothing, utensils, medicines. We calculated weights. What could we take which would not weigh much yet keep us well? How many kinds of dried foods were there? (There were not very many back in 1926.) Between blows with the caulking sledges the two men shouted suggestions: "If we can only take two or three cases of canned stuff, let's take two of canned milk, and one of tomatoes, and you can use the tomatoes for the baby too."

We were thrilled and confident there in the hot sun under the calm blue sky. (May is a magical month in Fairbanks.) Looking back on it, I'm surprised that we didn't panic over those lists and that outfit. What if we had forgotten something vital, such as spare engine parts or extra baby bottles? But I recall those days as blithely busy ones, taken up with buying, packing, visiting, showing off our smiling fat son to all our old friends, attending farewell dinner parties. There was only one shadow. All our friends, except Jess and Clara, thought we were crazy, if not criminal, to take the baby along into the Arctic. I should stay in

Fairbanks. What were we thinking of? The mosquitoes would eat him alive. What if he got sick? What if the men had to go off and leave me alone? What about wild animals? And weren't the rivers dangerous? And didn't the men have enough, with navigating and camping out and chasing geese, without a woman and baby to bother with?

I could still read all these thoughts on the faces that lined the bank on that sunny morning, May 25, when the lines were cast off, the motor sang a crescendo, and we made a big circle with our fifty-foot outfit and slid quickly past them all—shouts, smiles, tears, waving hands. The bend below town quickly banished everything. We were alone—three of us and a baby—and this fifty feet of boards and gear would be our home for four months.

Up ahead, the scow, fully loaded and covered with a tarp, then the little pointed decked-over bow of the motorboat, then the baby's place and mine, on the port side. I had a folding canvas chair; the baby had a four-foot wooden packing box which advertised to the world: "Mishawawka Ball Band Rubber Goods" (before our return it was repaired with a board emblazoned: "Darigold Creamery Butter"). In the bottom of this box we had a thick pad, a rubber sheet, and a baby-sized eiderdown sleeping bag made by his grandmother in Twisp. Here he sat, or jumped up and down, or slept, clad in khaki coveralls (also made by mother) and a little khaki sun hat tied under his chin. He also wore a baby harness, and whenever he was aboard, the leather leash attached to it was hooked into a stout screw eye in the bottom corner of his box. The boat was open, and the rushing, relentless water was right there beside us. Around my feet, stowed neatly, were the baby's small packsack of clothes, a rubber-lined Boston bag, another utility bag, and a denim case for my notebooks, reading matter, and other stray items. This was our five-foot-square home, all day, every day.

Behind us there was dunnage of all sorts, and in the starboard stern, on his stool at the steering wheel, Jess, tall and lean, his sharp dark eyes searching the river and shore for adventure and fun—sensitive to every change in mood of water or wind or the voice of his precious engine. At the port side, across from Jess, was Olaus, smilingly alert, his blue eyes searching the shore and water for any kind of animal life, or busy with his notebooks or his collecting kit, with rifles and binoculars close at hand.

In a few days our routine was established, and each precious bit of gear had its place. For now, we were purring along down the treacherous muddy Tanana, high cut banks on one side, low gravel or sand bars on the other, spruce and birch and aspen on the high banks, with "sweepers" leaning into the current; willow, roses, and high-bush cranberry on the opposite bank, lush in their new green. This is one kind of river scenery. The other kind appears when the stream cuts through hills. Then the slopes come right into the water and the whole aspect changes; the stream itself becomes straight, sedate, with none of that dimpling of tiny whirlpools all over it—clear sailing. We could relax and view the hills, those green slopes dotted with small spruces and satiny birches. The Tanana hills were a fairyland in May, with every shade of green on the grassy slopes, in herb and bush and tree; blue sky, feathery clouds, no mosquitoes. We were all relaxed and chattering, Martin jumping up and down in his new home, holding out his hands to the rushing water. The first big hurdle was past. We had *started!* The weather was good, and already we were feeling our unity, separated from whatever the rest of the world might do in the next four months. The boat, the wild river country, the search for those nesting waterfowl—this was our universe. We began to accept it, to settle into it.

We had had a great piece of good luck, too, on our second day, when we stopped at Nenana, and there was the *General Davis*, the river steamer on which we knew Otto was working. We had hardly dared hope she would be in port just then. I stayed by the boat and the baby, and in a very short time Otto was scrambling down the bank, Jess and Olaus at his heels. I was happy beyond words to see Otto, proud to show him our son, thrilled to hear about his courses at the college the winter before and to hear that Dr. Bunnell was trying to raise funds to send him out to the Bering Sea coast on the Coast Guard cutter next season to look for Eskimo village sites and artifacts. Otto was on his way, and this was a joy for us, but mingled with sorrow at having to leave him again. Once again he stood watching while we slipped away around a bend.

From the diary:

"May 27: We have been following a beautiful chain of hills. They rise gently in hummocks, free of underbrush, and jade green from aspen and birch with clumps of spruce for contrast. We are still following them as I write this, about 4 p.m. I am beside Olaus while he steers, the boy is asleep; Jess is up on the scow mending tent. The day has been hot, the sky strewn with puffy white clouds. Our little water caravan already seems like home.

"May 29: Our first camp is typical of many along the Yukon and the Porcupine: 'camped on a wide sandy beach under a high bank.' Camp routine was set by now. We landed; Olaus jumped ashore and tied the boat; then came back and picked up baby, box and all, while I followed with all the little bags. Jess by then had both tent rolls ashore. We picked a site for the tents. Olaus and I set ours up while Martin, tethered to a tree or his box, crawled about in an ecstasy of freedom and Jess built the supper fire. Into the tent went our sleeping bags, our kits, and I would delve into grub box and say something like: 'Jess, shall I make cornbread in the Dutch oven tonight? Do you know where the granulated eggs got put?'

"Now Jess is putting up his little tent, and Olaus is saying: 'Guess I'll get a mouseline out before dinner—it looks good back here in the woods.'

"Pretty soon there is stew, made the night before, cornbread, applesauce, tea. The baby has been made ready for bed and is having a bottle of warm milk in the tent. Jess has brought up the canvas stools near the fire. We eat in a leisurely manner. There's no need for any hurry, because night will not fall and though there is all the 'housework' to do now at day's end, I can take until midnight if need be.

"While we eat, two gasoline cans, split down the middle of one side, the edges rolled back (the universal Alaskan camp utensil), are on the fire, full of water. When we have eaten I proceed to the day's work—wash dishes in one can, wash baby clothes in another—while the fire crackles under beans or spaghetti or stew for tomorrow, dried fruit cooking for sauce, and baby cereal in a stout little double boiler. When everything is washed, and all the food is cooked, and the baby clothes spread over bushes to dry, and both grub boxes covered with a tarp, *then* I can heat a washbowl of water (the washbowl is the bottom half of a gas can) for myself and retire to the cozy security of our waterproof, mosquito-proof, paraffined linen tent. Here with warm water, soap, cream, and lotion, I could have a few moments of being just a woman."

It was nearly always midnight when Olaus finished putting up specimens and writing notes (he never for an instant forgot that this was a scientific expedition) and I finished my chores. Jess would have crawled into his tent much earlier, after writing in his diary, doing something to the motor, and mixing the sourdough for breakfast. So, at six A.M.: "Hey, you fellas, goin' to sleep all day?"

Then came the clatter of pans, the whang of the ax, the crackle of the fire. "Hey, Mardy, I've got Martin's bath water heating."

So another day—bright sunshine through the tent wall. Groan, moan, feel your stiff joints—is it worth it? Crawl out. The baby is bobbing up and down, all smiles. Get out there and wash. Thank goodness the long hair has given way to a short bob! Get out the baby's bath things; lay him on the rubber sheet, the bag of toilet articles beside you. Olaus lifts the door and shoves in the pan of warm water. When the baby is nearly dressed, all clean and smelling of baby talc, Jess has begun cussing the sourdoughs: "Gol-durn stuff, they don't look too good this morning. Cloudy weather yesterday; I bet the dough didn't 'work' enough. Oh well, they'll sure stick to our ribs!"

I clean up the bath things and reach for a Thermos bottle. Into a cup go five tablespoons of Dryco powdered milk. I fill the cup with warm water from the Thermos. Martin is reaching out and chuckling, and subsides into his box again with a bottle while his mother goes to breakfast.

As quickly as I can, I clean up the breakfast dishes while the men are striking camp. At the last minute, I put hot cereal from the double boiler into a small screw-top jar, with a bit of canned milk, and then get into the boat with the baby. As Jess cranks the engine I'll be spooning mush into a co-operative customer and the day will be well begun.

Noon on a sand bar—no mosquitoes. The broad bars of the Yukon are a world apart. Coarse gravel, little pools of fine sand, the bleached bones of trees, patches of stubbornly alive green things—lupine, vetch, grass, and silverberry bushes. Just enough to make a pleasing pattern, a little protection and shade, a place to tether the baby, with a longer leash so he can scramble about, chuckling, playing with the multi-colored pebbles. At times he would lie on his stomach very quietly, and run handfuls of pebbles through his fingers, watch them fall, and then pick up another handful. From what far-off granite and sandstone rib had these pebbles been cracked and crushed and carried down, and rolled and pommeled and scraped, and rubbed and polished by the great river?

On these bars of the Yukon we were careful where we tied the baby or set the grub box, for we would be in the midst of a colony of nesting arctic terns, and as their nests are merely slight depressions in the gravel and sand, and the eggs blend perfectly with the tweed of the gravel, we had to look about first. While I heated soup or stew for lunch the men would be tiptoeing about, searching for nests, cameras at the ready.

There were no prepared baby foods in those days (how they would have simplified life!), so we carried a small sieve to make purees for Martin. At noon he had his big meal; if we had goose, bear, or caribou stew made with the dried soup vegetables, some of this was put through the sieve for him. Sometimes he had tomatoes, mixed with a bit of our excellent canned butter; after that he generally had some kind of dried fruit sauce, made of apples, peaches, prunes, or apricots or any two of these cooked together. The baby would sit happily on the sand, eagerly accepting food as I knelt before him, bowl in hand. Then, while the rest of us ate lunch, he would have a zweibach to chew on (every few days he sprouted a new tooth, but with no discomfort).

These were the sunny May days on the Yukon. The river seemed to tolerate us kindly. We attribute personalities to all things of nature; I suppose we can't help it, being the self-centered creatures that we are. The Yukon has been both devil and angel to the various people who have traveled upon it. To us it seemed a kindly yet reserved host—a giant of enormous power disposed to accept us and give us safe passage this time. We were interlopers, of course. This world belonged to the river, to the birches and spruces on the cut banks, to the terns and plovers on the bars, to the black bears who sometimes ambled along the tops of the banks, to the unique black ground squirrels that scurried through driftwood piles behind the beaches. (Along this stretch of the river melanism—black pigmentation—seems to be prevalent in the ground-squirrel population, for which science has as yet no explanation.)

Gravel bars are havens in the north country, providing some refuge from the scourge of Alaska. If you step up the bank and into a lush undergrowth of the forest, you are immediately in a buzzing, whining inferno. So we looked for a bar on which to eat our lunch and set up camp at night. Here we sat and gazed about. Jess scrutinized the path of water we had come over and the track ahead for signs of bars, shallows, whirlpools, and snags; I watched the river, the whole sweep and motion of it, simply because the very fact of such great liquid power held me enthralled; Olaus searched the land with his gaze, for signs of nesting, for signs of mice and geese and ducks; his eyes followed the terns and plovers as they whirled over our heads and cried at us. Why were we disturbing their important business?

Time goes by; the river world changes. We cannot always have the accommodation of gravel-bar refuges. Every great river must have a section peculiar to itself. The Yukon has its "Flats." I hesitate to try to describe in words this tremendous, mysterious, fiendish region. The river spreads itself over nearly sixty miles of flat, willow-covered mud, splitting into thousands of channels, sloughs, and dead-end passages. A great volume of water pours over a low point; this must be the main channel. But a boat may struggle up it for three miles only to find it barred by a driftwood tangle. Over against the opposite bank there may be an ominous whirlpool. This is the Flats. And the strange thing is that in this perfectly flat-appearing land the heavy silt-laden water comes pouring through at eight miles an hour, laced with whirlpools, pricked by hidden snags, so that boats have to give their all to get upstream through this hundred-and-twenty-mile ordeal. And here there is no escape from the mosquitoes.

We hit the Flats dramatically. At the edge of the last range of hills at camping time—there were no gravel bars—we picked a fairly open-looking point of woods. Olaus stepped ashore with the line. And found himself gazing straight into the broad face of a big black bear.

Jess was ashore with his rifle by the time the big fellow had got his feet under him and lumbered into the willows. Olaus was holding the line and whispering frantically: "Give me my gun," and I was as awkward and slow as any woman could be in getting ashore. He was swallowed up in the bushes before I had found a place to tie the boat.

I stooped to pull the knot tight (I always knew my knots were not to be trusted), and the mosquitoes were there, a singing black cloud of them. We had hit the Flats all right. At the same instant my eyes fixed on a horrible sight at my feet. There under the willows lay two newborn moose calves, both dead, one partially eaten. No wonder Mr. Bear had been surprised—he had been engrossed in a feast. In all this stretch of country, we had landed right here in the midst of a wildlife tragedy.

I was fairly talking to myself. Don't stand here. Hurry into the boat and put the Citronella cheesecloth around the baby's neck, and try to find the other mosquito nets. No, not in this bag, nor this. I clambered over the load, slapping at bugs, getting more frantic with every second. Martin began to whimper; it was time for his supper, and the mosquitoes were biting. Finally, in desperation, I unfolded a very light blanket and draped it over his box. I knelt there and held the blanket over the beating fists and rising cries, and tried to sing "Three Little Kittens," his favorite song, to keep him quiet.

There was a shot, and another. If I live to be a hundred I shall never again hear a more horrible sound than the one that arose then from the willow depths. Was it a bear or a man? On and on it went, agony and despair intensified in every note. Oh, why didn't somebody do something? Martin was quiet; he was listening too. I held the blanket tight and tried to blow the mosquitoes off my bare hands, shifting my aching knees on the floor of the boat. The groans continued; it seemed an endless nightmare before another shot rang out, and then there was silence, then the voices of the men, shouting to each other. I had begun to think they had both been swallowed by the earth, not having sense enough, or not being in the right state of mind, to realize that they had to maneuver carefully to get a sure shot in those thick willows.

They came thrashing back triumphantly through the brush, to find a completely unreasonable, weeping young woman kneeling in the boat. They were thrilled over the adventure of the good bear specimen for the museum. I was hysterical because I had no nets, no fire, no hot water, and worried about my poor baby, wondering why I had come along anyway. No doubt the men wondered too that night!

Yet in an hour's time life was different. Baby was asleep in a safe tent. With a head net and gloves on, I had time to think of that other mother who had lost both her babies that afternoon. All up and down the sandy bank the willows were stripped of bark, where she had eaten, awaiting her labor, and the tracked-up beach showed the signs of her frantic dash after the villain had arrived.

The night before we reached Fort Yukon, we had slept on a particularly hard gravel bar, I guess. We had not rested well and were feeling weary, in no shape to cope with new or unexpected situations. Besides, we had been seventeen days on our own, seeing very few other people, and there is something about such independent, relaxed, unsocial life that breeds shyness. Somehow it is a great effort to step ashore at a real settlement, to greet a whole group of people, to find out what they are like and how you fit in.

The group of old-timers gathered on the bank to watch us land at Fort Yukon were friendly of course. But I thought they looked at one another a bit wryly when Olaus said: "Where's the roadhouse? We thought it might be a nice change to stay in one here, get cleaned up and our outfit sorted out."

"Right back there, behind the N. C. store, the only one there is," replied one old fellow.

Olaus put the baby on his shoulder, and we all trooped up to a very old, very dark-looking story-and-a-half log building. It was a lovely warm day, but the door was closed. When it opened we were assaulted by odors which hadn't even been mingled enough. The proprietor, a stout, dark, oily individual wearing a flour sack tied round his middle—which he had been wearing for months, it seemed—looked rather startled and then showed us unsmilingly to the bottom of a narrow, dark stairwell. Up there under the eaves, in stifling, oppressive, odorous heat, were two rooms. Jess, muttering to himself, went into the back one.

There was a tiny window in the front room. It was sealed tight. Everything was grimy and covered with dust—it hit suddenly with a sinister feeling. I winced when Olaus set our fairly clean baby down on the old quilt that covered the bed. A moment later

I was sobbing on his shoulder, and then I heard Jess's voice in the doorway. "You guys can stay in this hole if you want to; I'm going upriver above town and put up my tent."

"Wait a minute. We're going with you!"

An hour later we were all set up in the wonderful clean out-of-doors. Apparently the old-timers had expected this. They were waiting, with kindly advice, and we found ourselves in the trappers' colony on a beautiful green slough of the river above the town. Here Bill Mason, the leader of the group, had staked out an area for the use of white trappers, and here every summer the men of the North came to sell their furs, have some "town life," and outfit themselves for another winter. Ten months in the bush, two months in the village!

We had three happy days among these real northerners. We made our last purchases and had happy visits with Dr. and Mrs. Burke, the famous missionaries, in the big mission house where Mrs. Burke mothered and trained and loved as many as twenty children, orphans or children from broken homes. "Dr. Hap" had a way with babies, as he had with all human beings. He took Martin in his arms and disappeared upstairs with him, saying: "The baby and I both need a nap." Then Clara Burke and I sat in the huge living room and talked over our plans and our equipment. Even Clara, who knew the ways of the North as very few women ever have, was a bit skeptical about me and the baby. She asked me about the items I was taking along, and nodded her head. "I'm sure you'll get along fine. But you know Old Crow is the worst mosquito place in Alaska. Even the Indians stay out of there in the summer. You'll have the whole country to yourselves!"

Here was the real departure into the unknown. From here on we would be in territory that none of us knew. Jess had done a lot of talking with Bill Mason and all the rest, and was full of information about bad riffles, rapids, and swift water. But how did the country look?

2

The Porcupine

The Porcupine comes down between hills most of the way, cutting through one range after another in clean, surging strength. While the slopes rose steeply, even in cliffs, on one side, there were, nearly always, gentler slopes and broad benches and gravel bars on the other, so we still found open gravel for our stopping places. Now when we sat in the boat when it was tied up, we no longer heard the glacial silt of the Yukon passing the sides of the boat, sizzling like something frying in a pan. For the Porcupine is a clear stream, and that means a great deal. First, it is beautiful; the trees and vegetation go on down into the water and the rocks beneath lend color to the stream, so that the whole world here feels more crystalline and sparkling. Second, after weeks of trying to "settle" water in kettles by adding mustard, with no success, and of mixing the baby's powdered milk and food with, and washing his clothes in, the "gravy" of the Tanana and the Yukon, the clear water was a treasure. We found a beautiful sand-bar camp the first night, and we all proceeded to bathe, and wash clothes, and *drink!*

These are the gifts of the Porcupine: clear water, a straight-forward, honest, untreacherous current, plenty of flat sand and gravel bars to camp on away from the mosquitoes; a light breeze much of the time, which also helps to give respite from the mosquitoes; plenty of dry firewood on the beaches and in the woods. These are all the conveniences the traveler in the wilderness needs. Any other gifts, from whatever treasure trove, would be useless here. So this is the river of the trappers, the river they love. In addition, there was also plenty of food.

From the diary:
"June 12: At eleven-thirty we passed Black River and at five the mouth of the Sheenjek or Salmon River. But just then we spotted geese on a bar. I watched through the field glasses. Pretty! Twelve of them, standing in a row like tenpins. I steered the boat right up to the bar before they flew off, and the boys both whanged away. Two geese."

That was the Porcupine. Lazy hot days in the boat; all of us in shirt sleeves or no sleeves, getting sunburned; the baby, clad in a diaper, playing in his box. Sitting beside him, I wrote notes or read a bulletin on the geology of the Porcupine country, or through the glasses watched the shore for ducks, geese, bears, wolves, caribou, or foxes, and saw them all in the course of those twelve days. Back in the stern Jess steered and watched the water, lifting his glasses now and then. Sitting next to him, Olaus wrote notes or put up mouse or bird specimens, the collecting chest beside him. Sometimes he came back to play with Martin while I took a steering lesson from Jess. When the baby napped we might all three be up front together, watching the country, discussing the chances for success on our wild-goose chase.

At least once each day there was an adventure. At the mouth of Coleen River, on the lush goose-grass beach, we bagged a black bear. (The meat was delicious; we smoked some of it and it kept well.) One day we had an exciting time on a long open beach with a wolf, our first; but we were at such long range that he got away. Another day we spent an hour running round and round a yearling moose, photographing it. Another time we landed beneath a cliff where a colony of swallows was busy buildng nests, and Olaus climbed to the very top of the cliff to a hawk nest, to band the young. Martin ohed and ahed over the flocks of birds and stretched out his hands for them, and Jess took pictures of swallows and shouted a lot of humorous advice to Olaus as he climbed. For each evening by the campfire, some adventure to live over again. And each little event, each lovely vista, every wild creature, held importance for us. Our appreciation was keen, not diverted by other people, newspapers, radio, or too many

contacts. Have you ever noticed that books read in the wilderness stay with you a long time? Their entry into your mind is unimpeded.

We were eight days on the Porcupine without seeing another soul. On the morning of June 21 we were still threading our way between the imposing "ramparts"—high cliffs, red, vermilion, rust, and yellow, deeply scored and carved into pinnacles, castles, and rugged terraces. They seemed almost to form a great circle about us, upstream and downstream.

Suddenly Olaus pointed. "Look, an Indian graveyard, on that point."

And Jess replied: "Betcha a nickel Rampart House is around this next bend."

Sure enough, there soon came into view a surprising array of neat buildings on a high bench, the Union Jack shining in the bright arctic sunshine. Behind the village rose sharp grassy vertical ridges, cut by trails, clear to the skyline. "That's the International Boundary, I bet," said Olaus.

There was supposed to be a terrible riffle just below the post, but we found it no worse than others we had come through, and we didn't have to line; we chugged up to the landing beach very slowly, but we made it, and I knew Jess was proud of the little Ferro engine. All this while we had a view of the excitement we were causing. First a small darting figure, then more and larger figures, hurrying to the beach, and then from the building over which the Union Jack flew, two khaki-clad tall ones. They were right there to take the line when Olaus threw it. "Hi, first boat upriver!" Thus were we greeted by Royal Canadian Mounted Police Sergeant Charlie Young, who introduced himself and his assistant, a young Norwegian giant named Ellingson. I thought: "Yes, of course, just like the Curwood stories. All Mounties are tall handsome he-men. How do they do it?"

We had started very early that morning, and so we joined the two constables in a second breakfast. It seemed strange to be walking on a floor and sitting on chairs. The baby crawled around busily, exploring a different kind of world.

It was fun to be such welcome guests, the first boat upstream and with an accumulation of mail for the police. By the time breakfast was over, the two or three families of Rampart House were sitting quietly on the grass outside, just waiting to have a glimpse of the strangers. Down at the beach we could see several small boys, just standing there looking at our craft. They never touched anything.

Olaus had some mice and a duck which had to be put up, and Sergeant Young wanted to learn how. We all moved outdoors, and the whole group gathered around Olaus while he skinned the specimens on a big packing box. Three Indian women and a tiny girl were more interested in Martin, the first white baby they had seen. They sat and watched him, fascinated, as he crawled around on the grass. One fine-looking woman spoke English; she was the wife of the Russian trader, old Dan Cadzow. A jolly soul she was; we had a merry visit with her. I asked her then about getting moccasins for Martin at Old Crow Village; she said she wasn't sure they were available. An hour later the two other women and the little girl came back and handed the baby a beautiful pair of moccasins; they had made them, fancy-braid trim and all, in that hour!

Olaus took pictures of them with Martin, and then he and Jess accompanied them back to their house, to call on old Dan, a famous character of the North, who was crippled with rheumatism.

In the sunny headquarters house the two policemen were meanwhile pouring out to me all the unspoken thoughts of a whole long arctic winter, digging out from their stores all the delicacies they could think of for lunch and trying to find something the baby would be allowed to eat. He had a bath on the sergeant's table and a nap on his bed.

After all this fun and visiting, Olaus and Sergeant Young went through the formalities of crossing into Canadian territory in very short order. Our permits were shown and stamped. "There's no boundaries up here; it's just the North," said the sergeant. Then: "Now we have to have a drink on this. I make the best beer in the Territory. Wait a minute." And away he went.

Ellingson said: "He keeps it cold in a hole down by the water."

Olaus looked at Jess and me appealingly. He hated the taste of beer. Jess sat there with a diabolical leer on his face—he *loved* beer! The sergeant returned, oozing good will, carrying several bottles by the necks. Olaus downed one with best wishes for all concerned. Jess and I each drank two, to make it more enthusiastic. It was a hot day and the beer was really cold.

A few minutes later, as we were climbing back into the boat, the sergeant gave us still another gift, which Olaus accepted promptly—a big whitefish just taken from his set net, the kind they call "inconnu" up here.

We had talked about a little project. Here it was the twenty-first of June, and we were about a hundred miles north of the Circle; we had a feeling we wanted to climb up, out of the river, and see the midnight sun.

Half an hour above Rampart House, at six o'clock we found a beautiful camp. At the spot where a sparkling stream rushed out between rocky bluffs, there was a tiny grassy bench for the tents and a nice beach below. Up and down and around us were the high colorful ramparts; before us, the shining river. The sun was still high in the cloudless blue. It was hard to leave all this beauty, but we went into the tents and lay down. At eleven-fifteen we arose and got the baby up, sat him in a packsack, and tied him in. Olaus shouldered the pack, Jess took the cameras, I the glasses, and we started climbing.

We followed the bed of the creek for quite a way, jumping from rock to rock. Then we were climbing up a slate-shale slide, hanging on to little green willows or spruces to pull ourselves up. We came into a mossy spruce woods on top and followed through it back toward the river. Here we came out onto a narrow point where there was just about room for us all to stand, where we could see far up and down the valley of the Porcupine and up through the plateau our little creek was cutting. Beyond the plateau, the sun was just hovering on the horizon, a warm rose-colored ball, shedding vibrant pink light over the whole quiet arctic world. We sat there for a quite a while on top of the world, at midnight, the sun at our backs, the river before us and far below; we were talking of the folks nearest and dearest, and trying to realize where we were on this longest day of 1926, and wondering whether we would ever see the midnight sun any farther north. In this high quiet place the only sound was the singing of the many kinds of small birds in the spruces. I wonder if they ever rest in this season of color and light.

Old Crow Village is on the Porcupine, just below the mouth of Old Crow River. It is like all the river villages of Alaska; there's no other possible plan, I guess—a row of little cabins set a hundred feet back from the top of a high cut bank, and at the foot of the bank a narrow gravel beach where boats are tied. Here at the top of the bank on the sunny morning of June 26 stood one tall young white man and about fifty assorted Indians, watching intently as we approached. We all remarked how self-conscious this performance made us feel each time. Jess and Olaus stepped ashore first, amid a hum of Indian talk. Olaus turned and helped me step off with Martin, bareheaded, in my arms. Immediately we were aware of a sudden increase of excitement in the voices.

The young man introduced himself—Jack Frost! Then he stuck out a tentative finger toward Martin's fat baby hand. "A white baby! And with yellow hair too—long time since I've seen one. That's what all the jabbering up there on the bank is about. These women and kids have never even been to Fort Yukon. This is the first white baby they've seen. They'll sure be hanging around." He looked at me quizzically a moment. "Think you can stand it?"

We climbed the little cut to the top of the bank, and they were lined up, all smiles, ready for the hand shaking. Down the whole line we went. "Hello, hello, hello." I was so glad the baby didn't cry; he just scrutinized them all wonderingly.

Then Jack Frost took us into the trader's big clean cabin, and we had peace for a while—until Martin, crawling busily about, tried to climb the big kitchen range and burned his fingers. By the time Jack and I had bound them up with burn emollient every Indian in the village had gone slowly past the open door, looking in to see what the baby was crying about, and Jack had to explain and explain. After lunch I took Martin out, all smeared with mosquito dope, and sat down among the Indian women, where they were gathered under rigged tarps, with smudges going all around, working on moccasins and fishnets and other handwork. Smiling and gesturing, we had a good visit; there is no mistaking a friendly feeling, and these people exude good will. Every time the baby uttered a baby word or sound, they all chuckled and exclaimed.

We said our good-bys at three-thirty, with everybody gathered on the bank again. A young woman and a little four-year-old girl came up to me. The child handed Martin a package, another pair of moccasins, made since our arrival. The young mother spoke some English. "My little girl, she crazy about baby. She cry. She say: 'Oh, Mamma, make moccasin quick!'"

I was glad the chocolate bars were kept handy in the little dickey box in the bow. As we pulled out, the girl stood there with tears rolling down her face, hugging a big milk-chocolate bar to her breast.

3

The Old Crow

When a whole season's planning and effort is focused on one little piece of world, on one river, when it takes a whole precious month to reach it, that spot on the map takes on a great deal of importance. We had no other considerations to deflect our thoughts. Every bit of information, every conversation had been about Old Crow.

We came to a tall clay bluff, a brown tide staining the waters of the Porcupine. Then we turned left, over the lip of a sand bar. We were in it at last. A small stream compared with the Porcupine, it would be a big river in the Middle West; it twisted and flowed rapidly here at its mouth, walled by ramparts of clay and rugged wooded slopes. We camped on a wide gravel beach, the last one we would see for six weeks.

Here we met the much-touted Old Crow mosquitoes! Since we had been warned a thousand times about them, they didn't seem so awful. ("Do you know what you're getting into, with that baby?" "Even the natives stay out of that country in summer." "There's mosquitoes all over Alaska, but they're nothing compared to the Old Crow." "They couldn't be thicker unless they were smaller!")

So here, after a month of pure pleasure, began the real part of the trip. A mosquito routine was established. As soon as Jess reached for the lever to slow the motor for a landing, I reached for the little roll of mosquito netting and draped it over the baby, box and all. By talking and singing and making all kinds of funny sounds, I kept him under the net till the men got our tent set up. Then Olaus came, picked up the box, made a dash, lifted the netting door, shoved the box in quickly, and then let the netting down. I came along behind him with all the small articles. Crouching, I shoved all these objects in one at a time, closing the netting each time. Then I took off my stiff-brimmed, netting-draped hat, left it outside, wiggled in quickly myself, turned, and pulled the netting down securely behind me.

Inside there was a curious stillness, for only a few bugs had got in. From the Boston bag came a thick tin lid and the can of Buhach. A tablespoon of the yellow Pyrethrum powder went onto the lid and a match was set to it. It burned like incense with a delectable odor, and in a few moments the tent was entirely free of bugs. Buhach! How we loved it! It was the one thing that made life possible, that insured sanity.

Now I could undress the baby and let him crawl about while I fixed his supper, a jar of stewed fruit, ready since morning in the bag, a bottle of milk mixed with water from the Thermos. Then I gave him a talc rubdown, got him into his flannel nightie, fed him, and put him to bed, in a mosquitoeless haven.

Then I had to reverse the process. From a vacuumlike peace I crawled out into the buzzing inferno, grabbed my hat, draped the head net down, pulled the leather gloves out of my pocket, and buttoned down my shirt sleeves. By now the men would have smudges going around the central cooking fire, the grub boxes would have been brought up, and I could proceed to the night meal and my day's work. We could eat with the nets up if we sat in the smoke. As soon as we had eaten, the nets came down and the gloves went on again. Everything was all right as long as I had my hands in wash water, except that, of course, dozens of bugs dropped into the water and drowned, but the moment I pulled my hands out of the water they would be black with mosquitoes. Yet, with our routine established, and satisfied that it was the best we could make it, we were able to concentrate on other things. Conversation at meals was animated; we heard a lot about Jess's adventurous life in the real frontier Alaska; we talked about the camping we had done together in the past; we shared the plots of books we had read; we learned about birds and animals from Olaus's quiet stories of his many collecting trips; we conjectured a

lot on where we'd find the breeding grounds, or why we hadn't found them; and each night we relived the day's adventures. And let the mosquitoes hum.

But I won't try to say that, when, around midnight, chores done, we crawled in through the netting into that little oasis of stillness, we didn't sigh with relief and gratitude—every time.

From the diary:

"June 25: Finally came to the canyon, about five in the evening. I was thinking of Bill Mason's words: 'If you get through the canyon all right, there's nothing to the rest; it's different country from there on; just sluggish water.'"

If we got through! I sat on the seat near the men, Martin in my arms, with one of the big life-preserver vests pinned on to him with many safety pins.

As we started up into the fast water a gale of wind swept down the canyon, against us. We were halfway through but had a real drop to go over. Between groups of big rounded boulders, the whole river was boiling down through a very narrow channel.

We dropped in to shore in an eddy just behind this jumble of rocks, and on a beach made of boulders as big as tables, we stood to survey our situation. The wind was increasing; clouds were piling up; it was suddenly cold. The men built a fire behind a vertical rock; we heated some beans and the baby's mush and had supper close to the fire. The wind and cold had driven away the mosquitoes. Against the rocky wall the men found a little shelving space where, by laying alder branches, they could put up one tent. As the tent went up the heavy rain came. We all crawled in, and with the clamor and roar of rain and river in our ears, slept. One month from Fairbanks!

The morning came bright and clear, and we breakfasted on mush and coffee. Now we were about to try it. The rope "bridle" attached to the bow was tested, and all the stout line was coiled neatly on shore, Olaus and I holding the end. Behind us on the shore, harnessed firmly into his box with all his toys, the baby sat, watching the maneuvers.

Jess and his boat slid out into the stream. Then the current caught him and he slid down some more, to get straightened out. Soon he yelled: "Hold her!"

The coil of rope was going out fast now, and Jess and Olaus were both yelling: "Snub her, snub her!" I had the very end and all the rest was going—a panicky moment till I got a turn around a small boulder while Olaus took a new purchase and we both put our shoulders under and pulled. We drew in line, and pulled again, scrambling over and round the rocks. By now we were in the next little cove; we must be getting *somewhere*. Then we heard Jess shout: "We got 'er; we got 'er. Keep takin' in line; I'm comin' in now."

Now I could hurry back over the rocks to that packing case sitting all alone in the next cove downstream. The baby was not crying, but he gave a big chuckle when he saw me coming down over the rocks to him.

We were all back in the boat again and chugging away. I mixed a bottle for the baby and put him down for his morning nap. Then I heard Jess say: "Oh-oh, guess we aren't through yet. But I don't think this one will be bad. Just hop ashore here and give me a little pull."

So we hopped ashore blithely. "Guess we needn't take the baby ashore."

We had the line; Olaus had the loop at the end over his shoulders, but we hadn't quite braced ourselves when Jess, boat, and baby hit the current and went downstream like a streak. We were being suddenly dragged over the rocks, scrambling for footing, fighting to keep that rope. Olaus went down full length, I

crashed to my knees behind him, and we were still being pulled. Now Olaus was frantically working with the loop, trying to get it off over his head, and he was already in the edge of the current before he succeeded. I kept running with the rope, but of course that was futile. I ended up in a jumble of sharp rocks at the water's edge.

We picked ourselves up and looked out over the river. No red boat, nothing but boiling, churning water. We both raced downstream, tumbling over the rocks. I heard Olaus say, under his breath: "Hope the rope didn't get in his wheel."

But the picture in my mind was that other boiling place below. Could Jess get out of the current before he was carried down into that, boat, baby, and all? We pulled ourselves up over a little point of rocks. There below us was the eddy, and in it the boat, idling serenely, and Jess, standing up, coiling in line. I sank down limply onto the rocks. Jess looked up and grinned at us. "Hey! Took your baby for quite a ride, didn't I? I was thinking, out there when we went round the bend, 'My gosh, Mardy'll be wondering where her baby's gone.' I knew you couldn't see us from where you were. We'll make it O.K. next try. I know how the current is now."

And we did, with tremendous pulling. But Martin, still asleep, was carried ashore first! Gratitude swelled in our hearts as we traveled on into the "different" country.

Just above the canyon, in still, slack water, was an old trappers' cabin and clearing. Here we put up camp for the rest of that day. We were about to leave the hills and enter the great flat tundra of the Arctic, and Olaus wanted to hike into the Shafer Mountains, a long bald hill stretching for about seven miles along the east side of the Old Crow Basin. Higher and farther away in the southwest toward the village were the high blue hills called the Old Crow Mountains. Northward, just flatness.

There were no breezy sand bars here. In the clearing Jess built excellent smudges from rotten stumps—we were not quite out of the timber country yet—and without nets to impede us we accomplished a lot of camp work while Olaus was gone. Here was a chance to air all the bedding in the hot sun. Jess was always busy—cleaning and oiling the guns; making me another pan or utensil out of a gas can or making another canvas stool; patching his clothes—all to a running comment. Many a tale I heard; much practical skill I should have absorbed.

From the diary:
"June 27: The Old Crow is really the descendant of an enormous Pleistocene lake which occupied this whole region north of the canyon and the hills, so it winds and curves back upon itself in an amazing way. And often in the sandy clay banks we see lenses and layers of ice—the Ice Age still with us.

"Sometimes at night we are sure we are only a mile or two, overland, from our last camp. The country is alternating high yellow sand banks or mud banks or bluffs, and on the opposite shore low willow-grown mud shores or cut banks topped with small spruces on the mossy tundra, wild roses and red and pink Indian paintbrush blooming everywhere, the vivid light green of goose grass near the water—the deep, quiet, brown water.

"A great empty quiet land; its only voice the steady whine of the mosquitoes—until we round a bend and see, high up in a crevice or shelf of a mud bluff, a duck-hawk nest, and out over our heads come the parents, 'Ka, ka, ka'—but no syllables can truly convey the rasping, raucous, upsetting quality of that fairly intolerable cry. It was the only sound which, even above the roar of the engine, always woke the baby. He would rise up in his box and start imitating that cry, jumping up and down. With us it wasn't a matter of just passing a duck-hawk nest. We had to stop, and tie up under it, while Olaus, and sometimes Jess too, climbed up, banded the young, and took pictures while the two parents swooped and swung and made the whole wilderness ache with their protest.

"Two duck-hawk nests, three flocks of geese, several ducks, a bald eagle, and many small birds, singing. While we travel the breeze of our motion keeps mosquitoes away. Sometimes there are storms at night, so we have to hurry to get the work done and get under cover, but the days are bright and hot. Every time some geese go over Olaus calls to them, and Martin has amazed us by imitating this sound perfectly—a good little goose-caller!"

A fairly typical entry—typical of our first days on the Old Crow, the serene days before the thing happened.

4

By Main Strength

On June 28 we camped at Black Fox Creek, three tumble-down cabins atop a high grassy bank in a thick stand of spruces. No one was there of course. If another human being had appeared anywhere on this river we would have thought we were seeing things, for we were to be the only people in the Old Crow Basin that summer. ("Even the natives stay out of there.") But sometime long ago someone had had a winter camp here. We knew we were getting close to the end of timber.

Next morning, hot and fair, we were purring along as usual, the folding canvas canoe set up now and being towed behind us, every eye looking out for geese. "There's a slough coming in up ahead. Might be geese on that beach." Olaus reached for his glasses.

Suddenly we heard a "clank, clank"—not a loud noise, but ominous; then silence. The engine had stopped. "What the Sam Hill!" Jess exlaimed, and began jigging this and that and muttering to himself. Finally he said: "Well, guess we'll have to pole over to shore till I see what it is. It might . . . but I'm afraid it's the crankshaft."

The moment the motor died the mosquitoes attacked. It was a great relief to get into the tent which Olaus quickly set up in the thick moss on top of the cut bank. I lay there playing with the baby. He was the one perfectly serene member of the party. I heard metallic sounds from below, but no explosions from Jess; this was a bad sign. Pretty soon I heard him say in a strangely quiet voice: "Well, we might as well go up and tell Mardy."

They both came crawling through the netting. Olaus was smiling at me. "Well, Mardy, our days of mechanized travel are over. Do you mind?"

The crankshaft. I'd never known there were such things. Now I found out how important they were. Jess had brought along practically a whole second engine. In the bottom of the boat lay a spare propeller shaft; stored away in the lockers were dozens of spark plugs, three extra wheels, all kinds of repair parts. But none of these things broke. Only the one most expensive, vital part that breaks only once in a million times!

We were just reaching the waterfowl grounds; the work for which we had come had just begun. They had banded twelve geese so far.

Quite a long time they sat there, discussing what had happened. My mind was leaping on to "What next?" but Olaus had not said anything about that yet and I suddenly remembered the government contract signed in Fairbanks. Jess and his motorboat had been hired together. He was under no obligation to go any farther. Twelve geese banded so far.

Jess was sitting cross-legged, tossing a bolt or nut and catching it as he talked. Suddenly the piece of iron went sailing against the tent wall and Jess said: "Well, by Jesus, we don't need to be stuck! We came up here to band geese and by Criminy we're *going* to band geese. I'm ready to go on if you are."

Olaus heaved a big sigh, and a big smile appeared on his face. "By golly, Jess, do you really mean that? Of course I want to; I've never been stuck on an assignment yet; only, I hate to ask you . . ."

Jess went right on. "Hell, of course we can. We'll take the boat back down to Black Fox Creek and tie her up; there's a good bank there. We'll put all the stuff we need in the scow and pull her and pole her on up—they said it was sluggish water all the way to the head of the river. Must be about two hundred and fifty miles, I guess. But if there's geese anywhere in the country we'll find 'em, even without an engine!"

Three hours later the motorboat, with the canvas canoe trailing behind, was disappearing round the bend downstream, two paddles dipping in rhythm, both raised in a reassuring salute as they slid from view. I climbed the ten-foot bank above the wet sand beach and knelt at the tent door, holding the netting close to my face so I could see inside. Martin was sound asleep on our bed, clad only in a diaper, arms flung out wide. It was a hot day and the tent was warm. How safe, how defenseless! I rose and went back down to the beach. Except for the incessant din of the mosquitoes, the world was quiet and still. Across the brown stream a white- crowned sparrow sang a lazy midday song; there was no other sound in this green world under the warm blue sky. The river was empty, the other shore just a thick green wall. At my back, beyond the little tent, stretched the limitless tundra, mile upon mile, clear to the Arctic Ocean. Somehow that day I was very conscious of that infinite quiet space.

But it was better to get busy. They had left me a pile of firewood. In a flour sack lay two geese, skinned the day before for specimens. I built up a fire. I would make rice stuffing for the geese. Where was the rice? Ah, that was a question! Here along the beach, in a heap measuring about ten by twenty feet, were piled all our possessions, everything but the cases of gas and oil and the tools for the engine. These were on their way downstream to Black Fox Creek. I began poking and peering and climbing about over the pile of boxes and waterproofed bags. It took quite a while to find and assemble the food needed for the next day's cooking, but eventually the two geese were simmering in the Dutch oven, and the baby cereal and dried fruit were on the grate. By the time those three thick chunks of wood burned down, they would be cooked. I drew the tarp back over the pile of goods, looked again at the line running from the precious scow to be sure it was securely tied, took a bowl of cooked mixed vegetables for the baby, and climbed up to the tent.

Before going in, I looked out over the tundra once more. Wavering, hummocky, softly green, it stretched to the sky, here and there a stunted spruce, a small feathery birch, tussocks of white Labrador tea in bloom. A white-crowned sparrow flipped into a nearby birch, and on the tip of a small spruce a tree sparrow was singing blithely. There was no other visible life. I crawled into the tent, pulled off my hat and veil and gloves, and unlaced my high leather boots.

There the baby and I stayed, all that day and the following night—night in which the sunlight was only slightly less intense. I played with the baby when he was awake, tossing the red rubber lamb back and forth for a long time, playing peek-a-boo behind his box—all the little games I could think of.

When he lay quiet with his bottle, or slept, it was still again. Almost afraid to look, I gave the river a quick glance—empty; then out over the tundra—nothing moving, every little tree in its place—good. And nothing moved across the river on the green grass either. Just the wilderness itself, friendly, and normal. My eyes were looking, not for any life, but for a reassuring lack of it. If I had spied a human form coming across the tundra, I would have been terrified; a bear or a wolf would have seemed excitingly normal.

So every little while, all that day and night, I had to go out and be reassured by looking all about, reassured that the baby and I were still safely alone. At two in the morning I banked some coals around the Dutch oven and lay down fully dressed beside the sleeping baby.

Someone was in the tent! Then the nicest voice in the world. "Hello, darlin', it's four in the morning and pretty cold, and the skeeters are gone for a while, and Jess and I are awfully hungry!"

Bill Mason had told us about Timber Creek and the cabin he had built there; how they had whipsawed spruce for the floor and roof and set in two windows they had brought from Fort Yukon. Old Crow had been a great spring muskrat region then; they had taken the muskrats and left the country on the first water, ahead of the mosquitoes!

On the morning of July 4, with Olaus pulling and Jess poling, the scow and canoe arrived at Timber Creek. The creek came in on the right side, from the north, and strangely enough, just where it emptied into the river there was the last stand of timber, and well back from the high bank, close to the spruces and tall cottonwoods, was the cabin, still sturdy and solid. Last timber, last cabin. From here on we would really be in the Arctic.

Jess loved to make things out of nothing. In five minutes we had a broom made of brush, the cabin was swept out, and Olaus had tacked netting over the windows.

Moving into this old cabin was our Fourth of July, and it was a real celebration. The day was bright and hot, just as Fourths should be. There was a wonderful breeze, so rare in this valley. We pulled off our heavy shirts, nets, and gloves, and hurried back

and forth like small children playing house. This was a change, an excitement. In the vast quiet wilderness every little event was sharpened into thrilling poignancy.

Chattering incessantly, we were soon moved in; the floor was swept, a smudge built outside the door, the inside "Buhached," our gear in place. There were two built-in bunks, a table, shelves, stools—all waiting for us. Olaus spread a clean tarp on the floor in the back corner and tethered Martin to a bunk post. Here he crawled about, enjoying his new situation and all that space. And that very evening his daddy brought him great excitement. Olaus walked into the cabin with two golden-yellow downy goslings which he had caught and brought to the cabin to show Martin and me. He set them down at the edge of the tarp where Martin sat; they ran cheeping right toward him. The baby reached out his hands, gurgled "Oh, oh, oh," and bounced up and down in a frenzy of excitement. When one gosling came very close, Martin reached out to grab it. Olaus, kneeling there, said quietly: "Easy now, easy—go easy."

And the baby seemed to sense that there was something different, to be touched gently. He stretched out one fat finger and touched the soft downy thing, looked up at his daddy, and laughed aloud. The two little goslings gave him an exciting interlude, and perhaps his first sense of handling wild creatures with gentleness. When the baby had fallen asleep, Olaus took the little goslings back to the riverbank and turned them loose to grow up.

To keep the cabin cool, we cooked outside. But we ate inside, and can you imagine the joy of sitting at a table, on a chair, without head net or gloves? All this we savored, along with the roast goose, the last of our fresh potatoes, hot biscuits, chocolate pudding. Martin sat on his daddy's lap and chewed on a goose bone and then shared in the opening of our Fourth of July package.

Back in Fairbanks, when the outfit had been loaded, Eddie Clausen, manager of the Northern Commercial Company, had handed us a package carefully wrapped and tied. "This is for your Fourth of July, wherever you are."

Martin watched the unwrapping, squealing and reaching out with his hands. Sure enough, in among the jars and bars of candy, nuts, dates, and chewing gum, was a box of Arrowroot biscuits for him! That was a real celebration. When it was over, Jess grabbed his rifle, strode out to the edge of the bank, and fired three shots into the air. ("Hello, all you big and little creatures of the Arctic. We have arrived among you. Don't let us disturb you too much—we aren't very important, but we're proud of ourselves today for having got here!")

So for six days. From the diary: "We thought we were taking a holiday, but we have all been going at our various duties every minute. It is nice to be settled and making a little home even for a few days and we enjoy it. We have more leisurely meals, and enjoy the evenings and other times when we are all in the cabin working and visiting. Olaus has kept a mouse trapline going, done a little painting, explored about, collected birds. He and Jess have unloaded and sorted our gear, made repairs, developed films, kept smudge and fire going, carried water. A mammoth washing took us all of a day. Miraculously, there are a small tub and a homemade washboard here. I blessed whatever trapper made that board.

"I went out with Olaus the other night to set traps. We hiked back on a little birch-clad knoll, then down through the tundra. From the knoll we saw short mountain ranges here and there all around this flat timbered basin. The Old Crow Mountains looked dim blue. We found a new flower, a butterwort like a microscopic violet. The skeeters are unbelievable, vociferous, indescribable—you keep moving just to drown the noise a bit."

On one of those evenings at Timber Creek, Jess and I decided to take the canoe and go across the river to explore a bit. In the beautiful hot days the water had been dropping, and below the muck and mud and clay of the banks, we could see a broad layer of gravelly soil coming to view. We landed on this and started wandering along. Suddenly Jess said: "You know, Olaus has been talking about maybe finding prehistoric stuff, if the river ever dropped down to the gravel level; he said he thought any bones or such would be in the gravel—remember? Be a heck of a note if we could find something right here and take it back to him, wouldn't it?"

He stooped and began scrutinizing the gravel more carefully, and so did I. A basic human urge, somehow—wanting to *find* something! "By gosh, Mardy, look here!"

Jess held out a brown object to me. It looked like part of a huge tooth. Neither of us could guess what it was, but we really began looking then, and our excitement mounted, for we did find things, many of them—pieces of bones and teeth. Finally Jess and I both pounced on something at the very edge of the water. "Look! It's just like a beaver tooth, only three times as big!"

By this time we had a sizable pile of bones at one end of the strip of beach. "You stay right here," said Jess. "I'm going back to the scow and get a gunny sack, quietly. We're going to surprise Olaus!"

A few minutes later Jess and I stomped into the cabin, where Olaus was at the table busily writing notes. Olaus didn't look up. Jess dropped the sack of fossilized bones on the floor at Olaus's feet with a great clank. "Well, you've been talking about wanting to find some bones. Here they are!"

What excitement then, as Olaus spread them all out and began trying to identify them—prehistoric horse, parts of mammoth teeth, and yes, that *was* a giant beaver tooth, the best specimen of the lot. How keen the sensations of a little adventure when you are far in the wilderness with nothing to dilute them! What a divine thing, enthusiasm, and Jess had it. We chattered and laughed over those bones, and related over and over to Olaus every detail of our discoveries. Aside from all that, they really were interesting finds, and later found their way to scientists who were happy to use them as data for their studies.

5

Geese

"Will you love me in December as you do in May?"

Jess was standing on the decked-over bow of the scow, poling and singing. He had a very nice high tenor voice. I love to sing too. We both knew hundreds of songs, and I really believe this saved our sanity, our friendship, and the success of the expedition. Down on the floor of the scow, just behind Jess, the baby and I spent our days now in a four-by-four space under the light muslin-and-netting tent a field naturalist friend in Washington had insisted we take along. Life from June 29 on would have been fairly intolerable without it. Here in this space were the baby's box, beside it Olaus's collector's trunk, and, piled on the trunk, all the baby paraphernalia and other small articles needed during the day. My stool was set in front of the chest, beside, the box. And that was all; this was our world. By leaning forward and putting my eyes close to the netting, I could catch glimpses of the outside world. It remained unvaried for five weeks: Jess's booted legs, the tip of the red-painted bow, a green blur of grass and willows on the shore, maybe a bit of sky. Sometimes I caught a view of Olaus, trudging along on shore, the line over his shoulder. He was "pulling her by the whiskers," as the trappers say; Jess, experienced with the pike pole, leaned his weight on every stroke in a steady rhythm, all day long.

So we slid along, and sang song after song, and estimated our

progress, trying to pick out landmarks from the Geological
Survey maps. But the Old Crow throughout its middle course has
no landmarks; just high banks, brown stream, green shore.

Variation came when Olaus would signal frantically from
shore. The song would stop in mid phrase. Then we would
quickly haul up the canoe, and both men would get in and push
off, after a flock of flightless young geese which by now would
have taken fright and would be beating furiously through the
water. By this time I would be out on the bow, pole in hand. "If
we're gone too long, try to get to shore where you can hook a
willow, and wait for us"—the parting shot as canoe, men, and
geese disappeared around a bend upstream.

It was fortunate that the Old Crow *was* a sluggish stream. The
scow drifted now toward one shore, now toward the other. I
wound the bandanas tighter over my shirt cuffs to keep
mosquitoes from crawling in, tied the strings of the head net
tighter about my chest, leaned on the pole, and waited. If the slow
current took us close to shore, I reached out and caught a branch
with the hook. Then it was just sit there on the bow and hold it. If
it were near Martin's mealtime and he began to call and fret, I
could only pray that the bird banders would appear again
sometime.

In ten minutes—or an hour—they would come, bringing a new
story. "Hey, you should have seen your husband up there in the
mud, trying to catch up with an old goose before he got over the
bank." Or: "Jess should have been a football player; he made a
peach of a flying tackle after two young ones. Well, that's six for
us already today."

Sometimes the canoe would come in fast, sliding up to the
scow, and Olaus would reach over and dump a gunny sack at my
feet. "Don't worry; they won't hurt one another. We're going
after another bunch up here."

The banders' advantage was that in these weeks the adult geese
had shed their wing feathers and the young had not yet grown
theirs, so that all were flightless.

One hot day the sack contained six full-grown but flightless
geese. For forty interminable minutes I drifted, and poled, and
watched the river in vain for the canoe, while those poor creatures
never stopped squawking and wriggling. It was a big surprise for
me when, after finally being banded, they all went down the
stream again honking furiously, and unhurt.

Lunch was more ordeal than pleasure during these weeks. The men would try to build a fire for tea, but the willow, so much of it green, was poor fuel. Some days we merely went ashore with the tin grub box and ate a bowl of stewed fruit or tomatoes with pilot biscuits or cold sourdough pancakes and a bit of cheese. Bowl in hand, you loosened the string of the head net, poked the spoonful of food into your mouth, and quickly let the net down again. It was the same with all the bites. Even so, there'd be a few bugs to squash inside the net when lunch was over! This was merely taking in fuel for energy; it was no social hour.

Down in the tiny haven on the scow I heated mush or tomatoes or a bit of gravy on the Sterno outfit for Martin. He never came out of there until we camped at night. That is why we had to let him crawl about the tent as long as he liked in the evenings, and why Olaus romped and played with him every night. It was his only exercise during those five weeks.

Olaus has a biologist's scorn of allowing anything biological to disturb him. All creatures are a legitimate part of the great pattern he believes in and lives by. He ignored the mosquitoes with a saintly manner that made me furious at times. But one day he paid!

He and Jess had been chasing a lone white-fronted goose for a long time. As it was the first white-fronted goose of the season, it was worth a lot of time and effort. Olaus finally went ashore under a steep mud bank and waited for Jess to drive the goose to him with the canoe. From across the river, where I had hooked a willow, I watched the play. The goose swam upstream, Jess after it. Just as he came close enough to hope to turn its course, the goose dived. Jess waited and watched. As soon as the goose came up he paddled hard, trying to get ahead of it and force it to swim toward Olaus. The goose dived.

This went on for a half an hour. Every line of Jess's figure as he swung the paddle expressed determination; even under his head net I could see how his long jaw was set. The goose seemed fresh as a daisy. It rose each time with a quick sidewise glance at the canoe and a Bronx-cheer kind of honk.

Once she came up very near the scow. Jess came tearing past, talking to the goose. "God damn you, I'll get you if we have to go clear to the canyon together!"

Away they went around the bend; Olaus waved to me from across the stream, the kind of wave that said: "This is a funny life we're in, isn't it?"

Then the goose came swimming back again, paddling furiously, honking a little anxiously; right behind her Jess, also paddling furiously. And this time she decided shore was the place.

Olaus had lifted his net to watch the performance, and had also taken off his gloves—something Jess or I would never have done. Now he had to freeze into position, for the goose had begun to wade ashore at the spot where he was crouching. It padded determinedly up the bank. Suddenly it became aware of the figure there and hesitated. "Onk?" it questioned, and waited, watching Olaus. Then it put one web foot forward in the mud. "Onk?" again. Olaus didn't dare move an eyelid. Mosquitoes were setting in black clouds on his face and hands.

Out in the stream sat Jess, at ease in the canoe. Now it was his turn; he could make all the noise he wanted; he had forgotten his awful anger at that goose. "Heh, heh, heh," he said in his high-pitched voice. "How you like the mosquitoes, eh? Nice comfortable position you're in, isn't it?"

Olaus kept silent; he was as determined to get this bird as Jess was. The bird took another very tentative step, looked at Olaus, and asked him again: "Onk?" No answer. From out on the river: "Boy, don't you wish you'd kept your net on! How long d'you think this will take? Watch her now!"

The goose took three steps; it was feeling the nearness of the overhung bank and safety above it. Like a fox drawing his legs up imperceptibly for a pounce, Olaus moved his feet, so carefully. "Onk?" Spring! Pounce! He had it round the body by both hands; they were sliding down the slippery mud together, and Jess was whooping: "Hang on, don't let her slip—I'm coming! How do your mosquito bites feel? Boy, don't anybody ever say anything to me about foolish as a goose; they're about the smartest damn critters you can find!"

They were slow, strenuous hours, chasing geese like this. Yet practically every goose we saw was caught and banded. Either the Old Crow had been much overrated as a nesting ground or something strange had happened in 1926, for we never found the "hundreds of thousands" someone had described to the powers in Washington. The days were hot and muggy, and we felt almost a claustrophobia down there between those steep banks of thawing

Pleistocene mud, in a steaming, whining breathless world where insects were in full command. We human creatures were saved from insanity and death only by a few yards of cheesecloth and netting and leather. Sometimes the shield felt pretty thin. We longed for a breeze with passionate longing and welcomed a hard shower, because it downed the hordes for a while; and at least it substituted the sound of water for that other perpetual sound.

"Notice how much lower the banks are today? I think we're getting into different country." Olaus, always hopeful, always optimistic, was poling today.

Jess was on the line, over on the lower shore. His answer was prompt: "Can't be different country any too damn soon for me."

Five o'clock—the banks still lower, a clear sky. "Hey, Mardy, feel the breeze?"

I scrambled out from my "hole." What a feeling! Moving air! I looked up; the solid cloud of spiraling insects was gone; the wind had dispersed their formation, broken their absolute control of the land. "Can't I go ashore and walk a little? Martin's asleep."

I fell into step behind Jess, shoulder under the line. "Sure a lot more current here," he said. "Maybe we *are* getting into something different; even that old mud bank over there is pretty low. Looks as though it ends up ahead there. What's that?"

A dull boom, like a distant cannon shot, from upstream. "D'you hear that?" Olaus yelled. We threw our utmost into pulling, peering upstream. "Be a good joke if we found people up here after thinking we were the only ones in creation."

"I don't think it sounded like rifle fire exactly."

"Could some party have come over from the Arctic? You said it was only about eighty miles in a straight line now."

We rounded the next bend. "Boom!" Right there, near us. Then Olaus shouted, pointing; ripples were running out against the current in one place. In the mud bank on the opposite shore we saw a great lens of dirty brown ice. We watched. Crash! A big piece of ice suddenly dropped into the water, a rending, a crash, and a splash. Here was the exact northern shore of that ancient lake; the Pleistocene ice was being defeated by summer sun and the modern stream.

Suddenly Jess threw up his arm with a shout: "She's clear!"

I dropped the line and rushed to the very edge; there on our side

was clear, shining beautiful water. As though sighting a new planet, we looked down into the bottom, into the beautiful yellow gravel. Then we looked across, and halfway over, there was the dark line in the stream where the Pleistocene mud was still falling off with the ice. "Come on," Olaus shouted. "Let's get above that mud. Look, it's flattening out up here. We *are* in different country."

A mile above the lens of ice we made camp, to the accompaniment of that cannonading; it exploded regularly, every two minutes by the watch. We had, in the space of a few moments, emerged into another world. The gravel bank was low to the stream, flat as a floor, dotted with all manner of brave arctic bushes and flowers. Better yet, there was a breeze blowing, and best of all, we were on top of the world; we had come up out of weeks in that Pleistocene hole.

We threw off our head nets, gloves, and heavy shirts, and stood with the breeze blowing through our hair, gazing all around. We could see, far out over miles of green tundra, blue hills in the distance, on the Arctic coast no doubt. This was the high point; we had reached the headwaters of the Old Crow. After we had lived with it in all its moods, been down in the depths with it for weeks, it was good to know that the river began in beauty and flowed through miles of clean gravel and airy open space.

Latitude 68 degrees, 30 minutes.

We had a paradise camp for a few days. The men went out in the canoe and explored the river upstream. It became shallow rapidly, and they satisfied themselves that there were no other goose grounds. Martin had a heavenly time, turned loose in the air and sunshine. He had long since learned that gravel hurt his knees; he did not crawl, but walked on all fours like a cub bear. Here on a long leash he explored, crawling right over the low bushes, playing peek-a-boo behind them, scuttling away like a laughing rabbit when someone "found" him.

Jess caught some eighteen-inch grayling the very first night in the clear pools just above camp. The baby stood at my knee and kept begging for another bite and another bite while Jess kept saying: "It can't hurt him; it's good for him," till we realized he had consumed a whole big grayling.

Jess is a real fisherman, and getting these beauties, our first fish in weeks, lifted his spirits a little. But he was experiencing a letdown of sorts. He was drawing away from us, into himself. After all, I don't know how one could expect a trip of this kind to be all sweetness and light unless the personnel were recruited in heaven. Plenty of things could have affected Jess. Olaus and I were together; we were content; his Clara was miles, weeks, months, away from him, and she was to bear their sixth child in August before he could be with her again. Then his motorboat had let him down. Every one of those slow miles up the river since June 29 must have reminded him of how easy it all would have been with that engine. And now after the tremendous effort was over and we had reached the headwaters—well, there had to be a letdown.

It was hard having Jess lost to us. He became a very polite stranger. At meals: "No thank you," instead of "Couldn't eat any more of the stuff!" "Yes, please," instead of "Hey, Mardy, you going to eat all the stew yourself?" He was even more polite to Olaus. They were really on the outs. Before, they had been two old pals on a trip together; now Jess was a stiffly polite employee; Olaus was the boss.

It was good that, while Olaus explored, Jess went fishing. I didn't blame him for needing to get away by himself.

Three days' respite from the mosquitoes; then it was time to turn south, back into the mud, and brown water, and clouds of insects. We all worked at sorting and reloading the outfit, in polite formality. The baby's little nook was placed amidships now, to make room up front for the rowing. The handmade oarlocks were put in place, then the two long oars, which had been made from two spruce trees.

On that last evening, after the baby was asleep, Olaus and I slipped across the river in the canoe and climbed up onto the tundra. It was ten o'clock, July 26. The sun had just slipped below a distant blue ridge, but bright saffron light filled the northwest; the rest was pale blue. It was still daytime, but that very still, strange, exhilarating daytime of the arctic summer night, which can only be felt, not described. Here the flowing green-bronze tundra stretched as far as we could see—to the north, a few short ranges of hills; far to the south, rising pale blue off the flatness, the Old Crow Mountains again. In the morning we would be turning toward them.

We stood there for a long time, just looking. This might be our farthest north, ever. If we could only take a giant step and see the Arctic shore; we were so near.

Then our eyes came back to the near tundra, the velvety sphagnum hummocks, the myriad tiny arctic plants gleaming in the moss, in the golden light. The Labrador tea had gone to seed, but its sharp fragrance filled the air. In a tiny birch tree, a white-crowned sparrow, the voice of the arctic summer—"You will remember; you will remember," he sang.

6

Downstream

Downstream is a much different story. The weather was beautiful; rowing and floating was easy. It would have been joyous if we could have forgotten the mosquitoes, for by this time we were as used to them as we could be. But we were still cramped in our strict formality, and Olaus and I were wondering how long it would last. We were still far from home, and this sudden loss of one member of the party, in such a small party, was disturbing. Missing a chance at a bull caribou the second day down didn't help any. Olaus, after spending years on a study of the life history of the caribou for the Survey, was most eager to get at least one specimen from this far north.

The fourth day down. We were sliding along, no songs, no words, Olaus at the oars. We came round a bend. There on the beach stood a beautiful young caribou bull. Olaus backed on the oars, looked appealingly over his shoulder, and in a loud whisper, said: "Jess!"

There was no need to speak to Jess. He had come alive! His Springfield was at his shoulder as the bull turned to plunge up into the brush. I flung myself down close to Martin as the shot crashed over our heads. One shot, and the caribou fell.

"Got him—right in the neck—perfect!" Olaus shouted. And then, at last, Jess's high excited tones: "God damn—if I'd missed this one I'd have thrown this old blunderbuss right in the river.

Here's a good place to get ashore, right up here, Olaus."

Olaus gave me one quick look as he clambered toward the bow; it was as though steel bands about our breasts had been broken. We all burst into a flood of chatter at once.

"Where's that knife of mine? You sitting on it, Mardy?"

"No, maybe the baby swallowed it."

And so on, all morning. Jess had returned to the expedition! I was sure of it as I listened to the arguing up there on the shore over how to skin the specimen.

What delicious steaks and biscuits by a big campfire that night! What warmth of friendship rediscovered!

Did I say we had lived with the Old Crow in all its moods? There was one more. There had been a big rainy spell while we had been gratefully "at home" again in the Timber Creek cabin, putting up and cataloguing specimens, and working on another exciting prehistoric find. On the day after the joyous reunion Jess was taking his turn at the oars, and suddenly let out a whoop: "Hey, Olaus, look there, right above the beach! It's a tusk, a whole one! I'll swear it wasn't there when we came up. It's washed loose while we were upriver!" Jess rowed quickly to the shore. It really was a mammoth tusk, a whole one, and it took some tugging by both men to get it onto the bow of the scow. It was old, dark brown and dark green and tan and cream in color, and weighed 125 pounds on the steelyards. When we arrived again at the cabin at Timber Creek and found an old saw there, Jess and Olaus, and even I, spent all our spare time sawing that ivory into a few chunks so we could put it into the load and get it back to Fairbanks. But before we sawed it up we took pictures of all of us kneeling under the curve of that huge tusk!

When we said good-by to the little cabin on August 4, the weather seemed fine. Of course, the river was rising dramatically, willows standing in the water and very few high banks any more. A few inches of water can change the whole aspect of the country.

Two mornings later Jess began his breakfast clatter very early. "Hey, you guys, I don't like the looks of the weather; big black cloud bank up north there, and you hear that breeze?"

They took turns pulling mightily at the oars. Jess kept glancing back north; the cloud bank was coming, reaching higher into the sky. "About time we got back to that cussed old boat; I figure much more of this and she'll be swamped."

So that was it; the motorboat, tied to the bank at Black Fox all these weeks. Of course Jess was worried about her too!

In the tiny tent I began dragging out all the baby's sweaters and his brushed-wool snow suit; he soon looked like a fat brown teddy bear. I sat him inside his eiderdown bag, pinned another small blanket around his shoulders, and mixed him a warm bottle to keep him quiet under the covers.

There were thumpings and mutterings outside. "Here they are, way in the bottom of course. I *thought* there'd be some day we'd be glad we had 'em. Here, you put yours on while I row." Jess was hauling out the waterproof coverall suits.

Then I heard: "Here she comes! Wow!" And the wind struck. In a flash the world was dark, and cold, and even our low boat rocked in the wind; then came a sheet of water. I heard more thumping, and from outside, the sound of the big tarp being drawn up over our little haven. It was dark inside now, but we were dry and safe.

"Jess, for gosh sakes, let me row a little, will you? I'm freezing."

So it went for an hour, while the wind lashed at us and the rain came in torrents. Mosquitoes could be forgotten now. The baby had gone to sleep. I reached into the eiderdown and felt his little fat hand—warm as toast. Then my glance went to the floor. Between the floorboards I saw the glint of water—water right up to the boards, half an inch below the baby's box. "Hey, darlin', we've got a flood in here!"

"I thought so," Jess said. "I was just wondering when you'd holler. Just a blame good thing we didn't leave this bilge pump in the other boat. Here, go rescue your family, Olaus."

I perched on the trunk while Olaus pumped; the water began to go down. Then suddenly something was different. Olaus stopped pumping; we both raised our heads to listen. It was quiet; the rain and wind had stopped. Then: "Well, I'll be double-damned. Hey, look out here, you fellas—August fourth on Old Crow!"

It was snowing so heavily we couldn't see across the river: thick soft flakes, coming down quietly, purposefully. "I'm glad," cried Jess. "I'm glad. This won't fill that old boat down there so fast. And I bet you anything it will put the finish on the bugs too."

Pretty soon I heard a bump; we were stopped. Then came the clatter of tin cans and the crashing of axes. I was beginning to shiver. But then Olaus called: "Come on out, Mardy. Jess has used up two gallons of gasoline, but he's got a blaze going!"

In a tangle of big willows, a tall fire was blazing, the iron grub box and three stools arranged around it. Jess was holding the coffeepot over the fire with a camp hook. We had coffee and sourdough bread and jam while blobs of snow kept pelting down on us from the willows and the fire scorched us one side at a time. Olaus brought the baby out and held him by the fire while I spooned some stewed fruit into him, and we heated more water for the Thermos bottles.

At seven o'clock that evening, in a completely white world, we came to Black Fox and let out a shout of joy as we spied a red spot close in under the bank. "There she is, the gol-durned old wreck; still afloat anyway!" Jess's relief showed in his voice.

All these weeks I had lived with a Worry. Caught up in the interest and novelty of some adventure, I would forget; but then the thought would come again, a drowsy dragon lying only half asleep in the depths of my mind.

The dragon was the knowledge that back down those hundreds of miles was the canyon, and we had no power. Just once had it been mentioned—"Oh, if we hit it when there's plenty of water we can steer right through with the motorboat rudder."

They never spoke of it again, and I had a superstitious fear of asking any more questions. I was a woman and ignorant of rivers and such, and I'd better not let on that there was a big bogey living with me, a picture of those rocks, that plunging water, and a baby with us, a baby we had brought along against the advice of many people. And no other way to get out of this country.

On the night of August 10 we camped at the old cabin site just above the canyon. We were in spruce country again, and there was a stream just behind camp, where Jess stood blissfully pulling out big grayling, two at a time. We were busy and talkative, excited and not admitting it. For quite a long way upriver that afternoon we had been hearing a deep roaring voice downstream—the canyon.

Here in camp the roar was quite loud, crowding close in the background of every thought. At supper, Jess had stood by the campfire, looking out at the current, staring as though he would force that water to tell him its every secret. "I'm glad she *is* making a big roar; means there's plenty of water going through. We're lucky we had all that rain and snow."

Olaus made me a spruce-bough bed that night, the softest bed I'd had in weeks. But I awoke many times in the night, listening to the voice down there around the bend.

"Now! Give 'er the devil! Give 'er the devil!" And Olaus strained at the big oars like a man possessed.

We were out in the very middle of the stream, headed straight for the rocky gates below. The baby and I were on the open thwart just in front of Jess, life-saving vests pinned and tied on. We were sliding fast, closer and closer to that sound, and Olaus was pushing with every ounce of strength to give us more speed. "The more speed we can get up, the better chance I'll have to steer straight through with the main current," Jess had said.

Faster, faster—the shores were a green-and-yellow blur; we could feel the water rushing along beneath our keel now. We were between the walls, with a great swelling in the middle, the white water, the dark shadow under a satiny wave. Up, and down, slap; up, and down, splash! Out over the lip of a watery ledge, and a great flat "Slap!" that made the whole load tremble; white foam splashed on both sides. "Oh, oh, oh," Martin cried, and reached out toward the white spray. "Give 'er the devil—there's one more, you know!"

A wave, and another, and splash, and we were lifted in great arms, lifted over, and through, and there was smooth fast river ahead.

"Yay, yay, whee!" We were all shouting at once, purely spontaneously, expressing our boundless relief.

"You can relax now, Olaus," laughed Jess. "Just keep her headed and I can steer her; you sure put all you had into it back there! Did you hear the baby squeal!? He *liked* it!"

So on and on, a thousand things to say, now that the dread weight was lifted. I squeezed the rosy fat bundle in my arms, and the old drowsy dragon blinked an eye and slithered away out of my mind. Breath came freely, clear from the depths. It seemed almost worth living with fear for a time, so sweet was its departure.

"We'll be in Old Crow Village by suppertime." Olaus turned and smiled at me; he knew the mixture of feelings this would arouse—at the same time an eagerness and a reluctance to see people again, to get mail from the outside world. I wondered that the trappers ever actually got themselves in to the villages after ten months, seeing that only two months in the wild affected us this way!

"D'you know what?" Jess grinned at me. "I'm gonna sleep out tonight—no tent."

"Why—we could, couldn't we?"

Here was a fine thought. We were three days below Old Crow Village, back on the stately, beneficent Porcupine. The cloudburst and the four inches of snow had dealt the death-blow then and there to the hordes which had held the whole Arctic in their power all those weeks, and here on the Porcupine there were none at all. The relief one feels can hardly be put into words.

Our fifty-foot outfit, all together again, had a sail rigged on the bow of the scow. We had had sunshine and a fair wind every day, and the wind and the current, with Jess at the rudder, carried us briskly along, all out in the open. No hats, no nets, the whole wide world to gaze upon.

"You remember that wide gravel beach at Hanging Woman Creek? I think we'll camp there tonight—maybe see a wolf again."

Yes, I remembered Hanging Woman Creek. That was the place where the men had shot and shot at a wolf loping up that long stretch of beach, and couldn't hit him. When the excitement was over, Olaus realized he had been trying to shove a rimmed cartridge into his .30-caliber government rifle. The mystery of how that one wrong cartridge had got into the outfit was never solved, but he didn't get the one wolf specimen he had wanted. We had seen only three all summer, one a black one, way up the Old Crow.

There were the remains of a very old cabin at one end of this beach. "I suppose some Indian woman hanged herself here sometime," said Jess. "But that doesn't keep it from being a swell camping place just the same."

He had a roaring campfire going, and I sat beside the grub box seasoning a goose to go into the Dutch oven. It was six o'clock but still very warm. Martin, in a shirt, was bouncing up and down in his box. Olaus was spreading our sleeping bags on a tarp beside the box. This was camping out at its most delightful. Jess lifted the cover of the Dutch oven and banked coals about it. We all sat there quietly then, content. The baby and his daddy were tossing the caribou-skin ball back and forth (he had been showered with more gifts when we left Old Crow Village). With scarcely a whisper, the great strong river traveled past us on its never-ending journey; the wind had died, and it was very still. From the cotton-woods behind us the varied thrush uttered its one constant question, and the white-crowned sparrow spoke again—he was still with us.

There would be light for four hours more, but it was a subdued, soft light, for we were some miles south now and it was mid-August. Across the broad current rose the northern edge of the Ramparts, a high yellow sandstone bluff, golden in the late part of the day. Over it circled a golden eagle. A great bird and a piece of golden sky can give one peace. Watch him as he soars and dips, a graceful pattern with no self-consciousness, there before a golden curtain. The mind is loosed, and, emptied of all edged and clattering thoughts, goes freely floating out to meet the bird. We need such communion; we need to remember we are still animals. After all, intellect is new—how far can we trust it?

We lay under the stars after darkness had come and the fire had burned to dull embers. I wanted to look at the stars for a long time, but I kept drifting off, and as in a dream heard Olaus and Jess still talking back and forth . . .

"You know, Jess, I think it's been a success in spite of all the trouble. Out of the geese we banded there's just a chance they may get enough returns to give them just the information they want about the migration. And I know darn well we got a good bunch of specimens. That caribou from way up there is an important link in my study. I feel pretty good about it all."

"Yeh, I hope so. It still makes me sick every time I look at that old engine; but, you know, some ways it makes a fellow feel better to have a lot of trouble, and get the job done anyway."

There was silence for a moment, then: "Sure swell to be sleepin' out in the open again, isn't it?"

That was the last I heard.

"Hey, Olaus, listen!" Jess's voice in a loud whisper.

We raised up on our elbows, blinking. "What's the matter?"

"Wolves, by golly!"

White mist lay over the river; above it, the yellow cliffs and a rosy sky. It was dawn along the Porcupine. Then we heard it—a long-drawn-out musical sadness which was not loud yet seemed to fill the valley.

"Sounds like it's across the river," Olaus whispered. "There it is again—this one's further upstream."

"Ahoo-oo-oo"—starting low, rising, rising melodiously, falling, falling, down through several notes and fading to a complete stillness. The baby stirred under his covers, and raised a curly tousled head. We were all sitting up now, watching the sky grow a brighter pink, listening, waiting. Jess reached over to his dickey bag. "Where'd I leave those glasses? There! Say, I see one! On top of the bluff over there. See him?"

Through the glasses we could see the singer, silhouetted against the morning sky, sitting there quietly on his haunches. Then Olaus said: "There's the other one, coming." He handed me the glasses again. Long-limbed, moving along effortlessly in a swinging trot, the second wolf moved along the beach from further upstream. The wolf below began to climb up through a little gully. Soon they were together, and sat facing the river and us. Now a duet floated across.

"I guess we're camped on their home territory," Olaus whispered. "They're letting us know about it. Mardy, I wouldn't have missed this for anything. There is really the voice of the wilderness."

"Gives a fellow a kinda funny feeling, doesn't it?" Jess whispered. "This is something to tell Clara about!"

Starry night, rosy dawn, and wolves singing. I had a sudden feeling of climax. There were still long miles ahead of us before we reached journey's end and Clara. But from here on we would be sliding out of the wilderness, away from perfect solitude and unsullied country. Here, on the Porcupine with the wolves of Hanging Woman Creek, we would be leaving perfect at-oneness with the untouched.

UNITED STATE BIOLOGICAL SURVEY
DEPARTMENT OF AGRICULTURE

Washington, D. C.

No. 303147

DEAR SIR (OR MADAM):

You will be interested to know that information has been received that a Hutchins's Goose wearing the above number, banded by you on July 21, 1926, was killed at Clarimont, Alberta, October 14, 1926.

(SIGNED) *E. W. Nelson*
CHIEF

This was the only Hutchins's goose banded on our trip. But for the larger Canada geese there were returns, showing a pattern of migration:

No. 302113, shot at Rupert, Idaho, Nov. 17, 1926.

No. 303562, shot at Washoe Lake, Nevada, Dec. 11, 1926.

No. 303545, shot at Columbia River, Prosser, Washington, Nov. 20, 1927.

No. 303550, shot at Mantario, Saskatchewan, Canada, Oct. 28, 1930.

No. 303561, shot in Lassen County, California, Nov. 24, 1929.

PART IV:
SHEENJEK

1

North Again

We first loved Jackson Hole, the matchless valley at the foot of the Teton Mountains in Wyoming, because it was like Alaska; then we grew to love it for itself and its people. Olaus was sent here by the Biological Survey in 1927 to make a complete study of the life history of the famous elk herd; here we made our home for thirty years and here our three children, Martin, Joanne, and Donald, grew up. As this chapter opens they have all found careers, married, and given us three grandchildren. Joanne and Norman, in New York City, were awaiting their first child, which was expected to arrive in July, and I was torn between going on an expedition to Arctic Alaska with Olaus and being with our only daughter at such an important time. But Norm, a sociologist, was confident and comforting: "Don't worry, Mardy. She'll have the best of care. And just think—when 'he' grows up he can tell his pals: 'When *I* was born my grandmother was on an Arctic expedition!'"

May 1956. Ten years before, Olaus had left the government service to enter the struggle to preserve our remaining wilderness; he became director of the Wilderness Society, but still lived in Jackson Hole. In the absorbing, demanding, never-ceasing battle of these ten years, our thoughts were still in Alaska, and our news from up there after World War II was not always heartening. It began to appear that even the vastness of Alaska's wilderness

would not remain unexploited without some special legal
protection. Thoughtful people both in and out of Alaska were
concerned, for the Age of the Bulldozer had arrived. Scientists
like Starker Leopold, Lowell Sumner, F. Fraser Darling, and
George Collins, who had recently traveled in Arctic Alaska,
began writing and talking to Olaus.

One day when we were in New York City, Olaus called up

Fairfield Osborn, president of the New York Zoological Society. "I think Mardy and I should go to the Brooks Range."

"Well," Fairfield answered, "isn't that something that *we* ought to be interested in?"

So it had happened. We were going North again, our expedition financed by the New York Zoological Society and The Conservation Foundation, and sponsored also by our Wilderness Society and the University of Alaska, whose new president, our old friend Ernest Patty, was eager to encourage research in Alaska. On the staff of the university was one Otto William Geist, who had become an internationally known authority on Eskimo archaeology and the paleontology of Alaska. He was still working on the recovery of fossil remains from the dredging operations near Fairbanks, and he and his house near the university were awaiting our party.

When we left Jackson Hole on May 9, the co-owners of our former-dude-ranch home there were with us. These were none other than Olaus's brother Adolph and my sister Weezy, who had been married in 1932 and who had been the companions of much of our life in Wyoming. Now, with son and daughter both in college, and Adolph scheduled for more work in Mount McKinley National Park, they were going North again too.

Five of us were going north; the fifth was Bob Krear, of the University of Colorado, who had become a "third son" to Olaus and me.

There was one cloud over all the preparations: Jess would not be there to greet us, to help us in our planning, as in the old days. We had to keep reminding ourselves to be grateful for all those other times, and for the two summers the children and I had had with him and Clara in 1936 and 1937 while Olaus was out in the Aleutians, and for the time he and Clara had spent with us in Jackson Hole in 1948—Jess's first trip Outside in forty-four years. The memory of Jess's enthusiasm, his intense enjoyment of all the outdoor world, his unfailing sympathy and kindness, will never die.

The Brooks Range extends almost all the way across the top of Alaska, some one hundred miles back from the flat Arctic coastline. Although a composite of many mountain groups, it forms a continuous great mountain world one hundred miles deep

and up to ten thousand feet high—a massive northern rampart to all of interior Alaska. Our Endicott Mountains of the Koyukuk are part of this range.

The two weeks at Otto's house were over—commencement at the university, parties and visits and picnics, planning and making lists and buying and packing, fun and laughter and reminiscing. And on this half-overcast, mild first day of June, Olaus and I and Dr. Brina Kessel, a young woman professor of zoology at the University of Alaska, flew by the regular air service to Fort Yukon, traversing in sixty minutes what had taken two weeks in 1926, and there, with no delay, had been "inserted" with our baggage into a Cessna 180, equipped with wheeled landing gear.

The exploratory flights had been made the week before by Keith Harrington, a bush pilot for Wien Alaska Airlines, who was stationed at Fort Yukon. He had flown the two young men of our party, Bob Krear and George Schaller, up the Sheenjek River the day before and landed them, on wheels, on the ice of one of the lakes. So far as anyone seemed to know, this was the first such landing on ice in the Sheenjek Valley.

Olaus had pondered over what part of the Arctic this party should investigate. We were to make a detailed and concentrated study of a comparatively small area. We had been in the Koyukuk, which was to the west, and in the Old Crow and Porcupine area, on the eastern side. Other scientists had given good reports on parts of the northern side of the range, Herb and Lois Crisler having spent two years over there. The valley of the Sheenjek was the heart of the whole area which George Collins, Starker Leopold, and Lowell Sumner had suggested should be designated as an Arctic Wildlife Range, and at the same time the region least visited. The only scientific reports available were those on the geology of the area, by the early and incomparable pioneers of the U. S. Geological Survey—John Mertie, Gerald Fitzgerald, and their companions.

There are several ways of describing a river and its valley. For example, one of Mertie's Survey bulletins begins: "The Chandalar-Sheenjek district . . . consists of an irregular area of about 6,000 square miles that lies between parallels 66° 28′ and 69° north latitude and meridians 143° 25′ and 147° 35′ west longitude. This area includes mainly the valleys of the Sheenjek River and the East Fork of the Chandalar River from their headwaters in the Brooks Range southward to their debouchures into the Yukon Flats."

Then we can look at a topographic map of northern Alaska. We see that the Brooks Range extends across almost the whole width of Alaska, tapering into lowlands at the east near the Canadian border. In the last two hundred miles of the eastern part of the high mountains, three rivers, flowing from the crest of the range southward, can be seen: the East Fork of the Chandalar, the Sheenjek, and the Coleen. The last two, after flowing mainly south and a little east for two to three hundred miles, flow into the Porcupine, the great river which comes angling in from the northeast, from Canada. About twenty-five miles below the mouth of the Sheenjek, the Porcupine joins the Yukon.

For a better look at the area, let's go back to the Cessna. Brina, the efficient young scientist that she is, had a flight map in her hand and ticked off the features of the land as we flew over them, every few moments bringing the map forward over my right shoulder and pointing out something she had recognized and correlated with the map. She and Keith shouted confirmation over the roar of the motor. The day had been hazy, but pale blue sky showed ahead of us far to the north.

We flew over the brown tundra-like muskeg of the Yukon Flats' northward extension for half an hour. Then Keith shouted in my ear: "Weather is better ahead. We'll fly straight in."

The brown country, partially clothed in the dark green of spruces, now had small hills and shallow valleys, and we began to catch glimpses of the river, the river of all our anticipation and planning—the Sheenjek. It was free of ice and shone gunmetal silver, slanting down out of the north and disappearing eastward, to our right, to join the wide Porcupine. The fascinating thing about the view from aloft is that the whole earth north of you seems tilted up, so that those far mountains are at a level with your plane, and the river seems to be flowing down over a huge slant.

The top of the slope, still far off in the distant north, was a great curve of mountains—the Brooks Range. It was getting closer every minute—snow on top, some dramatic sharp shoulders shining in the hazy sunlight, but the lower slopes free of snow and black in the distance. So far all the lakes below us were open, black and shining. Then Keith pointed out, over a low saddle to the west, Old John Lake on the East Fork of the Chandalar, and through my glasses I could see it was all white, still frozen. We were now passing Helmet Mountain and the Koness River, the main tributary of the Sheenjek from the west; and far to the east, alone against the sky, a black pyramid, Spike Mountain. Here was the dividing line in temperature, it seemed, for the lakes now were white with just a black rim of water around their edges.

All this time Olaus, sitting on the baggage behind Keith, was watching the country with a serene, untroubled look—getting back North at last!

Suddenly we came between two sets of hills and saw before us a delta-shaped valley, all brown and dotted with lakes, and the river winding down through it and off to the right, to the east. And then the mountains were below us, reaching around on either side of the valley, and to the north, at the head of the valley, high, beautiful rugged peaks, from which the river must come. I took a deep breath and shouted to Keith: "What's this interesting-looking place?"

"Well, this is where you'll be making your home for a while."

Immediately we began to lose altitude, and in what seemed only a moment we were circling above a fairly long lake lying in a bend of the river—the river winding around the west end of the lake and then east again and on south. The lake was pinched almost into two separate segments, and there on the one nearer the river, on a little shelf above the frozen lake, we saw the three tents. Around we went, banking again, and down and down, and suddenly and as gently as a hawk, onto the ice, the wheels crunching merrily along, an hour and a half from Fort Yukon! "We're here! We're here! Isn't it lovely?" cried Brina.

And there came George, the tall warm-blooded one, running out onto the ice, with his red-plaid flannel shirt sleeves rolled to the elbow; and there was Bob, his movie camera on its tripod on the ice taking in our arrival. George's first words were: "Brina! Two ptarmigan nests with seven eggs already!"

That exclamation set the tone of our first weeks in the Sheenjek.

Then we quickly unloaded the packsacks and boxes. I took a postcard from the blue utility bag, and using the body of the Cessna as a counter, wrote a card to Otto, who would send cards to all our dear ones, telling of our safe arrival on the Sheenjek.

"Well, anything more you think of you need, next trip? O.K. See you about the fifteenth then."

And Keith was in the plane, and running down the lake, and into the air and gone like a bird.

Suddenly, standing there in the middle of that lake, a picture flashed into my mind of all the miles of Alaska we had flown over this day and how really far away we were, and for a moment I thought: "Dear me, did we really do this? And no chance to run back home!"

What Keith had said came to me then: "This is where you'll be making your home for a while."

We each snatched some pieces of gear and started toward shore. Over the gap between solid ice and shore the boys had laid brush and sticks to form a sort of bridge. They had done a great job. They had been here exactly twenty-four hours, and the tents were up, a grate set in place, all supplies under cover. The eight-by-ten tent, not mosquito-proof, had all the food boxes in it. On either side of it were the other two tents, and Brina's was already going up, a little distance away. The camp was on a fairly level little shelf; we were very lucky in this, for the land sloped rather steeply above and below, in mossy hummocks and knolls. We were delighted to see so much spruce, scattered, but some fairly tall. Somehow it gives life and color and comfort to any landscape. Olaus and I dug out our duffel and laid our beds in the little green Aberlite; and by that time there was a meal to think about.

But already we realized it was going to be hard to get camp work done and notes written, on account of this country and its animal life, for just then George shouted: "Grizzlies!" and he and Brina began scrambling to find the telescope she had brought. Across the lake, across the river, up the far slope in a yellow grassy swale—there they played, two of them, chasing each other. They were very pale in color, paler than the dry winter grass they rolled and played upon. Here was a welcome!

Bob's handsome dark brow was puckered with eagerness as he gazed at those far-away bears. "I wish they were just a little closer; I'd go after them!"

"I'm so glad you're the movie man, and not I," I answered. "All I have to do is look at things through my binoculars and enjoy them! Nice not to be responsible for getting them on film!"

I went into the cook tent to see what we could have for dinner. There were all the boxes—but where was everything? Suddenly I felt utterly blank and utterly weary. Stooping over the boxes, pawing around, I felt a kind of foolish panic. "My heavens, you've camp-cooked for years of your life," I said to myself. "What's the matter now? Well, one thing maybe is having to stoop and bend over everything—blood rushes to my head and I can't seem to think!"

Half an hour later, at six-thirty, the meal had been cooked— over a cheerful fire in the grate and one burner of Brina's Coleman stove—and we were happily eating—noodles with dehydrated cream-of-mushroom soup mixed in; wieners, four apiece, brought from Fort Yukon that day; knackebrod and jam; hot chocolate; and a candy bar apiece. We had arrived; we were established; we were ready for exploring and learning about this river country. It was a fine feeling, and our sleep was sound that night.

The next day the first thing was to have a close look at the river. The morning was warm and sunny. The river was perhaps an eighth of a mile from camp across soft mossy hummocks. On our side it flowed at the foot of a high sand bank; the opposite bank was low and bordered by willows. It was still at high-water stage, of course, and quite muddy, a steady, fast, inexorable but smooth-flowing flood, perhaps two hundred yards across. Half a mile upstream it made a beautiful wide curve and disappeared from view, and far upstream, above the brown tundra and lower ridges, were the high snow-topped peaks, ridge behind ridge, summit behind summit, displaying all shapes—towers and shoulders and pyramid peaks. At the curve of the river we could see a gravel bar showing above the surface. "The water is falling; maybe there will be tracks on that bar," said Olaus, the track-conscious one.

I was thinking about that Geological Survey bulletin again: "All the streams that drain southward from the eastern part of the Brooks Range within the Chandalar-Sheenjek drainage are characterized in their upper courses by a stretch of relatively sluggish water that is followed downstream by rapids. The Sheenjek River is no exception to this rule, and the main river, ten miles above the forks, changes to a sluggish meandering stream and continues thus for twenty miles upstream. Within this stretch the river is confined largely to a single channel and flows through a wide, lake-dotted valley floor with banks of sand and silt. . . . Upstream from this sluggish stretch of water the river is a typical swift mountain stream and the gradient steepens to its head."

We were in the middle of the "wide, lake-dotted valley floor," but in these early June days the river was not "sluggish"; it was carrying a load of silt and flowing swiftly. Looking downstream, we could see the low hills behind which Old Woman Creek flowed from the west to join the river. Old Woman Creek, one of the very few named features on the available maps of the region, had been our landmark for finding our unnamed lake, which the geologists in Washington had recommended as a camp site. The river flowed quietly over its smooth bed, but during the quiet nights by the lake we could hear the creek; it must be rushing over boulders to join the river, and it must be a big creek. I pulled the Survey bulletin from my pocket again: "All the larger tributaries of the Sheenjek except the East Fork enter from the west, thus rendering the Sheenjek drainage system markedly asymmetric. . . . Another noteworthy feature of the Sheenjek drainage is the marked tendency of a number of the tributaries that enter from the west to flow northeastward in approaching the main valley, thus creating the condition resembling 'backhand drainage.' This feature is believed to be due mainly to the controlling effect of the rock structure."

In this day and age it is a rare experience to be able to live in an environment wholly nature's own, where the only sounds are those of the natural world. Here at our lake all sounds were truly charming. Nearly always a little breeze was whispering through the small scattered white spruces on the mossy hillside; there was the splash of a muskrat diving off the edge of the ice; ptarmigan were crowing, clucking, talking, and calling all around us; tree sparrows and white-crowned sparrows sang continually—their voices were an almost constant background to all the other sounds. We heard the scolding chatter of Brewer's blackbirds and what at first seemed very strange up there in the Far North, the voice of the robin, our close friend of all the mild, domesticated places.

These were the voices of the hillside around the camp. From out on the lake, as the ice receded from the shores more each day (and the days were warm and never darkening), we heard other sounds, which were equally charming and exciting. Predominant in the lake chorus was the "ah-*hah*-wi, ah-hah-*hah*-wi" of the old squaw, and there was the churring sound of the white-winged scoters, the cheerful little three notes of the baldpate, and at times the excited voices of the gulls.

Our lake was about a mile long and half a mile wide, divided into two wings by a neck of tundra. Far across from us we sometimes heard the indescribably haunting call of the arctic loons, and then all the binoculars would be snatched up for a glimpse of these beautiful patricians of the North.

From the diary:
"June 3: As I sit here on this soft mossy slope above camp, writing, the writing has been very erratic because of those who live here. I have watched a band of fifty caribou feeding back and forth on a flat a quarter of a mile away; ptarmigan soaring and cluck-clucking and giving their ratchety call, all about; tree sparrows so close and unafraid; cliff swallows hurrying by; Wilson snipe and yellowlegs calling; gray-cheeked thrushes singing. The three young scientists are beside themselves with all there is to see and do and record. A great trio they are. Olaus has come back from a short hike toward the east end of the lake, and has now gone over to the river, saluting me smilingly as he passed and calling up to me: 'It's nice, Mardy.'

"The tree sparrow is singing, the wind is soughing through the thirty-foot-tall spruce at whose feet I sit, some unknown bird is clucking and talking, away in the distance. The only sounds we hear are the sounds of the land itself. I recall Lois Crisler's letter: 'The peace and vastness of that Arctic are haunting.'

"It is warm this morning—78 in the shade. And not a mosquito!

This is the perfect paradise period in the North. When the men were loading us and our gear at Fort Yukon, Masten Beaver, the Wien agent, said to me: 'Got plenty of mosquito repellent? They will arrive on the Sheenjek about June 16.'"

To all the usual sounds were sometimes added new, exciting ones. One night after we were all in our tents, we heard, far over toward the river, a short, sharp cry. "A fox, I think," Olaus said, and then we heard Brina, out of her tent, with her glasses: "Oh, I see him; a cross fox, way beyond the lake over toward the river, and there's an owl, diving at him—a short-eared owl, I think."

Our lives consisted of little episodes like this, and we were all completely absorbed in them. The sights and sounds of our days and our daylight nights were not of our making or doing; we were simply the visiting observers of spring in the Arctic's natural world, trying to be as unobtrusive as possible. Olaus and the three young scientists tried as much as possible not to disturb this natural world. Besides helping me with cooking and all the camp work, Bob's main job was to make a motion-picture film. On his back he slung his packsack loaded with extra film and camera parts, his lunch, and his notebook; around his neck hung his still camera and his binoculars; over his shoulder he carried the movie camera, already attached to its tripod. Thus prepared, he quietly tramped the tundra, the river bars, the mountain slopes, ready at any moment to take a picture.

Brina and George were co-operating on a study of vegetation and birds and mammals and their habitats. They had to mark and watch all the nests any of us found, but they did this quickly, tying small, strong pieces of muslin to nearby dwarf birches or willow branches and then immediately leaving the spot, to allow the mother bird to return soon. They also had to collect a few birds—those particularly interesting in this region—to be made into specimens for the University of Alaska's collection. They did this with a shotgun carrying very fine shot, but far away from camp. None of this collecting, however, was on a scale large enough to effect the ecology of the area in the least. The whole varied and fascinating population near camp was being studied, photographed, and observed.

In addition to their other activities, Brina and George were grouping the nearby region into convenient divisions for their habitat studies: the lake shore, the open tundra, the tundra pools, the dwarf-willow-birch borders of streams, the lower slopes of the mountains where the sparse white-spruce forest grew, the higher slopes of the alpine world. They wanted to know what the nature of the soil and the moss was, what plants grew there, what animals lived there. And as they tramped the country in a different direction each day, they took pictures, made notes, and collected plants of every kind. George was also making an insect collection for someone at the University of Wisconsin; for a fisheries biologist somewhere else, he was preserving the stomachs of all the grayling Bob caught for camp use; and for the archaeologists, he was always on the lookout for any signs of former inhabitants of the valley.

In a small spruce behind her tent, on the first day, Brina had set up a maximum-minimum thermometer where it would be in the shade at all times, and all summer at eight in the morning and eight at night either she or George took the reading. From this I remember that it was as low as 29 degrees on June 2, as high as 78 on June 16, and that the usual range was from 42 to 72.

These activities required equipment. Stored neatly in one corner of Brina's tent were her tin box of collecting tools, the laboratory scales for weighing mice and birds, and her plant press. In a neat row on one side of the cook tent were boxes of films, with small poles under them to keep them dry, rolls of cotton and cheesecloth, a stack of newspaper sheets for the plant presses, and a box of miscellaneous scientific gear, including increment borers for the tree-growth studies that were made later in the season.

As for Olaus, he wore his packsack like a part of his anatomy, for he had to carry his notebook, color pencils for sketching, extra films, and numerous containers and papers for collecting all kinds of scats, or droppings. We teased him a good deal about this activity. He had us all trained to save every small can, box, wax or foil envelope, or cardboard container. We would throw them in a pile beside the tent, and Olaus would retrieve them and use them for containers. As he tramped the tundra and enjoyed the song and flight of the birds, and every flower that grew, he was also ever alert for a track or a scat; and out of it all, before the summer was over, came an important ecological conclusion.

2

At Lobo Lake

It was easy here to forget the world of man, to relax into this world of nature. It was a world that compelled all our interest and concentration and put everything else out of mind. As we walked over the tundra our attention was completely held by the achievements of that composition of moss, lichens, small plants, and bright flowers, yet we were ever on the alert to identify every bird, to note every evidence of bears—moss and roots dug up, tracks in the mud at the edge of pools. And since our way always led by either the river or one of the many lakes, we were identifying shorebirds, ducks, grebes, loons, gulls. How could we be anything but absorbed?

The three young people and I worked hard the first two days getting the camp in order. Bob, the master camp craftsman, built a "cupboard" from scraps of poles and limbs, wire, and a few nails. He placed it against a clump of small spruces, just below the fireplace, so that all manner of things could be handily hung on the spruce branches; and being able to stand up to prepare food made my life entirely different! Brina, George, and I ransacked the whole outfit. We got the main food supply into the steel drum, whose clamp-on cover kept the food safe from bears, and placed it in the shade at the back of the cook tent. All the other supplies were set in a row on each side of the "cook tent," which we rarely cooked in. Near the kitchen we fixed a box of staple supplies,

along with another box, christened the "snack box," where all the food for lunches was kept. After this labor we soon settled into a routine of work and exploration.

Each morning after breakfast everyone delved into the snack box and packed his own lunch—Jersey Cream biscuits, cheese, raisins, apricots, figs, chocolate—and with rucksack on back, camera and binoculars slung on, set off. Thus four or five different localities were explored on each trip. And the big news in our lives, related each evening as we sat at dinner, went something like this:

George: "Three ptarmigan nests, one with seven eggs, two with six. Two tree sparrow nests. One yellowlegs nest. I marked them all. I saw three bands of caribou and got close enough to photograph a cow and calf, and by that little lake just north of this one I stood behind a clump of spruce and a beautiful bull with a good set of antlers came right by and I got two pictures before he heard the camera."

Brina: "I found a least-sandpiper nest and the female stayed right around me, making little sounds, and getting back on the eggs right there within five feet of me while I kept on taking pictures."

And Bob: "I got movies of a cross fox; maybe the same one we heard the other night. He still had a beautiful brush, and trotted and galloped clear across that flat by the river right in front of me.

I don't think these animals up here know about man—they don't seem to have fear."

Our lake, by far the largest in the region, was the richest in animal activity. On the days when we stayed in camp to write in our journals, put up specimens, or perform camp chores, the animal world still claimed us. The girdle of water next to the shore widened each day, but for ten days after we landed the ice was still a highway for animals. One afternoon Bob sat just below camp watching the performance of three muskrats. Suddenly they all dived. He glanced around. A fine big gray wolf stood above him on the slope. There is no knowing who was more surprised, but Lobo did not run; he merely turned and trotted back, and down to the ice. Bob called to us with utmost urgency in his deep tones. We all rushed out, and stood entranced, watching our first wolf going away unhurriedly to the far shore. And that is how our lake came to be named Lobo.

From the diary:
"June 4: Olaus got up ahead of the rest of us this morning. I drifted off to sleep again and was in the midst of some dream of a court trial when I heard Olaus's voice: 'Brina! Look out of your tent, out on the ice.' Then: 'Mardy!'

" 'Yes, I'm looking.'

"Walking across the middle of the lake in leisurely fashion, eleven caribou, three bulls with antlers in the velvet in the lead. The cows and a yearling stopped to drink off the surface of the ice at one point. The scene was so quiet, the sound of their feet on the slush ice such a lovely whispering sound.

"Now Olaus and I have been walking upriver, first above it along the ridge running back of our camp, then down to it, and now I sit on a patch of fine dry sand on one of the big sand bars this river makes at each of its bends as it comes down through here in broad sweeps, leisurely yet steadily. We have just made a detour into a small lake back of the beach where four species of ducks went about their living—scaups, pintails, white-winged scoters, and old squaws. I thought their 'Ah-hah-*hah*-wi' a half-sad, wistful, questioning kind of call, but Olaus says: 'Don't worry. They're happy!'

"We have walked the edge of gravel on these bars, looking for fossils for Otto and wishing he could come up and look with us. George says: 'If we could only find a giant beaver skull for Otto!'

"We have also watched a band of sixty-five caribou on a big grassy flat across the river—standing, feeding, lying down, finally ambling into spruce forest on a slope—but I'm sure they never knew about us. We are wondering whether they are going to stay in this valley to have their fawns, or whether they will be moving on further west. Looking with glasses back toward camp, I saw Brina and George stooping over something in the tundra, and in the distance Bob, with his movie tripod set up. 'There's your whole crew, Olaus, hard at work.'"

When we landed on the ice of Lobo on June 1, the snow was gone from the land and the prevailing color was brown; there was no green vegetation except for the little spruce trees. But there was one flower blooming, flat on the ground, a single deep red-purple saxifrage, a lone but definite announcement of winter's end—*Saxifraga oppositifolia*. Multitudes of others were crowding close behind it, and in only one week Lobo was a different place. The first week of June in the Arctic must be the most exciting time of the year. Dwarf birch, Labrador tea, heather, cranberry, all sorts of annuals and grasses and alpine blossoms came into bud, into leaf, into flower, so fast we were bewildered. The botanists could hardly keep up with the show. On June 5 George made a trip to the north shoulder of Table Mountain (the one named mountain), east of Lobo. We called this north shoulder "the Ridge." He came striding home across the ice at six o'clock, three and a half hours from the top, after a long day and many miles of hiking and climbing with nothing to eat but a pocketful of raisins. "What a country! Those clear mountain streams, and those slopes, full of flowers, and such valleys! And from on top, the mountains just go like this, up and down, up and down—you want to keep going, up one ridge and down another!"

Then he proceeded to empty onto the moss a gorgeous assortment of alpine flowers. These had to be sorted out, laid carefully flat on the plant-press papers, each sheet labeled with locality, date, elevation, and other pertinent information, and pressed between the blotter sheets of the press. All this had to be done before George would eat, and we were all clustered around him, trying to help, and admiring the tiny gentians, forget-me-nots, and others we did not even know.

Two days later Olaus announced at breakfast that he wanted to go "over to the mountain" to the foot of the Ridge. Brina and Bob and I looked at one another. Here was something I had hoped wouldn't come up just yet. A year before, Olaus had still been a patient at the National Jewish Hospital in Denver, about to be discharged after thirteen months and a miraculous recovery from military tuberculosis. Our expedition had been delayed exactly two years on account of this. The young folks and I had discussed going up the Ridge for a day, but had agreed we should wait a little, as we thought perhaps Olaus shouldn't climb much yet. So on this morning I said: "O.K., I'll go with you, if you're only going *to* the mountain; then another day we can all go and climb up where George did."

So what happened? After thirty-one years I should have known! We went to the top of course, and Olaus wasn't as winded as I was. He even went on over the top a little way, "to see what's on the other side."

Our route led around the base of the ridge on which we were camped. It extended back from camp and back from the lake, north along the river, then out across a big belt of tundra pools and scattered spruce forest to a rather large lake half free of ice. In it were twenty white-winged scoters, several greater scaups, and some pintails. Olaus sat down with the glasses. I said: "Come look here. There's something that looks like a grebe, and I don't know . . ."

Then followed the usual routine. He looked for a while, saying nothing, and then handed me the glasses. I, hesitating, said: "Well—horned grebe?"

"Yes, that's right; and I'm sure George and Brina haven't that one listed yet."

So that was a highlight of the day, news to carry back to Brina.

We had left camp at nine; at ten we were enjoying the lake and the ducks. At eleven we had sloshed and hopped and slogged across a great wet muskeg flat and were in the spruce again at the foot of the Ridge. At twelve we were halfway up, still in spruce and some willow, but at the edge of the great slate slide that marked that side of the mountain. There were alpine-type moss-covered rocks and mossy hummocks, with the roar of a stream in a draw near by. We went over to it and sat on soft hummocks in a fairyland of tiny moss plants, and ate our lunch, drinking ice-clear water from the stream.

We then began traversing, gaining altitude up over the treeless top third of the slope, among yellow, purple, and blue alpine flowers, with pipits "pipit-ing" and once the sudden "snore" of a rock ptarmigan which flew off in front of us. We were really climbing, but I think we both noticed the helpful difference from our home altitude in the Tetons of Wyoming, for here our base was only 2,500 feet rather than 6,500. We were only slightly out of breath, and felt no heart pumping. The weariness in our long-unused climbing muscles was the main reason for the stops. And it was this muscle-weariness that crept upon us toward the end of the long trek back at the end of the day. But the day was worth the price.

On top, across a carpet of mountain avens, heather, dwarf willows, and dozens of other lovely small plants, a balmy breeze blew. The sun was high and blazing. I lay flat on the moss and heather, hat over my face, and felt absolute content. This cannot be put into words. Here I was, privileged to lie on top of a mountain in the Arctic, an observer of the richness of this short summer pageant. Through half-closed eyes I looked across the valley to the west and north. The mountains made an unearthly beautiful frieze against the blue: numberless, snowy, streaked with dark rocks, various in shape—shoulders, domes, spires, and castles—and cliffs and screes on the slopes reaching to the darkness of the belt of forest. And then the broad valley, the winding Sheenjek, the countless lakes. I know nothing of painting, but I felt for a moment the urge a landscape painter must experience—to brush great strokes of brown and fawn and purple-gray and silver upon canvas. Gazing at such a scene, through half-closed eyes, from a mountaintop strikes through to your inmost heart. The place, the scene, the breeze, the bird song, the fragrance of myriad brave burgeoning mosses and flowers—all blend into one clear entity, one jewel. It is the Arctic in its unbelievably accelerated summer life. It is also the personal well-being purchased by striving—by lifting and setting down your legs, over and over, through the muskeg, up the slopes, gaining the summit—man using himself. This wondrous mingling of weariness and triumph and sudden harmony with the exquisite airs, the burgeoning life of the bird and plant world of the tops, is part of the "glad tidings," surely, which John Muir meant when he said: "Climb the mountains and get their glad tidings."

When Olaus came back from his "little look at the other side," we stood and took a long view before starting down. Facing west, we looked across the "wide, lake-dotted valley floor" with the river winding in great broad loops through it and on to the southeast. Far to our right, to the north, was the head of the valley, up against the crest, or backbone, of the main range itself, which runs east and west. From that crest, all the way to Table Mountain, short steep mountain masses, also running east and west, rise on both sides of the river. The mountain world here seems to multiply itself—mountain and valley, mountain and valley, all the canyons emptying into the Sheenjek. Each valley made me wonder what was at the head of it, what was on the other side. But the heart of the whole region is, of course, the river.

Coming down the little channels of turf over the limestone formation was fun, and when we hit the forest we followed it all the way back, avoiding the big muskeg flat to the north. The last miles through the springy soft moss stretched themselves out; we had to stop and rest several times though it was getting late and I thought Bob might be worrying about us.

We passed a lot of bear diggings. I said: "If we meet him now I'm just going to lie down and let him have me!"

"Oh, no, you won't. All you have to remember is to *stand*, not run."

I wondered about this—and still do! However, no bear appeared, and half a mile from camp, sure enough, we met Bob, who was out looking for us. Bless them, he and Brina had dinner all ready—vegetable soup, corned beef, mashed potatoes. And we found the weariness fading away in the stimulation of food and comfort and good company.

Lying in the little tent that night, bandana tied over my eyes to keep out the light of this twenty-four-hour day, I listened to the sounds of Lobo. The ptarmigan, robust and comical: "Come here, come here, come here—go back, go back, go back"; the tree sparrow, a cascade of sweet notes; the white-crown, plaintive, questioning, but strong. Always these three voices, and from the lake the ducks, the loons, the gulls. This was their world. We were the fortunate visitors.

From the diary:

"June 8: This morning we were up early, but were still fussing along with various chores when suddenly someone hissed: 'Caribou coming on the ice!'

"Bob grabbed his movie camera and went up the hill to shoot down on them, and Olaus went along with his still camera. The rest of us went on with packing our lunches until in the middle of a word I saw the whole bunch coming on up, right near camp. Brina and George dove for their cameras, I for my glasses, and we flung ourselves down on the moss. Seventeen caribou, bulls, cows, and yearlings, clicking along, right past camp, silhouetted against the ice, heels clicking on it—blue sky and low brown hills to the south behind them. This clicking sound is thought by some scientists to be a snapping of tendons in the ankle. They seemed not aware of us at all. Brina exclaimed in a hushed voice: 'How many people in the world ever get to see anything like this? How lucky can one be? The pattern of those long legs—the sound of their feet! What a memory to have!'

"And George: 'Yes, but it's *over* so fast—you have that *feeling* of the thing, and then it's already just a memory!'

"Bob and Olaus came back happy; Bob's only complaint was that he had run out of film. Olaus and I then left on another trip upriver, covering some of the same tundra muskeg, bars, and ridges that we had traveled over the other day, but going further, counting several bands of caribou, watching the ducks on their favorite pond again. We also came upon many quite recent bear diggings in the mixed tundra and spruce on higher ground, so that I found myself looking to both sides and behind as we went along. But it was good walking, and sweetly, tangily fragrant in the spruce taiga. One has to lift a foot a bit higher springing through the moss, but we've discovered that if we keep a very relaxed, almost lazy, attitude about it and just slosh and slog along with no muscles tense, it is not tiring, and certainly much easier than hippety-hopping through the tussock-type muskeg places. After so much of that in years past in the Koyukuk and the Old Crow, we bless the Sheenjek for its variety; we can nearly always avoid the tussock patches.

"We came down to the river again where a little muddy creek wound in from the east. It was too wide to jump and too deep to wade, so at its mouth we sat on a sandy bank and ate lunch and drank good muddy water. A beautiful blue day, and so quiet—still no mosquitoes! A pair of American widgeons drifted past, the male calling his whistling note now and then: "Whee, *whee* whew." Then from upstream came a long, lonesome "Wah, ah-a," and into view came a single bird. I handed Olaus the glasses. The same routine, he looking, handing me the glasses without a word, and I, quaveringly: 'A loon? Some kind of loon—it has a red throat!'

" 'Yes, that's right. red-throated loon, true bird of the Arctic!'

"So we sat watching as he floated by us and on down around the bend of the river, and as he went he kept turning his head, that beautiful soft gray head, to the left and right, as though searching the banks of the river for something, and three times as he went by us he uttered that long, dreamlike, lonely cry. 'Is he looking for another loon?' I asked.

" 'Oh, I don't know. Maybe. That's just the call they have,' the scientist said.

" 'Yes, but he sounds so lonesome; he sounds just the way I'd *feel* like sounding if I had lost *you* and couldn't find you!'

"We came home by way of the long wet sand bar, which bore wolf tracks, hundreds of caribou tracks, and one big moose track. We looked in every spot of gravel for fossil bones for Otto, but found none. Reaching camp, we found Bob and George just arriving jubilantly from their day southeast of Lobo at the grayling stream flowing out of a little lake, which Bob had discovered the day before. Five big grayling for our dinner!

"The day was warmer than ever today, and I could feel my face and hands 'cooking' despite nylon fisherman's hat, baby lotion, and mentholatum. But the land is deceptive; you are quite comfortable in the sun in cotton flannel shirt and heavy trouser and rubber pacs, because there is always a little cool breeze. There is no shade anyway; the sun is high and the spruces so scattered. And when the day is over, or rather when you call it a day and crawl in, and catch a glimpse of yourself in the camp mirror, you realize you are becoming the color of old leather, pouches swollen round your eyes, queer bumps on your cheeks. But it is part of the adventure, and none of us would think of criticizing this weather!

"June 10: Olaus and I had another long day afield. We were walking through ptarmigan all day, but it is impossible to find their nests except by sitting down somewhere and just watching the female until she goes to the nest—such protective mechanisms I never saw before. Even when Brina led me to the one on the hill behind camp and pointed right at the bird, it took me a few moments to distinguish the streaky brown feathers down at the base of a dwarf birch bush.

"At lunchtime we were far over near the base of the hills, and Olaus wanted to go across the big flat to the river and home that way. I was not bubbling over with enthusiasm, but we started across, through real old-time Alaska muskeg tussocks. You have to try to find a space for your rubber pac in the wet squishy moss between the tussocks, for if you step on top of one you will be tipped off balance every time. I was just beginning to worry about where we would find the energy for the return across these acres of 'footstools' when we came to an unsuspected stream, clear and sparkling, spread out in the grass. Olaus had to admit we couldn't cross this one without getting wet, so we sloshed and slogged back to the ridge and started the homeward trek. After about five hours I seem to reach a back-achy, heavy-in-the-legs state, in which I get pretty mad because Olaus went so far, and it's too far back to camp, and why do we *always* have to go so far, etc., etc. And always at this point some sweet inhabitant of this land furnishes relief. This time each of us found a tree-sparrow nest. Brina is making a study of their nesting and is delighted with every find. Mine had five eggs. Nice, the reciprocal living in the wilderness—the tree sparrow lines her nest with ptarmigan feathers!

"Then, as we finally neared camp, we found a pair of horned grebes in the little lake just north of our Lobo Lake, and a pair of Bonaparte gulls. We hope they are paired and staying so Bob can get movies.

"The rhododendron (*Rhododendron lapponicum*) so common all over our slopes here is just beginning to bloom—in a few days we expect our little world to be rose-colored. George had had another wonderful day—south, past the grayling lake and stream, and up on the slopes, east of the river. His great event that day was meeting and photographing a lynx. Brina had spent the day in the vicinity of the grayling lake, in the area which she calls Table Mountain ponds, chasing sandpipers, and brought in specimens of four different species.

"After dinner I decided to make a cake, to see if it was possible to make cake too from our famous flour mix which Bob and I had invented and mixed at Otto's house in Fairbanks. Here is the 'recipe':

> 10 lbs. white flour
> 10 lbs. whole-wheat flour
> 5 lbs. yellow corn meal
> 5 lbs. soy flour
> 3 lbs. wheat germ

"These ingredients were mixed well and put up in three heavy plastic bags.

"It was becoming cloudy and cool. Bob got a fire going in the Yukon stove in the tent, and we took cover for the first time. It worked remarkably well and the tent was cozy, and we were all grateful to our friend Jack McPhee, who had unearthed for us from the Northern Commercial Company warehouse in Fairbanks what must have been the last Yukon stove in town. This brought me one more realization of how life had changed in my home town. Every family used to have a Yukon stove—an oblong box of heavy tin divided into a fire box and an oven, with a door to each. They were stored in a cache or shed, and used on picnics and camping and dog-team trips. In 1956 we had had to scour the town to find one, but it was a treasure. Just a few little sticks warmed the tent, cooked a meal, baked a cake. The cake wasn't too bad either—at least it disappeared quickly; I sprinkled brown sugar and a few of the precious pecans on top of the batter before baking.

"At bedtime we got everything under cover, for it still looked threatening. Olaus and I lay in our beds, trying a Double-Crostic puzzle, and also enjoying the talk and laughter of the three young people in the cook tent, who were comparing bird notes and chatting. Olaus murmured: 'Sounds good, doesn't it?' and turned over and was immediately asleep.

"June 11: It did rain during the night, a gentle rain lasting several hours, but in the morning it was clearing, and after lunch the whole 'family' went off together for the first time, around the east end of the lake and over a ridge where in a fairly dense stand of trees George had found an old cache a few days ago. Under one tree lay an old hand-made toboggan, two axes and a saw, and an old pack frame. In a tall spruce, the trapper or prospector or whoever it had been, had hung a big canvas-covered bundle by a rope and then peeled the tree to keep animals from reaching it. This must have been many years ago. The tree had died, the rope had rotted and broken, and the bundle had fallen. Brina and I sat on the moss and watched while Bob and George cut the ties. Inside were two big bags of beans, one of barley, water-soaked and mouse-chewed; a heavy canvas pack case containing thread, tape, and some small tools. There was a heavy paper rice sack containing a collection of carpenter's tools and a whole set of drills. Finally, two new ax handles and on each of them written in pencil: 'Daniel Christian.'

"George tied everything up again in the canvas and put it under the sled. We wondered about this unknown man and the plans he must have had, and what had happened. The North has had many such incidents."

The next afternoon, as we were all working around camp, Brina with her sharp ears heard a plane coming from the west. Straight over it came, and George recognized it as the big Cessna on floats; it swerved over us and around, and went over to the river. Olaus and George took off right away, and Brina and I began frantically getting the mail ready in a heavy plastic bag. Then we dashed toward the river, but saw a whole group coming over the tundra. "Whoops!" said Brina. "They're coming in for coffee—better get the stove going!"

Keith was on his regular weekly run to Arctic Village over on the Chandalar, and he had brought with him Abraham John, the Indian storekeeper there, and his young niece, Jessie James, to give them a ride and to check up on us and on the landing possibilities. We were delighted, as we had been wondering how he could bring Don MacLeod in on the fifteenth, seeing that Lobo had not thawed out yet. But he made the landing and the take-off on the river with no trouble at all. We served chocolate and coffee and my baking-powder bread with peanut butter and jelly, and had a nice visit. Abraham told us about Daniel Christian. He must have left the cache there many years ago and never come back; he was an old man when he was found frozen to death in his cabin near Christian Village. They thought he must have been sick and unable to keep the fire going.

We also got out our maps and looked over the upriver situation with Keith, for Olaus wanted to move closer into the mountains later on, if possible. Keith munched a Jersey Cream biscuit, sitting on the mossy slope with his long legs curled under him, calmly scrutinized our maps, and smiled his slow reassuring smile. "O.K. One of these times we'll take a reconnaissance flight up there. It will be good to see some of that country anyway, now the lakes are thawing. Looks as though there's one at least we might land on."

Flying was such a mysterious business to me that I was forever marveling at the calm, unhurried efficiency of these bush pilots and their lack of conceit about their work.

Jessie James (which her uncle pronounced Jamis) was a regulation teen-ager—jeans rolled halfway up, bobby socks, ballet slippers (which got good and wet on the trip from the river to the camp), her short hair permanented and carefully done up in curls. She was very shy but had a nice smile, and she did volunteer that she liked the wild flowers and that at Arctic Village they did not have "this kind" (the rhododendron), so on the way back to the plane she and I picked some and I told her that the bouquet would prove to her family that she had landed somewhere.

The mosquitoes arrived on June 13, but were nothing compared with the swarm at Old Crow. Our breezy camp site was a blessing, and the repellent seemed to deal with them satisfactorily. Well smeared, knowing they wouldn't bite, one could ignore them, almost forget them, and this is what we did until late July, when they died away. But none of us ever said we enjoyed their song!

Next morning at six-thirty there was a cry of "Grizzly!" from George. I don't know how Brina got into her clothes so fast, but she joined the race. The three of them returned, puffing, just as Olaus got the fire going. It had been a small light grizzly, on the flat at the east end of Lobo. He had run off promptly, a fact I was not too sorry about. We proceeded to our breakfast of fruit, oatmeal, scrambled powdered eggs, and new bread, but midway in the meal George spied a big cow moose galloping along on the flat at the west end of the lake. I couldn't remember ever having seen a moose gallop. Olaus said perhaps it was because our Jackson Hole moose have no enemies and have become phlegmatic—like humans!

On June 14 George departed, pack on back, for a three-day exploration trip east and north along the mountainsides; Brina and Olaus and I went eastward too, then separated. She was working through the hillside habitat and we were headed for the first, or southernmost, of the Table Mountain group, where George had reported some great cliffs on top, with peregrine falcons—the duck hawks of Old Crow memories. Bob had gone off southwestward with movie camera and fishing gear.

This was the hottest day yet; we went over two lines of ridges, with long muskeg between, past the grayling lake and stream, over another ridge, down into the deep bed of a big mountain stream of clear water rushing over gravel. It was split into channels in such a way that it was easy to wade, and it seemed like a Wyoming mountain scene for those moments. And there we discovered the one and only cottonwood tree, a beautiful balm of Gilead at least thirty feet tall and still in the fragrant sticky bud stage.

After a long time of tramping upward through moss-floored spruce forest and then copses of dwarf birch, we at last came to the timber line, the bare heath dotted with purple anemones and yellow dwarf daisies and mountain avens, and this should have been pure pleasure. But there is a test involved in all this climbing. After miles of muskeg your leg muscles are heavy and complaining. The test, of course, is to keep your mind on other subjects. The best I could do was think of mountaineers and all the famous climbs I had read about. That helped some, but at last, as we neared the top, I said: "If I just sat down here, would you find me on your way back?"

"No," Olaus said emphatically, "I don't want to come back this way; I want to go down over there to the left, on that other slope. You're doing fine—just fine—you can make it!"

So I did. On the top there were no mosquitoes, and I went sound asleep on the turf with my hat over my face while Olaus went around the shoulder to the cliffs and back to join me, having seen no duck hawks.

How grateful we were that night to those two young people who had dinner ready when we got home and waited on us! We also learned that the helicopter we had spotted from on top had landed right on the knoll back of camp just after Bob had arrived home—Messrs. Foley and Myer, of the U.S. Geological Survey camp at Old John Lake. They "just dropped in" to see how we were getting along, which was very good of them. Olaus and I were sorry we hadn't been able to meet them. They were mapping the Sheenjek and surrounding country.

Talking about mapping led to a discussion of the future of this wilderness. When Keith came over unexpectedly on his Arctic Village run a few days before, he had said as we walked over to camp: "I know you want to be quiet up here and I don't want to disturb the atmosphere for you, but I thought I'd better find out about what time you thought you'd want to move on upriver."

Keith was sincere in this thought; he was not being facetious. One Cessna on floats skimming quietly onto a lake, and departing again, leaving no tracks, does not seem to alter the "spirit of the place." But suppose some real lovers of the wilderness were camped here and six float planes full of people came skimming in—what then? So it resolves itself into the same old problem—people and their attitudes and sensitivities. We cannot blame the plane, the motors, the machines, the inventions. In every phase of life, from the cold war to building new towns, machines will be destroyers or benefactors according to the way in which they are used by man. I could not help recalling a little piece I read in the *Wildlife Review* of the British Columbia Game Commission, about a couple who hiked many miles into the Canadian wilderness for a much-needed quiet vacation. It was wonderful. Two days later a plane came clattering in and landed on their lake—acquaintances of theirs who thought they "would just fly over and see how you were getting along."

We discussed this problem many times at our campfire (a campfire, by the way, which burned only dry dead trees and branches, never a standing tree), and we all agreed that many people could see and live in and enjoy this wilderness in the course of a season, if they would just come a very few at a time, never a party larger than six, and then leave the camp site absolutely neat. It is possible, and this attitude of consideration, and reverence, is an integral part of an attitude toward life, toward the unspoiled, still evocative places on our planet. If man does not destroy himself through his idolatry of the machine, he may learn one day to step gently on his earth.

3

Both Sides of the River

From the diary:

"June 16: All these days lately we had been talking about Don MacLeod and wondering whether he would really be able to pull himself away from all his patients in Jackson Hole, whether he could possibly get here right on the fifteenth. So yesterday was a day of great suspense. We kept busy, getting mail ready, getting the camp in order. Bob and I renovated and redid the arrangements in the cook tent so there would be room for people to sit and work, etc., and Bob arranged space for Don to sleep in his and George's tent. At five-thirty we had vegetable soup and chicken pot pie with biscuit bread in the skillet just about ready when Bob and Brina both cried at once: 'A plane!'

"What a happy scramble to get to the river in time; but Keith very thoughtfully circled over the camp first, so that we all four got to the bank in time to see him land downstream like a big seagull and taxi to a good landing beach. I fairly tumbled down the bank to the beach and got my glasses out and screamed up to Olaus, who was just arriving at the top of the bank: 'It *is* Don—it *is*!' and I could see that Don was grinning and grinding away with his little 8-mm movie camera as Olaus and Brina both scrambled to catch the rope from Keith; all the while Bob had been catching the whole scene from on top of the bank with his 16-mm. As Don stepped ashore and reached for Olaus's hand he turned to me and said: 'Look at that face of his, just look at that sunburn. Doesn't he look great?'

"With great glee everyone took a load of something to carry over to the camp, and when I said to Keith: 'Can't you stay to dinner?' he answered: 'Well yes, I guess I could; Eila and the kids went on the Wien Airlines tour to Point Barrow and won't be back till tomorrow.'

"Here was a real celebration, and to add to it, Keith handed me a flat package he had been carrying very gingerly. Mrs. Cheek, wife of the manager of the Northern Commercial at Fort Yukon, had sent us a big cake! I flipped quickly through the big bundle of mail looking for familiar handwriting from New York—yes, both young parents well, waiting, impatient. I rejoined our celebration with a light heart.

"Today was another beautiful hot day. Don was the first one up, building the fire at six o'clock. 'Don't know whether I can get used to this all-the-time daylight!'

"Right after breakfast Bob departed for the river to start assembling and inflating the big rubber boat which had come up on this load. Olaus and Don draped themselves with cameras and lenses, and lunch, and started off to the river bars beyond the west end of the lake. I stood and watched them go off over the muskeg, talking busily, and I knew how eager and happy Olaus was to be able to show Don some of his north country, and I realized that here and now was one of the great unforgettable moments of our lives. Two years ago today the doctors at the National Jewish Hospital had been shaking their heads. Today Olaus and the doctor who had so quickly diagnosed his trouble and packed him off to that wonderful hospital, were striding like young schoolboys across the arctic tundra!

"I went with Brina to investigate some nests Bob had located, and walking across the tundra with her was a fascinating lesson in botany and the study of habitats. Each inch or so of height in the swamp-muskeg complex carries a little different set of plants. Also intriguing are the polygons of frost heaves enclosing very wet green swamp; they look almost like rice paddies. Brina explained to me that scientists do not know everything about how these interesting formations come about; research on them is still going on, but the current theory is that they start as a result of contraction caused by cold, especially where the soil is fine-grained and not granular. Then the freezing of moisture from all sources causes enlargement in the cracks. By the fall of the second year of their formation, the water in the cracks freezes early in the season, being pure water, and once ice forms it attracts more water, which freezes too, and the cracks are further increased. By this process, ice wedges form around the edges of the original polygon. Each year the wedges get bigger and bigger and force up the ground around them, forming ridges, and vegetation grows over the top; thus there are vegetated ridges all round the circumference of these polygons, which are usually about ten to fifteen feet across.

"Brina and I smeared ourselves well with 6—12 and then approached the least sandpiper's nest to within five feet and sat down quietly. She came off, cheeping, walked all around us, went back, and settled on her eggs again. She did this several times, but it was more as though she were welcoming us to her home than that she was afraid of us.

"George returned from his three-day hike on schedule. We delayed dinner a little while tonight, and sure enough, as Don was cooking the big steaks he had brought with him he glanced toward the east trail and said: 'Here comes your other boy now.'

"George was limping. He had pulled a muscle in one leg and looked haggard, with hollows in his cheeks. He hadn't taken enough food, of course, and had traveled so far upriver that he had had to walk from three o'clock this morning in order to get back to us when he had said he would! He was glad to collapse on the moss. Brina gave him hot tea with honey immediately, and he then proceeded to savor the steak and mashed potatoes and fruit salad. And we had saved half of Mrs. Cheek's cake too."

On the afternoon of the seventeenth, George, in camp to put up specimens and recover from the pulled muscle, heard a plane coming, and Brina said: "Oh-oh, I bet it's John Buckley with all my stuff for the plots."

So it was—John Buckley, of the Fish and Wildlife Service wildlife research unit at the University of Alaska, one of our most enthusiastic helpers in all our plans for this study, and his pilot, Jim King. In addition to all the material which Brina would need farther upriver for her study of a few of the "random plots" they had marked from maps, they brought the mail and a huge apple pie from Mrs. Cheek. What a woman! John and Brina got out the aerial photos and discussed the work she was to do—all part of an extensive observation of wildlife ecology in many parts of Alaska, a long-range project Dr. John had undertaken in co-operation with the Air Force. From aerial photographs and maps, following some system of "random" selection, a number of spots all over northern Alaska had been marked on maps. Two of these fell in the upper Sheenjek Valley, one on the east side, one on the west. At each of these locations Brina was to mark off a plot, using twine and colored plastic flags, which could be seen from the air, for markers, and here she was to set traps at regular intervals, to trap resident rodents. She was also to make a study and census of the vegetative cover, the species of plants, and the types of soil.

Such methods are routine among ecologists for determining animal population, variation in numbers from time to time, and their effect on the plant cover of an area. I gathered that so far as the Air Force was concerned, they were interested in knowing what conditions their men might find in various parts of Alaska and what plants and animals could be used for food in case of forced landings or other emergencies.

Meanwhile Don and I made coffee and chocolate and brought out the pan of Logan bread Bob had baked the evening before, and we had a good visit, sitting there watching the scoters and widgeons and old squaws and getting all the news of the university. They left at five. They had a dinner engagement in Fort Yukon and were flying back to Fairbanks afterward. Ah, wilderness! When no plane appears in the sky, and we hear no sound of one, the whole world seems as remote as can be, and this world *is* as wild and untouched as it ever was. Then a plane speaks from the air and you realize it is after all only 130 miles by air from Fort Yukon; whereas the tortuous 260 miles of river, difficult to navigate, has all through the years kept this region untouched, the plane makes it accessible in a matter of an hour and a half. This feeling is hard to analyze. Mrs. Cheek takes an apple pie out of her electric freezer in Fort Yukon at noon, and we eat it with great gusto on the banks of Lobo Lake in the wilds at six o'clock.

It was nice to see these thoughtful friendly people, to feel their interest and support, and nice to get the mail—and also nice to have the quiet world close in around us again and revert to our own harmonious little routine.

As I went down along the lake shore after dinner to brush my teeth I suddenly heard that strange lonesome cry from way over east. I called the others, and we all stood on the brow of the hill in

the midst of the rhododendrons and listened for several moments to that infinitely wild call. To human ears, it seems a cry of measureless loneliness, like a soul alone since time was, condemned to loneliness for all time to come—the cry of the red-throated loon. To the loon, as Olaus said, it is no doubt the expression of spring urges and fulfillment of a cycle of growth.

There had been a little shower around noon that day, and as we stood in the rhododendrons the fragrance of the blossoms rose all round us. "Oh boy," exclaimed George, "those flowers—they just send me!"

During dinner a pair of lesser yellowlegs were going through a courtship performance just below camp at the edge of the water, the male springing into the air with wings folded close over his back.

By these little scenes and episodes the hours were filled and enlivened. And they were hours without pressures, without schedules, without bells or appointments. Each one decided his own activity for the day; the day flowed by; we gathered at dinner to exchange news and views and to enjoy being together.

From the diary:
"June 19: The past two evenings Don and the young ones have held a sort of infirmary in the cook tent before bed. From our tent Olaus and I listened and chuckled. We knew that Don was first

massaging George's pulled leg tendon, then doing something to Bob's ingrown toenail, with Brina enjoying the whole process immensely.

"At 3:20 A.M. I awakened and remembered that Brina wanted to be called then if any of us happened to wake up. She was going to go up to the first creek north again after an alder flycatcher she had seen, and she thought very early was the time to find the bird. I crawled out and went over to her tent—nobody there. Back to bed; pretty soon the rain started, and it really rained; a lovely sound on the tent and so cozy inside. Yet there's always the thought: 'How long does it keep on?'"

On the nineteenth Keith flew over from Arctic Village after his regular run there and with a soft "whoosh" landed east of camp and taxied gently up to us; at last Lobo was free of ice. He had with him Elias "Jamis," the chief of Arctic Village, a studious-looking little Indian who wore glasses. Keith had told us that all of these people were eager to get in the plane and have a ride, any time. Keith had come to see about moving us, and it was decided he would take a run upriver right then on a reconnaissance. Olaus, of course, had to go; I thought Don should go, but found myself being overruled and fairly pushed down the bank, just as I was. "Well, is there anything to be sick in, in the plane?"

Keith looked at me with his quizzical smile. "You going to be sick?"

"Well, no, I don't think so, but I'd feel better knowing there was something! Brina, bring me one of those plyofilm bags off the willow bush there!"

Olaus sat in back, I up front, with the aerial photos and map and my plyofilm bag in my lap. We were off in no time, smoothly, out over the river, cutting off all the meanders, flying past the mountain we were calling "First Mountain," which was west of the river, looking down on the shallow ponds displaying green and yellow algae around their shores. We passed a long narrow lake on the west, which was shown on the map, and then, on the east side, a smaller, more or less boot-shaped one; it was smaller than Lobo, but Keith said it looked deep enough and long enough to land on. But this lake was only about eighteen miles north of Lobo, and we were hoping for one a bit farther into the mountains. Soon we were passing a large creek coming in from the west; above this point the Sheenjek suddenly splits into braided channels, with great stretches of solid overflow ice, white with brilliant blue spots, all over the river flats. This ice, we gathered, was permanent ice but would not be safe to land on. Now the valley was narrowing and mountains stood "edgewise" in relation to the river, one sharp face after another, one narrow valley after another ascending at right angles to the river, rushing torrents coming down out of them. The whole eastern side looked sharp, austere, almost forbidding, a little vegetation on the steep deltas of the streams and along the river itself. On the western side the valleys seemed greener, more varied in terrain, with gentler slopes and in places what looked like real stands of cottonwood, with tall spruces. At one point, up ahead, there seemed to be a lake, but when we reached it it was another ice field, and by then we were almost at the head of the valley; we could see where the river branched right and left around a mountain ahead. I glanced back at Olaus and could tell that he was strictly looking for mountain-sheep trails! Any reconnaissance for camp sites, Keith and I would have to do! I looked at the map again. "That right-hand fork up there must lead over to the pass to the Kongakut."

"Yes, and up there at the left, see the glacier the Sheenjek comes out of? I guess we had better get turned around."

Keith turned. We had been flying low; it felt to me we were about halfway down the mountainsides, and now the valley seemed so narrow I didn't see how there was room to turn, but of course Keith did it easily, and we passed close to a golden-brown striated mountain on the western side. I remembered Don's words the night he arrived: "I'd fly anywhere with that fellow!" So would we all. I was concentrating so hard, trying to see lakes, river bars, mountain sheep, everything, that I felt cross-eyed, but there was no hint of sickness. In fact it was wonderful fun, and over too quickly. I so enjoyed the way Keith dropped over the brow of the hill on which we were camped and lit on Lobo like a duck, with hardly a jar. All this in twenty minutes.

It was agreed then that Keith would come on the twenty-sixth and move us to the boot-shaped lake; everyone thought it would be worth the move, to be really in the mountains, one day closer to the divide, and with Brina in a good position to reach the plots she was to set up. Our next week would be spent exploring the western side of the river, now that we had the rubber boat.

On the longest day of the year we had our first all-day rain, but we survived cheerfully. Bob kept the Yukon stove going, and it is just amazing how meals can be cooked and served in an eight-by-ten tent with six people present, with the added business of juggling all the boxes and cartons about so that the scientific equipment and the specimens are kept dry. Meals were fun, and also games of skill, but we managed a good dinner—rice, fried ham, and apricot tapioca pudding, which Don made. The skill is to balance your plate on your knees, find a flat place on the floor for your cup that is not occupied by another cup or a foot, watch your own feet so that you don't kick your neighbor's cup over, and move both feet and cup when some dish or pot has to be moved into or out of the tent. After we ate we set all the dishes out in the rain, and everyone kept busy, reading, writing, talking. At this point we were glad we had brought a little paperback library along. Don was reading *The Sands of Karakorum*, and Olaus a life of Nansen.

The men had had two wonderful days of exploring the mountains across the river, and on the third trip across Brina and I went along, with Don and Bob, on our first ride in the "*S.S. Sheenjek.*" Just back from the western bank of the river there was a shallow lake which we had to skirt to reach the low ridges behind. Brina left us here and went over into a real grove of poplar, quite rare this far north, to see what birds she might find. Bob, Don, and I climbed the low ridge running along behind the lake and followed the ridge southward, knob to knob, looking for fox or wolf dens, or anything. "Anything" turned out to be arrowheads; on one of those gravelly knolls I picked up one unmistakably worked piece. Immediately I remembered the letter of instructions from our young son Donald, who was studying anthropology at the University of Wisconsin. I had the letter, back in camp, and as I stood there holding this little piece of stone out for Bob to see I could hear Donald's quiet, deep voice saying: "If you find any evidences of old sites, there's a *right* way to do these things."

What great fun it would be to find something more. But none of us could find anything else at that spot and we went on. In any case, it was a fine day. Walking the ridges was easy and pleasant, and this was an ideal day for travel—cool and breezy but sunny, and no mosquitoes; and there was always the feeling of adventure, looking for whatever the country held, wondering what life was there long ago and what was there today.

Evidently these knolls were the favorite camp sites of the Indians when they went trapping and hunting, for we found many old tent sites, the bleached white tent pegs still in place. I could imagine that in the old days these knobs with their dry gravel and grass tops, and their breezes, would have been the only places where one could get away from the insects. On top of one of these we sat and ate lunch, looking close around our feet for artifacts, and far across the valley at the meanderings of the river, and listening to the roar of Old Woman Creek nearby to the south.

Later in the afternoon, after Bob had gone on ahead, Don and I started climbing the high ridge nearest the river. Don went off to one side to investigate a hole which looked like it might be a wolf or fox den, so I climbed to the summit of the ridge alone. As I reached the top, I saw right in front of me three posts, with carved pyramid-shaped tops; they were startling. Don came along just then and we walked over to examine these objects which seemed so surprising out here in the wilderness. We realized that they were the markers of an old Indian grave; rocks had been placed all over it. It was very small and must have been the grave of a child, but what work and care had been lavished on it! The tops of the posts, which had five sides, were evenly carved with great accuracy.

We stood there looking about, and it was borne in upon us strongly that this was the most beautiful and commanding view we had found yet. It took in the whole sweep of that part of the Arctic—the valley of the Sheenjek, the mountains of the Chandalar to the west and those of the Coleen to the east, the sweeping bends of the river, the myriad ponds and lakes, and Old Woman Creek, large and swift and noisy, coming in just south of the ridge on which we were standing.

When we rejoined Bob he told us that on the next and very last knob of this ridge he had discovered another grave, but of different construction; it was a sunken grave with narrow stakes all round it.

Now we had to hurry, and the straightest route took us across some muskeg with several little streams to jump over and I was really put to it to keep up with the two long-legged men. We were to meet Brina at the boat at four, but even at five we were a few minutes ahead of her. She had had a day too. She had climbed to the top of "First Mountain." "I was scared witless halfway up, but couldn't find a way to get back down, so I had to go on to the top, and then I found a way down on the sloping front slope facing the river."

I said to her: "I guess you won't be doing that again soon, will you?"

"Indeed I won't!"

Next day the men all went back to explore the region of the graves and Old Woman Creek. George's comment that evening was: "But what a place to be buried in! All that wonderful view of the mountains, and nobody else right next to you, and no old concrete slab holding you down!"

When we were planning this expedition, Olaus, in discussing it with Fairfield Osborn and some of the others, had spoken of it as a "sample adventure"—to gain intimate knowledge of one area as a guide to the planning for the whole big area we all hoped could be saved as wilderness for the future.

I thought of this phrase when the field party of the twenty-second, Don, Bob, and Olaus, finally arrived at camp, cold, wet, and excited, at 8:30 P.M. Bob, it seemed, had had one of the sample adventures.

They had gone clear to the top of the second mountain on the western side of the river, but before that, early in the afternoon, they had had an adventure. Bob, coming down from the gyrfalcon's nest on First Mountain to join Olaus and Don, came over a slope right above a bear, which Don and Olaus, far below, had sighted and were watching. Bob took many pictures, closer and closer. Suddenly the bear started trotting right up to him and he realized the bear didn't know what he was. He decided he had to get upwind so the bear would get his scent, and started running to the side. Then the bear started galloping. It was a close thing. Suddenly the bear, with a great "whoosh," stopped dead, whirled in his tracks, and ran. He was no more than twenty yards away when he slid to a sudden stop, leaving one mighty relieved and shaking boy behind him. He ran right down toward Olaus and Don then, and they both got pictures as he went by, not knowing at the moment what an escape Bob had just had, because they had been running to get into position for pictures. When Bob reached them, he was still white, they said.

He told us this was the closest escape he had ever had, and that once in combat in Italy, and on this occasion, he had the feeling of absolute finality. I said: "Yes, Bob, but how did you know what direction was upwind?"

"Oh, Mardy, you just know *instinctively!*"

I wondered. Then I said: "Bob, don't write this story to your folks; wait till you get home and then tell them."

Our travelers were mighty glad to rest, to eat, to be warm and dry. It was past eleven when we got to bed, infinitely grateful to have all the party complete.

4

Up the Valley

From the diary:

"June 28: Keith, with Abraham John to help, came at four o'clock on the twenty-sixth; they had been delayed at Arctic Village, but so efficient and methodical is he that he had made four trips and had us all settled on the upriver lake by seven. He said he was *sure* he had never flown in that much stuff from Fort Yukon for us! Olaus and Bob flew on the first trip, to select a site and get two tents up. Keith was back in twenty minutes. 'What's it like, Keith? Did you find a camp site?"

"'Yes, it's all right, I think. Yes, it *is* all right!"

"Another load was quickly stowed away, George and I the passengers this time. It was fun, flying those nine minutes— eigthteen miles, low over the country; it gave one the feeling of actually being a bird. George, sitting behind Keith, looked so eagerly, his brown eyes shining, at the big mountains up ahead."

As we taxied over the glassy water of this new lake, grayling were rising in little swirls on both sides of the plane.

So far as we knew, the only other white people who had visited this part of the Sheenjek were our friends Lowell Sumner and George Collins, who had been up there briefly, and a mapping party of the U.S. Geological Survey in 1952. When we first planned our trip, in 1954, I had visited the office of our old friend Gerald Fitzgerald in Washington, D. C., and one of his young men had given me the location of this lake and their camp. Olaus and Bob had easily found the site; one old oil drum was still standing there and a little box shelf was still nailed to one of the spruce trees. We all pitched in busily to carry the supplies from the two loads over to the camp site, and in no time Keith was back, this time with Brina, and Bob waved him in right in front of camp. Brina jumped from the pontoon to a mossy hummock with both arms full, exclaiming in her always vibrantly enthusiastic way: "Olaus, did you notice these gulls—mew gulls, aren't they?—and I bet they have a nest or young. Are they ever in a tizzy!"

The two gulls had been screaming and diving at us ever since the plane had first landed. Bob said: "Well, how would *you* feel if you thought you had this lake all to yourself and suddenly a whole horde of barbarians dropped in from the sky?"

As on June first, I felt my most valuable service would be to produce a meal, and I had with me the box of fresh supplies Keith had brought from Fort Yukon that day. By the time he landed on the lake for the fourth time, with Don, who was also greeted by the gulls, I had fresh potatoes boiling and pork chops and onions frying. And with all the constant demands on her, Evolyn Melville at the roadhouse in Fort Yukon had managed to bake extra bread for us, so we had the great luxury of real bread and jam for dessert.

But Brina is first and always a bird woman; when I saw her put down her piece of bread and jam and lift her glasses, I put down my coffee cup too and reached for my glasses as she said in an urgent low tone: "Look everybody—arctic loon!"

Apparently the bird was curious and intended to inspect this intrusion on his solitude. He floated up to within a few yards of camp, and this was the first really close look at this species for Bob and Don and me. Floating there on the glistening clear black water, black and white body in such infinitely artistic designs, he was an unforgettable picture. But the unbelievable thing about these birds is the velvety, luminescent, silver-gray over the head and the back of the neck. I don't think it can be described; it is the kind of perfection which strikes you with real impact, before which you can feel only awe and reverence. Don said: "You just couldn't find a prettier sight than this!"

And Brina, prayerfully: "Oh, I do hope there's a mate!"

By eleven-thirty camp was all set up, the supplies under cover, and all of us in our tents. All, that is, except George. He couldn't wait. An eighth of a mile east of camp, beyond gradually rising, mossy, hummocky slopes scattered with spruce, rose a dramatic, almost pyramid-shaped, gray limestone mountain, which became "Camp Mountain" for us; but George had to see what was up there right away. He came back and went to bed at 2 A.M. I didn't lie awake listening for him, but Don did.

After riffling through the mail—no letter from New York—I had dumped it all into our little tent; so when we were in our bags and I began shuffling through the letters, I noticed one with "W.O.D." in the corner of the envelope. A moment later Olaus said: "Isn't that wonderful? I didn't think he would really be able to make it!" And he called to Bob and Don in the tent next to ours: "Hey, Justice and Mrs. Douglas *are* coming after all, on the twenty-ninth! What do you think of that?"

We all put in a busy morning of settling into the camp. Don was building me a box cupboard and a table and a washstand shelf from old boxes and bits of boards left by the geologists. I remonstrated a little: "Don, I don't want you to spend your valuable vacation time on camp work."

"Mardy! That's part of the fun, you know," he replied, eyes twinkling behind his glasses.

Don was a forester before he went into medicine, and here on the Sheenjek he was the forester again, the outdoorsman, the expert camper. By noon we had a pretty handy camp. Olaus and Bob had built a "range" from two old gas cans, our grate between them, and mud to chink in the space behind.

Then to explore our new world. Bob could no longer resist those little swirls in the lake and stayed at camp, fishing. Don and Olaus and I set out to scout a route to the river, which here is far to the west of camp, half a mile over muskeg and grassy marsh. We went out by the northern end of the lake, the gulls attacking us fiercely, and sloshed through wet muskeg till we reached a small channel. We realized the main one had to be further on. Here we separated, Don going north and we south. The river here was crystal clear and flowing over gravel. What a change in eighteen miles—but of course it must be at least forty miles as the river flows. At this point I had a nosebleed and added quite a bit of red to the lovely clear water; I had to come all the way home with a plug in one nostril. Then we got into a tangle of willows; finally we struck out for camp along the southern end of the lake, and established the fact that this was the water route! By that time the sky was overcast and a cold wind was blowing; we were both wet to the knees and above. But at least we had found out how *not* to go to the river! We were hoping Don had found a better way. Staggering and splashing and teetering along over and on and off and among those muskeg footstools, I was suddenly inspired to deliver a little speech from the swaying top of one of the tussocks: "Well, we came to see what this country is like, and whatever it's like, that's what we have to know. So it doesn't matter, we'll have the knowledge anyway!"

Quite a speech!

Back in camp, I put thirteen grayling into the skillet, and cooked more of those delicious fresh potatoes, and applesauce, and everybody was happy again. Don had come home by way of the belt of quite heavy timber which lay at the northern end of the muskeg flat. He had found a woodpecker hole—the first indication of this kind of bird—but he still had to slog across half a mile of muskeg to get back to camp; there was no escape from it, north, west, or south. He said that north of the timber, out across the river valley, the whole flat was practically covered by the overflow ice, or "auf eis," as the geologists call it.

From the diary:

"June 28: Olaus and I are having a lovely day. We are now sitting close under the summit of the mountain behind camp, at the top of a wide couloir, or gully, beside a talkative stream of the most delicious ice-cold water, and here we had our lunch and are both sitting on moss clumps among the rocks, writing and looking—at the valley, our lake, the Sheenjek, and all the valleys and mountains, close and rugged, across it. We look directly into the mouth of a broad valley running back westward—from there on north runs the continuous mountain-and-valley series, the mountains abutting on the river, the valleys between running back west and east.

"Don and Bob and George set off north early this morning, to the timber and beyond. Brina is south of this mountain somewhere, doing vegetation studies. We have climbed slowly, seeing myrtle warblers, gray jays, robins, a rock ptarmigan right up under a cliff, rosy finches, pipits. The tiny dwarf forget-me-not is in bloom, also a white one. Here in the couloir grow scattered sturdy willows the seedheads and leaves of which have a sweet

fragrance. It is a gorgeous cumulus-cloud day with a breeze just right for carrying the mosquitoes away. The breeze is balmy, the sun hot, the whole atmosphere benign; and I hope I may always remember this scene. So it goes—one day of hard work and frustration and seemingly fruitless toil in the flats, another of heavenly airs and beautiful scenes and charming wildlife on the heights. And all in the same neighborhood! The name Sheenjek should mean 'land of contrast' instead of just 'dog salmon.'"

The one day up north simply whetted the boys' appetites for more exploration, and on June 30 Don, Bob, and George set off north again for a three-day trip, carrying quite heavy packs.

Soon after they departed Olaus and Brina and I also set off, for the day, to try to get across to the valley on the western side of the river where Brina was to set out one of the study and trapping plots for John Buckley's ecological study. She was eager to find these locations, to see if the terrain would allow her to measure off a satisfactory plot and do some trapping. We went back of camp to the hillside and traveled north along it through the timber. In a little open stretch of muskeg we flushed a pair of ptarmigan, and I nearly stepped on a downy young one, peeping and struggling down there among the tussocks. I held the little ball of fluff while Brina took pictures and the parents circled and fussed within twenty feet of us.

A few moments later we were approaching the belt of big timber and the big creek, and a goshawk suddenly flew low among the trees right in front of us, another record for the trip and a delight to Brina. At the creek we found Olaus taking off his boots to cross, and we did the same. The water was clear and icy and coming down among big rocks, like a Rocky Mountain stream in Wyoming or Colorado—more contrasts in the Sheenjek! Beyond the creek we walked through beautiful woods and grassy flats which were solid earth, not muskeg, out to the main valley bed and the great field of overflow ice, still three or four feet thick! This was a new experience, picking a route and walking in many circling detours, jumping across openings and fissures, across at least half a mile of this pale-green and blue and sparkling white expanse. It was a long trek finding the Sheenjek, for it flows at the extreme western edge of its valley here and beyond the overflow. The overflow was fine walking, and as we crunched along we tried to understand and to visualize what takes place here every winter during those months of sub-zero temperatures—the river, still flowing under its ice but blocked frequently by ice thickening down almost to the bed, forcing the water up and out over the flat valley gravel bed to freeze immediately, more water flowing over, freezing again, building up this whole field of ice so thick that it takes nearly all summer to melt away and add its flow to the river again, the larger creeks flowing in at the sides doing the same thing, creating their own "auf eis."

Finally we came to a sort of island, climbed a high bank, crossed the island, and there at last was the river, a narrow channel, quite shallow-looking, a tongue of gravel, another channel, another bar, then the main stream, and beyond it, the location of the plot Brina was supposed to mark out.

Should we try it? Should we take our trousers off? Yes, we would have to. So began the disrobing. Thank goodness for a good hot day. Rubber pacs off, trousers off; insoles and socks out of boots and into the packsacks; the boots on again to protect our feet and make our footing more secure. Olaus still had his big Stetson hat on and made a really ridiculous figure with long johns rolled up as high as possible, packsack on his back. "How silly can one get?" Brina laughed.

We all joined hands and went yelling and splashing through the first channel—easy. The next one was a lot deeper at its far side, with a loose gravel bank to scramble up onto. Now the big one. "Don't let's stand here—we'll freeze!"

Out we go. One third of the way across, the water was way above our knees and splashing up higher, the current pushing hard at us. We held hands tight. Olaus said in his always calm way: "I don't know about this."

Halfway. Olaus, still calmly: "No, we can't do this."

And Brina: "This water is *cold!*"

So back we go, to the gravel bar squlch, squlch, what heavy boots!

Lunch on the bar was pure pleasure, after we had most of our clothes on again, and our bare feet in a little patch of warm, dry sand. Brina reconciled herself to the fact that she could not do a plot on the western side; she would concentrate on the location mapped out on the eastern side a bit north of here. We knew we would have to turn back toward camp now, and leave the locating of the plot for another day, but we kept as close to the river as we could, to see new territory. This was not as simple as it sounds; it meant climbing up banks, through patches of thick willow waist-high, wading countless little sloughs, walking across others on ice, jumping through little streams which cut through the overflow. At one of these Brina and I hesitated and thought it over for a while. Finally she stood back, took a running leap, and made it. I stood there thinking of my shorter legs and my longer years; then I put all the force I could muster into my jump, and landed beside Brina with a jolt that pushed my spine right up into my head. Olaus elected to cross further up and in climbing the bank found a little mud patch with a perfect wolf track in it and promptly got out his bag of plaster (always in the pack) and made a cast.

For two hours we traveled through a beautiful dry mossy woods with the river on our right, and finally, across the big muskeg flat, we saw the white tents. But we still had the overflow and about six channels of the big creek to cross, where it made its way to the river, and then the half mile of muskeg to camp. It was not until that drag home across the muskeg that weariness began to set in; but once home and into dry footgear, with corned-beef hash cooking on the Coleman in the tent, we all felt fine. Strange, only three of us in the tent, so much room. It had been cloudy and cool when we got home, but the evening cleared off and was still and beautiful with the low sun bathing everything in gold; the

lake still as glass, grayling swirling, loons far out in the middle
(yes, there were two of them) and the gulls swooping and crying.

At three o'clock in the afternoon on July 2 we saw George
coming across the muskeg from the north. It was a hot day and
Brina hastened to mix up some limeade (we had found these
powdered fruit juices a great addition to our camp diet). George
was hot and dirty and bearded but in good shape and full of
enthusiasm, and between happy gulps of limeade told us of the
trip. "I went almost to the head of the river, to that divide into the
Kongakut. Boy! I hated to turn back, the country looked so
interesting ahead, but I met Don and Bob yesterday and camped
last night with them. I think they should be in in a couple of
hours. Bob was taking flower pictures and Don was studying the
spruces; he thinks there's some kind of disease in one patch of
woods up there. None of us saw a sign of caribou. I think they
must all have gone west of here to have their fawns."

At six o'clock we saw them coming, walking slowly, Bob with
the heavy camera on his shoulder and Don carrying a moose
antler. They were as happy over the limeade as George had been,
and we all compared notes as we ate a big dinner, Don's last
dinner on the Sheenjek—a thought we kept pushing to the back of
our minds. He and Bob had had the same experience we had
trying to cross the river, so they had given up the exploration of
one of the valleys on the west, which they had hoped to do, but

they had seen lots of country and taken lots of scenery shots, though they had seen no big game, and were happy about the experience and glad to be back in camp.

When Keith flew in at noon the next day, he had with him two U. S. Public Health nurses, very attractive young women who were traveling over the territory checking all the Indian villages and giving polio shots. I looked at these two young women, in their tailored slacks and cute little loafers and snow-white ankle socks, and looked at Brina. Her blue eyes were sparkling, and she winked at me. I knew we both had the same feeling—what a contrast to *us* in our faded denims and flannel shirts and rubber pacs!

The nurses told us there was now quite a bit of publicity in the Fairbanks papers about this expedition, since the Douglases were known to be coming up to join us. They were also delighted to be adding Don to their party for a few hours; I could see that he was going to be busy, both at Arctic Village and at Fort Yukon, since there was no doctor at either place.

The five of us stood on the shore and watched the little plane until it was a far speck in the western blue and we could no longer hear it. The camp suddenly seemed very quiet. Olaus said, "It's going to seem queer without Don; I only wish we could have shown him some caribou. Funny how they disappeared just before he got to Lobo and we can't find a one up here."

"Yes," Bob said, "but Don got a big thrill out of just being in the country, and we can be thankful the weather has been so good all the time; I wouldn't be surprised if we got a change pretty soon. I'm going up the mountain to get some more flower shots now while the light's good."

5

Tundra and Mountain

From the diary:

"July 5: Yesterday morning after camp chores were done and fresh beef stew for evening cooked, Olaus and I headed south from camp toward the high, broad green 'pass' at the south end of Camp Mountain. En route, Olaus took me through the lowland woods to a place he had found a few days before and which he called 'little Fairyland.' It is, too. A stream comes down under the rock slide of the mountain and emerges and runs through a thick stand of beautiful spruces, unusually large ones for this far north, some of them measuring twelve to sixteen inches in diameter. The distinctive and enchanting feature is that the forest *and* the stream dwell in a world of moss—dark-green moss, light-green moss, emerald-green moss, and golden moss. It is all over the stones and the bed of the stream, and under the trees is a deep springy carpet many feet thick, laced over with cranberry vines.

"Under the spruces are piles of flaked cones, but we saw no squirrels. Overhead, the voices of many birds, including the thrilling 'chick-a-dee' which we had not heard since leaving home in Jackson Hole in early May. With all the bird voices and the song of the stream, there is still a spirit of silence and withdrawnness about this place. Here is another example of the variety of environment to be found in the Sheenjek Valley, which at casual glance looks very uniform and rather stark. Neither this stream, at the southern end of the mountain, nor the big brawling bouldery one of the northern end—two very different habitats— can be found and experienced by flying over in an airplane, but only by going afoot, as the animals do. Here on the day he had discovered this little fairyland Olaus had met a lynx. The big cat did not run, but merely looked at him and then melted away into the thick growth of dwarf birch.

"From the fairy forest we emerged onto a broad slope of dry moss and grass and widely scattered small trees looking as though landscaped for a park. We ate lunch by a tiny stream there and then began climbing on up into the pass. We had had two short showers before this, but the sun shone warmly between them. We were almost at the top of the pass, so we thought, when we looked back and saw a great black cloud marching up from the south. We watched the storm clouds moving in, sliding over all the peaks, sending the advance streamers of mist up the middle of the valley. We felt the wind, and then the rain. And as we struggled on up the steep slope in the face of the storm, we both felt a real 'participation.' The environment is not tailored to man; it is itself, for itself. All its creatures fit in. They know how, from ages past. Man fits in or fights it. Fitting in, *living* in it, carries challenge, exhilaration, and peace.

"Now we made a dash for the last little clump of spruces and fairly crawled in under their branches, and sat and watched the storm and listened to the wind which came with it. The rain came, but a white-crowned sparrow in one of the spruces kept right on singing. In twenty minutes the rain stopped, but it was suddenly very cold. 'Let's go on. I'd rather move in the rain than freeze here.'

"Up we went, and the way was steep now, no more trees, only grass and lichen and sheets of mountain avens and heather with dozens of other flowers among them—a true alpine meadow all the way to the top. It was impossible not to see and appreciate all this prodigal wealth of plant life, even when the storm came on again fiercer than before, with strong wind driving rain which stung our cheeks. Thick swirls of mist moved across the tops of the slopes on all sides; the lower slopes and the pass itself were startlingly green below the gray mist. I had a sudden strong feeling that this could be the mountains of Wales. We went on through the pass until it began dropping toward little ponds in the valley which led around to the northern end of Camp Mountain.

'Someday soon we'll come up from the northern side,' Olaus said, 'and go all the way round and back to camp. But now we'd better go back the way we came. You look soaked.'

"I was, for I had left my rain parka in camp and worn only a light nylon jacket, but the rain was over now and we went back so fast, fairly running down the slope, that we were nearly dry and quite warm by the time we got back to camp and found the two blessed boys heating up the stew and making bannock over the outside fire. Brina had just come in from bird collecting, also a bit wet, but happy over having observed six gray-crowned rosy finches far up on the talus slope of Camp Mountain, at an elevation of about three thousand feet, and she had caught one. We ate our main course outside and then retreated to the tent for tea and Amazo pudding when another shower came along. Everyone crawled into his bed early.

"Here was another deep pleasure of summer in the Arctic: we usually went to bed rather early, all of us, and lay in our sleeping bags reading until we were good and sleepy. Small clothing bags and packsacks, plus the shirts and jackets we took off, made good high pillows for reading, and even when it was rainy it was light enough to read inside the light-green or white tents—and wonderfully cozy. Here at this latitude, 68° 36', the sun never sets from May 23 until July 20, and what the meteorologists call Civil Twilight is continuous from May 3 until August 9, all of which, in plain words, means it was never dark to any degree; the only approach to a sort of dusk was in late July, when the sun went behind a mountain for a few moments at a time, around midnight. Now and then we would hear the boys, in the next tent, commenting on something one of them was reading, and all the while, the songs of tree sparrows or white-crowned sparrows or the crying of the gulls and the loons. On this night after the fourth of July we kept waking, listening to gentle but steady rain, thankful for warmth and a dry tent. At eight-thirty this morning I heard George and Brina talking in the cook tent, so I just stayed where I was for a while. By the time I crawled out everyone was enjoying very good pancakes made by Brina and cooked on the Coleman in the tent.

"And then the sun came out, just as two beautiful big bull moose wandered slowly through the muskeg behind camp, unconcerned while Bob got some good movie footage."

Three days later Bob and Olaus and I set out early to make the trip all around Camp Mountain. It was a beautiful day—mildly warm, not hot, blue sky with a few white clouds making shadows on the mountains, a nice breeze to disperse the mosquitoes, so that we were not even conscious of them. We went round the northern end of the mountain, up and up, over the shoulder, on around through a pass high up, a lovely timberless alpine sort of valley. We traveled just below the limestone talus slopes and just above a series of little lakes. In one we found a pair of wandering tattlers, which was exciting. Olaus was sure they had young. And here we found a whole new series of flowers: buttercups in the water, delphinium, monkshood, polemonium. The high valley or pass was getting narrower and narrower, and we finally emerged into the beginning of the East Fork of the Sheenjek and realized that our broad pass of the Fourth of July dropped off into this, so we were soon up in it and tramping down toward home, coming by way of Fairyland, where Bob and Olaus planned to take some movies the next sunny day.

We found Brina and George in camp, both looking through glasses over toward the west. "I guess the Indians have arrived," George said.

Keith had told us that three Indians from Arctic Village were on their way, hunting wolves for bounty, with eight dogs packed with their supplies, and he had left with us a bag of tea, flour, and sugar for them.

Next morning George set off for the Indian camp "to say hello" and let them know the plane had left things for them. "Heck, might as well be neighborly," George said.

In this case, being neighborly meant traveling two or three miles to a split channel upstream after he got across to the river, wading the river in waist-high water and traveling the same distance downriver again and over to the camp, which was on a slope that appeared to be quite a long way back from the river.

As we were starting lunch, George and one Indian appeared on the far side of the lake, and Bob quickly went across in the boat to pick them up. They were both wet to their waists. "We'll have to carry the boat across and use it," George said. "That river is rising; it's deep and dangerous."

First we gave them both hot tea; then I stretched the stew a bit and made a batch of potato pancakes from our dehydrated mix; and Brina had made a chocolate pudding. The Indian, whose name was Peter, was young and nice-looking, and smiled and laughed at everything that was said. Olaus was soon asking him about Indian names for birds and animals and he seemed pleased and eager to give him all the information he could. When Brina urged a third plate of food upon him, he said: "Oh no, thanks—I had two plates."

But he accepted the third one when Brina insisted. Just then I heard George calling to me from inside the cook tent, and when I went in he said to me in a low voice: "Mardy, you know I'm sure they don't have any food left over there; it took them ten days to come through from Arctic Village. They gave me some Labrador tea to drink; they had a little flour they mixed with water and fried in porcupine grease, and I saw a pot with a porcupine paw sticking out of it; and the dogs looked as though they are starving. Ambrose, their leader, told me they would have to shoot a moose, though they hated to, because there didn't seem to be any caribou in this whole country. Gosh, d'you think we can give them a little?"

"Of course, naturally—but some of these dehydrated foods I'm afraid they wouldn't know how to cook properly. You help me find what you think best."

So after lunch Peter loaded his pack with the tea, flour, and sugar Keith had left, then we filled up his pack, as much as he could carry, with beans, rice, dried applesauce, and some other things. He kept saying: "Thank you very much, thank you very much."

The boys took him across the lake in the boat, then carried the boat across the muskeg to the river, put him across it, and left it tied up on this side for future use. The Indians planned to go on upriver on the western side, to the head of the river, cross over to the head of the East Fork of the Chandalar, then travel south along it, back to Arctic Village (which is certainly a misnomer, being as far south as it is, compared to all the expanse of really arctic country. No one seems to know how it was named). This route they mean to travel is almost the same as George plans to follow on his back-pack trip, which he and Olaus have been discussing and planning. If George makes this trip it will mean that our party will have, in various ways, pretty well explored this middle area of the region, as Olaus had planned, so that with the reports from other trips and other scientists they will have a fair idea of the topography, vegetation, and animal life of this whole area, from the Canadian boundary to the Canning River, and from the Arctic Ocean to the latitude of Lobo Lake. This area, roughly 215 miles east to west and 100 miles north to south, we all hope will become an Arctic Wildlife Range, of about nine million acres, so that one great representative unspoiled piece of arctic wilderness can be kept as it is, for basic scientific research and for recreation and inspiration for everyone who cares enough about untouched country to come and visit and leave it without the marks of man upon it.

George would be photographing and taking notes on the topography and vegetation of the country at the head of the Sheenjek, and over west into the Chandalar drainage, but he would be especially looking for signs of mountain sheep, and for caribou and wolves, and observing the bird life. Olaus has a strong belief that valuable scientific data are accumulated *on the ground*, afoot, with eyes and ears alert, notebook and camera ready; and in George he had an earnest disciple.

The next morning Bob said he had heard four shots in the night, and after breakfast we saw a big smoke over at the Indians' camp, so we hoped they had got some game for food and were smoking it. We hoped the shots did not mean they had killed wolves, although we would, of course, rather have the bounty go to the natives than to some white hunter flipping around in an airplane for the "sport" of it. We had seen only three wolves on the whole trip so far, and it appeared that there were certainly no more than enough in the country to keep the caribou herds in balance. Olaus, tramping the country every day, collecting scats and other evidence, was making an ecological study of this whole question. He was, through scat analysis and field observations, constructing a fairly clear picture of the interrelationships among the animals. One chain of events goes like this: A wolf kills a caribou—in nearly every instance, naturally, a lame or sick one. The wolf cannot eat all of the meat. A grizzly quickly finds the wolf kill and has a meal. The foxes may be next on the scene, or a lynx or a wolverine. This story is unfolded by analyzing scats of all these species.

It is clear that the bear is largely a vegetarian but enjoys a meal of meat whenever provided from a caribou carcass or by digging out a ground squirrel from its burrow. And the ground squirrel, found all through the Sheenjek country, also largely vegetarian, likewise enjoys a bit of protein when he can find it—a bird's egg or even the dead body of another squirrel.

Supporting this whole chain of life is the plant cover, which furnishes the main diet of the bears and squirrels, the nesting sites and cover for the birds and the small rodents, and, very importantly, the food of the caribou. So we are back at the beginning again!

Olaus and Brina had had many discussions of the value of one really sizable area being left alone, as a basis for comparison for all other wildlife studies. Under the provisions for the proposed wildlife range suggested by the Tanana Valley Sportsmen's Association that spring, hunting and trapping would not be prohibited, but we knew that the number of Indians and Eskimos who went into this area was so small that they would have no unnatural impact on the country; over the centuries a very few, from the Arctic and from the south, had only intermittently come into this area. There was always plenty of game nearer home; as a result, this whole region had been left almost completely untouched, and to us this was a warm, exhilarating thought!

From the diary:

"July 10: Martin's birthday! What memories it brings, of thirty years ago at the Timber Creek cabin on the Old Crow, where I made a cake with raisins in it, and baked it in the fire hole Jess had made in the sand bank and lined with old scraps of tin he found around the cabin; and Olaus had made one candle by dripping wax into a tiny roll of paper; and the baby had got the idea—he blew the candle out himself!

"Thinking thus makes us realize too how different this part of the Arctic is from the Old Crow Valley—so much richer in all life, so much more varied and spectacular, being in the mountains; and how much *poorer* in insect life, to our great joy. And yet, how glad we are that we had that Old Crow adventure—one more whole region that we can see in our mind's eye, one more region about which there is some scientific knowledge. Olaus is writing a birthday letter to Martin now, and we hope he and Alison and the two little girls had a good vacation at Moose.

"In the middle of the morning we noticed a flag waving over at the Indian camp. George went off immediately and soon returned with Peter and his beautiful Malemute dog. Peter had been hunting all night and got two wolves, and was going to return to Arctic Village on the plane if Keith came over on his Arctic

Village run and would take him. The other two Indians are going on upriver; they have not got any wolves yet.

"Keith did come in, and had with him, just for the ride, Margaret Sam, a very attractive Indian girl from the village, who was feeling a little woozy on arrival and glad to have the cup of tea we made for her. She had her stylish curly hair bobbed too, like Jessie James, a flowered cotton skirt, a black cardigan sweater, and moccasins topped with white fur inside of rubber galoshes. This seems to be the accepted footgear; Peter had the same. She sat and smoked a cigarette and said a few words to Peter in Indian, but he didn't seem to make much response.

"When Keith got out of the plane, he handed me, with a grin, a small package. It contained the two pairs of white baby moccasins from the Fourth of July raffle at the village; the lucky number was thirteen! He said that Don had won a pair of men's moccasins and he would bring them over next time. He also said that they had stayed in Arctic Village over an hour last week, while Dr. MacLeod attended to some of the Indians. Those nurses weren't going to let him get away easily. They came on down to Fort Yukon, and I think they kept him busy all afternoon there helping them give polio shots!

"Olaus and I had a lovely day yesterday, up in the big deep woods at the northern end of our flat, along the big creek. At the creek we had lunch and sat on the rocks and wrote for a while; there were fewer mosquitoes there. Olaus searched for fallen trees, large ones, and sawed sections with the little Swedish saw and counted the rings. He and the boys have all been doing this, and we already realize how slowly the white spruce grows in the arctic environment. Most of the trees seem to require over 30 years to reach a height of 5 feet, and about 100 years to attain 20 feet. The oldest tree they have found so far is 10½ inches in diameter 8 inches above the ground, and from the increment borings that Bob made, we found it to be 298 years old! In this stretch of forest along the big creek, where there is comparatively good shelter, the trees are taller and quite dense, a real forest floored with deep moss.

"While Olaus was busy with the saw, I wandered through this forest looking for birds. You stand and listen. When you hear an interesting call or song, you go toward it until you find the bird. This is a happy kind of detective work, and this time it did bring

forth a new species for Brina's list, a gorgeous male pine grosbeak
who sat on a dead limb right in front of me for several moments, a
glowing spot of rose color in all that green world. There were
juncos, myrtle warblers, and gray jays. Finally I came to a group
of squirrel trees, and when Olaus came along we went over to
examine them. There were the cone middens and the little holes in
the moss, and up in a nearby tree a winter nest. 'Aren't we ever
going to see a squirrel? How can they keep so hidden?'

"'I don't know. It's a queer place up here—everything is so
secretive.'

"Just then my eye caught a movement and I raised the glasses,
and there he sat—a beautiful little animal, gazing down at us,
perfectly quiet. We walked over slowly, and stood under his tree.
He went up onto a higher branch, still silent, just gazing at us—a
self-sufficient little aristocrat of the woods. Down home at Moose
our pine squirrels would have been telling us what to do in six
different languages.

"We plodded home straight across the flat—through water,
over tussocks, hopping along on little mossy ridges. We flushed
out a mother ptarmigan and four downy young, and a young
longspur.

"A beautiful evening. We were in bed reading. About ten-thirty
we noticed a golden light in the tent; we looked out through the
nylon-netting front onto a misty golden sunset, if we can call it
that (the sun doesn't set; it just goes behind the mountains
upriver). Olaus immediately crawled out to take a picture, and so
did George. Everyone had a hard time sleeping, what with the
sky, whose colors kept changing and intensifying for a long time,
and our gull and loon neighbors, who were all in a great frenzy
over something and producing the most amazing variety of
screams and calls. Here is a special kind of experience, lying snug
in a tent, so close to the water, hearing all these sounds, lifting
one's head to see such beauty reflected in the still, black sheen of
water.

"July 12: The three young folks were up and off very early
yesterday morning, to begin a long day's work on Brina's study
plot before George leaves on his trip. They would first have to
locate the spot carefully, from the aerial photographs and the
maps, then measure it off and drive stakes and run the heavy
twine all around it and erect the blue and red flags at a corner, and
then set the small mammal traps at regular intervals and make a

listing of the vegetative cover by species. With three of them working, they hoped to do this in one day. Then Brina would go back up to stay overnight for more trapping. Bob came back at seven o'clock, striding into camp at his tireless pace. 'I've found the way to go upriver I'm sure; all the way from that plot of Brina's, must be five or six miles; you can travel on that overflow ice. Sure beats muskeg hopping! We got the plot surveyed and traps set for small mammals. They were doing the vegetation survey, and three people couldn't work at that, so I came on in.' "

After he had eaten, Bob started fishing, but soon had to drop his rod and run for his movie camera as the sun slid behind the triangle mountain across to the west, casting its rays through the big valley which opens from the west, making a romantic painting of the whole scene—mountains rising one behind the other in a golden mist, the nearer velvety sidehills a livid, burning bronze-green. I remembered Otto's words as I stood and watched. "You will see beautiful skies up there."

Brina and George came home about nine-thirty, but it was not until breakfast the next morning that Olaus and I heard the story of the day's adventure. They had asked Bob not to mention it when he got home, for fear I would worry about their getting back.

As the three of them were going north and had just crossed the big creek, they stepped up into the deep woods (where I had been wandering around identifying birds the other day). Bob remarked: "What a contrast! This is just like stepping into a tropical jungle all of a sudden."

George replied: "Yes, I bet unseen eyes are watching us."

And at that instant a huge grizzly reared up out of the moss and brush in front of them! Bob was in the lead; he hurled his movie tripod at the bear and shouted. The bear wheeled, fell to all fours, and galloped off toward the creek. The three young folks just stood there for a few seconds, looking at one another. Brina said she could just *feel* how white her face was, but when George said: "Brina, your face is white," she answered: "Never mind! So is yours!"

In spite of the presence of a bear in the area, Brina was off the next morning, by herself, to stay up at the plot for two nights to do some more trapping. But she and George had come back by the open river route too, and that was the route we would all use from then on! Bob's comment on the bear episode was: "You know, this running into grizzlies is getting darn monotonous for me!"

After Brina had departed for her lone trapping vigil, George and I began to get his supplies ready for his big trip north, west, south, and back east to camp. He was to leave on a Friday, and he and Olaus had figured about nine days for the trip, so that if he had not returned by a week from Tuesday, when Keith would come in again, it would be time to make some search flights— horrible thought, but best to plan as wisely as we could.

George got out the laboratory scales from Brina's tent; we packed all his supplies in Pliofilm bags, weighed each one, and listed everything, George translating grams to pounds to satisfy my curiosity. I wasn't a scientist, and grams made no clear picture in my mind. Altogether, he was to carry twenty pounds of food, his whole pack weighing sixty pounds. The food included: concentrated meat bars, 1,200 calories each, cheese, brown sugar, brown rice, oatmeal, MPF (multiple-purpose food) dehydrated campers' stew and soups, dried peach and apricot granules, raisins, instant chocolate drink, tea bags, instant whole-wheat cereal, dehydrated potatoes, chili beans and corned beef, Jersey Cream biscuits, candy bars, and Logan bread. We hoped the amount was enough to see him through for twelve days if necessary. I made a whole batch of Logan bread, the stand-by of Alaskan mountain climbers, named for Mount Logan; it is full of nutriment, having in it, besides the famous flour mixture, brown sugar, honey, molasses, powdered milk, margarine, and raisins. Bob baked it in the Yukon stove; then we cooled it, cut it in squares, split these, buttered them generously, and packed them in Pliofilm bags, which George laid carefully in the top of his pack.

When we awoke on the morning of the thirteenth, George was gone. We knew he had planned to start about five; we had laid out food for him the night before, and I hoped he had eaten well before starting off.

Olaus and Bob and I spent most of the day taking movies in Fairyland and out on the big overflow-ice field beyond the mouth of its stream, and, back in camp, helping Bob get more movies of the lone young offspring of our pair of gulls, which he had finally discovered in the grass and reeds near camp. The parents were complaining, but by now they had become somewhat reconciled to our living there with them. They had even found some benefits in it, for they had discovered that one of us was a fisherman and that he cleaned the fish at the edge of the lake beyond camp. Before long Olaus noticed that whenever Bob went to the edge of the water, for any reason, the two gulls arrived on the scene immediately. Any of the rest of us could go down to wash, or dip water, or rinse clothes, and they paid no attention. They knew Bob! And they shared our opinion that arctic grayling is a delicious fish.

The next day we three wended our way northward with empty packs to meet Brina and help her carry back the equipment from the plot. A memorable cool, breezy day, just right for hiking, and no mosquitoes out on the ice and the gravel bars. We met Brina coming through the willows at the agreed meeting place. She had had success in trapping voles and brown lemmings, and through this trapping had a satisfactory estimate of their distribution in the area of the plot. She said she "wouldn't have missed the experience for anything," but was willing to have Bob and Olaus deprive her of some of her load. Just before she met us she had seen a reddish-colored wolf loping away in the willows.

The diary for that date:
"Another beautiful evening in camp. It has just happened that for several nights lately I have wakened at 12:30 A.M., and there is the sun, shining gold between two lower peaks upriver. The whole environment has a steady, serene beauty that sings, that will stay forever, that soaks into one's being."

6

Caribou

All these weeks at our still unnamed lake we had seen no sign of caribou; so it was really exciting on the morning of the fifteenth to hear Bob report that he saw a calf, already able to run away quickly, on the hillside back of camp. And early the next morning Olaus saw one beautiful young bull, with a full set of antlers in velvet, in the scattered small spruces behind camp.

All that day we lived in a terrific tearing wind—a most dramatic moving pageant of clouds of every description racing across the valley, pouring over the peaks, sailing on over the passes to the east toward the Coleen, until finally, toward evening, the sky was all blue and bright again. Just before dinner I walked up the slope behind camp toward the mountain, and stood and searched the whole visible world with the glasses. I especially searched the western landscape, for Olaus was sure the caribou had all been somewhere to the west all this time, having their calves. White caps still dotted our lake, but the landscape was quiet; nothing moved except one of our gulls, startlingly white against the blue sky. After the wind, it all seemed breathlessly still, as though we were all waiting for something.

After dinner, as Bob and Brina and I were finishing the camp work and Brina gathered her gear to go set mousetraps as usual on the southern side of the lake, the three of us suddenly stopped what we were doing and looked at one another. We were conscious of a strange sound, way over toward the river. "Surely there couldn't be a cat train way up here," Brina said.

"Oh, Brina, what a horrible thought!"

"Well, it sounds just like a freight train coming along in the distance," Bob said. "Could it be some wind still blowing in one of those canyons over there?"

"Well, I just don't know," Olaus said, and went to the wood pile and started sawing some dead branches he had carried in. Brina disappeared with her traps. I was about to go into the tent to read in comfort when Bob and I heard a strange little faraway sound, like a short low hoot of an owl, blurred by distance, and with a screen of gull cries in the foreground. "Olaus, will you please stop sawing and come here and listen?"

He did, got his hat and coat and my glasses, and said: "I'm going to walk over that way and see if I can find out. Sounds like an owl of some kind."

A few moments later Bob called to me: "Mardy, are your glasses here? There's something out on the flat, over toward the river; a big bunch—boy, are they kicking up the dust! Yes, it *is*—caribou, caribou!"

There was a wild scramble now—Bob getting his movie camera and going off on the run, his camera on its tripod over his shoulder; and I running in the other direction to find Brina. Now, over my shoulder as I ran across the mossy hummocks, I could see a long dark line of figures beyond the first woods by the lake shore. I went shrieking: "Brina, Brina!" Finally I saw her, and she looked up. "Come on, come on—caribou!"

She came running over the tussocks, snatched her camera from her tent, and we both ran over toward the open tundra. There stood Olaus, calling to us: "My camera!"

Back I galloped over the tussocks again, got the Contax and the light meter from the tent, ran back, and kept running, because Olaus was going as fast as he could toward the hill slope. Away out on the edge of the flat and toward the mountain I had a glimpse of Bob's red jacket. By now the great herd covered the flat, and the sounds it made were fantastic.

Brina and Olaus and I kept going uphill, trying to get above for a good look, and finally we collapsed on a high slope, on the grass, and settled down to look and listen. They were traveling steadily along, a great mass of dark-brown figures; bulls, cows, calves, yearlings; every combination of coloring, all bathed in the

bright golden light of this arctic night. The quiet, unmoving landscape I had scanned so carefully from the ridge before dinner had
come alive—alive in a way I am not competent to describe. The
rightful owners had returned. Their thousands of hoofs, churning
through the gravel and water of the creeks and the river, had been
the great mysterious "train" we had heard and puzzled over. Now
they added their voices. Individually, the voice is a low or
medium "oink, oink," very much like that of a big pig.
Collectively, they make a permeating, uncanny rumble, almost a
roar, not to be likened to anything else I can think of. But the total
effect of sound, movement, the sight of those thousands of
animals, the clear golden western sky, the last sunlight on the
mountain slope, gave one a feeling of being a privileged onlooker
at a rare performance—a performance in Nature's own way, in
the setting of countless ages, ages before man. How fortunate we
were, to be camped at one of the great crossroads of the caribou!

Bob came climbing up the slope and sat with us. Olaus and
Brina were trying to count now, and the vanguard of animals was
beginning to move rapidly on up through the woods at the
northern end of our mountain, up through the woods this side of
the big creek, into the valley leading over toward the Coleen. But
the herd still occupied the whole length of the big muskeg flat
clear to the river, which stretched for at least a mile. Now some
were feeding, some even lying down, and the background chorus
continued. Calves ran here and there, and we were glad to see
them. Small groups split off and came back toward our camp.
There were many bulls in dark summer coat, with great antlers
looking black against the sunlit green muskeg. Some had black
patches of new hair on their backs like saddles, light underneath;
some were still in faded winter coats. Every kind and variety was
here; something, in some valley west of here, had brought them
together into this 1,600-strong herd of talking, grunting
pilgrims—they traveled as though they had a goal and knew the
way and were not stopping.

Bob got some nice shots, he thought, before the sun moved
behind the tall mountain across from us. But now the light was
fading and the breeze came cold on the slope. It was past ten
o'clock and we knew we should go back and get some sleep. We
didn't want to; it was a scene we wanted to watch for hours. Brina
said: "Oh, look, how beautiful it all is; this is something I want
always to remember!"

And Bob: "This is terrific! This *makes* it!"

This was the culmination of all the good things the river and the mountains had already shown us. Here was the living, moving, warm-blooded life of the Arctic—out of some far valley to the west of this region, into some far valley to the east—with the wisdom of the ages, moving always, not depleting their food supply, needing all these valleys and mountains in which to live.

As we made our way slowly down over the mossy slope, in light that was still golden over the whole landscape, Bob voiced the thought of all of us: "I hope they can always have all this country to travel back and forth in."

Bob set off early next morning, into the pass, and during the morning we saw two more herds of caribou of several hundred each, traveling more quietly than the one the night before. We knew Bob would see them up there and get some pictures.

The big wind seemed to have taken the mosquitoes far away into the east, and there was a sweet stillness in the air, without that song! Brina and I rearranged the whole cook tent again, to make more room. When we finished and stepped outside it was sunny and still and warm. I looked at her. "What do you say, Brina? You know, we've been talking about it ever since we landed here. I think it's now or never."

"O.K. I'm game if you are." And she went to her tent for her towel and soap.

After settling Olaus by the fireplace with his notes, we walked over to the little bay of the lake south of camp, shed our clothes, and plunged in. Wow! Cold and clean and wonderful—a swim out about thirty feet, and back, and out in the sun for a moment, and in again, and soaping, and out again. I felt as though ice packs were tied to my arms and legs, but that soon passed and was followed by absolute tingly well-being. When we got back to camp Olaus looked up and smiled. "Well, it *sounded* fine!"

In fact, it had sounded so fine that a little later we saw him, with soap and towel, headed for the little cove! And when Bob came home from getting some fine caribou shots, he did the same. It turned out that this adventure was the only thing the rest of us could hold over our rugged George. He never got into the lake!

From the diary:

"July 18: Yesterday, though it brought no baby news, was a full and interesting day. The mail was made ready and then, because we rather expected the two Indians to come over, I made a big stew and cooked fruit for lunch, then started washing clothes. (Our big food drum and the old Geological Survey one, standing on end together, made a fine kitchen table.) At ten there was still no signal smoke from across the river, so Bob set off anyway and soon returned with the two Indians and introduced them all round—Ambrose William and a younger one, David Peter. They had not signaled because the river had dropped again and they got across without needing the boat. Olaus was sitting outside making a drawing of a brown lemming Brina had caught, and the two sat near him on gas-can seats; Brina joined them, and while I finished the washing I listened to a most interesting four-way conversation about animals, birds, Indians, and Eskimos. Olaus began taking down Indian names for birds, and David Peter became so interested and amused that he was soon volunteering names. He has a wonderfully sweet smile. He was trying to give Olaus a name for a certain duck; he hesitated, searching for a word, and said: 'I no speak very good English.'

"Olaus laughed. 'Well, I don't speak very good Indian either!' They were discussing our loons, and Brina brought out the Peterson guide, and both the Indians were very much interested in all the pictures. Then I brought out Olaus's *Field Guide to Animal Tracks*, and Ambrose was immediately absorbed in that, looking closely at every picture.

"We had a very jolly lunch, but afterward the sky became overcast, with a cool breeze. Brina went into the cook tent to put up mouse skins and Olaus went to help her and they invited the two guests inside too. Ambrose had such a thin-looking jacket I was afraid he was cold, and I think he was glad to get inside. At three o'clock Brina, with her sharp ears, heard a plane coming. It was Keith, but in a different plane, and we knew that what he had feared last trip had happened; they had had to take away the Cessna to put it on a different run for a while. This Aeronca was about the same size, but much less powerful than the Cessna 180. As he came low we saw that he had a passenger, a stranger.

"The passenger—a Mr. Robinson, from Olympia, Washington—introduced himself to Olaus as he jumped out onto the mossy landing place, and Olaus introduced all the rest of us, including Ambrose and David. Mr. Robinson is an attorney working for the state attorney general, but he also writes a column of some kind for the Seattle *Post-Intelligencer*. He is a big fellow, simple and friendly in manner. He at once found out that Bob was the photographer and had a lot of questions about cameras and photography up here—which gave me a chance to riffle through the mail; but there was no news from New York. So Brina and I went in and started the Coleman and put on hot water and soon had the whole crowd in the tent—seven of us; it is marvelous what that tent can hold. With a Jersey Cream box in the middle of the floor, and cups and spoons on a box behind Brina, we made hot chocolate for Keith and Olaus, coffee for Mr. Robinson, and tea for the Indians and me. Everybody had a big visit for about forty-five minutes. Mr. Robinson was asking Olaus questions about this wilderness area, the Wilderness Society, and the conservation movement in general. Then he began asking Brina and me our impressions of this country—a very clever questioner. We brought Ambrose and David into it too, asking them about the caribou herd and the moose. At this point Olaus and Keith were having a discussion of the Quetico-Superior country and the fight over the exclusion of airplanes in the canoeing country. Keith had been in the middle of that battle; he feels that if airplanes are to be excluded there, motorboats should be also, and Olaus agrees with him.

"There followed a general discussion on the possible uses and future of this area. Mr. Robinson mentioned having been in Palm Springs last winter and hearing of the fight over building a tramway up Mount San Jacinto, and said how difficult he feels it is for anyone to fight such 'hard, tough customers as those hotel and resort owners.' Also, that if the Military wants any area it is very difficult to win out. He also mentioned the attitude of some people near Olympic National Park, the shortsighted view of 'dollars for the present and hang the future.' By this time I was rather wondering just what Ambrose and David were making of all this talk! Keith feels, and I think we all agree, that the airplane can service this region with no development in here at all, for only float planes need be used. He says they are starting to prepare an air strip at Arctic Village for emergency landings in winter for the Wien Airlines C-46's that fly to Barter Island, and he thinks this is all the development needed for a long time, and this is *outside* the proposed wilderness area. As he says, the plane leaves no tracks and, in this region, there is really no other way to get in with gear for an extended stay. Even small boats, with any kind of load, would probably have difficulty getting up this far, and it would take weeks. The upper river rises and falls so rapidly, because of the glaciers in some of the canyons above here; today Ambrose and David waded across with no trouble, whereas a few days ago George and Peter had barely been able to get across. Here again arises that all-important question of people having consideration for one another, so that there will be only a few people at a time on these fragile lake shores.

"Mr. Robinson then insisted on taking pictures of everybody (Olaus had not shaved and looked real woodsy). Keith told us how disturbed he is about this plane. He can't even get from Fort Yukon to Old Crow Village on a tank of gas. He had tested it out, staying close to the Porcupine, and sure enough ran out of gas. He had to plop down on the river, ram the plane's nose onto a sand bar, and put in a can of gas.

"So we all stood there, wondering about the take-off. Keith had told Brina to watch, so she'd know how much gear she can take with her when she has to leave next week! He made his usual long taxi out to the northern arm of the lake, then gunned the engine and came down the whole length of the lake, but as we held our breaths we realized the plane wasn't going to rise. He slowed, swerved, came in so close we were expecting the plane to come into the little trees on shore, but then turned in time and went off for a second try. Same thing all over again. 'Well,' Brina said, 'we may have Mr. Robinson with us tonight. Good thing you have that extra mummy bag!'

"This time Keith swerved and came right by us, close. We thought he was going to land, but he turned, gunned it, went straight across the lake, on a little puff of crosswind, and raising one pontoon and then the other, managed to lift the plane and get over the little trees on the western shore and on around, dipping over our heads, all of us waving madly as off they went. 'Well! How do you like that?' I said to David. 'Oh my, oh my,' he responded, shaking his head.

"Someone at Fort Yukon—Keith thought it was the Cheeks—had sent up a whole fresh frozen king salmon weighing about twenty pounds. Ambrose had brought us a beautiful piece of moose, so we gave them half the salmon, along with a few other things, and they assured us they now had enough of everything to see them home to Arctic Village. They had received a box of supplies on the plane too. It will take them two weeks to get home—three days to walk across to the East Fork of the

Chandalar, then a few more days to hunt and shoot caribou, build a skin boat from the caribou skins, and load the dogs, meat, and everything into the skin boat, and then the rest of the time traveling down the East Fork to Arctic Village. If they get seven caribou they can make a thirty-foot boat; if five caribou, a shorter boat.

"Now they loaded up their packs and came to shake hands all round. 'Thank you very much; you sure treat us good,' said Ambrose, and 'Good-by, sir,' when he shook my hand!

" '*Mahsik, mahsik,*' David said, smiling. This is their word for 'thank you,' which they had taught us earlier in the day and which we all had been using.

"It was a moment of real feeling on the part of every one of us. We had had a good day of fellowship and fun and sympathy, and we stood rather sadly, watching them trudge away across the muskeg again. It had been a full day for us all.

"With evening, as so often happens, the blustery overcast day was gone. Now there was sun and a bright sky and a warm gentle breeze. Olaus and I felt the need of walking, and went up the slope of Camp Mountain, over a moss-covered rock slope, up under the shallow cave in the rock face which is filled by one of the largest eagle nests ever. Olaus had discovered it soon after our arrival; it is centuries old, it seems, and must be six to ten feet across. The rock all around is covered with the red lichen that so often grows under and around nests, and Olaus thinks the nest fertilized the amazing thick growth of moss on the slope beneath. Here also are flowers of many kinds, white and blue and yellow, and lichens of other colors, and even some kind of fern in the little rock niches. A beautiful little spot at the foot of that stark gray limestone mountain, with life and music furnished by a whole family of phoebes, flitting from rock to rock, uttering their sweet 'phoebe' over and over, answering one another. A little symphony, and a symphony of soft colors on the birds, too.

"It is colder at night now. We've been tying down the front flap of the tent, which makes it much warmer. Ambrose said: 'Dis country—first of August, daytime all right, but nights cold!'

"As I write, Olaus and I are north of camp, up by the mouth of the big creek, where he has been making plaster casts from many of the tracks of our caribou migration, and writing his notes while sitting on the creek bank. He remarked this morning that he 'couldn't write notes on a high plane in the tent, with all that chatter about food, different flavors, etc., going on.' (He had been sitting in the corner of the tent writing while the rest of us got breakfast.) This I can see, but it got me to thinking a bit too. I think this is one of the reasons for the relaxed, unstrained, harmonious atmosphere of our camp. The people are sensitive enough to appreciate and ponder over all the beauties, the scientific interests, the meanings of this wild country, and at the same time are interested enough in camp routine, food, menus, new tricks with our limited variety of food, to make camp life fun and not at all boring; and all are mature enough not to be annoyed by any petty inconveniences.

"One of the things Ambrose told me was the story of Chief Christian, grandfather of the Daniel Christian whose cache we had found. Ambrose said that he himself is the only one who has come over into the Sheenjek nearly every year, but once long ago he was over here with Chief Christian. 'Dat Chief Christian, he's a good man. You know, one time he kill white moose? Dat moose now Fairbanks at dat school?' (I told him I knew the moose and had seen it, mounted, in the University of Alaska museum.)

"'Chief Christian, he give dat moose; he want it in school, for kids to see. He give it to government for dat; then government, he gonna pay him one hundred dollars for it, but he don't want that either. He want to *give* that moose for school, for kid. He's a good man.'

"We talked to Ambrose about naming this lake; he said they have no name for it, but 'I guess call it Last Lake, dat be all right. Dis the last lake. No more good lake up above here—some small lake, but no good.'

"So our lake is named—at Last! We explained to the Indians our Lobo name and what it means, and they thought it a good name too."

7

To the Head of the River

As we were busily getting dinner on the evening of July 19, George suddenly appeared, walking between the tents, looking a bit thinner, but well and with a happy smile on his face, the soles of his tennis shoes tied with string over his rubber pac soles, which had come completely loose from the leather tops! Other than that, all was well, and we were delighted to have him back in camp a day earlier than planned. Olaus and I had been planning a five-day back-pack trip to the head of the river, and now we could leave with free minds. George, after doing full justice to the grayling and all the rest, got out his map and showed us where he had gone—to the head of the Sheenjek, over a pass into the head of the Hula Hula River, which runs into the Arctic, over into the next watershed and into the East Fork of the Chandalar, and so south and home again—eight days of hiking. And he had been in the midst of some of the caribou migration too. (One group had passed, unawares, close to him as he lay in his sleeping bag watching them.) He had seen a few mountain sheep, far up at the head of the river, one of the main objects of the trip, and had also had a close look at a grizzly, close enough for a good picture.

Next morning, a sunny cloudless day, Olaus and I set out, each with a well-loaded Trapper Nelson pack, and with all three of our wonderful young people taking pictures of us as we left.

By noon, taking the river-bar-and-ice-field route, we had

passed Brina's plot, seemed to be above all the ice, and were traveling along on the gravel bars close to the river. The river was now sparkling clear, and in places where old snags or large rocks lay in the bed, we saw huge grayling.

After lunch by the river we found a wonderful route, along a well-worn animal trail, at the foot of the hillsides on firm ground, down into dry creek beds and out, and through patches of spruce woods for several miles. Then we came to another ice flow, where a creek came down off the hillside, and there on the opposite edge stood a beautiful young bull caribou, seemingly asleep standing up. We hoped to get close for a picture, but he must have heard our steps on the soggy ice, for he suddenly came to life, looked around, gazed at us, puzzled, for a long time, and went off slowly, stopping to look back at us several times. We wondered if this had been his first contact with humans.

At five o'clock, when we were both feeling our packs a little and were about to start looking for a camping place, we found ourselves in a thick jungly growth of every kind of bush and tree known to this region, all spread across the many mouths of a stream coming down out of a canyon. So we were climbing down banks and wading shallow streams and climbing up out again. We were really grateful to see the end of this stretch, but when we emerged we found that we were a long way back from the river and the lovely gravel bars, and confronted with a long, long gentle slope made up of nothing but wet ground covered with the tallest, meanest tussocks either of us had ever seen, and no way to get out of it in any direction except to cross it.

We rested a bit, leaning our packs against a bush, and watched a longspur flitting and soaring and glissading down through the air uttering his bubbly carefree notes, and then a caribou appeared at one side, probably the same one we had seen before. He looked at us and then went swinging off across all that muskeg, flinging his long legs out to the side effortlessly. "Oh me!" I sighed. "If we could only travel like that!"

The caribou was out of sight before we felt like shouldering those packs again and starting our ordeal, for we knew it could be nothing else. I think my watch said forty-five minutes, but it seemed hours to us, slogging between the tussocks, trying once in a while to step from one to the other. Unbalanced by our packs, we fell, time and again. Sometimes I helped Olaus get up again, sometimes he had to help me; then we tried to stay down in the water in between, but in places the tussocks were so close together you could not do that, and had to step up, and try to teeter along! But there was no way out but to go on, and of course that is just what we all do when we have to.

But all things come to an end, even tussocks in the Arctic, and finally we stepped off the last one, onto a solid shale slope leading behind a little hill between us and the broad river flats. We dropped the packs; then Olaus picked up mine, put it on, and said he would walk on over toward the little hill to reconnoiter. When he came back I was crouched by his pack, crying big wet blotches onto its khaki cover. "I'm not unhappy," I sobbed. "I guess it's just that the spirit is willing but the flesh is weak; I can't seem to keep back these pesky tears."

"I know," Olaus answered. "I felt like crying myself a few times crossing that place. Never mind, I think I found a place where we can camp, and believe me, we won't take this same route coming back downriver!"

Over against the rocky-shelving side of the hill Olaus had found a little mossy spot where we could camp; it was a little wet, but there was a sort of shelf where we could spread our sleeping bags, and willows grew close to the rock, with enough dead branches for fuel for a tiny fire. It was seven o'clock. A cold wind had started to blow, but the camp site was sheltered, and somehow as soon as a fire is burning, life always seems possible, even joyous. I managed to get a kind of stew made from dried beef-noodle soup, MPF, and potato granules, and we ate that with Logan bread and instant hot chocolate, and were warm and satisfied. We dried our socks at the fire, put on dry ones, and crawled into bed. While I had been getting supper Olaus gathered some dry moss from the rocks above us and made a fine bed, building up the edges with rocks so we wouldn't roll off. Our one air mattress was set crossways, and the head and foot of the bed were built up with moss; we lay in our down bags on top of this, with Don MacLeod's nylon tarp under and over us. Wonderful peace—not a sound in the world except the faint singing of the river far across the flat. Lying there gazing up at the steep slope that ended in rugged gray limestone just across our tiny valley, we named over the birds we had seen during the day: Bohemian waxwings, ptarmigan, one shrike, many semi-palmated plovers and spotted sandpipers, and two pigeon hawks, a new addition to the bird list, and then we were asleep.

From the diary:

"July 21: The moisture collected on the nylon tarp was frozen when we awoke, and the ice was quite thick on the water we had left in the little pan and our two Sierra Club cups. But we had slept, and finally at six o'clock the sun appeared over the tops of the steep mountains on the eastern side of our tiny valley and gave us courage, and Olaus got up and built the fire. He had prepared kindling the night before. I lay snug and relaxed, face up to the blessed sun, and listened to the strike of the match, the whisper of kindling starting, the crackle of the fire. Breakfast— oatmeal with butter and brown sugar, Jersey Creams and butter, and a cup of water. We started off at eight o'clock, taking a last grateful look at our little haven and wondering what a grizzly might think of that mossy bed!

"This was a day to remember, a good day—heavenly clear and warm, reminding us of the Indian-summer days we have in Jackson Hole in the fall. It was a day of following the river (never would we stray away from it again!) on the bars, on the firm slopes just above the water, over gravel and sand, on and on, but all good traveling except for one stretch where the bed of the river consisted of mud and boulders, which took more watchful stepping. We rested frequently, our first stop being on a nice sand-and-gravel bar where we had our morning wash and Olaus found a wolf track and made a cast.

"We had lunch on top of a little rocky promontory where the river flowed close under, and we had to climb up and over. On the mossy top we ate and rested, and I fell sound asleep, bandana over my face, in the warm sun, and dreamed we were back in New Zealand walking through some beautiful bush with some of our dear friends there, as we had in 1949 when Olaus was investigating the introduced wapiti down there. I was a bit startled when I woke and found myself lying above the Sheenjek River in Alaska, with Olaus sitting calmly writing notes. 'Mercy, how long did I sleep?'

"'Oh, about twenty minutes, I guess.'

"'Really? I've been clear to New Zealand and back!'"

At three-thirty on this second day of hiking we were nearing the dividing of the river. The crest of the range, rugged and snow-flecked here and there, seemed very close. I thought the big green-sloped mountain which divided the main stream of the Sheenjek and the valley leading over to the Kongakut couldn't be more than three or four miles away, but I couldn't get Olaus to make a guess. Scientists never want to commit themselves to anything!

We were passing the northern end of another large field of overflow ice which had been caused by a creek over on the western side. A long tongue of heavy spruce and willow growth stretched out from a creek coming in from the east just ahead of us, and by the time we had trudged through the mossy forest and literally squeezed through a belt of very big and very dense willow, and had come out onto the gravel of one of the many mouths of the creek, I was deeply happy when Olaus said: "I think we'll camp here."

My pack had been taking on extra pounds in the last mile, but I had only to remind myself of yesterday's ordeal to feel happy again; and as soon as I shed the pack I felt fine. While Olaus went on upcountry a little farther to look around, I started a fire under some rice and kept busy gathering willow branches to fill out our bed, which was to be on the sand between two willow bushes. A belt of these bushes and a four-foot bank sheltered us from the wind, and setting up our primitive housekeeping was fun. Olaus returned just in time for dinner—cheese and rice, a meat bar, Logan bread, hot chocolate. By eight o'clock it was already so cold we were glad to get into bed, but before crawling in I cooked some apricots for the morning.

From the diary:
"July 22: We had a good sleep. Olaus was up at four-thirty to go upriver a little way to pick up a wolf-track cast he had made last night. I fell fast asleep and dreamed I had gone back to Jackson Hole again just for the night and had to get back to the Sheenjek to hike with Olaus today! I was walking with our friend Lucille Oberhansley in her garden and she was showing me the tall delphiniums she was growing, and a moment later I was going down the road into the town of Jackson and met our Joanne, who said to me: 'Mommy! What are you doing here? Don't you know Daddy is expecting you to hike with him to the head of that river in the morning?'

"And then I woke, sat up in my sleeping bag, looked across to those beautiful green-and-brown mountains across the river to the west, and thought: 'Dear me, what time is it?' And just then I heard a long coyote howl! Olaus was coming! Six o'clock—time to scramble out of here and cook breakfast. I think Olaus had been thinking that I might be worrying (he had been waiting for the sun to be just right for a picture of some cotton grass), instead of which I had lain there sound asleep and back in Jackson Hole!

"This was to be our day to get as close to the head of the river as we could, and then back to this camp. There were no trees to hang things in, away from animals, so we just took a chance, put all the food into one pack, and left our beds as they were. Olaus carried one pack with our lunch and his notebooks, and at seven-thirty we started over to the river, to cross its many little shallow channels and to follow up the western side of the main stream. It was heavenly without a pack, and a heavenly cloudless day, our Indian-summer weather continuing, and no mosquitoes.

"This was our farthest north, a perfect day we shall always cherish. As I sit writing this, we have just crossed one of the unbelievable, tremendous deltas of gravel and turf which characterize this main fork from the moment it branches.

"Apparently every canyon and opening in these limestone-talus-slope mountains has been spewing out gravel for centuries. We nave never seen anything quite like it anywhere else in the North. Whatever the cause, it has been going on for so long that the depth of these delta deposits is sometimes hundreds of feet, so that as we crossed them the river was far below us and we traveled between them along the top of a quite high bluff above the river. One of these deltas, or alluvial fans, or whatever the geologists may call them, was so wide it took us forty-five minutes to walk across it.

"The caribou were all gone east apparently, but all along here we walked on their centuries-old trails, very definite, sometimes crossing bare talus, but all wonderful walking. The distance from the actual mouths of the little canyons to the river was in most places at least half a mile, all gradual slope and covered with a charming heath of dry moss and every kind of small alpine plant, a beautiful place to walk, and enlivened by flitting longspurs, pipits, phoebes, and even one horned lark.

"On a knoll from which we had a wide, long, far-reaching view up to the crest of the range and what we knew must be the head of the river, we stopped for quite a while, and looked through my glasses and took pictures. Our farthest north, and our last look at it for this trip—how beautiful, how quiet, and how blessedly *itself*. Olaus was looking at what he was sure were sheep trails across some of the talus on the opposite side of the river, and wished he had some time to explore over there. But then he turned to me and handed back the glasses, and smiled. 'I know I shouldn't be so greedy. I should be grateful I'm up here, and have seen this much!'

"At the head of the valley, northwest from us, high in the sky, it seemed, were the snow-covered peaks, with glaciers in their sides; these must be the glaciers George mentioned. Out of one of these comes the Sheenjek. Canyons, folding in and shouldering into one another, sharply knife-edged and rugged, and all of a dark-reddish and purple tone, cut their way into the heart of the mountain range under the crest.

"The river as far as we went was wide, with a heavily braided gravel floor; from the top of one of the bluffs on the way back, I counted seven channels across at one place. But above here it must soon be compressed into its canyon, for it is not many miles from here to its source and the divide.

"We came fairly romping back over the high gravel, grass, and sedge delta slopes. We saw again the violet-green swallows near the forks, swooping blithely about in high willows at the river's edge, feeding their young, which were fledged, perched on the branches, calling for more. Here we also saw two more pigeon hawks, soaring above the ridges. The swallows give us a new addition to the bird list, and Olaus thinks this will make eighty-six species for Brina's report. How each one enriches and enlivens this summer arctic world!

"We crossed four channels of the river to get back to our eastern side and camp, and then, as we were nearing camp, I slowed down a bit to admire a particularly lovely clump of rock fireweed, and saw, just beside it, a large, perfect bear track! Olaus came back to take a picture of it, and then we looked at each other, and there was no need to say what we both were thinking. Then Olaus laughed and said: 'Well, we'll soon know, anyway.'

"It was only about an eighth of a mile to camp; our pace was a little faster; and what a thrill of gratitude, to find our little haven untouched, the pack with the food in it sitting against the rocks just as Olaus had left it!

"After supper and quite a long process of drying boots and socks, Olaus had just slid into his bag when I caught a movement in the willows and said: 'Darling, there's a fox looking at me!'

"It was a small cross fox; he came trotting on over, circled below the bed where Olaus lay cheeping like a young bird, came around a big willow, stopped and looked at me, trotted closer, shrank back, came closer yet, then really looked up at me. It was an experience, to watch this animal, to see sudden suspicion of something fearful come into that mind; his whole face changed, the ears went back, and his eyes seemed suddenly to 'flare' with a topaz light. Even so, he did not run away; he kept trotting off and then coming back, sniffing at a can Olaus had plaster in down by the tiny stream; then he went over to our food pack and sniffed all around that. All this while a wandering tattler out on the bar was crying and swooping toward the fox, but he paid no attention to her. He finally trotted off toward the hill, looking back now and then, half loathe to leave, still curious.

"July 23: Now we have said good-by to that little spot which was so friendly to us and are homeward-bound for Last Lake. We might just get there before the plane comes in for Brina, and surely there must be some news about that baby who was supposed to arrive around Mother's birthday, the eighteenth. We left our little camp at seven, and of course the packs seemed much lighter. And still the cloudless blue-and-gold weather. We took care to stay with the river except for a couple of short detours through some willows, and now at nine o'clock we are taking our first rest. We have to go over this knoll and down again, where the river is pouring its crystal flood over some great rocks of beautiful green and blue-green color and of a texture like jade. There is a structure of this rock through the valley here; it seems to run east and west. From this knoll we have a beautiful view back upstream to the parting of the river—our last glimpse of the great yellow delta fan, our last glimpse of the northernmost tongue of spruce, just above our camp. Olaus is sitting below me on the slope here, drawing an arctic poppy—our flower."

We camped that night among fairly large spruces on the steep bank of the main river, and there met mosquitoes again. But we had a strip of mosquito bar with us, to lay over our heads, and in the cooler hours of the night the song died away. When we reached the northern edge of the ice field the next morning, we found that these few hot days had had tremendous effect—the ice was nearly all gone. We walked on bare gravel most of that distance, only now and then finding a stretch of ice solid enough to hold us. Halfway through this stretch, as I slogged along, half aware, thinking of Joanne and the baby, I realized that Olaus had suddenly veered off to the side. I stopped, startled, and then saw him coming to me with hands cupped together. He held them out to me. There was an entrancing little white and black spotted ball of fluff little larger than a golf ball, struggling and cheeping frantically. "Downy young semi-palmated plover," Olaus said. "Isn't he nice? I'll let him go now; I just wanted you to see him."

And when he set the little thing down, it went streaking off across the gravel at terrific speed, and we saw the parent bobbing and calling. We had seen these birds all the way along the bars, but this was the first young one we had been able to see—they blend so perfectly with the tones of the gravel.

Just before noon we tramped quite untired into camp and found all three of them still there. Brina's gear was stacked neatly in a pile, and they were lying about in the wonderful still air and hot sun, waiting for Keith, but they all sprang up and began helping us out of our packs, getting lemonade for us, then soup, insisting we sit and be waited on. It was wonderful, to get into clean clothes and wash up, to sit on a mossy hummock, to be served drink and food; then to continue to sit or lie, hat over face, the others all lolling near by, talking over the whole trip, and getting their news. They had had another visit from the geologists from Old John Lake (who took down our suggestions for naming Lobo and Last Lakes, and Double Mountain just upriver from here) and from David Peter, who had brought them a piece of caribou. He and Ambrose had departed on the twenty-third. Finally we decided there was a good chance Keith might not come that day. Bob and Brina cooked dinner, still keeping me in the status of guest, and, of course, while we were eating here he came, in a Cessna 180; but it turned out it was "Andy" Anderson from Bettles and *his* 180; Keith was with him. Keith said he expected to have his 180 back again by the twenty-ninth, when he was to bring the Douglases in. The minute he hopped out he looked at me, and said quickly: "There's no telegram, but I think there's a letter from your daughter."

And thank goodness there was one, saying they were still waiting, and not too patiently, but all well. A letter was never more gratefully received, for my thoughts had been with Joanne all the way upriver and back.

Andy, of whom we had heard so much through the Crislers, such a fine-looking and pleasant person, had to get back to Bettles that night, so they loaded up and were off in a few moments. We did not say good-by to Brina, only "See you in Fairbanks." And the Cessna was off the lake and gone. No trouble taking off with that one! Brina had promised to help band ducks at Minto Lakes but would be back in Fairbanks when we arrived.

From the diary:
"July 25: I lay awake in the heavenly comfortable bed in home camp last night, thinking over the trip, deeply aware of what a really different experience it had been, these past few days; Olaus and I alone, making our way through country new to us both, containing no sign of man except now and then some old tent poles or pegs of an Indian camp. And that happy, happy day, hiking on up the Sheenjek and back to our willow camp. This is the value of this piece of wilderness—its absolutely untouched character. Not spectacular, no unique or 'strange' features, but just the beautiful, wild country of a beautiful, wild free-running river, with no sign of man or his structures. For this feature alone this Arctic is worth preserving just as it is. Our hope is to leave it as lovely as we found it, with every possible sign of our short occupancy obliterated."

8

Autumn in August

From the diary:

"July 26: Very strange, to wake this morning and not hear Brina's cheery vibrant voice out by the fireplace!

"We kept busy. Bob wanted to get a movie of river travel in the rubber boat, so all four of us went across the muskeg to the river where the boat was tied. It was lovely out there on the open bar by the river. I wonder why I am always so happy on river bars? Bob gave us instructions, then went downstream and got set up, gave us an elk bellow as a signal, and we got into the boat and started down, George rowing. At the end of the long bar he had to make a very quick turn into a rapid channel that ended right by the camera, and he worked frantically to make it, but it was fun. We all feel it would be a great thing to make the whole trip down by river someday. Coming back, I carried a load of camera equipment and the three men carried the boat across the muskeg and we all got in at the lake, and spent a long time going back across to camp, stopping to enjoy and photograph six young least sandpipers on a tiny mud bar. The gulls, both parents and the one young, who is growing big and flying about now, protested our presence a little, as did a female pintail with three big young, but they all finally subsided and the sandpipers paid no attention to us at all. The lake was still and glassy, the air balmy. We all felt limp and relaxed and content just to sit in the boat watching all these nice neighbors. The two loons came quite close also. They are a constant joy, but still a mystery—never a sign of nest or young.

"The evenings have been really lovely. But the whole experience up here has a flavor, an essence that will not be expressed in words. I get so tired of saying 'lovely'—but where are the words? Anyway, the lake is like glass, reflecting the purple-brown mountains; the sun is low above the mountains; the sky gold, the whole camp site and Camp Mountain behind it shimmering in a pale burnished light. And that is only the setting. Out in the lake the two loons are floating together and calling 'Ah-ah-ee,' two voices together, questioning, blending, belonging in this far, quiet arctic world; over on the shore our gulls are in spruce treetop perches, now and then suddenly going into a chorus of crying; and close to camp, in the scattered trees, four cock ptarmigan are going full tilt with all the ratchety calls, the clucking, the cackling, the talking. On our first night back from upriver, when I thought I would simply blank out all night, I kept waking and lying there listening to the sounds, looking out onto water, mountains, and trees etched black against the water. That night all the birds were on the alert, and sometimes all speaking and crying at once. I lay there and prayed to remember always the feeling of this place.

"This morning we have ransacked once more all the boxes in the cook tent, and Bob and I went through the foodstuffs left in the steel drum, got everything into smaller cartons, and packed one box of surplus to be shipped out on Sunday. Now we can arrange the cook tent so the boys can sleep there; their tent will be fixed up for the Douglases. I know Mrs. Douglas must be an outdoor person or she wouldn't even be coming with him, but I have never met her, and I feel a bit apprehensive. I do hope she won't find this camp too primitive to bear. Olaus is, as always, entirely unworried. He was on the famous C & O Canal hike with Justice Douglas and is sure everything is going to be just fine. Of course, I keep reminding myself that there is no use worrying; there isn't a thing I can do to make this world up here less primitive!"

On the night of the twenty-seventh it rained. All day on the twenty-eighth it rained. The Douglases were due on the twenty-ninth, a Sunday. In the evening of the twenty-eighth the rain stopped, and the morning was half clear, with patches of blue sky showing, and our spirits rose. We well knew that after the phenomenally good weather we had had all season, we might be due for a storm, yet we hoped our guests could at least have a sunny introduction to the Sheenjek.

The boys had moved their beds into the cook tent, making a good arrangement, so there were still seats (gas cans and boxes) for six, with their beds rolled back in a corner. We had done everything we could to make camp tidy, and the weather was improving every hour. We had lunch outside, and just before one o'clock we heard the plane coming. It circled over camp and went over to the northern end of the lake, and as it went over George exclaimed: "It's still the Aeronca. Boy, I bet Keith is fit to be tied!"

We all assembled by the landing place. My heart was thumping, for not only were we to greet important guests, but there *must be* some baby news this time! So I suppose I was looking pretty anxious as that plane taxied in to the landing spot—was there baby news, and what would Mrs. Douglas be like? When she stepped out onto the pontoon and reached for Bob's hand, I thought: "Oh dear!"

Trim, petite, blonde, every hair in place, chic gray flannel suit, nylon hose, brown calf loafers. But I needn't have worried! The first thing she said to me was: "I've got my blue jeans, and rubber pacs just like you said, as soon as I can get into our duffel."*

From that moment there was nothing but joy in having these guests in camp. Bill Douglas now leaned out, blue eyes sparkling, and said calmly, as though they had had lunch together the day before: "Hello, Olaus."

Then Keith, having stopped the motor, climbed out on his side, grinned at me, and said: "Yes, we brought the news this time. It's a son. Mr. Douglas has the telegram in his pocket for you!"

Benjamin Olaus Miller had arrived—Joanne was "radiant." Olaus handed the telegram back to me and smiled. I knew he was thinking: "See, I told you everything would be all right!" He didn't say it. Mrs. Douglas said: "My, I just know how anxious you must have been for that news! I'm glad we could bring it."

So now with light heart to try to make the guests comfortable. The boys carried their duffel into their tent while I got some lunch ready for them, and before she ate, Mrs. Douglas changed to camp clothes, and still looked chic!

We served lunch by the outside fire; the sun was shining

* Mrs. Douglas was the former Mercedes Hester Davidson; the Douglases were divorced some years later and both later remarried.

fitfully. I said: "Justice Douglas, will you have some more soup?"

He looked at me, held out his bowl, and said: "Bill."

A few minutes later: "Justice Douglas, can I make you a cup of cocoa?"

He looked at me with that direct blue gaze again. "Bill."

So I learned, and so did the boys; and Mrs. Douglas said: "My name is Mercedes; they call me Merci."

From the diary:

"July 30: After lunch yesterday we found the Douglases hadn't had much sleep on the trip up, so they fixed up their beds and both went to have some sleep, and then it poured rain, nearly all afternoon. We read mail and the Seattle Sunday papers they had brought—strange to see a newspaper, they seem so out of place up here. Toward dinnertime it stopped raining and tried to clear up, but we had dinner in the warm cook tent; caribou steak, cheese-rice, fresh tomatoes, fruit jello, *and* a wonderful big angel-food cake from Mrs. Cheek!

"The evening was producing another pageant of storm cloud, mist, sunlight, and mirror-still lake, and Merci was fascinated, and busy with their camera. And then we heard a fox barking up on the hill behind camp, and Bill said: 'Sounds good, doesn't it?'

"It was overcast this morning, but has not rained, and the sun still tries to shine through. The boys are busy doing the last jobs to finish out the scientific aspects of this expedition—making more increment borings in various sizes of spruce trees, George still trapping mice and finishing the plant collection. Merci and Bill and Olaus and I made a first short trip south of camp, to the Fairyland and the ice sheet beyond it and back. Bill gazes all about at the mountain peaks and the passes, and I know he wants to explore them all. They were entranced with our Fairyland too and took many pictures—Bill reading off the light readings from his meter while Merci snapped the pictures."

On Tuesday, Olaus and Bill took a short hike south of camp, and to Olaus's joy they had, from atop a low ridge, a view of several beautiful big bull caribou traveling eastward and with glasses watched them until they disappeared up the pass into the Coleen. Then the rain came again, and the men turned back to camp, but Bill was jubilant over seeing the caribou, and said he had never realized what really regal animals they are. In the cook tent, the rest of us were keeping busy and happy. Merci, who is

absolutely the most efficient person I know, had even thought of a scheme for comfort while sitting on gas cans knitting; she and I sat back to back, comfortable, she knitting unconcernedly away on complicated-looking Argyle socks for her son Michael, I finishing, at last, the pale-yellow baby sweater for Benjamin. The two boys were busy putting up specimens—several mice and one longspur—and at times we would all burst into song, "The Happy Wanderer" and all sorts of other tunes.

Olaus had set mousetraps up past the southern shoulder of Camp Mountain, and on Wednesday morning, with the weather much nicer, he set off early to collect them, and later in the morning Bill and Merci and I set off toward the northern end of the mountain, into the pass of our Fourth of July showers, to meet Olaus. We had several showers this time too, on the way up, but hot sunshine in between, and the alpine meadows up into the pass were almost as beautiful in their seed stage as they had been in the flowering stage, and Merci found so much to admire and to identify that she opened my eyes to the beauty of flowers in seed too. Her father is a horticulturist and she knows plants. She kept exclaiming as we trudged upward: "What beautiful stuff underfoot. I have never walked on such beautiful ground."

As we neared the top of the pass we were glad for warm clothing and ponchos, for the rain came pelting down as it had on the Fourth of July. But there is a unique fascination about that high tundra-and-mountain country; even in the rain it was beautiful. We slogged on northward through the pass, approaching the point where we could look down into the little ponds; then I heard Merci, ahead of me, calling: "Olaus, Olaus!"

She turned and shouted back to us: "He doesn't hear me!" There, down by the shore of the first pond, which seemed far below us in the mist, came Olaus, looking at things along the water, oblivious, and there, at the other end of the pond, stood a huge bull moose, feeding in the water, also oblivious! Merci's light musical voice was entirely absorbed in the great space, in the rain and the mist, but eventually Olaus looked up, saw the moose, and saw us far above him on the tundra slope.

On the way back to camp the rain stopped and the sun came out. Merci and Olaus stopped here and there to dig up a few plants which seemed to belong to the lily family and which she wanted to take with her to the scientists at the Bureau of Plant Industry, to see if they would grow back home, and as we trudged along Bill told us of the plants he had collected on his far travels; he told me of the four hundred species of plants he had brought back from Persia, sixty of which had not yet been identified. What impressed me most about this was the far-ranging interest of this man of the law. What a divine thing curiosity is!

From the diary:

"August 2: How jubilantly I mixed pancakes outdoors this morning, for it was a vibrant, sunny clear morning. In the night there had been such spectacular sunset, or sun-behind-the-mountain, skies. Merci, Olaus, and George had all been out of their beds, taking pictures; I lay warm in my sleeping bag and listened smugly and rather guiltily to talk about 'What time are you giving? I'm giving it a twenty-fifth; I want to stop down as much as possible.'

" 'Well, I'm giving it faster. What does your light meter say?'

"At ten-thirty this morning Bill and Merci and I, with lunch, set off for the northern end of Camp Mountain, going high along the side of it and over one little shoulder after another, then following the caribou trails up into the gap toward the Coleen, where we ate lunch. Here there were a few persisting flowers in bloom, poppies, grass-of-Parnassus, vetch, and five-finger, and Merci was delighted with them all. How I wished she could have been at

Lobo during the rhododendron display! We found one large buffalo-berry bush, rather rare up here, loaded with berries in the most amazing profusion; I have never seen one so loaded, even in southern Wyoming, where they are common.

"On the way back we met Olaus. He and Bob had been out getting some movie shots Olaus wanted of certain plants, and we wonder now how many sunny hours there will be for motion pictures, for just at five o'clock it started to sprinkle and we realized our beautiful day had suddenly changed. Fortunately we had made caribou stew and cooked apricots in the morning, and we now had to move inside to eat. At every dinner hour the two boys are full of questions to ask Bill about the far places he has seen, so we have heard many a fascinating story. Last night he was telling of the early colonization of Tasmania, when the Aborigines were hunted down and exterminated like vermin. And he mentioned other kinds of exploitation, in Asia, and he looked across at Olaus then and said very earnestly: 'You know, Olaus, the people don't forget these things.' . . .

"August 5: This morning very early it was raining, but at seven it seemed to be trying to clear again. Bob had been up early and had done some fishing, and we had a grayling breakfast, and the sun was really warm, in a blue sky. Bill had been gazing across the lake, across the flat, across to the mountain on the western side of the river, many times in the past few days and remarking in his quiet way: 'That looks like a nice mountain to climb over there,' and 'Have any of you been over to that mountain?' And at breakfast he remarked that he was feeling quite fit, and it was such a nice day, and almost the last day too . . .

"So—Merci and I packed some lunch, and the four of us got into the boat, rowed across the lake, hauled the boat out, and started across the muskeg to the river. I was loaded with lunch, cameras, glasses; the others started with the boat, Merci on one side toward the back, Olaus and Bill on opposite sides toward the front, hopping and stumbling over the tussocks; and soon we discovered that all the rain had made the water everywhere so much deeper that it was going to be a really wet journey. Under these conditions a five-man rubber boat is no small package. After an eighth of a mile Merci turned to Bill and said: 'Bill, we just can't do this.'

" 'No, I guess we can't; we'd better turn back. We can explore somewhere on this side of the river, can't we, Olaus?'

"We were all willing to get back to the lake and into the boat. Bill rowed to the northern end of the lake then, and we walked on up to the mouth of the big creek, showed them the caribou crossing, and ate lunch on the drier heath near the creek, basking in sunshine. Olaus and Bill both lay back on the comparatively dry moss, and talked about their boyhoods. But Merci and I were interested in something in the here and now—blueberries! At last the little flattened bushes I had been watching all summer had produced ripe berries, and Merci and I are both berry-pickers. The only way to do it was to crawl, almost roll, in the moss from one patch to the next. Merci picked enough to fill her Sierra Club cup to the brim; I picked a few less. We ate all we could hold, fed the two men all they would eat, and put the rest in a Pliofilm sack to take home to the boys. There is a special satisfaction in being able to stay north long enough to pick blueberries. I only wished we were staying long enough to pick some of the cranberries I knew would soon be ripe in the little Fairyland. How closely, how perfectly, all this plant life is scheduled—between May 20 and August 10—to come out from under the snow, to bud, to bloom, to mature seeds, to disperse them, to retreat into warm safe earth again. Yesterday, over at the retreating edge of the ice flow near Fairyland, Merci and Olaus had been photographing mountain avens and saxifrage, blooming where the ice had recently melted away off their patch of earth; blooming six or seven weeks behind all their brothers and sisters on higher ground away from 'auf eis.' But still going through their whole cycle of growth, hurrying to make seed before night and cold came again.

"We tramped through the big woods, the woods of the grizzly, the squirrel, the woodpecker, and out on the bank of the big creek we showed the Douglases the remains of the big old cache, uprights of stout trees, out in the middle gravel bar of the creek; it seemed a strange place for a cache. And today, on the bank near there, Olaus and Bill discovered a fresh beaver-cut poplar tree, the first sign of beaver work we have found up here. Olaus thinks it probably marks the northernmost beaver family on the Sheenjek.

"So home in leisurely fashion across the muskeg, Merci and Bill stopping to admire and photograph mosses and lichens. Olaus and Merci also dug up two clumps of rhododendron, one for her to take back to Washington to plant in their garden, one for Otto to plant in his garden at Fairbanks.

"August 6: Merci and the boys and I had packing and chores to do in camp, for this is our last day. But Olaus and Bill went off on another short hike, up toward the pass to the Coleen. It was a partly overcast day, but cleared toward evening. Trying to use up the extra stove gas, and the last scraps of dead wood at our woodpile, the boys kept a nice fire going, and we had our last dinner outside: corned beef and onions and noodles, blueberries and milk and Fig Newtons.

"The sun was shining low through the big valley over to the west—no smoke from an Indian camp over there now. The lake was mirror-still and the grayling were rising all over the glossy black surface; the loons were drifting about out in the middle, and then came close to shore, and Merci ran for her camera. They were calling now and then and we all stood very quietly, listening. What magnificent creatures; what a poignant beauty they have added to our summer. At the same time our gull family were perched in their favorite treetop perches at the northern end of the lake. The sun now shone from a silvery gray cloud in the west, shining on the white tents and the gray Camp Mountain, turning it to burnished silver. Bob and I stood watching, listening to the soft 'plop' of the grayling.

" 'Mardy, you know, we're going to miss this. All the nights I have enjoyed lying there in the tent, listening to this.'

" 'Yes, so much about this country and the whole experience that I guess we all feel and can't put into words.' "

Keith was to come in at nine o'clock on the morning of the seventh and take Bill and Merci out on the first trip, so they could have more time in Fairbanks. Sally Carrighar and Otto were making arrangements for them, and the Bar Association and Ernest and Kathryn Patty at the university were planning a reception for them.

After this last visit with the loons in the golden light, we all went to bed feeling more hopeful about the weather, but before dropping off to sleep I heard George's voice: "Bob, I don't know about that sky down south. Do you like the looks of it?"

The moment I awoke I thought: "Oh good, it isn't raining anyway." But how dark it was! I twisted around in my bag and pulled the tent flap open. Black tree silhouettes, black water, nothing beyond—a world darkened and muffled by dense gray fog, right down to the water level across the lake. Then I heard the crackle of a fire. Someone was up and about. A few moments

later, when Olaus had dressed and gone out (it was never possible for both of us to dress in that little tent at once), I heard Bill's voice: "Good morning, Olaus. You know, I don't think any of us are going anywhere this morning!"

As we ate breakfast the fog seemed to be thinning a bit in the south. Merci said: "I don't see how anyone can be flying, but we're all packed; we can roll up the beds in a hurry if he does come."

At eight-thirty the clouds in the south had parted some more, like a tunnel in the mist with lighter sky beyond it. At nine o'clock Bob shouted: "Here he comes!" and there, through that tunnel, appeared a plane, very low, and as he fairly skimmed the treetops behind camp George cried: "Hooray! He's got the Cessna!"

Keith climbed out of the plane, the usual calm, relaxed smile on his face. "Sometimes handy to have a river to follow! I was flying about fifty feet above the Sheenjek a good part of the way up here; I was sure glad it got thinner instead of thicker after I passed Lobo! But it's breaking away down south now; I think we'll get you all out of here today, and I think we'd better, because the forecast for tomorrow isn't very good."

In half an hour they were gone—no good-bys; we would see them the next day in Fairbanks. As Keith climbed into the plane he called: "I'll be back here about twelve-thirty."

Best to keep busy—push back all the thoughts of all the favorite places you would like to hike to once more, of the full beauty of the arctic autumn foliage we were going to miss. Scour all the camp kit with steel wool; help Bob pack it all away. Go into our tent and from the bottom of the little packsack get out the one clean pair of trousers and the plaid Viyella shirt Mary Hamilton had made for me. Find the little plastic box of hairpins and the little cosmetic kit, and get the two clothes bags and everything else out of the tent.

A few mintues later, as I was putting the last hairpin into the braid on top of my head, George came by with arms full of dunnage. "My gosh, *lipstick* yet! I guess that means this trip is really coming to an end!"

Then Olaus came and dropped our tent, all rolled up, on the growing pile of bundles by the shore. I looked at the package and a strange feeling of finality flooded through me; all that comfort and protection of the past weeks, rolled up into a little light-green bundle. From the shore where he was stacking dunnage Bob called to us: "Have you folks noticed something different about camp this morning?"

George and I joined Bob at the shore and looked out over the lake. The fog had lifted and the mountains across the river were showing, quiet and gray through wisps of white mist. "Doesn't it seem quieter somehow?" Bob said. And as George and I still looked mystified, Bob went on: "The gulls are gone! All three of them!"

"Well, then," George said, "I guess it's time for us to go too, but gee, how I hate to leave this country! I never had a summer go by so fast."

We all turned to go back to the work of packing again, and saw Olaus, with two old gas cans in his hands, tramping across toward the talus slope at the foot of Camp Mountain. He was going to crush and bury the last vestige of our camping here, but more than that I knew he was going for one last look at that slope, at the old eagle nest, the lichens and mosses, the plants in seed, the sweep of tundra and forest to the north, the free land, the home of free creatures, his beloved Arctic, and I knew he wanted no one with him just then. I turned and looked through tears out over Last Lake and suddenly realized something else. "Bob, aren't the loons gone too?"

At seven o'clock that evening Keith was back at Fort Yukon with the two boys and the very last of the gear. As they had lifted from

Last Lake and flown out low over the river, there on a bar of the river were a large grizzly and her two cubs. The mother stood on hind legs and watched as Keith flew over her and on south. Good-by, grizzly bear, your valley of the Sheenjek is all yours again—all yours. But thank you for sharing it with us a while. As David Peter taught us to say: "*Mahsik!* Thank you! May you always have this wilderness."

PART V:

RETURN TO THE MOUNTAINS

1

Again North

On a morning in April 1957, Olaus and I were having breakfast in the coffee shop of the Hotel Florence in Missoula, Montana, where we were staying for a few days.

The bellhop came in from the lobby paging Dr. O. J. Murie. Weezy was calling from home at Moose. "We have just heard from Alaska. The Tanana Valley Sportsmen's Association and the university are inviting Olaus to come up and attend some meetings and discuss the proposal for the Arctic Wildlife Range. And John Buckley wrote to tell you to try to get there by May 14 for commencement, because they really are going to give Otto a doctor's degree!"

Olaus and I returned to our breakfast table so full of emotion that the woman at a nearby table looked over at us, smiling. I leaned over to her and said: "We're going back to Alaska—that's why!"

May 14—commencement at the University of Alaska—a warm sunny day with a brisk breeze blowing, billowing out the gowns in the long academic procession, making everyone clutch his cap as they all wound down the path into the gymnasium packed with young and old. We were sitting with Ted and Audrey Loftus, with Sally Carrighar and Mary Jean Pewe, whose husband, having to march with the faculty, had given her his motion-picture camera and instructions to get a movie of Otto receiving his degree.

Dr. and Mrs. Gilbert Grosvenor, of the National Geographic Society, were on the platform; they were to receive honorary degrees, as was Dr. McKenzie, president of the University of British Columbia, who delivered a fine commencement address. We were all happy about these degrees, and there was generous applause for them.

Otto's citation was read last, and when Ernest Patty and Elmer Rasmuson, the chairman of the Board of Regents, turned to him, and he stood and came forward, the audience stood as one man and there was a real ovation. The community was expressing its approval of the action of the Board of Regents, and its joy over the proper recognition, while Otto was still alive and most active, of his years of devotion to the cause of science and the growth of this new university, of work with little or no pay, of stretching meager funds, of enduring many long cold trails, stormy seas, hard manual labor, tedious hours in excavations and makeshift laboratories, of hazardous travel of all kinds. But perhaps more than all that, this ovation meant a recognition of the great kindly spirit of the man, Otto William Geist, his generosity, his solicitude for anyone in trouble, of any color, race, or creed. There was a living tangible emotion in that long applause. Through my own tears I glanced at Mary Jean at my side; she was struggling with the camera, aiming it at the platform, but I didn't see how she could focus through all those tears, and her hands were shaking.

Afterward, out in the warm sunshine, Olaus and I finally made our way through the crowd of people who were congratulating Otto. He held out his arms to us both. After a moment Olaus said: "Well, Otto—a long way from Bettles, isn't it?"

"Yes," Otto answered, "a long way from Bettles!"

We just stood there looking at one another for a while, and then Otto thrust at me the leather-bound book, the degree. "Here, you look after this for me; I'll lose it if you don't."

This trip was evangelism, not adventure, and we did not go back to the Arctic. Olaus was speaking and showing slides of the north country before every possible organization in both Anchorage and Fairbanks and, on the way home, in Juneau. Later in that year he was back in Washington showing the Sheenjek pictures before other groups and finally for the Secretary of the Interior, Fred Seaton.

And then three years went by, filled with all the facets of the struggle to save some wilderness in every part of the United States.

On December 7, 1960, I walked out to our Moose post office for the mail and our postmaster Fran Carmichael said: "There is a telegram for you." (We had no phone in those days.)

I floated back that half-mile through the woods on a cloud, burst in through the front door. "Oh darling, there's wonderful news today!"

Olaus was at his table at the back of the room, writing. I held out the telegram to him; he read it and stood and took me in his arms and we both wept. The day before, December 6, Secretary Seaton had by Executive Order established the Arctic National Wildlife Range!

2

Sheenjek Again

In 1957, early in the year, and again in 1959, Olaus had had surgery; he was hospitalized in Denver for lymph gland operations. But through it all he held to the dream of going north to the Sheenjek again, and in 1961 he was feeling so well that it all seemed possible and I was again immersed in planning. Food lists, clothing lists, equipment lists, plane reservations—1956 all over again, except that this time we should be arriving on Lobo Lake without our three wonderful young friends.

But first there was Fairbanks on a sunny May day, and Ted and Audrey Loftus at the airport to meet us, and an hour later Otto arriving from the university and with him our dear friend Ivar Skarland the anthropologist. We were back in Alaska again! It was May 14 and we were to have thirteen lovely days of visiting and preparing for our trip. What a difference it makes in any expedition, to be sent off with a background memory of companionship and fun, and concern by so many friends, great people!

The other great comfort was that Keith Harrington was still the Wein bush pilot at Fort Yukon. At two o'clock on May 27 he landed us with the ski plane on Lobo Lake in fine weather. Somehow very strange, these first moments, yet a good feeling; how familiar, how nostalgic, peaceful and welcoming, but I could hear the voices of those three young people, see them in every familiar spot here at our same old camp place. As before, it was the only place where the ice was still fast to the shore. Keith helped carry all the gear, looked it all over, looked at us, said: "Are you all right now?" There would be nine days here alone, and then on June 6 Keith would fly in, landing on the river with floats, to bring in our dear friend Charlotte Mauk of the Sierra Club.

Now in 1961 we soon realized that the 1956 summer had been an unusual one; we had really lived in Paradise for two and a half months—fine weather almost always, a gentle breeze to help keep mosquitoes away. This time we had the Arctic on its own terms—at some time nearly every day it rained, though never all day long. We learned to grasp the sunny hours and make the most of them, and the whole sequence only wedded us more strongly to this beautiful independent world, with all its natural living going on all around us, in all weather. We simply learned to make the most of the bright spots, ducking into the cook tent and using the Coleman stove to make meals when the clouds came close, dashing out the moment the sun came out, for immediately then the world of Lobo would come alive again, singing and clucking and chirping and splashing, and soon after our arrival the flowers were all there too. How unbelievably fast they bud and bloom and glorify the whole landscape!

From the diary:
"Tuesday May 30: Sat a long time on the northern point of the ridge north of camp, watching our first old squaws in the pond below. Olaus was getting some good movie shots (and that of course is the main object of this trip) until the storm clouds were deep blue and closing over and we hurried back to camp. It blew, it rained, it was cold, and the big tent needs resetting and tying, for water came in. We tried to read; Olaus tried to sleep. I read aloud a few of Henry James' incalculably involved sentences in *The Ambassadors* which should have put him to sleep. And then suddenly it cleared, at two o'clock, and we were immediately very warm again in the sun.

"Wednesday May 31: Calm, quiet, sunny, after the storm. The usual background of tree and white-crowned sparrow song, ptarmigan talking, Wilson snipe sounds in the distance, and three pintails being very raucous there in the little lane of water next to shore. As I sit here writing I am constantly picking up the glasses to identify another bird. The new birds today are myrtle warbler, rusty blackbird, golden eagle; Olaus saw a short-eared owl and I heard the exciting whistle of the upland plover, and the mew gulls are here too. Arctic paradise! Not even one mosquito! They will arrive June 15. These are deeply happy days for the two of us alone here.

"June 1: It rained all night, but after lunch of bread and jam and applesauce things looked much better and we set off with both cameras and made our longest hike yet—north on the ridge, down across ponds to another low ridge east and on in a big circle back to camp. Much to photograph and many birds, and how strange, almost unreal, it seems at times, recognizing this queerly bent tree, that old set of caribou antlers, this little knoll, that old fox den. It seemed they were all welcoming us back."

The caribou migration—bands of cows and calves moving from the east—and Charlotte arrived at almost the same time, so Charlotte's ten days with us were made up of caribou-watching and flower-picture-taking. Charlotte had a fine new camera and was bent on close-up flower pictures, and this was exactly the right time. There was more rain, but in between we hiked, and photographed, and lay on mossy knolls watching bands of caribou flowing over the tundra scene, swimming the Sheenjek, spreading out over the flat on the west side. Charlotte also watched the last ice melting in Lobo while muskrats and ducks appeared in every lead, and the old squaws and baldpates kept up their constant conversations.

From the diary:
"June 10: No rain, cloudy but no wind, so pleasant to sit outside. Charlotte even took pictures of me making pancakes on the outdoor fire. As we were eating bread and cheese with tea for lunch I looked across the lake and there was a huge dark blob traveling along the bank—a great dark grizzly, our first this trip! This was a great performance. For an hour and a half we watched him. He was headed west around the far side of the lake, but when he reached the west end he stopped, sniffed, turned around and retraced his steps. Every once in a while he stopped, to dig, to sniff or investigate something, but always keeping so close to the bank that we had a perfect view the whole time. Finally he

decided to continue back eastward, but then he came to a little spruce tree, deliberately walked right over it for a nice scratch, decided that felt pretty good, turned back, did it over again. Charlotte and I walked along on the hillside east of camp, to keep the bear in view, but he finally disappeared into some brush in the distance. We continued on to the end of the lake; saw grayling trying to come up into little channels in the grass, saw two beautiful eared grebes; more flowers in bloom. The Sheenjek's famous flower, the rhododendron, is coming out fast, a rosy glory. I spied a ptarmigan uphill from us, sitting calmly on the lower branch of a small spruce surveying his world, and I stood very still while Charlotte made a very careful stalk and got very close-up pictures of him. Charlotte is a big girl, but so nimble, and her face was shining with joy at every little adventure this afternoon. I was glassing over the rugged east peak of Table Mountain and found a band of caribou high on the mountainside. And then coming back down the slope to camp we found a white-crowned sparrow nest—five eggs. Altogether a lovely day, clear and sunny this evening. Cooked dinner outside, Drilite chicken and noodles; Sierra salad. On the lake this evening there are: old squaws, pintails, white-winged scoters, surf scoters, baldpates, Barrow's goldeneyes, scaups."

Charlotte's last day, June 14, was a beautiful day and she got lots of flower pictures. On the fifteenth in late afternoon Keith arrived with our two fifteen-year-old guests, Edward Zahniser and Stephen Griffith. And on that day, as I had predicted, the mosquitoes arrived too. (I had promised Charlotte she would not have many mosquitoes.) Edward, poor child, had been airsick all the way from Fort Yukon, but was cheerful as could be, and made such a quick recovery that he had caught two grayling by five o'clock, and from that date on we never lacked for fish.

The weather pattern continued the same all that last twelve days. So our pattern continued likewise: dash out and hike somewhere in the morning, get pictures (the boys each had a camera), get plaster casts of animal tracks, (they loved doing that), watch the sky, try to get back to camp before the clouds begin emptying. One day we managed a long all-day hike eastward, but the twenty-first of June all-night expedition we had planned, to the top of Table Mountain, was never realized; the skies were too ominous. However, the boys were ever cheerful, and thrilled with the little adventures they could have. One day they wanted to go eastward to explore and Olaus let them go, and then wondered if they would be all right! "I wonder if their parents would think this a wise thing."

But they came slogging home wet and happy; they had had a lot of fun photographing a belligerent cock ptarmigan. One entry in my journal says: "Rainy afternoon. Olaus in our tent; boys and I in the Duluth tent. I took the socks I was knitting off the four needles, and now each boy is learning to knit on two needles. I don't think this is what their parents sent them to Alaska for, but anything to keep serene while this ordeal of weather goes on."

On June 27 we packed up and waited for Keith; we had done everything we could, had taken down the boys' tent but not the other two; the boys and I had resorted to geography word games by four-thirty when we finally heard the plane. Keith took the boys and a load of stuff and said he would be back early in the morning for Olaus and me.

At five-fifteen Olaus and I were again alone on the Sheenjek as

on May 27. We ate rice and macaroni cooked together, butter and brown sugar on it, Jersey Creams and applesauce—just about the last of our food.

Then the clouds rolled away, the sun shone warm. We took a last walk over to the river. We could never have enough of that view, the graceful bend the river made just there, the high banks glowing with rhododendron, the dark accents of the spruce trees, all so real and so peaceful. We looked and looked, and then we looked through tears. At last Olaus said: "Well, I guess I can't look any longer."

PART VI:
AFTERWARD

1

1967 Alaska

When I came home alone to the ranch at Moose in May 1964 and walked onto the big front porch, and dear Fred, who was living in one of the cabins, put my bags down, I thought: "No, I can't do it. I can't stay here; I can't stand it."

There were all the places of Olaus's being, not only the log house he loved so much, his study, his desk, the bedroom, the bed, his place at the table; but outside, the trails to the beaver pond and down to the river; the far beaver pond where he sat on a grassy bank on his last walk and wrote some paragraphs about how he felt about grass and sky and birds. All too much; not bearable.

But how could I move away, and where else could I take up life again? And there were people just then depending on my being here.

So—get busy—do the spring cleaning, greet the friends who come, try to get to sleep at night without thinking, without remembering.

And after those first days a new feeling came into me. It was almost as though this loved log house put its arms around me. There was warmth and purpose again and each day made its specific demands and carried me through. Even the nights of tears were followed by days full of activity. Spring bloomed inexorably and carried all with it, and life and people continued their demands.

It was good to have these responsibilities; I had less time to think of myself. It is good to have entanglements with many people; in time of crisis they demand your attention and give you no time to brood. If Lois's stovepipe won't draw and you and Fred struggle all day with it, there's one day not given to introspection. And if people keep dropping in, you soon know the pattern of your days and there are no empty hours, so you are carried along until one day you realize that the grief and the missing are never going to go away, but that on top of them somehow you must build a rich experience of living, woven of involvement with others' joys and sorrows, and their partial dependence on your listening, and of your own still active curiosity about life. Perhaps I am most thankful for that. My father called it: "That divine thing, curiosity." Over and under everything, I am curious about it all.

The other sustaining thing is of course the beautiful world of Moose; the ranch, the valley, the creatures. This is the other great thankfulness. So many people have to try to find solace and solutions in city streets. I have a walk to the beaver pond and solace always.

But with it all I think I needed the sudden exciting lift at the end of that first summer without Olaus—the flight, on two hours' notice, to Washington, D.C., to be present in the Rose Garden when President Johnson signed the Wilderness Act.

All the succeeding summers have been easier. And Alaska is still there, and keeps calling me back.

There was involvement with Alaska all the time, because in those first years alone I kept an apartment in Seattle for the winters, and Stewart Brandborg, Director of The Wilderness Society, knew I needed to be busy, so I was made a part-time consultant, and in working with Brock Evans, the Northwest Representative of the Sierra Club and the Federation of Western Outdoor Clubs, found myself more than fully employed; also I gradually realized that I was no longer the secretary, the listener, the note-taker, but the writer and deliverer of speeches, the testifier at wilderness hearings, the writer of brochures, even the lobbyist at times. But always, Alaska calling.

All through the years, whenever our dear friend Mildred Capron was here with us in between her travels all over the world making films and becoming a superb film lecturer, Olaus would say to her: "You know, Mildred, you must do Alaska some day."

So, in 1967, Mildred and I left Moose on a sunny May 10th and headed north in her Ford Club wagon rigged as a camper and by August 17 and our return had added 10,000 miles to her speedometer. We drove to Prince Rupert and the ferry to Wrangell, and it rained; to Petersburg, and it rained; to Juneau and it was lovely. Flew to Fairbanks for commencement at the university (where I became a Distinguished Alumnus). Back to Juneau and to Glacier Bay for five great days; flew to Sitka and it was beautiful, on Memorial Day weekend; back on the ferry to Haines and four wonderful days; on to the Interior, to Anchorage, to Homer and by ferry to Kodiak for six days; then to Kenai and the Moose Range and a canoe trip and a flight over the Kenai Mountains; to Anchorage, to Palmer and the dairy farms, to Fairbanks and over the Steese Highway toward Circle; to Mount McKinley National Park and there were Weezy and Ade, carrying on the grizzly studies; to Camp Denali and Ginny Wood and Celia Hunter; to Valdez and by ferry to Cordova and the salmon run; back over the highway to Tok and the Taylor

Highway to Eagle on the Yukon; and then to Dawson and Whitehorse and Carcross and the White Pass & Yukon railroad to Skagway and return; and finally by car all the way home to Moose, and Mildred had a fine lecture film, "Alaskan Summer."

In the diary I kept on that trip:

"We were not long on the ferry out of Prince Rupert before getting the 'feel' of a new Alaska. There was a fascinating mixture of people on board. Going through Wrangell Narrows, quiet, under a slow bell, at dusk, everyone watching the very close shores, a young man, a piledriver operator in the timber business, was talking quietly: 'Never a dull moment in the new state of Alaska if you keep your eyes and ears open for what's around you; and we don't have much artificial amusements up here, so we keep our eyes and ears open for what's around us.'

"The new Alaskans—the young men love the life; some of the wives do, some don't. The young mechanic who was towing us in for repairs at Tok said: 'I love hunting in the fall, snowshoeing all over in winter, but my wife hates it.'

"In Fairbanks a taxi driver told Mildred: 'I came up here twelve years ago for two weeks. Never been back. No desire to go back.'

"At a cannery near Haines a young fisherman was mending his nets: 'I wouldn't live anywhere else. Always something beautiful to look at. Wake up in the morning, look out the window—always something nice to look at.'

"Why do they love it? Most of all the land itself I think, even though some of them are busy altering it, busy killing the thing they love, making it like all other states. But most of Alaska's new people love it. Will there be enough who care? The struggle will be between these two, both new: one group thinking of a whole life, the other of making money and getting out. As for the old-timers, the sourdoughs, they live in nostalgia, and can they be blamed? There were, in spite of hardships, so many charming things about the old life; dog teams, sternwheel steamers, absolute freedom. If a prospector didn't strike it in one creek, there were plenty of others to try. At Fortymile we stopped to take movies at the roadhouse, where they were raising Siberian huskies. One of the partners said: 'So where is there to go any more? Up at Barrow they say there's only two dog teams left; everybody's got those skidoos, and natural gas piped into their houses. So where is there to go any more? Fortymile is the only place left I guess; the folks there don't *want* all that new stuff.'

"My own overriding thought is: while all this is going on, what is being left for the one industry which can be most lucrative, non-destructive, self-perpetuating, for all time—a commodity in short supply in other world markets—the industry of simply letting people come, look, and enjoy Alaska?

"We talked to so many tourists, and what were they looking for? Size, vastness, magnificence, naturalness, informality of life, happy people, enthusiasm about Alaska, mountains, glaciers, waterfalls, great trees, whales, seals, porpoises, birds, all the other wildlife? Yes, but also glimpses of old Alaska and of everyday life of people. I saw tourists stopping to look at a garden in Fairbanks, admiring the cabbages, the peas, the flowers, and talking to the white-haired sourdough working in it. At Miller House on the Steese Highway we stopped in to see if they served breakfasts. The old proprietor said: 'No, we don't do that any more, but come on in and light your pipe and set and visit a while anyway.'

"I hope there will be an Alaska for the young mechanic at Tok, for the old sourdough who doesn't want the new stuff, for the young student who wants to explore glaciers, for the Indian or Eskimo who still wants to live in his village, for the young university professor and his wife who merely want to live simply, in the woods, and for the young fisherman who wants to keep on fishing in his own small boat, and 'look out every morning at something nice.'"

2

Another New Alaska—1975

As Mildred and I drove home to Moose in 1967 we often talked about what might be next for Alaska. It happened the next year—oil at Prudhoe Bay. And what was next after that was the suit by the Natives of Alaska and the passage of the Alaska Native Claims Settlement Act, in 1971. Under the terms of that Act some of the great land itself may be saved. How could I possibly stay "uninvolved" in this great challenge?

The involvement came with a long distance call from Anchorage just one hour after Mildred and I had returned, on May 1, 1975, from our usual month of April on San Juan Island, Washington, where I own a little house. The National Park Service was calling, transmitting an invitation from the Alaska Humanities Forum, and adding one of their own. Would I speak at a forum on "Alaska Lifestyle—1990," in Anchorage on June 8? And would I stay on for a month or more and visit areas I had not known before which are included in the proposals for National Parks and Wildlife Refuges under the Settlement Act?

At least I had a month in which, along with all the spring work at Moose, to mull over and worry about what I could possibly say about Alaska, on the very day after I landed there after an eight-year absence. It was a task I felt far beyond my ability, complicated by the fact that at first they told me I would be the last speaker, on the second day, and then they changed their

minds and sent word I would be the first speaker, and the three other speakers were all professors and eminent people! Hard to be the last speaker, always fearful that the others would have already said it all, and hard to be the first one, not knowing what on earth the other three were going to say! Only one thing to do—say what you really feel about Alaska:

"How much of Alaska for change, for development, for profits, for jobs, for more population? How much for the land itself as it now is, with all its potential gifts of subsistence living, of scientific discoveries, of healthful recreation, of inspiration? On this point do we have to split and declare war? I plead for a plan under which there will always be room for a healthy economy, for a healthy population, with a great deal of Alaska left alone.

"I think my main thought is this: that perhaps Man is going to be overwhelmed by his own cleverness; that he may even destroy himself by this same cleverness; and I firmly believe that one of the very few hopes left for Man is the preservation of the wilderness we now have left; and the greatest reservoir of that medicine for mankind lies here in Alaska.

"This sounds radical perhaps. And I don't mean to be saying that all of the modern inventions and discoveries and development are bad for man; I remember the old days, and I know they were not *always* the 'good ole days!' What I am trying to say is that somewhere along the line we have lost control over the beings we have created. We have learned to need all the comforts and refinements, and things and gadgets which all the technology has presented to us; we are constantly being bombarded with beguiling messages about how badly we need this or that. Big corporations, big bureaucracies, feed on themselves, become such entities in themselves, so imbued with the great American dream that Growth is a God and that the thought of decreasing size and a steady-state society is anathema, that to me they have become terrifying. In all this complexity of *things*, where is the voice to say: 'Look, where are we going?' And underlying all the meetings and talks and plans, lies the great doom-thought: when all of Alaska's non-renewable resources are dug out, piped away, cut down, what lifestyle then?

"Here I submit once more my theme: that man, too clever, too far away from Earth, is unhappy. I believe that Man needs Wilderness for five reasons:

1. For space.

2. For scientific research—for man's benefit of course, but also for that of all creatures, plant and animal. There are all kinds of things to be discovered in the natural world which can be discovered nowhere else.

3. For watershed protection—for a healthy earth.

4. For physical recreation of all kinds.

5. For what it gives man's spirit.

"Yet Man, for all his ego, is not the only creature. Other species have some rights too. Wilderness itself, the basis of all our life, does it have a right to live on? Having furnished all the requisites of our proud materialistic civilization, our neon-lit society, does it have a right to live? Do we have enough reverence for life to concede to Wilderness this right?

"I submit to this Forum, in all sincerity, that when all the non-renewable resources are gone, Alaska could still have a resource which will support a healthy economy and a happy life for her people. And that this happy possibility for Lifestyle 1990 depends on how much of unspoiled Alaska is saved NOW."

Thus the Alaska 1975 adventure began with a speech, but that was the end of speech-making.

I stayed at a motel in Anchorage not far from the Alaska Task Force office of the National Park Service. Breakfast at seven, to the office at eight. If we were not flying somewhere, if I was not running to some meeting, I studied and made notes on Environmental Impact Statements (and there were eleven of them) and discussed them with some of the enthusiastic and dedicated Task Force members.

But my other obligation was to talk to people wherever I went, and listen to them. Very few escaped me! I always sat on the banquette in the motel dining room, and could almost always very easily get into conversation with the diners on either side. To them, I was just an old Alaskan, back home for a look around. Where did they come from? Were they just visiting, where had they been, what was their occupation, what did they think about all this talk of National Parks and Refuges?

This was a game I had never played before, but it became amazing fun. In airport departure lounges, in airplanes, in all the stores, in restaurants, in buses, in museums and in hotel lobbies, people were willing to talk, and everywhere I went I over-heard many interesting conversations too. The driver of one airport limousine in Anchorage became so eloquent about his love of hunting, fishing, canoeing ("Where else in the world could you have all this?") that we got all tangled up in the Fourth of July parade!

On that night in early May when I had said to my dear friend Bob Belous, "Yes, I'll come," I knew I was committing myself to a lot of flying, and I'm not crazy about it, but that was the price of seeing some incredible country, and I didn't worry.

We flew to Lake Clark three times; to Twin Lakes twice. We flew to Talkeetna and all around the proposed extension to Mount McKinley National Park, into the vast amphitheater of Ruth Glacier and out again, over the Harding Icefield—simply unbelievable—and down over the Kenai Fjords.

I flew to Fairbanks three times en route to other places, and once to stay four days to meet with several groups of people. On June 27 I flew to Kotzebue. Bob Belous had flown up there the day before. After a sandwich at the new and very modern Nul-Luk-Vik Motel, built and operated by the Native corporation, we went back to the airstrip and took off in a Cessna 185 with Don Ferguson. Bob said: "I wouldn't take you on this flight with anyone else."

We flew north, over the tundra, over low hills, over strips of small spruce forest, and ponds and ponds and ponds. Suddenly there before us a great expanse of golden sand, the Kobuk Sand

Dunes, in the heart of the proposed Kobuk National Monument; ripples and mounds of sand, twenty-five square miles of it, with a sparkling clear grayling stream cutting through the middle of it.

We flew on north to the Kobuk and landed at the little village of Ambler, and were immediately surrounded by an escort of Eskimo children who were all smiling and calling: "Hi, Bob! Hi, Bob!" and who went with us every step of our two-hour stay. It was an exciting two hours for me because here I met old friends from Jackson Hole, Keith and Anore Jones, Ole and Manya Wick, and Don Williams, all of whom were living here with the Eskimos, in the same lifestyle, in little cabins in the spruce-dotted tundra along the river, and seeming so well and happy and content. Something to think about.

We flew over some more beautiful valleys westward to Cape Krusenstern, and low over the beach ridges and looked down into the old house pits of this most important archeological area, the proposed Cape Krusenstern National Monument. In a few minutes we were approaching a long sandspit and Bob said: "See—we are going to land right there between those two oil barrels."

Don brought us down without even a thump, and we walked half a mile up the sandy-grassy beach to a group of tents, the sealing camp. Here we met and had a memorable visit with Bob Uhl, who has lived in this area for thirty years, a well-educated man of Quaker faith who only leaves his Bering Sea wilderness to help organize Quaker meetings in other Alaskan localities. He has a lovely Eskimo wife, Carrie, and they live the life of the Eskimos. In winter they move back to a low range of hills nearby, where there is a tongue of timber, and here they have their log cabin winter home. We had coffee and pilot bread and smoked fish in seal oil, in their tent, and a great deal of talk about possible lifestyles for the young generation, and what is possible for them in Alaska now. Our host walked back to the plane with us. "I don't want to miss a minute of this visit."

In half an hour we were back in Kotzebue. What an afternoon it had been! We found notes pinned to both of our doors at the hotel. Gary Everhardt, then Director of the National Park Service, and four other Park Service people had arrived, and Brina had come in a day early from her field work on the Seward Peninsula because she knew we would be there and we needed to make final plans about the Arctic Wildlife Range trip on which she was joining me, July 8 to 12. So we all had a great visit and a long walk through the village and along the beach—broad daylight of course and the village full of activity, including motor scooters!

When Bob and I returned to Anchorage the next day we found our dear friend Ted Swem had arrived from Washington, D. C. Ted was then head of the Alaska Planning Group in the Department of the Interior. On July 2 he and I flew together to Fairbanks on the early morning flight. The Fish & Wildlife Service was cooperating with the National Park Service on Gary Everhardt's trip into the Brooks Range to see the Gates of the Arctic National Park proposal, and at Fairbanks Ted and I were met by Averill Thayer, Manager of the Arctic National Wildlife Range, whom I had known since 1967 when Mildred and I had had a canoe trip with him and the Dave Spencer family. Ted was to wait and come on north later in the day with the Director's party, but here was Ave, tall, slim, keen blue eyes, quiet as ever, ready to take me and some of the baggage north to Bettles.

We took off in the Beaver at nine o'clock, a sunny morning and a nice smooth flight, much of it right over the pipeline. Very clearly we could see the long green sections of pipe being lowered into the trench, the haul road paralleling it, trucks crawling along; every few miles a side road leading to a gravel pit or a huge field of parked equipment of all giant kinds. It was no simple "pencil mark across a sheet of paper" as someone had said, but a broad and portentous scar across an empty and innocent land. But at one point I drew Ave's attention to a beautiful winding river below us and passed him a note "What river?" (He had head phones on) and he shook his head, and I was glad to know that there were some nameless rivers left in Alaska, so I passed him another note: "There's a land where the mountains are nameless, and the rivers run God knows Where." Robert Service could still find some of his north un-named.

Ave also turned at one point and flew low over the famous bridge being built across the Yukon; I could hardly believe I was seeing all this.

Before noon we landed at Bettles, five miles upstream on the Koyukuk from our old Bettles, this one built on a huge gravel bar, with the few buildings back against the spruce forest. In two hours we had flown into a different world and I was back on the Koyukuk again after fifty-one years.

The two-story Bettles Lodge, run by a very friendly couple, the Beards, was like a true old Alaskan roadhouse, the difference being that the men talking, reading, playing solitaire were not dog mushers and prospectors, but smoke jumpers and helicopter and airplane pilots.

Celia Hunter was coming on the Park Service plane and my things were put into the twin bedroom she and I were to share. I began visiting with the pretty Eskimo woman who was getting the rooms ready and soon discovered that she is the daughter-in-law of Oscar Nictoon who was the cabin boy on the *Teddy H.* all those years ago! Now I realized that I really was stepping back into long-gone chapters! When she found out who I was she said: "Oh my, oh my, my parents have walked up from the village, the new Eskimo village is just below here—I think they will be sitting out in front there on the grass now; you must go talk to them."

This was Frank Tobuk, brother of David who had been the pilot on the *Teddy H.* The moment I spoke my name he said: "Oh—Murie, oh yes! We remember. We remember those good times."

Then he said: "Did you know David's daughter Rhoda is here; she is married to the F.A.A. man. You must come see her."

So Frank and his sweet smiling wife Dora and I walked over to the row of two-story houses of the F.A.A. and Frank opened the door of one and called: "Come, I have brought somebody to see you," and this lovely looking woman came to the door. I said: "I am Mrs. Olaus Murie," and she said: "Oh, oh, oh," and laid her head on my shoulder and began to cry, and we were both crying. But what a great visit we had! Rhoda had been ten years old when we were on the *Teddy H.* and she remembered all about it. Now she has a beautiful daughter and the daughter and her fiancé were there too. They were to be married a few days later, on July 4th.

Gary and his party arrived in late afternoon, and late that evening Rhoda, and John Musser her nice husband, took the whole party down river in their big poling boat with outboard. So there I was, on this beautiful calm evening, landing again at Bettles in a poling boat. This was a stepping back in my life which was hardly to be borne. The old village is empty, the willows and cottonwoods and alders have taken it; the cabins sinking away. I found ours, and stepped in, alone, for a few moments. It was completely empty, one corner sagging into the ground.

Outside, Rhoda and Celia and all the men were standing quietly

by the boat, waiting for me. Nothing was said. We traveled back up the shining river and into the modern world again.

Celia and I flew with Ave in the Beaver next morning, westward to Walker Lake, a ten-mile long gem in a gorgeous ring of mountains, and there John Kauffmann of the Task Force, with his young helper Bill Resor, had a camp all set up for us. The helicopter came soon with Gary, Bob and Ted. Weather was perfect and the men went to a nearby lake to fish and came back at supper time with fish and a jubilant story of watching a grizzly with three cubs, so the long evening by the campfire was rich with wildlife stories and earnest talk about how to best preserve this matchless habitat. When Ave took Gary and Celia back to Bettles on his first trip the next day he took them up the North Fork of the Koyukuk and was able to show them thirty mountain sheep!

On the beach at our camp I had been talking to the young helicopter pilot. He said: "I think the whole thing should be a national park with no hunting. There's only one animal left in the country that's fairly safe from sport hunting; that's the mountain goat, because we haven't yet invented a contraption which can get right up in front of one of those!"

Ted and Bob and I flew all the way back to Fairbanks with Ave in the Beaver, stopping only a little while at Bettles to load gear and to say good-bye to Rhoda and her family, who were in the midst of a crisis of trying to fit a huge roast of moose plus a huge turkey into the oven, for the wedding party the next day.

The next adventure was a second trip to Twin Lakes to take film to Dick Proenneke, and this time he was at home in his exquisitely built cabin, spotless, every item of his living in its proper place. He insisted on making sourdough pancakes for our lunch, after I had sniffed at his sourdough pot and declared it absolutely right. (I consider myself a real sourdough expert.) Dick passed me a plate with two good-sized pancakes on it and said: "Now you put butter and honey on those," and I did. Then he said: "Now, when I have them for lunch I do this," and he reached under the counter, brought out an onion, peeled it in an instant, put two slices on top of the cakes and said: "Now you eat that." And I did. And it was good! But I had two sissies with me. Ted stated that he is allergic to onions, and Bob just plain wouldn't! But all three of us and our jovial pilot Charlie Allen were delighted to have a visit with the forthright sensitive soul who is Dick Proenneke.

More meetings in Anchorage, more study in the Park Service office, more discussions about all the hoped-for areas to be presented to Congress, their great variety, their boundaries, their potential. Suddenly it was July 8 and time for my last trip, this one as the guest of the Fish & Wildlife Service, and I flew to Fairbanks again on that early morning flight. Ave met me at the airport and took me to the Fish & Wildlife Service hangar, where he locked in the office my bag with town clothes for the return trip. For the present trip I was properly garbed in shoepacs, levis, red flannel shirt, and carrying a down parka loaned me by the Park Service. In a few minutes Celia arrived, having driven up from Camp Denali in the wee hours of the daylight night, and one of Brina's graduate students brought her along soon after.

The four of us were soon in the air in the Beaver, flying over the beautiful White Mountains and on to Fort Yukon to wait for Dave Spencer, in charge of all Alaska refuges, who was flying another Beaver up from Anchorage. The two men were on a regular check of the area, and we were fortunate enough to be invited to go along.

Neither Ave nor Dave is given to idle chatter. They are not men who believe in telling people any more than is good for them to know. All I knew about this trip was that we were going to the Arctic Wildlife Range, going on over to the north slope (where I had never been) then going to see the proposed southward extension of the range. I was more than content with this. It was enough to know that Brina and I were going to have another Arctic adventure together and that Celia, long-time friend and now a member of the Land Use Planning Commission, was to be with us. Ave said when we were ready to leave Fort Yukon: "You and Brina will ride with me this afternoon; Celia will go with Dave; we'll camp at Sheenjek Lake." (Sheenjek Lake is west of the Sheenjek Valley and I had never been over there.)

We took off. We flew north over tundra ponds. In five minutes we had left all signs of man and were in the Land itself, and it was like June 1956 all over again for Brina and me. After half an hour I realized that we were not cutting across as Keith had done, but following the Sheenjek—my first inkling that we were to see the Sheenjek Valley at all.

Brina was in front beside Ave. After another hour she turned and said: "Lobo Lake coming up!"

We flew low over it. I had not recognized it because the tiny dirt island in its middle had washed away with the recent years.

We flew on north. There was Last Lake, same as ever—two tents right there where ours had been. There were the boot-shaped mirror water, the green tundra, the forested slope, the silver-gray shining "Camp Mountain" behind, the river on our left, the rugged mountains above and along it, the same quiet, the peace, the welcome. Ave circled and turned south again. Brina reached back and held my hand. I wiped tears all the way back to Lobo.

With a cow and calf moose feeding and resting on the shore below us, we had a lovely camp at Sheenjek Lake. I woke at five o'clock in the morning and got up and went for a walk up the ridges through all the lovely alpine-arctic growth and the moss—like coming home.

After breakfast we all flew southwest to Arctic Village in order to refuel, and then flew north up the East Fork of the Chandalar and through the mountains by a pass where the colors of the mountains, stone and rock and shale, were gorgeous; emerged onto the green tundra of the north slope and after a while Celia, who was flying with Ave and me that morning, said: "Look! There's the ice—Arctic Ocean ahead." In a few moments we were flying along the coast—water next to the shore, but all else ice as

far as eye could see and in no time it seemed, we were at Barter
Island—DEW Line station and airstrip and the Eskimo village of
Kaktovik. The men refueled the planes; we ate lunch beside them,
flew on east to the Canadian border, turned, topped off the fuel
again at Barter, flew west and landed on one of the big lagoons
which line the coast behind the gravel ridges of the shore. The
water in these lagoons is almost fresh. It was a warm sunny day;
we lay on the sand and sucked chunks of ice which Dave brought
from the outside shore, and Brina said: "Where are the palm
trees?" And then, across on the landward side, we spotted three
snowy owls sitting in a row on some humps of tussock!

On west, across the Canning River, out of the Wildlife Range,
and immediately there were the signs of man—tracks in the
tundra, helicopter pads, a gravel road leading off nowhere to
where some drilling might have been done; piles of oil drums. A
relief to turn back into the pristine range again. And then, near
the mouth of the Sadlerochit River we found a bank of musk oxen
which had been transplanted from Nunivak Island in the winter.
They went into a circle, but we could see they had three calves.
And they were standing in a bed of lupine! I could see this because
I was using my binoculars. Ave was being careful not to fly too
low over them.

The only buildings inside the range are those of the Naval
Arctic Research Laboratory at Peters Lake, and Ave had the keys
so we were semi-civilized that night. This is a beautiful spot, and
we roamed over the slopes the next morning so that it was nearly
noon when Dave and Brina took off from the lake, and were out
of sight by the time we were airborne. This was our last day, and
Ave was to show Celia and me the proposed extension to the
range and then meet the others at Arctic Village. Celia, the old
flyer, was in the co-pilot's seat. We had flown about ten minutes
and had just come out from the narrow steep defile of Eagle Creek
when there was a sudden terrific clatter from the engine; even a
mechanical ignoramus like me knew that something was very
wrong. Ave grabbed the radio transmitter but didn't have time to
say much, he was too busy with the plane, turning it immediately
to get out of that steep valley and back into the Sadlerochit, wider
and gentler. Celia said: "There's a pond over there." Ave said:
"What do you think?" Celia replied: "Too small." Ave said:
"Grab your sleeping bag and hold it over your face." I reached
back of the seat and threw to Celia the big down parka, then got

my sleeping bag and followed Ave's orders. With my left eye I could see the turf coming closer and closer, then we went Bang, Bang, Bang—and there we were, on the floats, on the turf, nobody even bruised. Celia and I both at once: "Oh Ave, how perfectly marvelous; what a wonderful job—we're alive!"

He didn't answer, just got out of his seat, ran around, opened both doors, and said: "Get out! Get out quick!"

I have no memory of getting out of that plane, but I was on the ground, and Ave said: "You go over there and stand, and Celia will help me unload." and he began throwing everything out, helter skelter. I thought: "Why can't *I* do anything?" So Celia and I were both grabbing things and running and dumping them some distance away—but nothing happened.

Half an hour later we had two tents set up; all the food and the Coleman stove in Ave's tent which was larger. An orange disaster cloth spread on the ground and weighted with rocks; the radio beacon set out on the slope. We had everything we needed, and we knew that after some hours Dave would do something. We were never worried at all. Even if nobody came, we knew we could walk the ten or fifteen miles cross-country to Peters Lake where they would be sure to find us. The only reaction, beyond the intense gratitude, was that none of us wanted to eat or drink anything for some hours. Finally about three o'clock (we landed at exactly noon) Celia made tea for us and hot cocoa for Ave and took it down to the plane where he was sitting with the radio but unable to raise anyone. We walked a bit, over to the pond and watched some northern phalaropes going round and round, but the mosquitoes were terrible (they had been no trouble at our other campsites). We had plenty of mosquito dope, but stayed in the tent most of the time. I wrote my notes; Celia tried to read. Finally she said: "My gosh, shipwrecked and not even a deck of cards!"

I said: "Oh? That's what *you* think. Go over to our tent and look in the side pocket of my pack; you'll find two decks of cards."

So I taught Celia to play Russian Bank, on the humpy, bumpy floor of that tent—and she beat me!

At eight o'clock we cooked some of the freeze-dried food—chicken and noodles, and some of June Thayer's good whole wheat bread and some jam, and we all felt fine. At ten Celia and I went to bed; at midnight I saw Ave going into his tent—he had been at the radio all that time. At 1:30 A.M. I was sure I heard something that was not just the roar of the river. I woke Celia and we both yelled at Ave; he got out and ran down to the plane, Celia crawled out of her sleeping bag and put on her pacs and said: "Don't you come out in all these bugs."

She was soon back, and said yes, Ave had been able to talk to that plane, which was circling round and round, and it was the Army C130 rescue plane from Fort Greeley, looking for us. He told Ave that from twelve thousand feet, with naked eye, he had spotted the orange disaster cloth; and then he said that a helicopter from Deadhorse (the landing strip for Prudhoe Bay) would be coming in about an hour and a half. Celia said: "Now they know we are all right, why can't they wait until eight in the morning to rescue us?"

We got our stuff together and stayed in the tent out of the bugs, and at 3:30 Celia and I knelt at the little back window of our tent and watched the helicopter land just a few feet away. When I crawled out of the tent a nice looking young man was reaching to help me, saying: "I'm sorry about this."

"Sorry? Why sorry? We're alive—you don't know how grateful we are!"

Ninety-six miles to Deadhorse, apple juice and crackers and conversation with the two young rescuers. When we had got our personal gear into the helicopter, and Ave was the last one to climb in, the pilot had reached back and taken Ave's hand and said: "Congratulations! That was a mighty fine job you did setting that machine down!"

After all that, we actually did sleep for two or three hours, upstairs in the staff house of the flying service which had rescued us. And at noon we were in a Wein plane bound for Fairbanks. Eighty-five degrees in Fairbanks, and we in our flannel shirts and rubber pacs. But June Thayer was there to meet us, and I went out to their home, while Celia took off in her truck to do grocery shopping for Camp Denali—right back to the practical world! The lovely thing at the Thayers was a big pitcher of ice cold lemonade, and getting into my other clothes. In a little while Ave went in to the airport to meet Dave and Brina, who all this time had been chugging along from Arctic Village.

Brina had spent the night in her little tent on the shore of a lake at the end of the airstrip of Arctic Village, watching a lot of interesting birds, eating Logan bread, while Dave took off to fly back over the route to look for us. He didn't happen to fly down the valley we were in, found no trace of us so then radioed to Barter Island and to the Army Rescue. He then had to fly on to Barter to refuel and there at two in the morning he heard that we were all right so he got a few hours sleep and flew all the way back to Arctic Village, arriving there at 10:00 A.M. and it was then Brina learned we were safe. And after all that, Dave flew right on all the way back to Anchorage that night, after talking to me on the phone from the airport. Then Ave brought Brina home and we had a happy dinner with the Thayers and they took us home to Brina's, where a bath and bed were all I could think about, but Brina did a lot of housework before she finally went to sleep.

Back in Anchorage—more meetings, and parties, and discussions, and good-byes, and Bob took me to the airport for another early flight, this time south. In the departure lounge, a last earnest talk: how can we do the best for Alaska?

It was clear most of the way to Seattle and I watched the glaciers, the mountain peaks, the rivers, unroll beneath the plane, and thought about the whole fantastic experience. What could I say to Gary Everhardt, or to anyone, which could express what Alaska can mean to us all? I guess it is this:

When I think about that return to the part of Alaska which has meant so much in my life, the overpowering and magnificent fact is that Lobo Lake is still there, untouched. Last Lake is still there, untouched. Although the instant you fly west of the Canning River man is evident in all the most blatant debris of his machine power, east of the Canning the tundra, the mountains, the unmarked space, the quiet, the land *itself*, are all still there.

Do I dare to believe that one of my great-grandchildren may someday journey to the Sheenjek and still find the gray wolf trotting across the ice of Lobo Lake?

3

Outside—1975
to 1989

Fourteen years—at Moose most of the time, but with more trips to Alaska, in 1976, 1980, 1985 and 1987; and to Australia and New Zealand.

The summers have been busy at Moose: ten grandchildren romping through the woods, interesting visitors arriving, and sessions with classes from the Teton Science School, the field science school across the valley.

I am a member of the council of the Wilderness Society, and thus I am involved in all wilderness preservation concerns and with the people who are active in those efforts. I have given too many speeches, testified at many congressional hearings, received more honors than I could possibly deserve. I have so much to be grateful for that it is hard to find words to express it. The natural beauty of my surroundings here in Moose is a great blessing.

The overriding thought throughout my days is that there is still hope for the preservation of the beloved natural world of both the Lower 48 states and Alaska. Perhaps my strongest perpetual hope, after these intervening years, is, as it was in 1975:

"Do I dare to believe that one of my great-grandchildren may someday journey to Sheenjek and still find the gray wolf trotting across the ice of Lobo Lake?"

Yes, I do still dare to believe!

About the Author

MARGARET E. MURIE was born in Seattle, Washington. She attended the public schools in Fairbanks, Alaska, spent two years at Reed College in Oregon, one year at Simmons College in Boston, and was the first woman graduate of the University of Alaska. Two months after her graduation she married the biologist Olaus J. Murie. She worked closely with him during his years as biologist with the U.S. Fish and Wildlife Service and, after 1946, as director of The Wilderness Society. Since her husband's death in 1963, Mrs. Murie has continued writing and working in the cause of conservation, and in 1976 was honored by the University of Alaska with a Doctor of Humane Letters degree. Mrs. Murie lives at Moose, Wyoming, in the Teton Mountains.

More outdoor adventure books
are available from Alaska Northwest Books™, such as:

Our Arctic Year, by Vivian and Gil Staender.
An Oregon couple, both wildlife lovers, record their experience of living for one year in the Arctic tundra. No comforts, no humans. Only birds, nature, and an unspoiled land. With more than 100 color photographs and drawings.
149 pages, softbound, $12.95 ($16.45 Canadian), ISBN 0-88240-238-2

Alaska Blues: A Fisherman's Journal, by Joe Upton.
Commercial fisherman Joe Upton has won awards and high praise for his journal of a salmon season in Alaska. In the words of famous author Ernest K. Gann (*The High and the Mighty*), Upton's photographs and storytelling make Alaska Blues ". . . one of the most unique sea sagas ever written." With 204 photographs.
236 pages, hardbound, $14.95 ($18.95 Canadian), ISBN 0-88240-098-3

Kootenay Country: One Man's Life in the Canadian Rockies, by Ernest F. ("Fee") Hellmen.
Kootenay Country is an easy-reading account of author "Fee" Hellmen's life fishing, hunting, and as a big-game guide in the rugged East Kootenay Valley of British Columbia. Beginning in the 1920s when Hellmen was a boy, this selection of anecdotes chronicles the adventures, dangers and pleasures inherent in a life in the Great Outdoors. With 14 photographs and a map.
204 pages, softbound, $9.95 ($12.95 Canadian), ISBN 0-88240-357-5

Skystruck: True Tales of an Alaska Bush Pilot, by Herman Lerdahl with Cliff Cernick.
From seat-of-the-pants Alaska bush pilot to captain for Northwest Airlines, Herm Lerdahl lived an exciting story in the 1930s and 1940s. From Lerdahl's journals, author Cliff Cernick, veteran Alaska newspaper editor, has recreated the excitement, danger and rewards of flying. With 15 photographs and a map.
169 pages, softbound, $9.95 ($12.95 Canadian), ISBN 0-88240-356-7

Ask for these books at your favorite bookstore, or contact Alaska Northwest Books™ for a catalog of our entire list.

Alaska Northwest Books™
A division of GTE Discovery Publications, Inc.
P.O. Box 3007
Bothell, WA 98041-3007
Toll free: 1-800-343-4567